Understanding Oracle APEX 20 Application Development

Think Like an Application Express Developer

Third Edition

Edward Sciore

Apress®

Understanding Oracle APEX 20 Application Development: Think Like an Application Express Developer

Edward Sciore
Newton Center, MA, USA

ISBN-13 (pbk): 978-1-4842-6164-4   ISBN-13 (electronic): 978-1-4842-6165-1
https://doi.org/10.1007/978-1-4842-6165-1

Managing Director, Apress Media LLC: Welmoed Spahr
Acquisitions Editor: Jonathan Gennick
Development Editor: Laura Berendson
Coordinating Editor: Jill Balzano

Cover image designed by Freepik (www.freepik.com)

Distributed to the book trade worldwide by Springer Science+Business Media New York, 233 Spring Street, 6th Floor, New York, NY 10013. Phone 1-800-SPRINGER, fax (201) 348-4505, e-mail orders-ny@springer-sbm.com, or visit www.springeronline.com. Apress Media, LLC is a California LLC and the sole member (owner) is Springer Science + Business Media Finance Inc (SSBM Finance Inc). SSBM Finance Inc is a **Delaware** corporation.

For information on translations, please e-mail booktranslations@springernature.com; for reprint, paperback, or audio rights, please e-mail bookpermissions@springernature.com.

Apress titles may be purchased in bulk for academic, corporate, or promotional use. eBook versions and licenses are also available for most titles. For more information, reference our Print and eBook Bulk Sales web page at http://www.apress.com/bulk-sales.

Any source code or other supplementary material referenced by the author in this book is available to readers on GitHub via the book's product page, located at www.apress.com/9781484261644. For more detailed information, please visit http://www.apress.com/source-code.

Printed on acid-free paper

To my parents, for their many years of unwavering love and support.

Table of Contents

About the Author

Edward Sciore is a recently retired associate professor in the computer science department at Boston College. He taught college students for more than 35 years. His research specialty is database systems, and he thoroughly enjoys teaching the wonders of database technology to captive students.

About the Technical Reviewer

Armando Plascencia has been a database engineer and software architect in multiple software languages, building systems and solutions for enterprises since the early days of information technology. Specializing in all things Oracle, Java, Linux, Open Source, and APEX, Armando is a natural principal architect. He thrives in dynamic, complex environments, where he leads teams of diversely skilled individuals, one business challenge and deadline at a time. Being an avid learner has made Mr. Plascencia a master technologist. Attending conferences and reading dozens of books each year keep his skills up to date, but teaching others is what keeps him honed and sharp to new technological iterations and innovations. A strong believer in the power of positive thinking and ongoing service to others (Armando and his mother recently made enchiladas for a team filming a documentary about death, grief, and surfing), Armando cares deeply about the larger context of our world, as well as the people who are special in his life. Armando's creed is that writing code, drinking coffee, and developing strong relationships are the foundations of everything. Outside of work, Armando enjoys running, cycling, designing, and working on landscaping projects and the hunt for the perfect cup of Java.

"It was an absolute pleasure to be associated with Apress and I want to acknowledge the amazing work of this author."

—Armando Plascencia

Acknowledgments

First and foremost, I would like to thank the APEX user community. Numerous people routinely and generously share their APEX knowledge by writing blogs, creating demonstration APEX sites, and answering all kinds of questions on the APEX web forums. I learned much from them. This book is my attempt to give something back.

I also want to thank my Apress editors, Jonathan Gennick and Jill Balzano. Jonathan convinced me to write the book, and then to revise it. He provided guidance and encouragement every step of the way. Jill was always supportive and smoothed out the inevitable bumps in the road.

Most importantly, I want to acknowledge my wife Amy. She has accompanied me through all three editions, listening to my ideas, helping me resolve technical issues, working through the APEX examples, and pointing out passages in the book that needed clarification. She is a relentless proofreader. I could have written the book without her, but it would not have been anywhere near as good. Thanks.

Introduction

Application Express (otherwise known as APEX) is a web application tightly coupled to an Oracle database. It has several uses: you can use its `SQL Workshop` tool to query and modify the database, you can use its `App Builder` tool to create your own web applications that interact with the database, and you can run the web applications created by you and others.

The app builder is especially interesting because it provides a simple, nontraditional way to build web pages. You do not specify code for the page directly; instead, you choose from a set of built-in templates. There is a template for the overall page and templates for each kind of component that you want to put on the page (such as reports, buttons, etc.). Each template has a set of properties, whose values determine where each component is located on the page, what it looks like, and how it behaves. You create a page simply by choosing templates for the components you want and assigning values to their properties.

The APEX app builder saves the property values for each component in its own database. When a browser requests one of your application's pages, the APEX server extracts the property values relevant to that page from its database, constructs the HTML code corresponding to those values, and returns that code to the browser. This process is called *rendering* the page, and APEX is called an *HTML generator*.

The advantage of using an HTML generator such as APEX is that you can build web pages without any knowledge of HTML (or CSS, JavaScript, or PHP). Moreover, because APEX is tightly coupled to an Oracle database, it automatically handles the intricacies of database interaction. APEX makes it possible to easily create good-looking, highly functional, and database-aware pages with only a rudimentary knowledge of SQL.

Why This Book?

Designing a page with APEX seems straightforward—all you have to do is choose the components you want and then assign the appropriate values to their properties. Choosing components is straightforward, but assigning property values is not. A page and its components have many properties, and you have to know the purpose of those properties to know what values to assign. These properties range from the essential (such as the *source query* of a report) to the obscure (such as the *static ID* of a report). Some properties (such as the *HTML expression* of a report column) are hooks that allow you to insert customized HTML or JavaScript code into the generated web page.

The purpose of this book is to gently lead you through this cornucopia of properties. To that end, the book develops a demo web application that illustrates various APEX techniques for building typical web page functionality. The pages of this application start out simply and gradually increase their level of sophistication. With each page, I introduce a few new properties, discuss their purpose, and illustrate their usefulness. By the end of the book, you will have been so immersed in the world of APEX properties that you should feel confident enough to tackle any website project of your own. And if your project requires even more sophistication than appears here, you should be comfortable enough to use properties that are not covered, perhaps by looking at the documentation, examining the numerous prepackaged applications provided by Oracle, checking a web forum, or even figuring it out on your own.

Another way to build web pages in APEX is to rely on wizards. APEX provides wizards to generate common components, such as report pages and data entry forms. Each wizard asks you a series of questions (such as "What is the name of the page?" "What table do you want to display?" "Should the page have an entry in the navigation menu?") and then uses your responses to generate appropriate components having appropriate properties. The advantage, of course, is that you don't need to know anything about properties. The disadvantage is that wizards tend to produce "one size fits all" pages, in terms of both their appearance and their functionality.

Wizards can take you only so far. If you want any kind of control over the look, feel, and behavior of your page, you need to get involved with its properties. This book provides the guidance you need.

Demo Application

As this book explains each part of the APEX app builder, it guides you through the development of a small application, named Employee Demo. I encourage you to build your own version of the application as you follow along. You can run my version of the application by going to the URL apex.oracle.com/pls/apex/f?p=91392:1. You can also download the source code for the application from the Apress website and import it into your own workspace.

Unlike demo applications in many books, this application does not "do" anything particularly interesting. Instead, each page is constructed to illustrate one or more techniques. Some of the pages have similar functionality, to illustrate the trade-offs between different implementation techniques.

The Employee Demo application uses the DEPT and EMP database tables available to every APEX workspace. The DEPT table lists the departments of a company, and the EMP table lists the employees in those departments. Their columns are as follows:

```
DEPT(DeptNo, DName, Loc)
EMP (EmpNo, EName, Job, Mgr, HireDate, Sal, Comm, DeptNo)
```

The key of DEPT is DeptNo, and the key of EMP is EmpNo. Each table has a built-in sequence for generating unique values for these keys, as well as an associated insertion trigger. If you insert a record into one of the tables and omit a value for the key, the trigger will automatically generate a key value from the appropriate sequence.

The Employee Demo application assumes that the EMP table has been modified to have an additional column OffSite of type char(1). An employee will have the value 'N' for this column if the employee works in the department office and 'Y' if the employee works offsite. For your reference, here is the SQL code you will need to add this new column to your EMP table.

```
alter table EMP
add OffSite char(1);
```

After altering the table, you will also need to assign an Offsite value for each existing employee. In my Employee Demo application, the employees SCOTT, ALLEN, WARD, and TURNER work offsite; the others work onsite. Chapter 1 describes how to import the tables if they are not already in your workspace and discusses the APEX tools needed to make these modifications to them.

Required Background

This book is for people who are comfortable using a database system and want to learn how to write nontrivial web applications in APEX. Many of the techniques used to write APEX pages involve various skills in the following database and web design languages and technologies.

SQL

The most important skill you need is the ability to write SQL queries. All data access in APEX is performed via SQL statements, and the value of many properties involves SQL in some way. The more fluent you are in SQL, the more sophisticated your reports and forms can be. This book assumes that you are comfortable with SQL. For the most part, the Employee Demo application uses relatively simple SQL statements, but occasionally I include something more complex (such as an outer join or nested query) to illustrate what is possible.

HTML

This book also assumes that you have a basic familiarity with HTML—in particular, how tags such as <p>, <b>, <a>, and <img> can be used to format text and display images. I will ignore advanced features such as JavaScript and CSS.

PL/SQL

APEX uses PL/SQL to specify behavior. PL/SQL is Oracle's programming language; its main feature is an embedded SQL syntax that makes it easy to write procedures that interact with the database You should have a rudimentary understanding of programming, although prior knowledge of PL/SQL is not necessary. This book introduces PL/SQL in Chapter 7 and uses only basic features of the language.

APEX

Finally, this book does not require you to have prior experience with APEX. Although it is possible to follow the book without actually using APEX, doing so seems rather pointless. So you should get an APEX account. The easiest and best way to get an account is by going to the apex.oracle.com site. Because I created my Employee Demo application from there, you should see the same screens that appear in this book.

Distinguishing Screens from Pages

APEX is a web application that is used to create other web applications. Thus, APEX has a home page, and its various tools have their own sets of pages. Throughout this book,

I describe how to use APEX to build a page of an application. This can lead to some strange sentences, such as "Clicking the Run button from the application's APEX home page runs its home page." To avoid such confusion, I denote all APEX pages as "screens." The previous sentence becomes "Clicking the Run button from the application's home screen runs its home page," which is less awkward and hopefully less confusing.

New to This Edition

Although APEX is a polished and highly functional application, it is (and always has been) a work in progress. The APEX developers have been relentless in their quest to improve the system and have not been shy about making large changes to the functionality of APEX and its user interface.

The previous edition of this book was written in 2015, just as APEX 5 was introduced. Since then, the user interface has undergone a series of significant changes. In fact, when I recently read through my APEX 5 book, I was dismayed to discover that its screenshots and instructions were often inaccurate and occasionally meaningless. Many APEX properties are now in different locations, sometimes with different names. New component types (in particular *forms* and *interactive grids*) have replaced old ones and have different functionality. Clearly it was time to revise the book.

The most significant additions to this book are the two new chapters on Forms and Interactive Grids. In APEX 5, a "form" was a static content region containing an intricately configured set of items and built-in processes. Now APEX has a dedicated Form region, which automatically generates the preconfigured items and processes for you and provides an easily understood set of properties for managing them.

Interactive grid regions have replaced the "tabular form" regions of APEX 5. They provide the same basic functionality as tabular forms—namely, the ability to update a report's values in place—but interactive grids are easier to use, more powerful, and have a cleaner semantics. In fact, the Interactive Grids chapter (Chapter 11) of this book is much shorter than the older Tabular Forms chapter because interactive grids require much less explanation.

CHAPTER 1

The SQL Workshop

Congratulations! You are on the brink of learning how to build APEX web applications. But before you can begin, you need an APEX account. There are several ways to obtain an account: you can register for a free account through the `apex.oracle.com` website, you might be given an account to an APEX server at your job, or you can even install an APEX server yourself and create your own account to it.

No matter the circumstance, your APEX server will have an associated URL. Invoking the URL from your browser takes you to a login screen. Figure 1-1 shows the login screen used by the `apex.oracle.com` server.

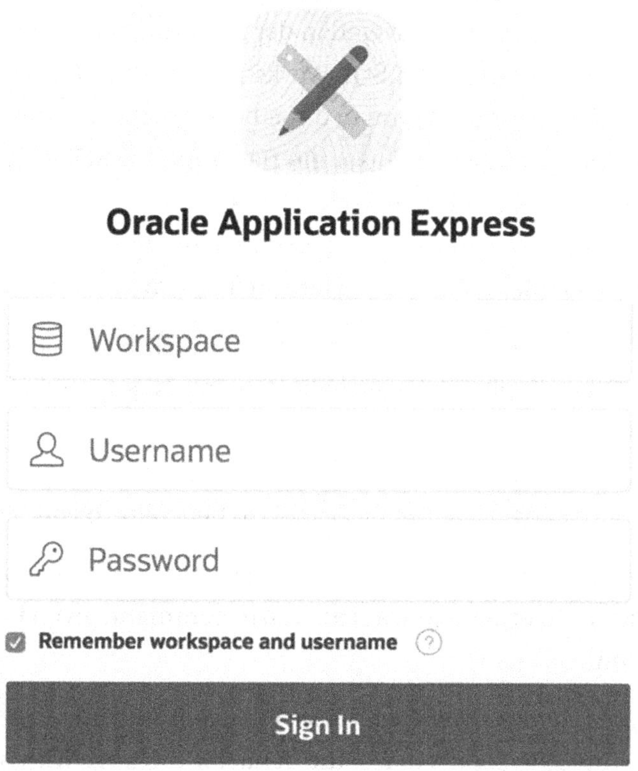

Oracle Application Express

Workspace

Username

Password

Remember workspace and username

Sign In

Figure 1-1. *APEX login screen*

© Edward Sciore 2020
E. Sciore, *Understanding Oracle APEX 20 Application Development*,
https://doi.org/10.1007/978-1-4842-6165-1_1

Entering your credentials then takes you to the APEX home screen, the top of which is shown in Figure 1-2.

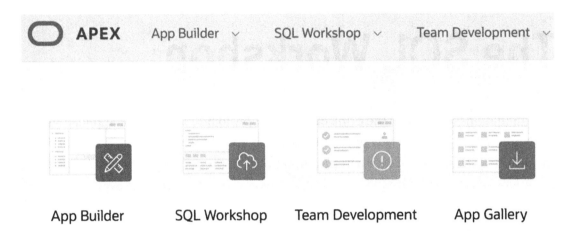

Figure 1-2. *APEX home screen*

The APEX development environment contains several tools. Of primary importance is the App Builder tool, which will be covered in depth starting in Chapter 2. We begin here by looking at two tools in the APEX SQL Workshop: the object browser and the SQL command tool. These tools allow you to directly access the database—the object browser lets you manipulate a graphical user interface, and the SQL command tool lets you execute SQL statements and PL/SQL code blocks.

Although the SQL Workshop tools are not essential for application development, using them can make your life much easier. Here are five ways that they can help:

- *The object browser reminds you of the database objects and their structures.* For example, a typical application involves several tables, each of which can have numerous columns. It is often impractical to memorize the details of each one. When building a page that references a table, you can use these tools to help refresh your memory.

- *To modify the structure of the database.* For example, these tools are the easiest way to execute the `alter table` command given in the introduction.

- *To modify the contents of the database.* For example, you might want to insert or modify records to test the behavior of a page with new or altered data, or to reset the database after testing the page.

- *To examine the contents of the database tables.* After running a page, you can verify that the database updated correctly.

- *To debug an SQL statement or PL/SQL block.* By executing code in the SQL commands tool first, you can verify that it produces the expected result before you actually assign it as the value of some property on a page.

To get to the SQL Workshop, click the SQL Workshop button on the APEX home screen. Figure 1-3 shows the resulting screen. From this screen, you can click the Object Browser or SQL Commands button to get to the desired tool.

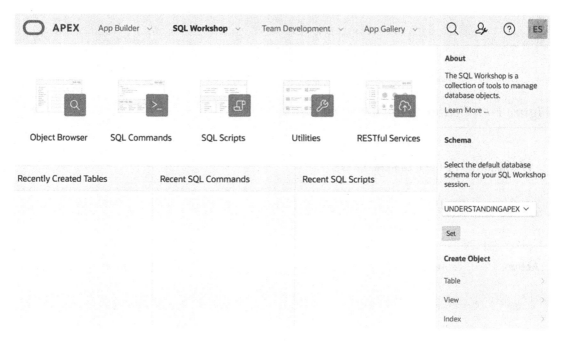

Figure 1-3. *SQL Workshop home screen*

Downloading Tables

This book makes frequent use of the sample tables EMP and DEPT. If your workspace does not contain these tables, here is how to load them. Click the arrow of the SQL Workshop tab, select Utilities, and then Sample Datasets; see Figure 1-4. Figure 1-5 shows the resulting screen, which lists the available tables. Click the Install button for the EMP/DEPT dataset, and follow directions.

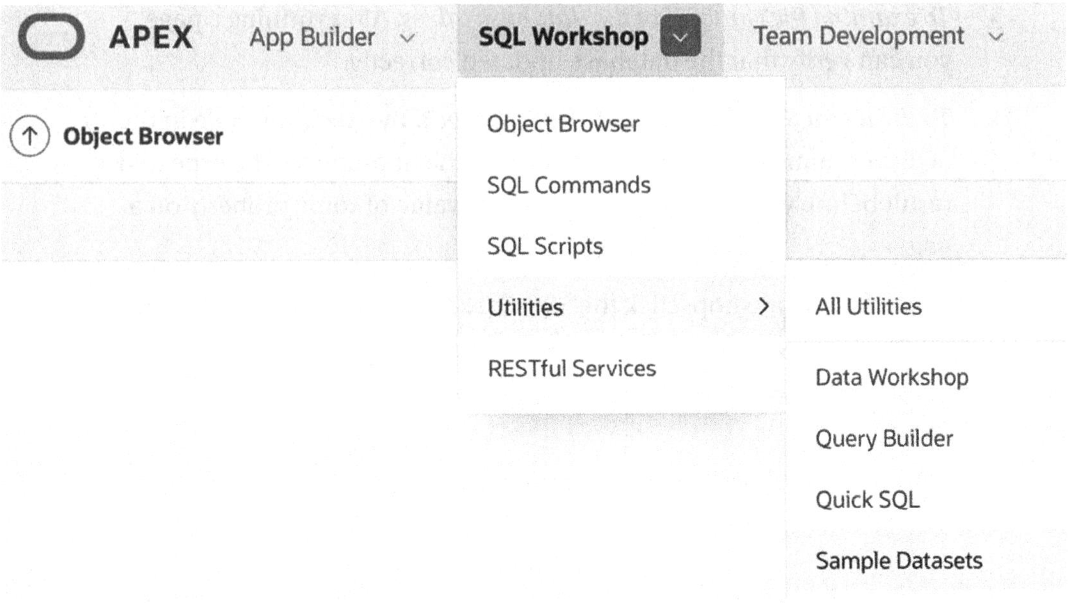

Figure 1-4. *Getting to the sample datasets*

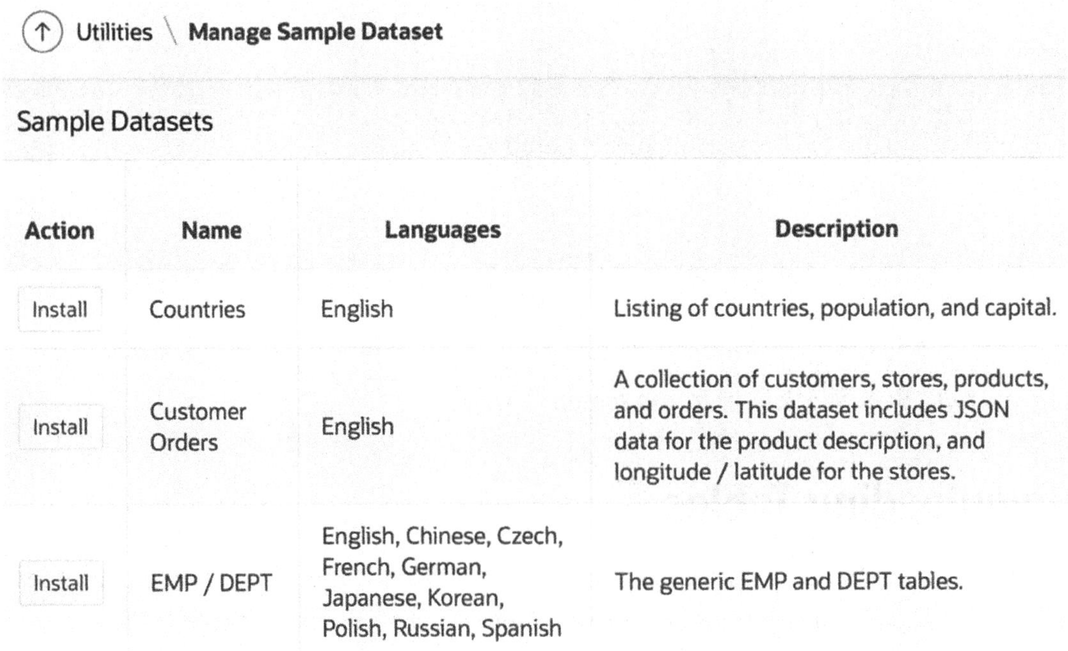

Action	Name	Languages	Description
Install	Countries	English	Listing of countries, population, and capital.
Install	Customer Orders	English	A collection of customers, stores, products, and orders. This dataset includes JSON data for the product description, and longitude / latitude for the stores.
Install	EMP / DEPT	English, Chinese, Czech, French, German, Japanese, Korean, Polish, Russian, Spanish	The generic EMP and DEPT tables.

Figure 1-5. *The Sample Datasets screen*

To verify that the tables have been installed, return to the SQL Workshop home screen (as shown in Figure 1-3). Entries for EMP and DEPT should now appear in the Recently Created Tables region.

Object Browser

The object browser lets you interact with your tables quickly and easily. From it, you can examine the description of each table—that is, the types and properties of its columns and its constraints, indexes, and triggers—as well as its contents. You can also use the object browser to make simple changes to the description or contents of a table.

The home screen for the object browser displays a list of table names along its left side. Clicking a table name displays information about that table. For example, the screen for the EMP table appears in Figure 1-6.

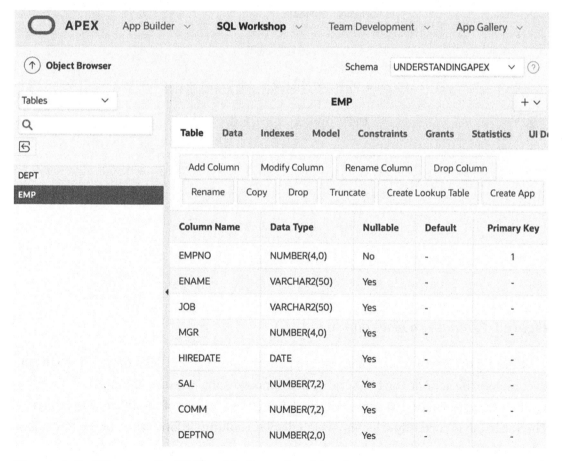

Figure 1-6. *Viewing the EMP table from the object browser*

5

The main portion of the screen displays information about each column of the table. Above this information is a series of buttons that let you modify it. As an example, recall that the introduction discussed the need for an `Offsite` column; let's add that column to the table now. Clicking the `Add Column` button displays a form for you to fill in the details of the new column. Figure 1-7 shows how I filled in this form.

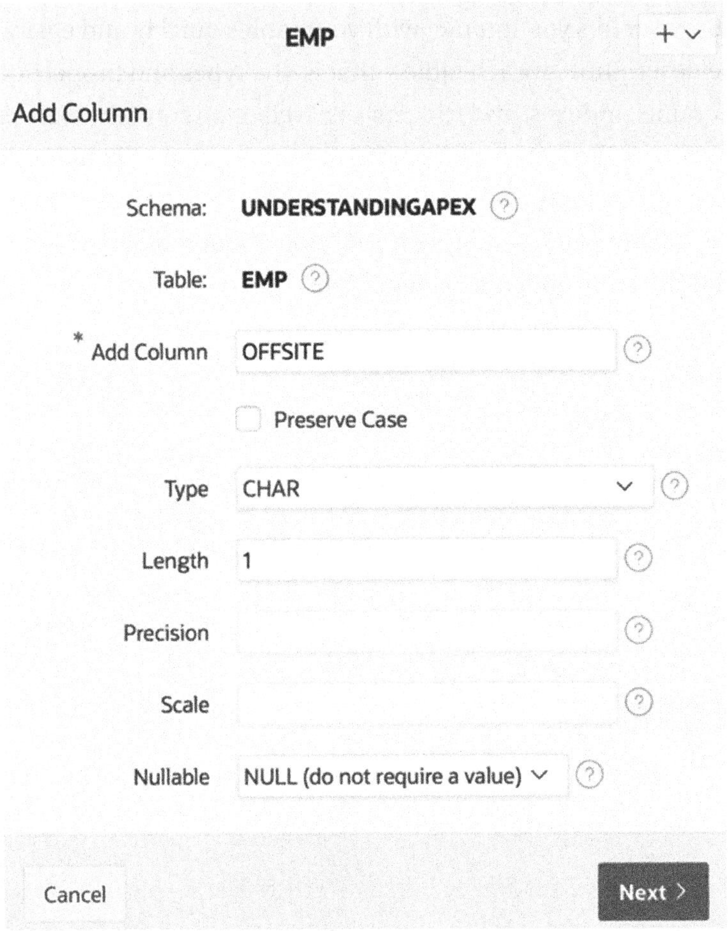

Figure 1-7. *Adding a new column to EMP*

Clicking the `Next` button takes you to a confirmation screen; from there, click `Finish` to complete the action. The `EMP` screen should now display the new column.

Returning to Figure 1-6, observe the tab bar above the row of modification buttons. The `Table` tab is currently selected, which displays column information for the table. The other tabs show you other kinds of information and provide appropriate ways to view and modify that information. For example, clicking the Indexes tab displays the current indexes for the table. Figure 1-8 shows the three indexes for EMP. Clicking the name of an index displays additional detail about that index.

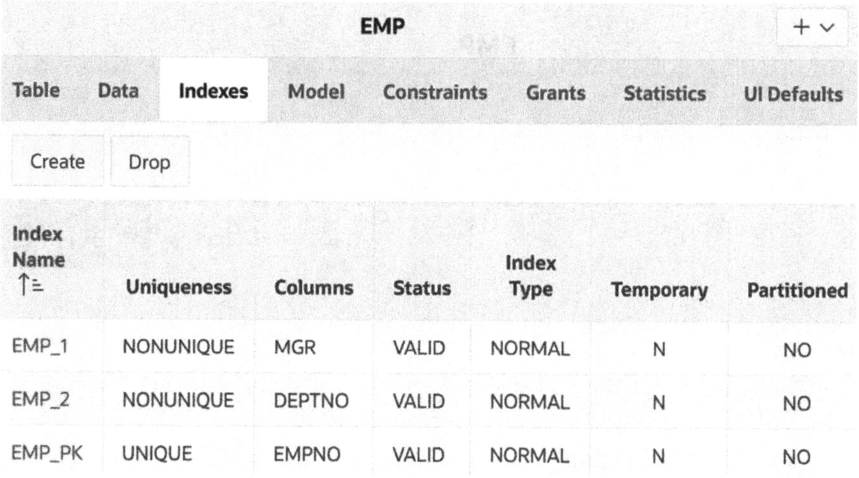

EMP								+ ∨
Table	Data	**Indexes**	Model	Constraints	Grants	Statistics	UI Defaults	

Create	Drop

Index Name ↑≞	Uniqueness	Columns	Status	Index Type	Temporary	Partitioned
EMP_1	NONUNIQUE	MGR	VALID	NORMAL	N	NO
EMP_2	NONUNIQUE	DEPTNO	VALID	NORMAL	N	NO
EMP_PK	UNIQUE	EMPNO	VALID	NORMAL	N	NO

Figure 1-8. *Browsing the indexes of EMP*

Finally, consider the Data tab, which displays the contents of the table. The top of this table appears in Figure 1-9. Note that there is a button to insert a new row and an edit link at the beginning of each row.

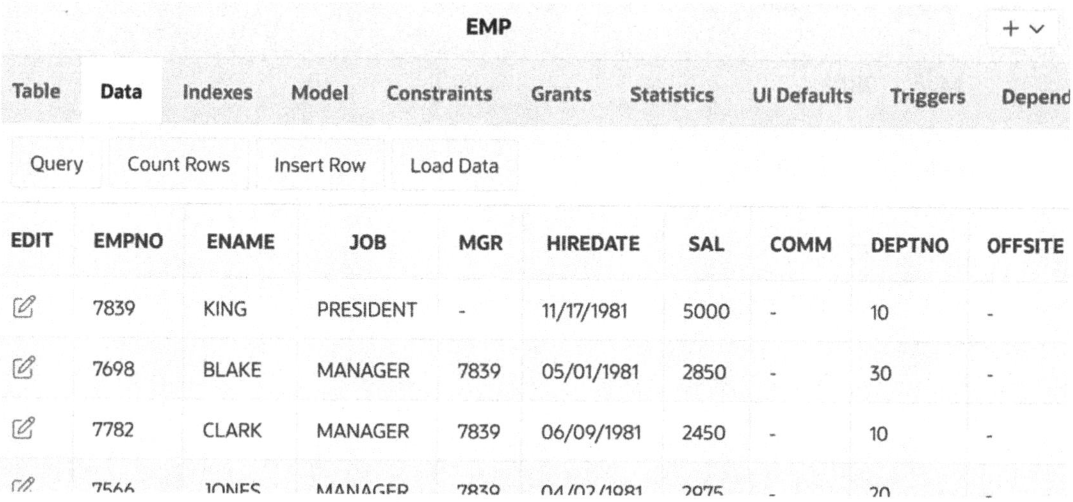

EMP									+ ∨
Table	**Data**	Indexes	Model	Constraints	Grants	Statistics	UI Defaults	Triggers	Depend

Query	Count Rows	Insert Row	Load Data

EDIT	EMPNO	ENAME	JOB	MGR	HIREDATE	SAL	COMM	DEPTNO	OFFSITE
✎	7839	KING	PRESIDENT	-	11/17/1981	5000	-	10	-
✎	7698	BLAKE	MANAGER	7839	05/01/1981	2850	-	30	-
✎	7782	CLARK	MANAGER	7839	06/09/1981	2450	-	10	-
✎	7566	JONES	MANAGER	7839	04/02/1981	2975	-	20	-

Figure 1-9. *Viewing the contents of EMP*

Clicking a row's edit link displays a form for modifying it. Figure 1-10 shows this form for employee 7698. Clicking the Apply Changes button performs any modifications that may have been made to the column values; clicking the Delete button deletes the record.

Figure 1-10. *Editing the contents of employee 7698*

If you wish, you can edit this record, setting the value for Offsite to **N**. You can then proceed to edit the other records, setting their column value to **Y** or **N** as desired. Given the tediousness of this approach, however, it is easier to use the SQL command tool, which is discussed in the next section.

SQL Command Tool

Most of the actions that you can perform in the object browser correspond to one or more SQL statements. In effect, the object browser is merely a convenient way to formulate and execute simpler SQL statements. If you want to perform more complex activities, use the SQL command tool.

The SQL command tool divides the screen into two sections. You type an SQL statement or PL/SQL block into the top section, and the result appears at the bottom. Figure 1-11 shows the screen after executing the SQL statement select * from EMP.

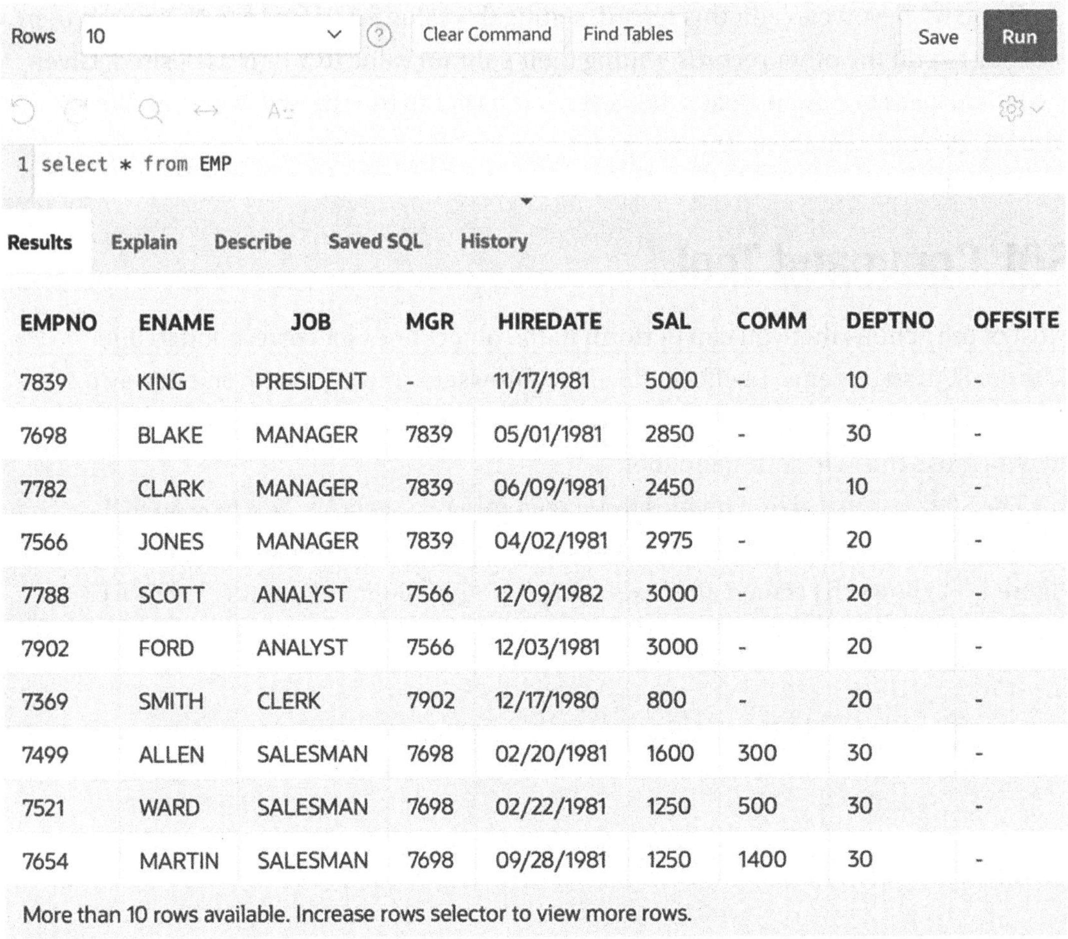

| Rows | 10 | ⌄ | ⑦ | Clear Command | Find Tables | | Save | **Run** |

↺ ↻ 🔍 ↔ A≈ ⚙⌄

```
1 select * from EMP
```

⌄

Results   Explain   Describe   Saved SQL   History

EMPNO	ENAME	JOB	MGR	HIREDATE	SAL	COMM	DEPTNO	OFFSITE
7839	KING	PRESIDENT	-	11/17/1981	5000	-	10	-
7698	BLAKE	MANAGER	7839	05/01/1981	2850	-	30	-
7782	CLARK	MANAGER	7839	06/09/1981	2450	-	10	-
7566	JONES	MANAGER	7839	04/02/1981	2975	-	20	-
7788	SCOTT	ANALYST	7566	12/09/1982	3000	-	20	-
7902	FORD	ANALYST	7566	12/03/1981	3000	-	20	-
7369	SMITH	CLERK	7902	12/17/1980	800	-	20	-
7499	ALLEN	SALESMAN	7698	02/20/1981	1600	300	30	-
7521	WARD	SALESMAN	7698	02/22/1981	1250	500	30	-
7654	MARTIN	SALESMAN	7698	09/28/1981	1250	1400	30	-

More than 10 rows available. Increase rows selector to view more rows.

Figure 1-11. *Using the SQL command tool*

APEX displays only 10 of the 14 employee records. The reason is due to the select list labeled Rows at the top of the figure, whose value specifies the maximum number of rows to display. By default, its value is set to 10; if you want more rows displayed, you must first select a larger number. This feature is intentional. By forcing you to explicitly specify the output size of your query, APEX protects you from yourself. Suppose, for example, that you execute a multi-table query in which you forgot to include the join conditions. The resulting output could easily have billions of records that, if not truncated, would cause your APEX session to be unusable.

To the right of that select list is a `Find Tables` button, which is useful if you need to be reminded about the tables and their columns. Clicking this button displays a window similar to the object browser. You can scroll through the available tables; selecting a table shows its column information. Figure 1-12 shows the result of using the `Table Finder` window to display the DEPT columns.

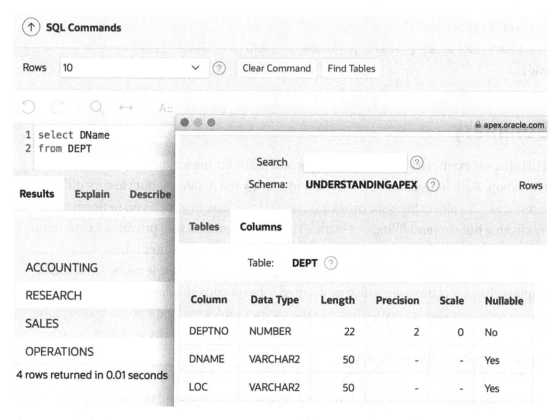

Figure 1-12. *Using the Table Finder window*

You might have noticed from Figure 1-11 that the EMP records still do not have values for `Offsite`. In the introduction, I stated that all employees work onsite except SCOTT, ALLEN, WARD, and TURNER. The easy way to handle this is to execute two update commands: the first one sets everybody's `Offsite` value to N, and the second sets the four chosen records to **Y**. You can either run each statement individually in the command tool or combine them into a single PL/SQL block and execute it. The code for the latter option appears in Listing 1-1.

Listing 1-1. A PL/SQL Block to Assign Offsite Values

```
begin
    update EMP
    set OffSite = 'N';

    update EMP
    set OffSite = 'Y'
    where EName in ('SCOTT', 'ALLEN', 'WARD', 'TURNER');
end;
```

Summary

This chapter examined the object browser and SQL command tools in the APEX SQL Workshop. Both tools allow you to view and modify the database, but via very different interfaces. The object browser provides a visual interface, in which you perform tasks by clicking buttons and filling out forms. The SQL command tool provides a command-based interface, in which you perform tasks by executing SQL statements.

The object browser is ideal for performing common and simple tasks. As its name implies, the object browser is also well suited for exploring the database. The point-and-click interface makes it easy to discover the various tables in the database and explore their columns. The object browser also does not require familiarity with SQL, so it is especially suitable for casual users.

The SQL command tool, on the other hand, assumes that the user is both familiar with the database structure and proficient in SQL. The command tool is therefore suitable for experienced users of the database. If you know the appropriate SQL, you can perform many tasks much more easily from the SQL command tool than from the object browser.

CHAPTER 2

Applications and Pages

This chapter begins an examination of the APEX app builder. You will learn about the basic tools for creating applications and pages—notably, the Create Application wizard and Create Page wizard—and use them to build a multi-page application that can be run from any browser. You will also see how to use the APEX page designer to modify the properties of the pages in your application. Although these pages will have no content to speak of, the techniques in this chapter provide the basis for the content-creation techniques of subsequent chapters.

Creating an Application

To use the app builder, you need to get to its home screen. Figure 1-2 illustrated two ways to do it: you can click the App Builder tab in the APEX menu bar, or you can click the large App Builder button on the APEX home screen. Either way leads you to the screen shown in Figure 2-1.

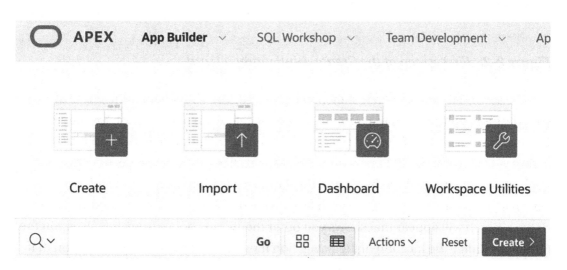

Figure 2-1. *App builder home screen*

© Edward Sciore 2020
E. Sciore, *Understanding Oracle APEX 20 Application Development,*
https://doi.org/10.1007/978-1-4842-6165-1_2

Figure 2-1 shows the two buttons you can use to create a new application: a large
Create button at the top left and a smaller green Create button on the far right of the
search bar. Clicking either button brings up the Create Application wizard.

The first screen of the wizard is shown in Figure 2-2. It asks you to select an
application type. You are creating a new application, so click New Application. The
middle button lets you create an application from an existing spreadsheet (or similar)
file, and the rightmost button lets you import a prebuilt application from the APEX
application gallery. Later, after you have become comfortable with APEX, you should
explore the application gallery. It contains many interesting applications—some provide
solutions for typical database tasks, and others illustrate advanced features of APEX.

Create an Application

New Application

Add pages on existing data,
select application features, set
your theme, and configure
other options.

From a File

Upload a CSV, XLSX, XML or
JSON file, or copy and paste
data, then create your
application.

Productivity App

Install one of many included
Sample and Productivity Apps
from the App Gallery.

Figure 2-2. *First screen of the Create Application wizard*

The second wizard screen is shown in Figure 2-3. You should enter the name of
your desired application in the text field at the top left of the page; I chose **Employee
Demo**. The remainder of the page shows the default configuration of the application and
invites you to customize it. For example, the Appearance property asserts that the new
application will use the Vita theme and display its navigation menu on the left side. You
can change this appearance if you wish by clicking the "set appearance" button at the
right. A screen will appear that shows you other themes to choose from and gives you the
option to change the location of the navigation menu. You can also choose the icon that
the app builder uses to identify your application.

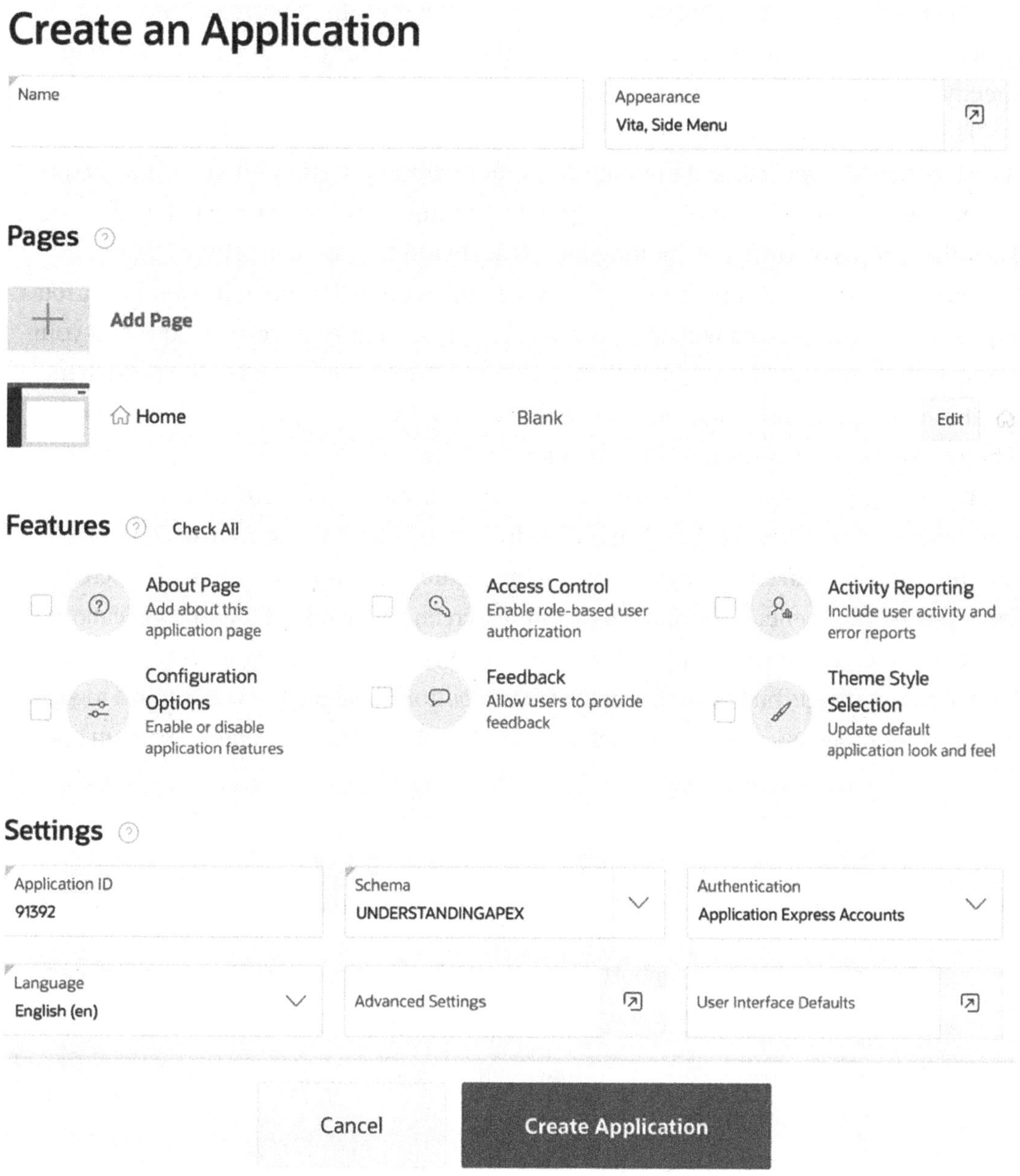

Create an Application

Name	Appearance
	Vita, Side Menu ↗

Pages ⑦

＋ **Add Page**

| 🏠 Home | Blank | Edit 🏠 |

Features ⑦   Check All

☐ ⑦	**About Page** Add about this application page	☐ 🔑	**Access Control** Enable role-based user authorization	☐ 👤	**Activity Reporting** Include user activity and error reports
☐ ⚙	**Configuration Options** Enable or disable application features	☐ 💬	**Feedback** Allow users to provide feedback	☐ 🖌	**Theme Style Selection** Update default application look and feel

Settings ⑦

Application ID 91392	Schema UNDERSTANDINGAPEX ⌄	Authentication Application Express Accounts ⌄
Language English (en) ⌄	Advanced Settings ↗	User Interface Defaults ↗

Cancel   **Create Application**

Figure 2-3. *Second screen of the Create Application wizard*

The Pages section of the screen asserts that the new application will have a single blank page, named Home. You can edit that page by clicking the Edit button, and you can add additional pages. Although this ability can be useful for experienced developers, it is not necessary—you can easily add and edit pages after the application has been created. It is simplest to leave the default pages as they are.

The Features section allows you to specify several useful features common to typical websites. These features can be added at a later point, so there is no need to specify them now.

The Settings section contains some additional settings. The Application ID value is assigned by the wizard, and uniquely identifies your application on the APEX server. My Employee Demo application was assigned the number 91392; yours will be different. The other property worth mentioning here is Authentication. The value of this property determines how people log in to your application. The default is Application Express Accounts, which will allow users to log in only if they have an account on your workspace. The other option is Database, which will only allow users of the underlying database to log in. For the moment, keep the default. Chapter 13 will revisit this choice when it examines the various authentication options.

When you are ready for APEX to create your application, click the green Create Application button. You will be taken back to the app builder home screen, which should now display an entry for your application. Figure 2-4 shows that screen after I created Employee Demo. In general, the app builder home screen has an entry for each application you create. These entries can be displayed either as rows in a report (as in Figure 2-4) or as icons. Look at the two toggle buttons to the right of the Go button in Figure 2-4. The leftmost toggle displays the entries as icons, and the rightmost one displays them as a report. Try them out.

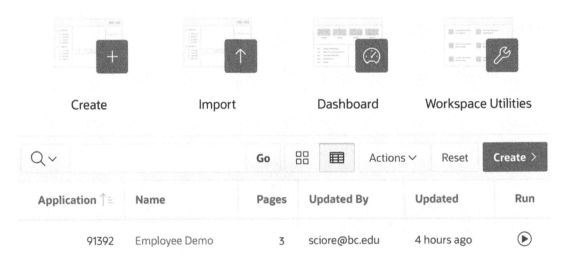

Figure 2-4. *An updated app builder home screen*

Editing Application Properties

Clicking the name of an application's entry takes you to the home screen for that application, which has an entry for each of the application's pages. For example, the initial home screen for my application appears in Figure 2-5. The screen has entries for three pages: a global page, the home page, and a login page. Note that the entries in the figure are displayed as icons. It is also possible to display them as rows in a report, using the same toggle buttons as in Figure 2-4.

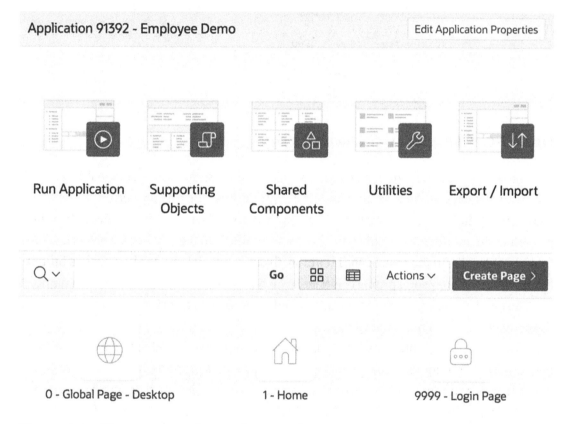

Figure 2-5. *Home screen of a newly created application*

Each application has numerous customization properties. Clicking the Edit Application Properties button at the top right of the home screen displays a screen of properties, the top of which is shown in Figure 2-6.

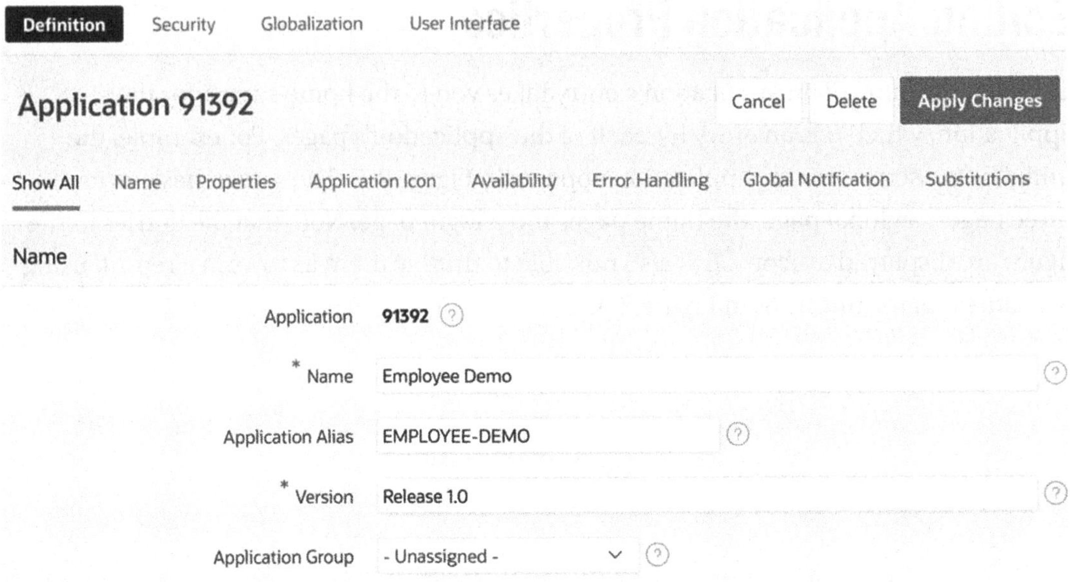

Figure 2-6. *Editing an application's properties*

The screen organizes the application's properties into *sections* for manageability. Figure 2-6 displays the Name section and its five properties. The first property, Application, holds the ID assigned to that application and cannot be modified. The other properties are modifiable; simply type the desired value into the text box (or select a value from the select list in the case of Application Group) and click the Apply Changes button. For us, the only interesting property is Name, which lets you change the application name.

The label of some properties contains a red asterisk. The asterisk means that the property must have a non-null value.

To the right of each property is a small question mark icon. Clicking that icon displays help text for that property, which is especially useful when a property is unfamiliar to you and you want to understand its purpose. As an experiment, click the help icon for each of the properties in the Name section and see if their purpose is what you expected.

Looking again at Figure 2-6, notice the row of tabs above the Name section. The first tab is labeled Show All, and is currently selected; the others are labeled by section names. The Show All tab displays the properties of all sections in a single screen. Clicking one of the section tabs displays the properties for that section. Again, clicking the help icon for the properties in each section is a useful exercise, if only to get a sense of what kind of customization is possible. Most of the properties will seem obscure because you have not delved very deeply into APEX. Certainly none of them (apart from Name) is interesting at this point.

Your application has still more properties. Look at the four links at the top of Figure 2-6, labeled Definition, Security, Globalization, and User Interface. Note that Definition is selected, meaning that you have so far seen only the definition properties. Click the other three links to get a quick look at the other properties. The security properties govern various security restrictions and are the subject of Chapter 13. The globalization properties allow you to modify the time/date settings. And the user interface properties govern certain page display issues. Here, the Logo section is of interest—it lets you manage the logo that appears at the top left of each page of the application. By default, the logo is the name of the application, but you can specify any desired text or even an image. For example, you may have noticed that the APEX screens all have an image-based Oracle logo. We will return to the Logo properties in Chapter 3.

Deleting an Application

There are two ways to delete an application. The right side of the application's home screen contains a task labeled Delete This Application; clicking the link performs the deletion. Alternatively, on the application's global properties screen (refer to Figure 2-6), you can click the Delete button to the left of the Apply Changes button; this button appears when the Definition properties are shown.

Running an Application Page

A web application is a collection of web pages. By *running a page*, you are asking APEX to render it in your browser. The term *running an application* is shorthand for running its home page. There are two ways to run a page: from within APEX (as a developer) and from outside of APEX (as a user). Each is considered in the following sections.

Running a Page from Within APEX

The easiest way to run an application from within APEX is to click the big Run Application button on the top left of the application's home screen (refer to Figure 2-5). Alternatively, you can go to the entry for the application in the app builder's home screen (Figure 2-4) and click its Run button.

To run an arbitrary page of an application, you must open the page designer for that page. (The page designer will be discussed later in this chapter, but you can find a screenshot of it in Figure 2-12.) Click the green arrow button on the top right of the designer to run the page.

Whichever way you run your newly created application, you will discover that the application asks you for your name and password, as shown in Figure 2-7. This is a consequence of the authorization scheme that you specified when you created the application. Recall that you specified authorization by "Application Express Accounts," which means that people can run the application only if they have an account in the application's workspace. In other words, the window of Figure 2-7 is asking you for the same username/password that you use to log into APEX.

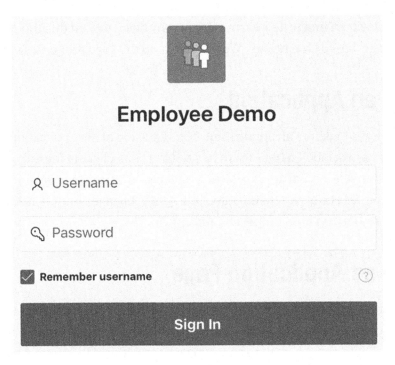

Figure 2-7. *Logging into your application*

If you are the administrator of the workspace (which occurs when you register for an apex.oracle.com account), then you are likely to be the only person having an account in the workspace. If you would like others to be able to use your application, then you have two choices: you can create additional accounts in your workspace, or you can use another authentication method. These options will be discussed in Chapter 13.

Once you have logged in successfully, APEX will display the requested page. Figure 2-8 shows the home page for your application as it currently stands. The *navigation bar* runs along the top. At its left is the logo, which by default is the name of the application. At its right is your username; clicking it lets you sign out. The *navigation menu* runs down the left side of the page. It currently contains a single entry labeled Home. Clicking the icon to the left of the logo toggles the visibility of this menu. The page contains a breadcrumb region titled Employee Demo that is otherwise empty. The page has no other content because, of course, you have not yet specified any.

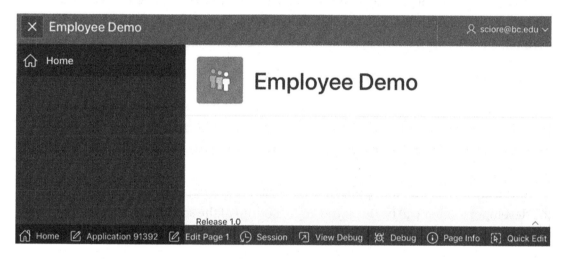

Figure 2-8. *Newly created home page run from within APEX*

Figure 2-8 also shows a row of buttons along the bottom of the page. These buttons, known as the *developer toolbar*, appear whenever you run a page from within APEX. Three buttons are particularly useful for building and debugging your application. The Edit Page button takes you to the page designer for the current page so that you can edit it. The Application button takes you to the home page for the current application so that you can work on a different page. And the Session button pops up a window that displays the current state of the application so that you can verify that it is behaving correctly. This latter topic will be discussed in Chapter 6.

If you wish, you can remove the toolbar from your application. Look again at the Application Properties page of Figure 2-6, and note that it has a section named Availability. This section has the property Status, which specifies how the application is accessed. The default value is usually Available with Developer Toolbar, which specifies that the toolbar will be visible to developers. If you don't want the toolbar, change the value to Available.

Running a Page from Outside APEX

The APEX Create Application wizard assigns an ID number to each new application. You can see from Figure 2-3 that my Employee Demo application was assigned the ID 91392. This number is displayed throughout the app builder; in fact, it has appeared in every figure since then (except Figure 2-7). APEX also assigns an ID number to every page of an application. By default, the ID of the home page is 1, the global page (to be discussed in Chapter 4) is 0, and the login page is 9999.

To run a page from outside of APEX, you need its URL. This URL consists of some characters that identify the APEX server, followed by the application ID and page ID. For example, the URL for my Employee Demo home page is

```
https://apex.oracle.com/pls/apex/f?p=91392:1
```

Up through the characters f?p=, this URL is the same for every APEX application hosted by the apex.oracle.com server. The characters following the equals sign are the application ID and page ID, separated by a colon. If you omit the page ID from the URL, APEX assumes that you mean page 1.

If you are logged into the application's workspace when you submit this URL, then the developer toolbar will be displayed at the bottom of the screen just as if you had run the application from within APEX. Otherwise, you will see the page without it, exactly as a regular user does.

Creating a New Page

There are several ways to create a new page for your application, but the most direct way is to click the Create Page button on the application's home screen (refer to Figure 2-5). Doing so brings up the Create Page wizard. You should use this wizard to create a second page for your application.

The first screen of the wizard, shown in Figure 2-9, asks you to choose the page type. For now, I suggest that you create only blank pages; the other page types are shortcuts intended for experienced developers (or clueless beginners). For example, a Report page is simply a blank page containing a report region.

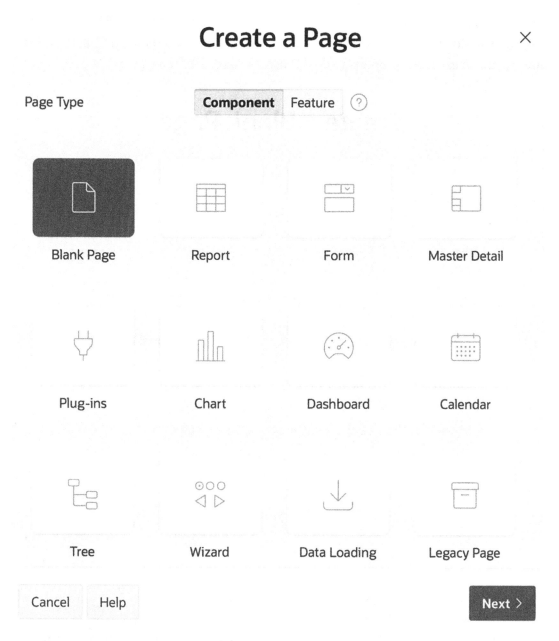

Figure 2-9. *First screen of the Create Page wizard*

The second wizard screen asks for the name, number, and mode of the page; see Figure 2-10. Feel free to use the page number suggested by the wizard. Enter **Region Practice** for the page name, and set the mode to Normal. (The other modes will be discussed in the "Property Editor" section.) The Breadcrumb property specifies whether the page should display a breadcrumb. Breadcrumbs will be discussed in Chapter 4; for now, set the Breadcrumb property to don't use breadcrumbs on page.

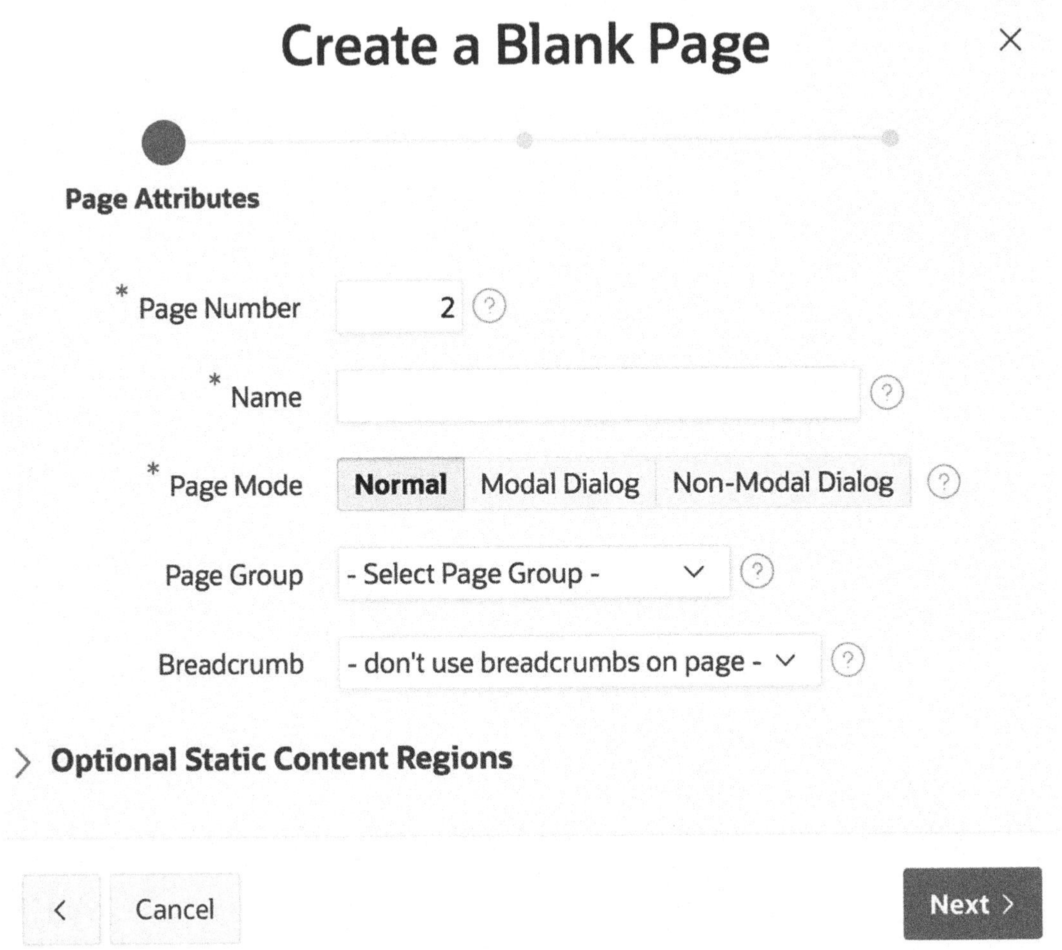

Figure 2-10. Second screen of the Create Page wizard

Figure 2-11 shows the third wizard screen, which asks you to specify whether the page should have a navigation menu entry. Selecting the Create A New Navigation Menu Entry option causes the screen to display items for you to specify the name of the entry and its parent. These options will be discussed in more detail in Chapter 4; for now, use the values **Region Practice** and No parent selected, as shown in the figure.

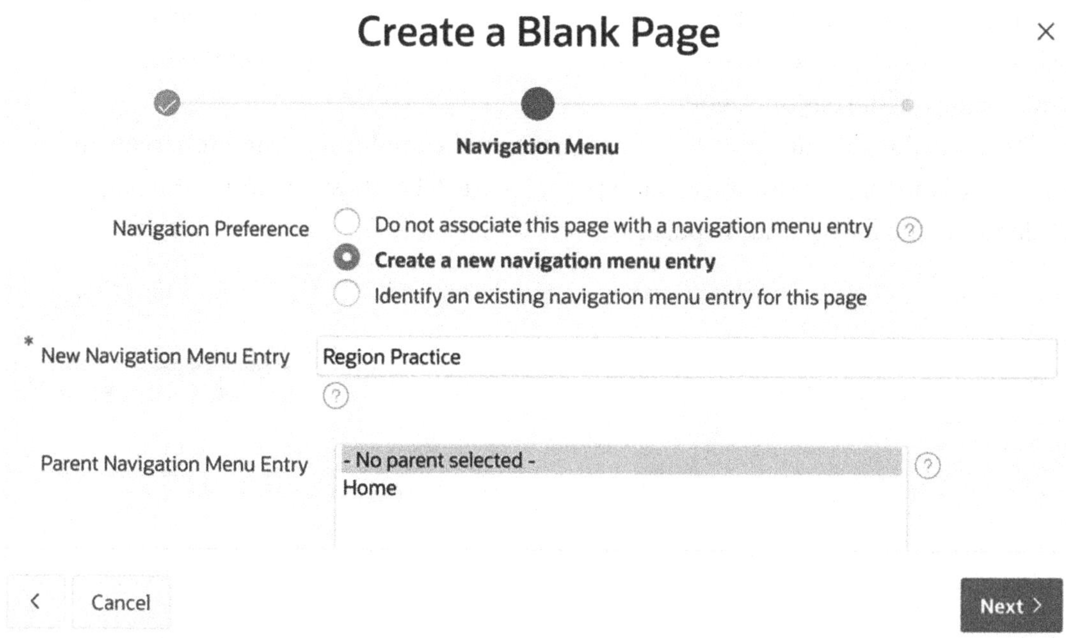

Create a Blank Page   ✕

Navigation Menu

Navigation Preference   ○ Do not associate this page with a navigation menu entry ⑦
           ● **Create a new navigation menu entry**
           ○ Identify an existing navigation menu entry for this page

* New Navigation Menu Entry   Region Practice
           ⑦

Parent Navigation Menu Entry   - No parent selected -   ⑦
           Home

<   Cancel   Next >

Figure 2-11. *Third screen of the Create Page wizard*

The fourth wizard screen (not shown) asks for confirmation. When you click its Finish button, APEX will bring you to the page designer for your new page. But before you delve into the page designer and its use, you should take a look at the page you just created.

Return to your application's home screen (Figure 2-4), either by clicking the link on the page designer's breadcrumb or by clicking the App Builder tab and then selecting the icon for your application. The screen should now contain an icon for page 2. Run your application and observe that the navigation menu now has two entries. Click the Region Practice entry to see your new page. Note that this page has even less content than the home page, because it is missing the breadcrumb. Also note that you can move between the pages by clicking their navigation menu entries.

Page Designer

The APEX page designer screen lets you manage the properties and content of your pages. Because a page can have several kinds of component and each component can have numerous properties, the page designer is extremely dense and can be daunting for beginners. In this book, you will learn about the different parts of the page designer gradually, on an as-needed basis. Each time a new APEX feature is introduced, you will also see how it relates to the page designer. This section introduces the basic functionality of the page designer.

To get to the page designer for a page, begin at the application's home screen and click the name (or icon) for the desired page. Figure 2-12 shows the top of the page designer screen for your home page.

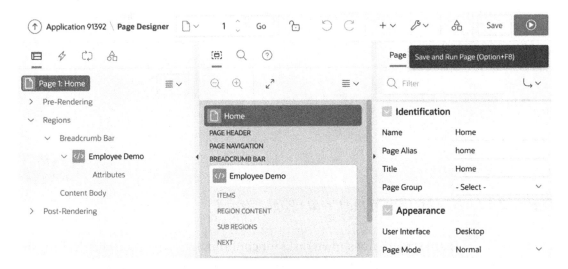

Figure 2-12. *Page designer for the home page*

At the top of Figure 2-12, to the right of the breadcrumb, is a toolbar that consists of several buttons. Here are some immediately useful ones:

- The undo and redo buttons (to the right of the lock) restore the page to a previous state in the typical way.

- The utilities button (labeled with a wrench) has a menu item that lets you delete the page.

- The save button saves your changes to the page.

- The run button (on the right of the save button) saves the page and then runs it.

The page designer supports an iterative page development methodology. The idea is to edit the contents of a page from within the page designer and then run the page. After examining the output, you return to the page designer and repeat the process until the page is satisfactory.

Below the toolbar are three vertical panels that form the heart of the page designer. The left panel displays the components on the page. The right panel specifies the properties of a selected component and is called the *property editor*. The middle panel provides utility functions.

The middle panel has three tabs, which correspond to the utility functions *layout*, *page search*, and *help*. The layout tab, which is selected in Figure 2-12, displays a visual representation of the page layout. You can change the size of the middle panel by dragging its left and right borders, and you can click the icons at the top of the panel to move between the tabs.

The left panel, which shows the page's components, has four tabs: Rendering, Dynamic Actions, Processing, and Page Shared Components. The panel can display the contents of only one tab at a time. You select the tab you want by clicking one of the four icons at the top of the panel. This book focuses on the Rendering and Processing tabs and begins with the Rendering tab. The Processing tab will be introduced in Chapter 7.

The Rendering tab displays the components that determine the page's appearance. These components are displayed as a tree. The root of the tree denotes the page. It has three child nodes, corresponding to the three stages of rendering the page: *pre-rendering*, in which components are initialized; *regions*, in which the components are rendered; and *post-rendering*, when cleanup activities occur. For readability, the rendering tree for page 1 is reproduced in Figure 2-13.

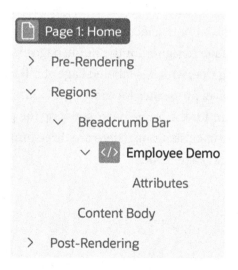

Figure 2-13. *The rendering tree for the home page*

The vast majority of components on a page are in the Regions subtree, so let's explore it more closely.

The real estate of a page is divided into *positions*. For example, the Breadcrumb Bar position runs along the top of the page, and the Content Body position encompasses the main central area of the page. Each region in a page is assigned to a position.

The Regions subtree is structured as follows: its child nodes denote page positions, and each position node has a child node for each region assigned to that position. Thus in Figure 2-13, the two children of Regions correspond to the positions Breadcrumb Bar and Content Body. The position Breadcrumb Bar has a child that denotes the region Employee Demo, and the position Content Body has no regions, and thus no children.

In addition, each region node has a child node named Attributes, and it may have other children, depending on its type. The purpose of these nodes will be covered in Chapter 3.

If a node in the rendering tree has children, then it will have a collapse/expand arrow to its left. Clicking an arrow expands the node to show its children; clicking it again collapses the node to hide the children. You can also right-click a node to recursively collapse or expand the node's subtree.

Property Editor

The property editor is the right panel of the page designer. Its role is to display the properties of whatever component is selected in the left panel.

For example, go to the page designer for the home page and click the root component of the rendering tree, which is labeled Page 1: Home. The right panel will then display the page-level properties for that page. Figure 2-14 displays the top portion of the property editor for the home page, showing the properties for the page's Identification and Appearance sections. There are three properties worth mentioning at this point: Name, Title, and Page Mode.

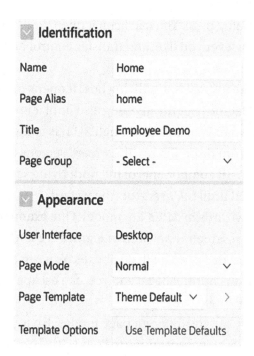

Figure 2-14. *The property editor for the home page*

The Name property identifies the page from within the app builder. You gave the page a name when you created it, and you can change the name here if you decide on a better one.

The Title property identifies the page to a user. Browsers typically display the page title in a browser tab. The property currently has the value **Employee Demo**. For fun, change its value to **This is my home page**, rerun the page, and observe the change in the browser tab.

The Page Mode property specifies how the page is to be used. There are three possible values: Normal, Modal Dialog, and Non-Modal Dialog.

Most pages in a web application are normal. A browser displays a normal page by simply replacing whatever page was previously there. The history of a browser tab (or window) can be thought of as the sequence of accesses to normal pages.

A non-modal dialog page opens in a new browser window. Such pages are typically used as auxiliary pages, peripheral to the primary flow of normal pages. You saw an example of a non-modal page when you examined the SQL command tool in Chapter 1. Its screen, shown in Figure 1-11, is a normal page. But when you click its Find Tables button, the Table Finder window pops up, as shown in Figure 1-12. The content of that window is a non-modal dialog page. You can keep it open for as long as you want, move it around on the screen however you like, and transfer control between it and the current normal page whenever you want.

A modal dialog page corresponds to a dialog box. It opens on top of the current normal page and will not let the user do anything else until it is closed. The app builder's Create Page wizard, shown in Figures 2-9 through 2-11, is composed of modal pages. Although you cannot tell from those figures, the wizard screens appear on top of the application's home screen. All components of the underlying screen (such as buttons, links, and tabs) are disabled until the user exits the wizard.

As a side note, not all wizards in APEX are modal. One example is the Create Application wizard, whose screens appeared in Figures 2-2 and 2-3. These screens are normal pages that masquerade as modal dialog boxes. You can tell this in two ways: they do not sit on top of a previous normal page, and you can escape from the wizard at any point by clicking a menu bar tab.

It is good practice to try out the different page modes. Go to the page designer for the Region Practice page and set its page mode to Modal Dialog. You cannot run the page directly (because a modal page can be displayed only on top of another page), so instead run the home page and then click the Region Practice menu entry. You should observe the modal nature of the page, as shown in Figure 2-15. Then re-edit the page in the page designer, set the page mode to Non-Modal Dialog, and repeat the experiment. Observe that the page still cannot be run directly. When you run the home page and click the Region Practice menu entry, the Region Practice page will open in a new independent browser window, as shown in Figure 2-16. When you are done, set the page's mode back to Normal.

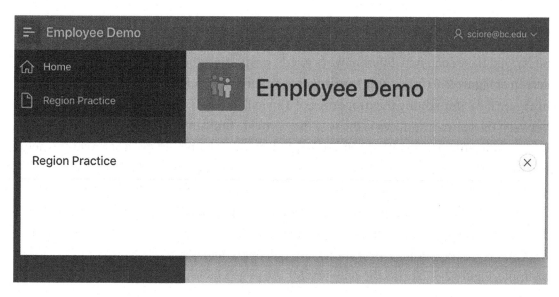

Figure 2-15. *Region Practice as a modal dialog page*

Figure 2-16. *Region Practice as a non-modal dialog page*

Accessing Built-in Help

So far, you have seen two different ways to edit properties: the Application Properties screen of Figure 2-6 (for editing the properties of an application) and the property editor in Figure 2-12 (for editing the properties of a specified page). One interesting difference between these two interfaces is the way they provide built-in help. To read the help text for an application property, you click the question mark icon to its right. To read the help text for a page property, you use the Help section of the page designer.

Recall that the top of the middle panel of the page designer has three tabs: Layout, Search, and Help. When you select Help, the middle panel will display help text for the currently selected property of the property editor. As you move from one property to the next in the property editor, the middle panel displays the help text for that property. For example, Figure 2-17 shows the help text for the page's Name property.

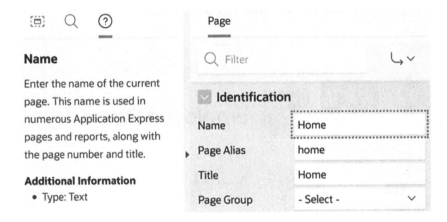

Figure 2-17. *Using built-in help*

Summary

In this chapter, you began your journey through the APEX app builder. You saw how to create an application, populate it with pages, and run them from a browser. You also saw how to use the APEX page designer to view and change the properties of a page.

So far, the pages in your application are devoid of content. The remaining chapters of this book examine the different types of content you can add to your pages. Chapter 3 introduces regions.

CHAPTER 3

Regions

A page's content is divided into rectangular areas called *regions*. Consider, for example, the APEX SQL Workshop home screen of Figure 1-3, which shows seven regions. Six of these regions have titles: `Recently Created Tables`, `Recent SQL Commands`, `Recent SQL Scripts`, `About`, `Schema`, and `Create Object`. The seventh region, which contains the five large buttons, is untitled.

Each region has a *type* that denotes what kind of content it can contain. The regions in Figure 1-3 belong to three different region types:

- The `Recently Created Tables`, `Recent SQL Commands`, and `Recent SQL Scripts` regions contain reports and have the type `Classic Report`.

- The `Create Object` region contains a list of links and has type `List`.

- The `About`, `Schema`, and untitled regions have type `Static Content`.

A region can also contain *controls*—that is, items and buttons. In Figure 1-3, the Schema region contains a select list item and a button, and the untitled region contains five large buttons. Because APEX considers a region's controls to be distinct from its content, any region, regardless of type, can contain controls. This chapter focuses on a region's content; controls will be discussed in Chapters 5 and 6.

APEX supports many different region types. This chapter covers four fundamental types: `Static Content, Classic Report`, `Chart`, and `Interactive Report`. Subsequent chapters introduce other region types: `Breadcrumb` and `List` in Chapter 4, `Region Display Selector` in Chapter 6, `Form` in Chapter 10, and `Interactive Grid` in Chapter 11.

© Edward Sciore 2020
E. Sciore, *Understanding Oracle APEX 20 Application Development*,
https://doi.org/10.1007/978-1-4842-6165-1_3

Creating and Deleting Regions

To create a new region for a page, go to the page designer for that page. Right-click the Regions node of its rendering tree and select Create Region, as shown in Figure 3-1. APEX will then add a region component (named New) to the rendering tree as a child of the Content Body folder. This component will also have a child of its own, named Attributes. See Figure 3-2.

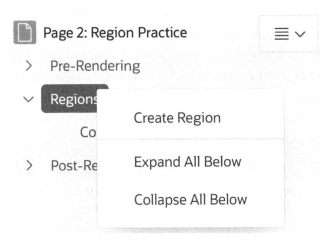

Figure 3-1. *Right-click the Regions node to create a new region*

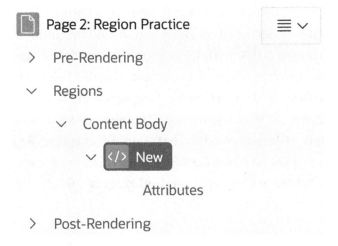

Figure 3-2. *APEX adds a new region to the page*

It might seem strange that APEX uses two components in the rendering tree to represent a single region. The reason is that the properties of these components have separate concerns. In particular, the region component (here labeled New) contains properties common to all regions, whereas the Attributes component contains properties specific to the region's type. The type-independent properties will be discussed in the next section, with the type-specific properties following.

If you want to delete a region, simply right-click its component in the rendering tree and select Delete. For example, the breadcrumb region that came with the home page is useless. Go to the page designer for page 1, find the Breadcrumb region in the rendering tree, and delete it. See Figure 3-3.

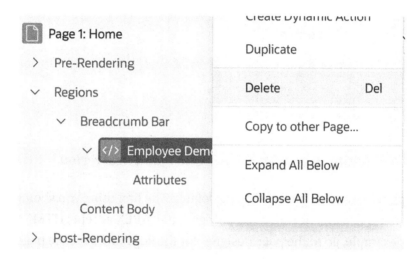

Figure 3-3. *Deleting a region*

Type-Independent Region Properties

To edit the type-independent properties of a region, first select the region's node in the rendering tree. The property editor will then display all type-independent properties for that region and their values. These properties are grouped into *sections*, according to their purpose. Here, I will discuss four important sections: Identification, Source, Layout, and Appearance.

Identification and Source Sections

Figure 3-4 shows the Identification and Source sections for the New region of the Region Practice page and their properties Title, Type, and Text. The Title property identifies the region and describes its purpose. This value is typically displayed in the region's header when the page is rendered.

Identification

Title	New
Type	Static Content ∨

Source

Text	↗

Figure 3-4. *Identification and Source properties for a new region*

A new region is assigned the title New by default. The first thing you should do after creating a region is to assign it a more meaningful title. APEX accepts HTML formatting tags here. For example, go to the page designer for the Region Practice page, select the New region in the rendering tree, and change its Title property to this:

```
<i>My First Region</i>
```

Then, create two more regions on the page, having this title

```
<b>My Second Region</b>
```

and this title

```
<span style="color:red">My Third Region</span>
```

Save and run the page. It should look like Figure 3-5. Note that each title is displayed in the header of its region, in italics, bold, and red, respectively.

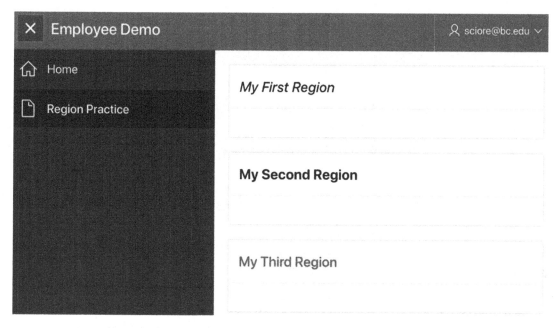

Figure 3-5. *Three regions on the Region Practice page*

A region's content is determined by its Type property and Source section. The type of a region specifies what kind of content it holds, and the Source section specifies the actual content. For example, if the region's type is Static Content, then its Source section contains the text the region should display; if a region's type is Classic Report, then its Source section specifies the table that the region should display.

New regions are assigned the type Static Content, and its source text is empty. For fun, let's assign some source text to the regions My First Region and My Second Region. I went for something simple, namely, **This is my first region** and **This is my second region**.

You change a region's Type property by selecting a type from its list of possible types. For example, change the type of My Third Region to Classic Report. When you do so, the Source section changes so that you can specify a report; see Figure 3-6. By default, the property editor expects the report to display an entire table: the source type is Table/ View and the Table Name property is empty, awaiting the name of a table. The property editor places a red error indicator next to the property name to remind you to enter the table name. It is quite insistent on this point—it will not let you save the page until the error is cleared up. So enter **DEPT** as the table name, and watch the error icon disappear.

Figure 3-6. *The default Source properties of a classic report*

Alternatively, the source of a report can be an SQL query. To try it out, change the source type to SQL Query. This will cause the Table Name property to be replaced with the property SQL Query, again with a red error indicator. Enter the query **select * from DEPT** and watch the indicator disappear.

Figure 3-7 displays the result of running the revised page.

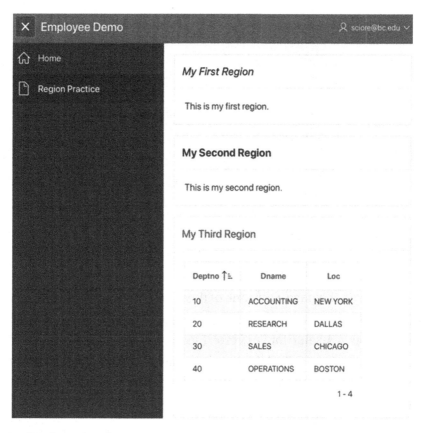

Figure 3-7. *Each region has a non-empty source*

Layout Section

A region's Layout section contains properties that specify the location of the region on its page. These properties are shown in Figure 3-8.

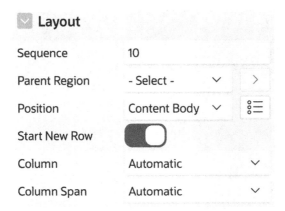

Figure 3-8. *Default Layout section for a region*

The `Parent Region` and `Position` properties provide two different ways to specify the region's location on the page. Only one of these two properties can have a value. A value for `Parent Region` means that the region should be located within a specified region, called its *parent*. A value for `Position` means that the region should be located at a specific position on the page. By default, a new region is located in the `Content Body` position, as shown in Figure 3-8. You can change the position by selecting from its drop-down list, as shown in Figure 3-9.

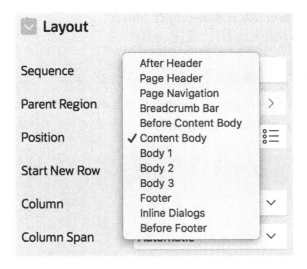

Figure 3-9. *Possible region positions*

These positions are listed in the order they appear on the page, from top to bottom. Most positions have specific purposes. For example, the Content Body position is the primary location for general-purpose regions, the Page Navigation position is intended for the navigation menu along the left side of the page, and the Breadcrumb Bar is for breadcrumb regions.

Note   Some of these positions (namely, After Header, Body 1, Body 2, Body 3, Footer, and Before Footer) are *legacy* positions. That is, they exist only to support applications written with older versions of APEX. New applications should not use them.

The set of possible region positions is determined by the page's *template*. When a page is created, it is assigned the default template defined by the application's theme. For example, the default page template for the Universal theme is called Standard.

It is possible to change a page's template. Select the component for the page in the rendering tree, and look at the Page Template property in the Appearance section. At the moment, the template is set to Theme Default. You can change the template by clicking the property's select list. For example, change the template for the Region Practice page to Right Side Column, as shown in Figure 3-10.

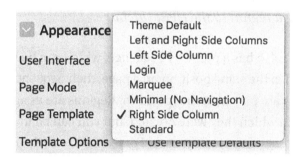

Figure 3-10. *Page template options*

Now choose a region (say, My Second Region) and reexamine its list of Position values; you will discover that in addition to the values in Figure 3-9, there is also the value Right Column. Set the position of My Second Region to Right Column and rerun the page. That region should now appear as a right sidebar, as shown in Figure 3-11. (I added more text to the source of the second region to make it more sidebar-like.) Note that the sidebar region has an arrow icon at its top left. Clicking the icon toggles between displaying the sidebar and hiding it.

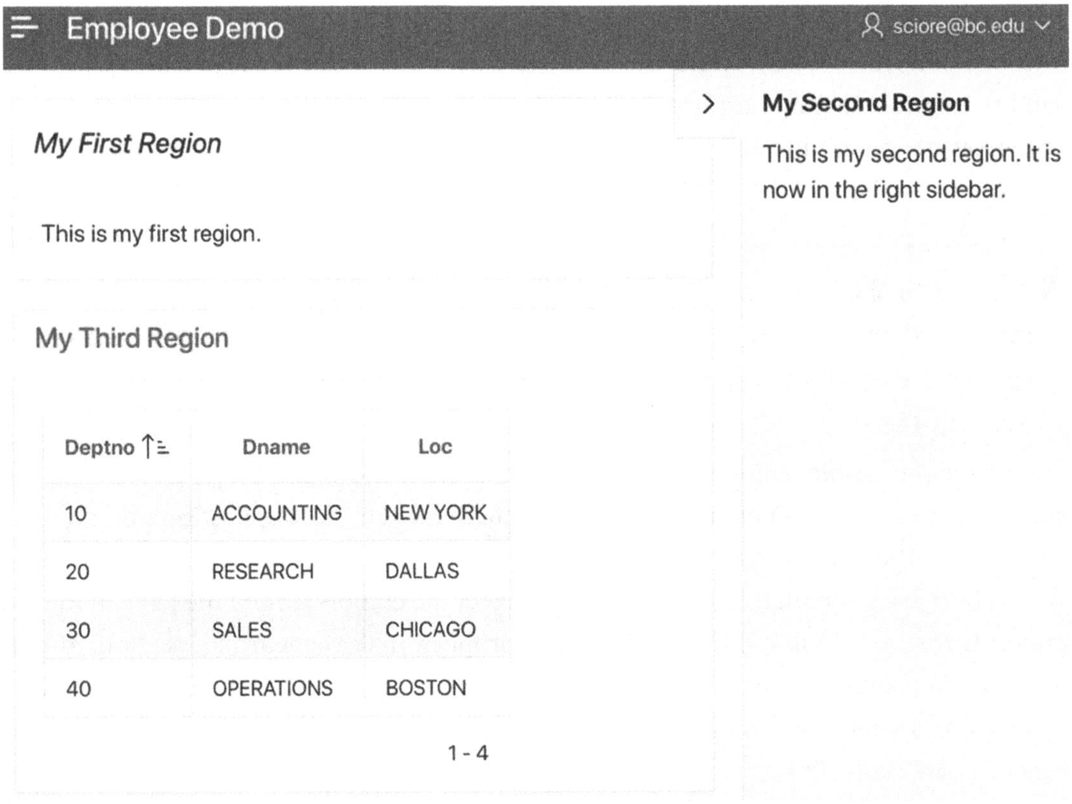

Figure 3-11. *Adding a region to the right sidebar*

The Layout section also has a property Sequence, which can be seen in Figure 3-8. If two regions are located in the same position on a page, their Sequence value determines the order in which they are placed in that position. Regions are assigned sequence numbers in the order in which they were created, but you can change that order by simply assigning different values to Sequence. For example, the My First Region and My Third Region regions are both located in the Content Body position, with sequence numbers of 10 and 30, respectively. If you change the sequence number of My Third Region to 5, the rendered page will look similar to Figure 3-11, except that My Third Region will appear above My First Region.

Although it is good to experiment with placing regions in various positions on the page, most regions on a page are usually located in the same position (in particular, Content Body). In this case, the remaining properties of the Layout section determine the relative location of the regions within that position.

The regions in a position are organized in a grid; each region is assigned to a row and column of that grid. APEX positions the regions according to their sequence number. The first region is placed in the first column of the first row of the grid. Each subsequent region is then placed in one of the following ways:

- In the same row and column as the previous region (in which case it is displayed beneath the previous region)

- In the next column of the current row

- In the first column of a new row

The Start New Row and New Column properties of the Layout section allow you to specify which option to use. Figure 3-12 displays these properties for a region that is placed in a new column of the same row. Figure 3-8 showed the case when a region begins a new row; note that in this case, the New Column property is unnecessary and thus not present.

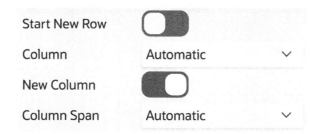

Figure 3-12. *Specifying row and column region positioning*

After assigning each region to a row and column, APEX then determines the size and location of the regions within the position. To do so, APEX uses the values of the Column and Column Span properties (shown in Figure 3-12) to determine the offset and width of each region in a row.

The Column property specifies the offset of the region within its row. APEX divides the width of a position into 12 "grid points"; the value of Column is a number from 1 to 12, denoting one of those points. A value of 1 specifies that the region begins at the far left of the position; a value of 7 specifies that the region begins in the position's center. The Column Span property specifies the width of the column. Its value is also a number from 1 to 12, denoting the width in grid points.

For example, Figure 3-13 shows yet another configuration of the Region Practice regions. Here is how you can create that configuration starting from Figure 3-11: Begin by changing the page template back to Theme Default, moving My Second Region back to the Content Body position with the others, and changing the sequence number of My Third Region to be the smallest. Then set their Grid properties as follows:

- My Third Region starts a new row, its Column value is 3, and Column Span value is 8. That is, its width is two-thirds the size of the position and centered.

- My First Region starts a new row, its Column value is 1, and the Column Span value is 4. Thus, its width is one-third the size of the position and left justified.

- My Second Region does not start a new row. Its Column value is 9, and the Column Span value is 4. Thus, its width is also one-third the size of the position, but right justified.

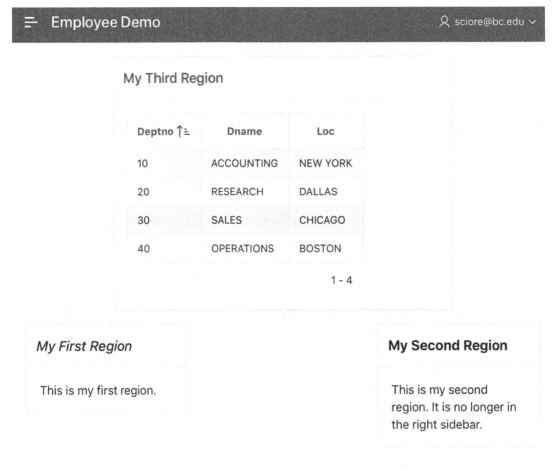

Figure 3-13. Another way to display the Region Practice regions

If you do not need such fine control over the placement of the regions in a row, you can assign the Automatic value to their Column and Column Span properties (as in Figure 3-8). In this case, APEX will place the regions in the row according to its best judgment.

Appearance Section

Figure 3-10 showed the Appearance section for a page, whose properties allow you to configure the page's template. Similarly, each region also has a template, which is specified by the Template property in the region's Appearance section. Figure 3-14 shows the various values for this property.

Figure 3-14. *Options for a region's Template property*

The Standard template, which is the most common, displays the region's title in a border across the top. Many of the other templates have special purposes, such as Alert, Inline Dialog, Login, Title Bar, and Wizard Container.

The Collapsible template is similar to Standard, with the addition of a small button in the top-left corner. Clicking the button toggles between hiding the body of the region and displaying it. A region using the Buttons Container or Blank with Attributes template is untitled; the main difference between these templates is that a button region has a border, whereas a blank region does not.

Drag and Drop

Turn your attention to the middle panel of the page designer, and in particular the Layout tab. Clicking this tab causes the middle panel to display a stylized representation of the page's content. The panel has an area corresponding to each region position, and each area contains a representation of the regions assigned to that position.

For example, consider the Region Practice page as it appears in Figure 3-13; its grid layout is shown in Figure 3-15. From it, you can see the three regions in the Content Body position, displayed in approximately the same way that they will be when the page is rendered.

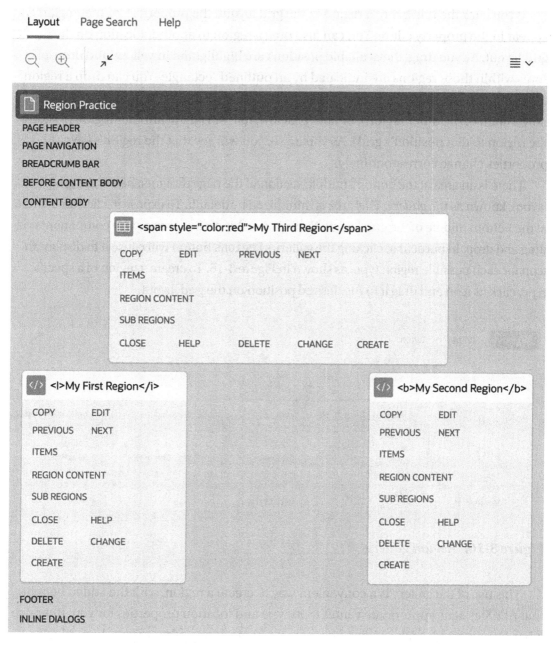

Figure 3-15. *Page layout area*

The grid layout gives you a visual approximation of the layout of the rendered page while you are designing it. When you change the `Position` and `Layout` property values of a region, the grid layout will change accordingly.

If you click the title bar of a region in the grid layout, the properties for that region appear in the property editor. You can also drag a region to another location on the grid layout. As you drag, the available positions are highlighted in yellow, and drop-off spots within those regions are indicated by an outlined rectangle. You can drop a region to an empty position, the Sub Regions section of another region (so that the region is now a child of the other region), or above, below, left, or right of another region (to add the region to that position's grid). As you do so, you will see that the region's Layout properties change correspondingly.

There is an area at the bottom-middle section of the page designer, below the grid layout, known as the *gallery*. This area is minimized by default. To expose it, click the handle at the bottom middle of the grid layout. You can use this area to create page components via drag and drop. In particular, clicking the gallery's Regions button will cause it to display an icon for each possible region type, as shown in Figure 3-16. To create a region of a specific type, click its icon and drag it to the desired position on the grid layout.

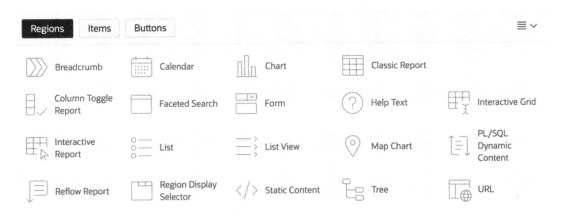

Figure 3-16. Region gallery

This use of the gallery is a convenient way to create a region, with the added benefit that APEX assigns appropriate values to its type and location properties for you. But once it has been created, such a region becomes the same as any other region. In particular, a region's properties (including its type and location) can be modified at any time, without restriction, regardless of how it was created.

Static Content Regions

A *static content region* can display text or formatted HTML code. The APEX screens contain several examples of static regions. For example, consider once again the SQL Workshop home screen from Figure 1-3. The region titled About on the right side of the page is a static content region whose source is the displayed text. The source contains HTML tags that cause Learn More... to be formatted as a link.

You can do similar things to your demo application. Let's beef up the home page to contain four static content regions. Figure 3-17 shows what the page will look like. The goal of this section is to learn the concepts needed to create this page.

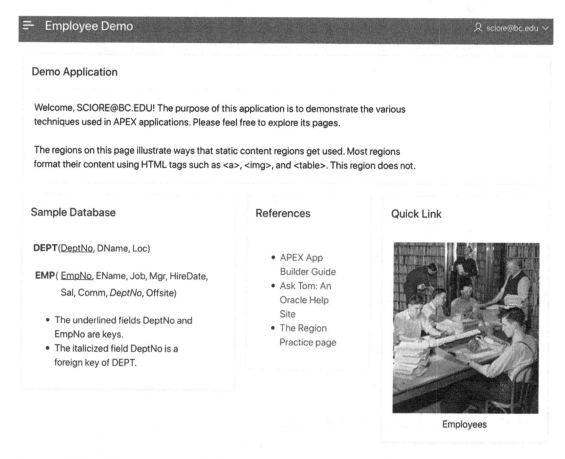

Figure 3-17. *Home page with four static content regions (photo courtesy of Library of Congress, Prints & Photographs Division, LC-H261-4562)*

The first step is to create and position the regions on the page before you assign any content to them. To do so, perform the following tasks:

- Go to the page designer for the home page and create four new regions. These regions by default will have the type Static Content, which is what you want.

- Assign the titles Demo Application, Sample Database, References, and Quick Link to the regions, in that order.

- Place the regions in the Content Body position, and use their Layout properties to specify their placement on the page. In particular, the Demo Application and Sample Database regions start new rows, and the other two regions start new columns. The Sample Database, References, and Quick Link regions should have column spans of 5, 3, and 4, respectively.

At this point, you can run your home page and verify that it has the intended structure. The page should look like Figure 3-18.

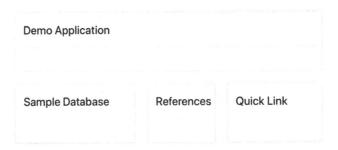

Figure 3-18. *Structure of the home page*

The next step is to add content to these regions. The following sections address the relevant issues.

Formatted vs. Unformatted Text

The source of a static content region is the text to be displayed. APEX can interpret this text in two ways: as the characters exactly as written or as HTML code to be formatted. The property that specifies this option is called Output As, and it appears in the Settings section of the region's Attributes node in the page rendering tree. Figure 3-19 shows this section with the two possible values of the Output As property.

Figure 3-19. *Type-specific properties for a static content region*

An `Output As` value of `HTML` specifies that the region's source contains HTML code. APEX will send this code as-is to the browser when it renders the page, so that the browser can format the source accordingly.

On the other hand, a value of `Text (escape special characters)` specifies that the source should be displayed exactly as it appears. In this case, APEX needs to transform the text so that there are no HTML tags for the browser to execute. It does so by replacing certain characters (such as < and >) with different characters that happen to print the same (such as < and >). This transformation is called *escaping* the characters. The result is text that looks like HTML code, but really is not.

The `Sample Database` region of Figure 3-17 illustrates several kinds of formatting:

- The description of the `EMP` and `DEPT` tables makes use of the bold, italic, and underline tags.

- To get the fields of `EMP` to line up in two rows, it uses a borderless table having two columns: the first row consists of "`EMP(`" in one column and the fields in the second column, and the second row consists of nothing in the first column and the remaining fields in the second column.

- The bullet list is implemented as an unordered list in HTML, and each bullet point is a list item.

Consequently, the region's `Output As` property needs to be set to `HTML`. The source code for the region is given in Listing 3-1.

Listing 3-1. Source of the Sample Database Region

```
<p>
<b>DEPT</b>(<u>DeptNo</u>, DName, Loc)
</p><p>
<table border=0>
<tr>
    <td><b>EMP</b>(</td>
    <td><u>EmpNo</u>, EName, Job, Mgr, HireDate, </td>
</tr>
<tr>
    <td> </td>
    <td>Sal, Comm, <i>DeptNo</i>, Offsite) </td>
</tr>
</table>
</p>
<ul>
<li> The underlined fields DeptNo and EmpNo are keys.
<li> The italicized field DeptNo is a foreign key of DEPT.
</ul>
```

Now consider the Demo Application region. Its content is unformatted and in fact contains HTML tags that should not be formatted. So the Output As property for this region should be Text (escape special characters). Its source appears in Listing 3-2.

Listing 3-2. Source of the Demo Application Region

```
Welcome, &APP_USER.! The purpose of this application is to demonstrate the
various techniques used in APEX applications. Please feel free to explore
its pages.

The regions on this page illustrate ways that static content regions get
used. Most regions format their content using HTML tags such as <a>, <img>,
and <table>. This region does not.
```

The beginning of this listing makes reference to "&APP_USER." This string is called a *substitution string,* and APEX interprets it as the name of the user. This topic is addressed next.

Substitution Strings

The APEX server has several built-in variables that hold information of interest. Here are three useful ones:

- The variable APP_USER holds the username of whoever is currently logged in. If the application does not require users to log in, the value of the variable is **APEX_PUBLIC_USER**.

- The variable APP_ID holds the ID of the current application.

- The variable APP_SESSION holds the ID of the current session.

To refer to the value of a variable from within HTML text, you prepend the character & and append the period character (.) to the variable name. Such an expression is called a *substitution string*. In other words, the substitution string for a variable named X is written "&X.". When the APEX server renders a page, it textually replaces the substitution string by the value of its variable.

For example, the substitution string &APP_USER. appears in the source of the Demo Application region. When the APEX server renders the page, it textually replaces the substitution string with the value of the variable APP_USER, which in this case is **SCIORE@BC.EDU**.

Referring to APEX Pages

The References region contains a bullet list of three entries. The first two entries contain links to external web pages; the third entry is a link to the application's Region Practice page. The source of the region appears in Listing 3-3.

Listing 3-3. Source of the References Region

```
<ul>
<li><a href="https://docs.oracle.com/en/database/oracle/application-
express/20.1/htmdb/index.html">
      APEX App Builder Guide </a></li>
<li><a href="http://asktom.oracle.com/pls/apex/f?p=100:1">
      Ask Tom: An Oracle Help Site </a></li>
<li><a href="f?p=&APP_ID.:2:&APP_SESSION.">
      The Region Practice page</a></li>
</ul>
```

The HTML `<a>` tag specifies a link; its argument is the URL of the target location. The first link in the listing is a typical link, which refers to a page on an external website. The second link refers to a page of another APEX application—in particular, page 1 of application 100 on the APEX server at `asktom.oracle.com`. Note how the link uses the "f?p=" notation, as described in Chapter 2.

The third link in the listing refers to page 2 of the current application; thus, it can be written as a relative reference. It uses the built-in variables `APP_ID` and `APP_SESSION` to refer to the current application ID and session ID. The reference looks like this:

`f?p=&APP_ID.:2:&APP_SESSION.`

The concept of a session will be covered in Chapter 6. For the moment, it suffices to know that APEX uses a session identifier to indicate related page accesses. By passing the current session ID into the URL, you ensure that the current session will continue when the link is followed. Note that the second link in the region did not include a session identifier. This was appropriate because the link was beginning a new session with the Ask Tom application.

Referring to Local Images

An HTML `<img>` tag displays an image; its argument is the URL of the image file. If the URL is a reference to a file on another web server, an absolute URL works fine. However, if you plan to store an image file on the APEX web server, then you should use a relative URL. The format of this URL is determined as follows.

The first thing to do is upload the file to the server. Go to the home screen of your application, click the `Shared Components` button, and find the `Files` section as shown in Figure 3-20.

Figure 3-20. *Files section of the Shared Components screen*

You have two options to choose from: Static Application Files or Static Workspace Files. The difference between them is one of visibility. An application file can be referenced from a specific application only, whereas a workspace file can be accessed by any application in the workspace. Whichever option you click, you will be taken to a screen that lets you choose your file. Then click the Upload button to upload it.

To display your image file using an HTML <img> tag, you must specify its location on the server. However, APEX will not tell you where it stored your image files; instead, it provides you with built-in variables. There are two variables, APP_IMAGES and WORKSPACE_IMAGES, whose values hold the path to your application images and workspace images on the server. You use substitution strings to access the value of these variables. For example, I uploaded the employee photograph to a file named employees.jpg and saved it in APEX as an application file. You should do the same with a picture of your choice. The HTML tag to display this file is

```
<img src="&APP_IMAGES.employees.jpg">
```

Note the two different uses of the period character in this tag. The first one is part of the substitution string notation and will be replaced by the path to the image directory when the page is rendered; the second one is part of the filename.

With this in mind, take a look at the source of the Quick Link region in Listing 3-4.

Listing 3-4. Source of the Quick Link Region

```
<div align=center>
<a href="f?p=&APP_ID.:3:&APP_SESSION.">
<img src="&APP_IMAGES.employees.jpg">
</a><br>
Employees
</div>
```

This code uses the <img> tag to display the employees.jpg image and then uses <a> and </a> tags to wrap this image in a link. Consequently, clicking the image takes the user to page 3 of the application (which means that the link will be nonfunctional until the next section, in which page 3 is created).

Chapter 2 discussed the possibility of using an image as the application's logo. To demonstrate this possibility, I created a stylized image of the words "Employee Demo," saved it in the file Logo.jpg, and uploaded it to APEX as an application file. I then configured the application's logo as described in Chapter 2. That is, I clicked the Edit Application Properties button in the application home page, clicked the User Interface tab, and modified the properties in the Logo section, as shown in Figure 3-21. A screenshot of the logo appears in Figure 3-22.

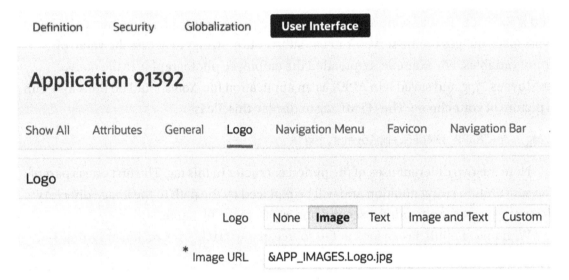

Figure 3-21. *Specifying an image logo*

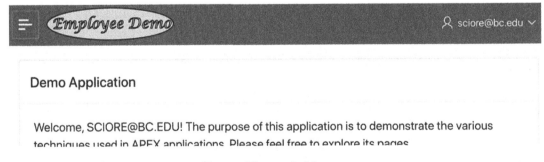

Figure 3-22. *Logo corresponding to Figure 3-21*

Classic Report Regions

Earlier in this chapter, you had a brief encounter with a classic report region, when you created a report in the Region Practice page having the source query **select * from DEPT**. This section examines classic reports in more detail. Page 3 of the Employee Demo application contains two regions, titled Default Report and Formatted Report. Figures 3-23 and 3-24 display the reports from these two regions.

Empno ↑≞	Ename	Job	Hiredate	Sal	Deptno	Offsite
7369	SMITH	CLERK	12/17/1980	800	20	N
7499	ALLEN	SALESMAN	2/20/1981	1600	30	Y
7521	WARD	SALESMAN	2/22/1981	1250	30	Y
7566	JONES	MANAGER	4/2/1981	2975	20	N
7654	MARTIN	SALESMAN	9/28/1981	1250	30	N
7698	BLAKE	MANAGER	5/1/1981	2850	30	N
7782	CLARK	MANAGER	6/9/1981	2450	10	N
7788	SCOTT	ANALYST	12/9/1982	3000	20	Y
7839	KING	PRESIDENT	11/17/1981	5000	10	N
7844	TURNER	SALESMAN	9/8/1981	1500	30	Y
7876	ADAMS	CLERK	1/12/1983	1100	20	N
7900	JAMES	CLERK	12/3/1981	950	30	N
7902	FORD	ANALYST	12/3/1981	3000	20	N
7934	MILLER	CLERK	1/23/1982	1300	10	N

1 - 14

Figure 3-23. *The default employee report*

Name	Hiredate	Sal	Department	Offsite
FORD the ANALYST	Dec 03, 1981	$3,000	RESEARCH	✖
SCOTT the ANALYST	Dec 09, 1982	$3,000	RESEARCH	✔
ADAMS the CLERK	Jan 12, 1983	$1,100	RESEARCH	✖
JAMES the CLERK	Dec 03, 1981	$950	SALES	✖
MILLER the CLERK	Jan 23, 1982	$1,300	ACCOUNTING	✖

1-5   6-10   11-14

Figure 3-24. *The formatted employee report*

Both reports have the same source, which is the following SQL query:

```
select EmpNo, EName, Job, HireDate, Sal, DeptNo, Offsite
from EMP
```

The formatted report differs from the default report in the following ways:

- The columns EmpNo and Job are not displayed.

- The column headers for EName and DeptNo have been renamed, and the header for Hiredate is in italics.

- The records can only be sorted by employee name or salary.

- Employee names are accentuated by writing them in a larger font and in bold and include the employee's job.

- Hire dates are formatted differently from the default report and are links.

- Salary values are formatted as currency and aligned right, and values over $2,500 are colored red.

- Department values are shown as department names instead of department numbers.

- Values for the Offsite column are displayed as images instead of text.

- Fewer rows are displayed at a time, with pagination controls.

This section will show you how to use the type-specific properties of report regions (together with some additions to the SQL source query) to build the formatted report. Begin by following these steps:

- Create a new blank page named Classic Reports and having page number 3. Tell the wizard to create a navigation menu entry for the page, also named Classic Reports.

- Go to the page editor for this page and create two new regions. Title the regions Default Report and Formatted Report, and place them in the Content Body position of the page.

- Set the type of each region to be Classic Report having the source query given earlier.

- Configure their Layout properties so that the Formatted Report region starts a new row. (Or if you prefer to see the reports side by side, set the properties so that Formatted Report does not start a new row.)

At this point, your page should display two identical regions that look like Figure 3-23. Figure 3-25 depicts the top of the resulting rendering tree for this page, showing the components for the Default Report region. (The components for the Formatted Report region are similar and thus omitted.) Note that APEX created several components for each report: a component (labeled with the region name) that contains the type-independent properties, a component (labeled Attributes) that contains report-specific properties, and a component for each column of the report that contains the column-specific properties. The following sections examine these column-specific and report-specific properties.

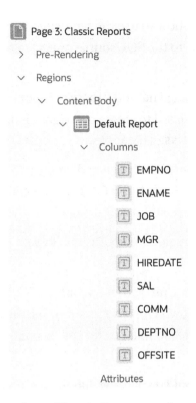

Figure 3-25. *Rendering tree for a Classic Report region*

Column-Specific Properties

Each column in a report has its own set of properties. When you select a column node in the rendering tree, the property editor shows you its column-specific properties. These properties are grouped into several sections, which are discussed next.

Identification

Figure 3-26 displays the two properties in the Identification section. The Column Name property is the name of the column. The column name comes directly from the source query, and therefore this value cannot be changed.

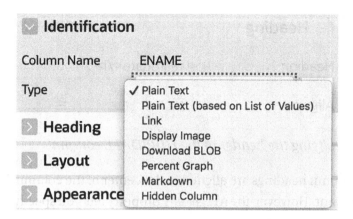

Figure 3-26. *Specifying the type of the ENAME column*

The Type property specifies how APEX should display the column values. The possible type values are shown in Figure 3-26. The type Plain Text is the default and says to display the value as is. The type Link says to display the value as a link, the type Display Image as an image, and the type Percent Graph graphically. The type Hidden Column says not to display the values at all.

In the Default Report region, all columns are plain text. The columns of the Formatted Report region have the following types: ENAME, SAL, and OFFSITE are plain text, EMPNO and JOB are hidden, HIREDATE is a link, and DEPTNO is plain text based on a list of values. In your application, you can change the type of the two hidden columns now. However, you need to wait until later in the chapter before you can change the type of HIREDATE and DEPTNO.

Column Heading

A column's Heading section contains two properties for customizing the column's report header. The Heading property contains the value that is displayed in the column header. By default, this is the column name, but it can be changed. For example in my application, I changed the header for ENAME to be **Name** and the header for DEPTNO to be **Department**.

In general, the value for Heading can include HTML code, such as formatted text or an image. For example, Figure 3-27 shows my HTML code for the header of HIREDATE, which causes APEX to display the string **Hiredate** in italics.

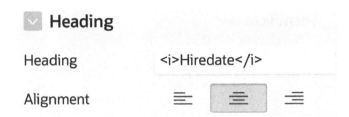

Figure 3-27. *Specifying the header of the HIREDATE column*

By default, column headings are aligned in the center of the column. This is almost always what you want. However, the `Alignment` property lets you specify a different alignment if for some reason this seems appropriate.

Column Layout

The `Layout` section contains two properties for customizing the display of the columns. The `Sequence` property determines the order in which the columns appear in the report. The `Column Alignment` property specifies the alignment of the column values. By default, column values are aligned to the left. Figure 3-28 shows the `Layout` section for the SAL column, in which the alignment is set to the right.

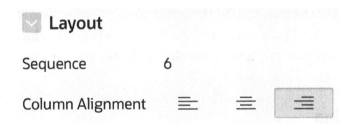

Figure 3-28. *Specifying the layout of the SAL column*

Sort Order

APEX divides the issue of sorting into two aspects: how it sorts the records when it first renders the report and whether the user can interactively re-sort the report by clicking column headers. If a report's source query has an `order by` clause, the records are sorted in that order and cannot be altered by the user. Otherwise, these aspects are determined by the properties in each column's `Sorting` section. Figure 3-29 shows the `Sorting` section for ENAME.

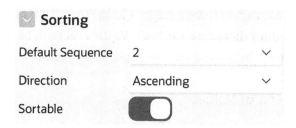

Figure 3-29. *Specifying the sort behavior of the ENAME column*

The `Default Sequence` property specifies the initial sort order. Each column that participates in the initial sort order will have a value for `Default Sequence`, with the primary sort column having value 1. In Figure 3-29, `ENAME` has sequence 2. Not shown is the sequence property for `JOB,` which has sort sequence 1. Together, they imply that the report will be rendered with the rows sorted by job, and two employees having the same job will be listed alphabetically by name (as you can see in Figure 3-24).

The `Sortable` property specifies whether a user is able to interactively sort on the column. By default, all columns are sortable. In the `Formatted Report` region, I turned off sortability for all columns except `ENAME` and `SAL`.

The initial sort sequence is completely independent of sortability. For example, the `Formatted Report` region is initially sorted by the `JOB` column, even though the column is not even visible.

List of Values

Consider the `DEPTNO` column in the formatted report. It displays values from the `DEPT` table, even though the report mentions only the `EMP` table. How can this be?

The answer is that the values in the column have not changed; they are still department numbers. However, you can set up a correspondence between department names and numbers and tell APEX to display the name corresponding to a given department number. This correspondence between the return value (the department number) and its display value (the department name) is called a *list of values*.

Formally, a list of values is a two-column table. The first column holds the display values, and the second column holds the corresponding return values. One useful way to specify a list of values is to use an SQL query. For example, the list-of-values query for the `DEPTNO` column is simply this:

```
select DName, DeptNo
from DEPT
```

When you assign a column to have the type Plain Text (based on List of Values), the property editor displays a List of Values section. Figure 3-30 shows the section with the property values filled in.

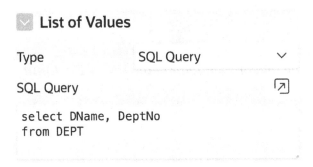

Figure 3-30. *Formatting the DEPTNO column using a list of values*

Format Masks

You occasionally might want to display a number as a string having a particular format. For example, you might use a comma to separate every three digits, you might have a prescribed number of digits to the right of the decimal point, or you might prefix the number with a currency character. Date values can also be written in different formats. In each case, you can use a *format mask* to express your desired format.

A column's Format Mask property is in its Appearance section. Figure 3-31 shows how I filled in the property for SAL. The icon to the right is a "quick pick" button. Clicking it brings up a list of common formats; selecting a format places its mask in the property's text box. If you are not familiar with the Oracle format mask syntax, you can get a reasonable understanding by examining the various masks. For example, 9 denotes an optional digit, 0 a required digit, G a thousands' separator, D the decimal point, and so on. Such an understanding makes it possible to modify the mask to fit your needs.

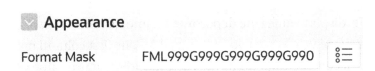

Figure 3-31. *My format mask for SAL*

For example, to get the mask for the SAL column, I chose the currency format $5,234.10 from the format list, which produced the mask FML999G999G999G999G990D00. However, because the EMP table stores salary values in whole dollars, I did not want to display the decimal point and the two digits to its right. So I removed the D00 from the end of the mask.

The mask for HIREDATE was created similarly. An examination of the various date format masks shows that DD denotes the day, Mon the three-character abbreviation of the month, and YYYY the four-digit year. I combined these elements to create my desired format mask, which is shown in Figure 3-32.

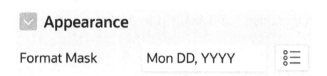

Figure 3-32. *My format mask for HIREDATE*

For a complete description of format mask syntax, search the Oracle SQL documentation for "format models."

Column Formatting

Columns of type Plain Text have a section called Column Formatting, which has a property named HTML Expression. This property allows you to format a column value by wrapping it in an HTML expression. For an example, look back at the formatted ENAME column of Figure 3-24. The name of each employee is in a large bold font, and the employee's job appears after it. Figure 3-33 shows the HTML expression corresponding to this format.

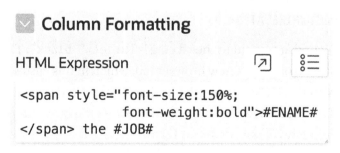

Figure 3-33. *Formatting the ENAME column*

This expression requires some explanation. To begin, consider what HTML expression you would write for the employee named FORD. To make the name large and bold, you can place it inside <span> tags. The resulting expression would look like this:

```
<span style="font-size:150%;
              font-weight:bold">FORD</span> the ANALYST
```

This expression is almost what the HTML Expression value should be—the only difference is that the employee's name and job need to vary for each row of the report. APEX makes this possible via the following convention: for a column named X, the term #X# denotes the value of X in the current row. Thus, you should replace FORD in the preceding expression by #ENAME# and ANALYST by #JOB#, resulting in the expression from Figure 3-33:

```
<span style="font-size:150%;
              font-weight:bold">#ENAME#</span> the #JOB#
```

Note that the expression #JOB# makes sense, even though the JOB column is not visible in the report. In fact, one of the common reasons for having nonvisible columns in a report is so you can use their values elsewhere in the report.

Link Columns

The HireDate values in Figure 3-24 are formatted as links. In particular, clicking a hire date (say, Dec 03, 1981) redirects the browser to the URL http://www.infoplease. com/year/1981.html, which gives the current events of that year.

One way to implement this functionality is to wrap the hire date in an appropriate HTML expression. For example, the link for Dec 03, 1981, would be the following:

```
<a href="http://www.infoplease.com/year/1981.html"
   target="_blank">#HIREDATE#</a>
```

Note that the second argument to the <a> tag is target="_blank". This argument causes the target page to open in a new browser tab, which in this case seems reasonable.

The problem with this HTML expression is that it always redirects to the page for 1981, regardless of the hire date. We need a way to extract the hire year from the hire date, which unfortunately is not possible in HTML.

However, it is possible to extract the year from within an SQL query. The idea is to have the SQL source query compute a new column, whose value is the hire year. The following query does the job:

```
select e.*, extract(year from e.HireDate) as HireYear
from EMP e
```

A consequence of using this new source query is that HIREYEAR will now be a column of the report. Since you don't want to see it in the report, you should set its type to Hidden Column.

After you modify the source of the Formatted Report region to be this query, you can format the HIREDATE column by using #HIREYEAR# in its HTML Expression property, as follows:

```
<a href="http://www.infoplease.com/year/#HIREYEAR#.html"
   target="_blank">#HIREDATE#</a>
```

Although this technique works, a better way to format a column as a link is to set its Type property to Link. Doing so causes the property editor to display a Link section. This section has the property Target, whose initial value is No Link Defined. Clicking that value opens a modal Link Builder page, in which you specify whether the target is a page of an APEX application or an arbitrary URL. In this case, select URL and enter the target URL into the text box that appears, as shown in Figure 3-34. Then click the OK button to return to the property editor.

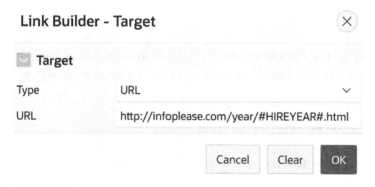

Figure 3-34. *Using the Link Builder page*

You can then enter the appropriate values for Link Text and Link Attributes into the Link section, as shown in Figure 3-35. Note that you need to enter the "http://" portion of the URL in the link builder, even though the Target property does not display it.

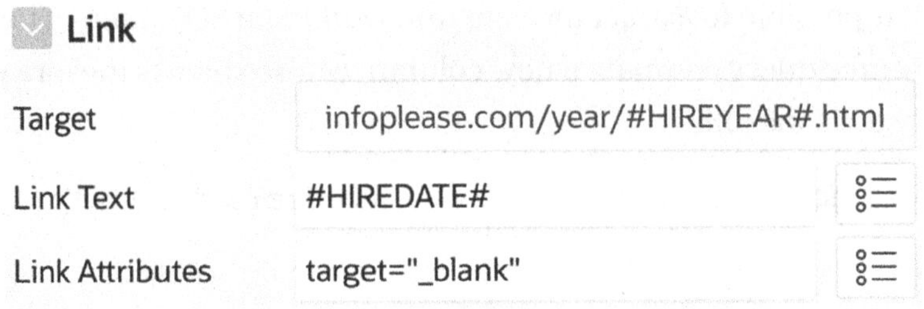

Link

Target	infoplease.com/year/#HIREYEAR#.html
Link Text	#HIREDATE#
Link Attributes	target="_blank"

Figure 3-35. *Link properties for the HIREDATE column*

Conditional Formatting

Recall that Figure 3-24 displays salaries in red if their value is over 2500. It is easy enough to use the HTML Expression property to format SAL values in a particular color. For example, the following expression makes all salary values red:

```
<span style="color:red">#SAL#</span>
```

But how do you write an expression to make only some of the values red? Because HTML by itself cannot perform calculations, you must again rely on SQL to do it for you. The idea is to have the SQL source query compute another new column, called SalColor, whose value is the color of the salary value. Here is the desired query (new code is in bold):

```
select e.*, extract(year from e.HireDate) as HireYear,
       case when e.Sal>2500 then 'red' else 'black' end as SalColor
from EMP e
```

After you change the Formatted Report region to have this query as its source, you can format the SAL column by assigning the following code to its HTML Expression property:

```
<span style="color:#SALCOLOR#">#SAL#</span>
```

You can apply the same technique to the OFFSITE column. In the formatted report, an Offsite value shows an image of a green check mark if its value is **Y** and a red check mark otherwise. Assume that these two images have been saved to APEX as the application files checkgreen.jpg and checkred.jpg. (You can download these files from the Apress website.) Then a value of **Y** should be formatted as the following HTML expression:

```
<img src="&APP_IMAGES.checkgreen.jpg">
```

The value of **N** should be formatted as follows:

```
<img src="&APP_IMAGES.checkred.jpg">
```

The way to distinguish between these two file names is to extend the SQL source query so that it computes a new column, named OffsiteImage, whose value is either 'checkgreen.jpg' or 'checkred.jpg'. The SQL query now looks like this (new code is in bold):

```
select e.*, extract(year from e.HireDate) as HireYear,
      case when e.Sal>2500 then 'red' else 'black' end as SalColor,
      case when e.Offsite = 'Y' then 'checkgreen.jpg'
          else 'checkred.jpg' end as OffsiteImage
from EMP e
```

After changing the source of the report to this query, you can format the OFFSITE column by assigning the following code to its HTML Expression property:

```
<img src="&APP_IMAGES.#OFFSITEIMAGE#">
```

Finally, you should set the type of columns SALCOLOR and OFFSITEIMAGE to Hidden Column.

Report-Specific Properties

It is now time to consider the report-specific properties of a classic report. These properties are associated with the region's Attributes node in the rendering tree and handle issues such as pagination and record grouping. Figure 3-36 shows the Layout and Pagination sections for the Formatted Report region.

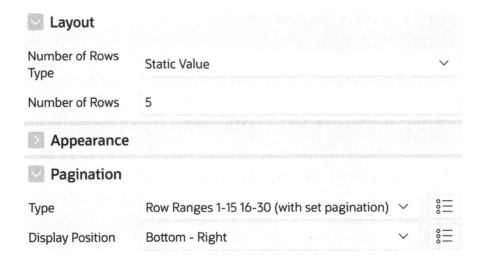

Figure 3-36. *Report-specific properties of a classic report region*

The Number of Rows property specifies how many rows of the report to display at a time. By default, the value is 15, but I changed it to 5 in the Formatted Report region. The pagination Type property allows you to select the format of the pagination controls. The option shown in the figure was used for the Formatted Report region in Figure 3-24. The best way to understand the other options is to try each one on your report to see its effect.

Using the Source Query for Formatting

Although the previous sections have focused on how to use APEX to format the rows of a source query, it is important to realize that you can get many of these same features by using a more precise source query. Here are some examples for the Formatted Report demo region.

Instead of hiding a column, it might be more appropriate to simply not include it in the query. In particular, the EmpNo column serves no purpose in the formatted report and is better off being left out of its source query entirely. On the other hand, the columns Job, SalColor, OffsiteImage, and HireYear are needed for the formatting of other columns, so they must appear in the source query and therefore must be of type Hidden Column.

Instead of changing a column's heading in the property editor, you could change the column's name in the source query. An example is the EName column, which was renamed as Name. The alternative is to use the AS keyword in the source query, like this:

```
select EName as Name, ...
from EMP
```

If you don't want the user to be able to change the sort order of the records interactively, it is easier to specify the sort order in the source query than to set the sortability property of each column individually.

Instead of using a list of values to format the DeptNo column, you can modify the source query to be a join of the EMP and DEPT tables like this:

```
select e.EName as Name, ..., d.DName, ...
from EMP e join DEPT d
on e.DeptNo = d.DeptNo
```

In this case, it is hard to say which of these two approaches is better than the other. The list-of-values approach requires that APEX search the list of values for each row of the report, which is potentially more expensive than simply doing the join in one shot. On the other hand, the list-of-values approach is simpler and more directly conveys the intent of the designer.

The rule of thumb is that the source query should specify *what* you want displayed, whereas the column properties should specify *how* you want them displayed. In some cases (such as hidden columns), this distinction is clear. In others (such as using a list of values), it is less so.

Chart Regions

A *chart* is a visual way to display data points. A data point consists of two values: the x coordinate, called the *label*, and the y coordinate, called the *value*. As an example, let's build a page named Charts, which will be page 4 of the application. This page contains two chart regions, which are shown in Figures 3-37 and 3-38.

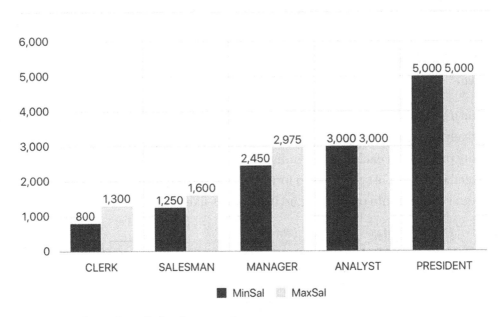

Figure 3-37. *The Salary Info chart region*

Employee Counts

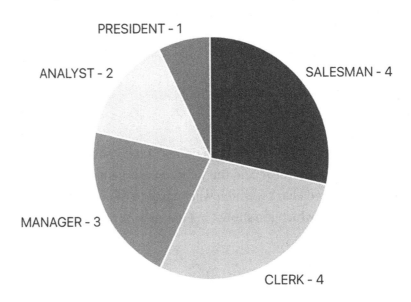

Figure 3-38. *The Employee Counts chart region*

The bar chart consists of ten data points, giving the minimum and maximum salaries of employees at each job. These points are organized into two *series* of five points each.

The pie chart consists of five data points, one for each job. The label of each point is the name of the job, and the value is the number of employees having that job. The chart displays a section of the pie for each label in proportion to its value. For example, two of the fourteen employees are analysts, so the size of the ANALYST section is two-fourteenths the size of the pie.

Creating a Chart Region

To build this page, begin by creating a new blank page named Charts, and add to it two regions of type Chart. Name the first region Salary Info and the second region Employee Counts. Figure 3-39 shows the resulting rendering tree for these regions.

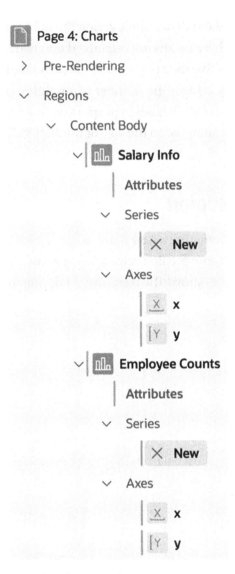

Figure 3-39. *Rendering tree for the two chart regions*

From this figure, you can see that a chart has four kinds of properties: type-independent properties (denoted by the region name), chart-specific properties (denoted by Attributes), properties specific to each chart series (denoted by Series), and properties associated with the chart axes (denoted by Axes). By default, a chart is created with one series (named New), but you can rename the series and add others.

Each series in Figure 3-39 is flagged with a red error indicator to tell you that the chart needs further configuration. Details of this configuration are discussed next.

Configuring a Chart

Every chart needs a *source*, which is an expression that specifies the chart's data points. A common source is an SQL query. If the chart has N series, then the query will have N+1 columns—one column contains the labels, and the other columns contain the values for each series. For example, the series for Salary Info has the following source query:

```
select Job, min(Sal) as MinSal, max(Sal) as MaxSal
from EMP
group by Job
order by MinSal
```

You specify the source of a chart similar to how you would specify the source of a report. The chart's Source section contains the three properties you need. Figure 3-40 shows the values of these properties for the Salary info region. You should also make similar changes to your Employee Counts region, using the following source query:

```
select Job, count(*) as EmpCount
from EMP
group by Job
order by EmpCount desc
```

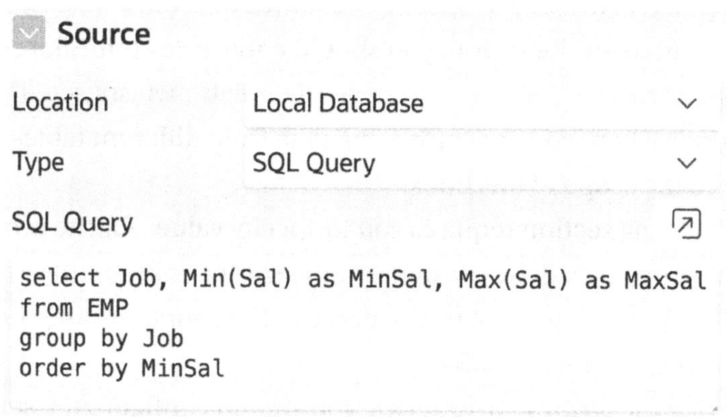

Figure 3-40. Specifying the source of the Salary Info chart

Configuring a Chart Series

After you have configured the source of a chart, you can configure each of its series. The relevant properties for a series are in its Identification, Source, and Column Mapping sections. Figure 3-41 shows these sections for the series created for Salary Info.

Identification

Name	MinSal

Execution Options

Sequence	10

Source

Location	Region Source	∨

Column Mapping

Series Name	- Select -	∨
Label	JOB	∨
Value Aggregation	No Aggregation	∨
Value	MINSAL	∨

Figure 3-41. *Specifying a series for the Salary Info chart*

The Identification section allows you to choose a name for the series. Because this series will hold the minimum salaries per job, I named it MinSal. (You will also need to create another series to hold the maximum salaries, but not yet.)

The Source section is where you specify the source of the series. Since you have already defined a source for the region, you should choose Region Source. Your other option, not discussed here, is to have each series define its own source. This flexibility is useful in situations where you are comparing data from different tables, but leads to complexity beyond the scope of this book.

The Column Mapping section requires you to specify values for the properties Label and Value. The Label value will be the name of the source column that holds the labels, in this case JOB. The Value value will be the name of the source column holding the values for this series, in this case MINSAL.

After configuring the Salary Info series, you should configure the series for the Salary Info chart, using Figure 3-41 as a model. When you are done, the error indicators should have disappeared from your page and you should be able to save it. If you run the page, you should get the output shown in Figure 3-42. These charts are pretty good, but are in need of customization. This topic is discussed next.

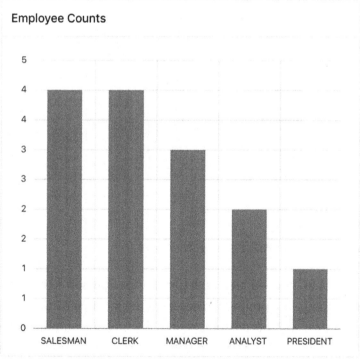

Figure 3-42. *A first approximation to the Charts page*

Multi-Series Charts

The Salary Info region currently has one series, which displays the minimum salary per job. You can easily create a second series to display the maximum salary per job, as follows. Right-click the Series node in the region's rendering tree and select Create Series. Then configure that series like you did the previous ones: rename the series MaxSal, and set its source and column mappings appropriately. The result should be the multi-series chart shown in Figure 3-43.

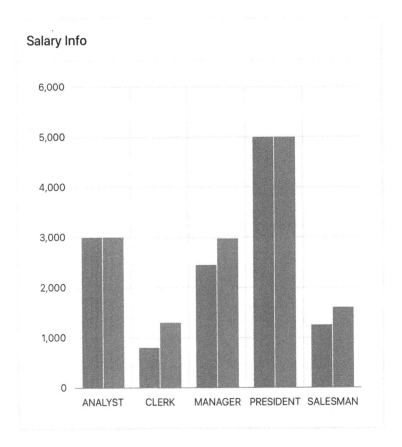

Figure 3-43. *Adding a second series to the chart*

Although the data looks good, note that the chart is now sorted by Job instead of MinSal. What happened? The problem arises from the fact that APEX allows each series to define its own source, and this flexibility entails significant complications. (What if the sources have different label sets? What if they have different sort orders?) APEX consequently has two chart-rendering algorithms: a simple one that ignores these complications and a sophisticated one that requires a separately defined sort order to resolve the complications. Figure 3-44 illustrates the relevant properties. The `Attributes` node of the chart has a section `Multi-Series Chart Data`, having two properties. The `Fill Gaps in Chart Data` property indicates whether to use the simple or sophisticated algorithm. Its default value is on, which denotes the sophisticated algorithm; turning it off specifies the simple algorithm. The `Sort Order` property is visible when the `Fill Gaps` property is on, so that you can specify the chart's sort order.

Figure 3-44. Multi-Series Chart Data properties

Fortunately, this complexity is irrelevant if all the series in your chart use the same source. All you need to do is turn off the `Fill Gaps in Chart Data` property, and sorting goes back to normal.

Customizing a Chart

APEX supports several chart types. The default type of a new chart is a bar chart, but you can use the `Chart` section (from the `Attributes` component of the rendering tree) to change it. For example, go to the `Chart` section of your `Employee Counts` region and change its chart type to `Pie`.

APEX automatically assigns a color to each series in a bar chart. It does a reasonable job of choosing chart colors, but sometimes you want to choose your own. Each bar chart series has a `Color` property in its `Appearance` section, as shown in Figure 3-45. You can type the name of a standard color (such as "maroon"), you can choose a common color from the quick-pick menu on the right, or you can use the color picker to choose a color from the color wheel. The `Salary Info` chart of Figure 3-37 specified the series colors MAROON and GOLD.

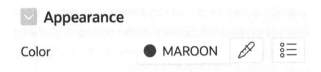

Figure 3-45. *Specifying the color of a bar chart series*

APEX also assigns a color to each label value of a pie chart, using a palette of bright colors. But suppose you want a different palette. It's not immediately clear how to use the Color property in Figure 3-45, because it applies to the entire series. For example, if you set the color to MAROON, then every segment in the pie chart would be maroon. What you need is a way to specify a color for each label.

The idea is to change the chart's source code, as follows:

```
select Job, count(*) as EmpCount,
case job when 'ANALYST'   then '#D6EAF8'
         when 'CLERK'     then '#AED6F1'
         when 'MANAGER'   then '#5DADE2'
         when 'PRESIDENT' then '#3498DB'
         when 'SALESMAN'  then '#1B4F72'
end as JobColor
from EMP
group by Job
order by EmpCount desc;
```

The JobColor column calculates a color for each job. The specified color values correspond to the blue palette shown in Figure 3-38. Figure 3-46 shows the revised Source section for the Salary Info chart.

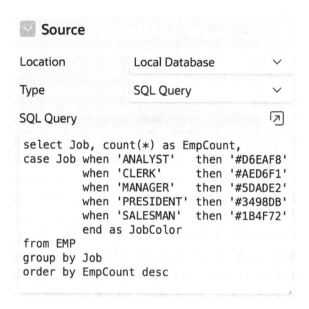

Figure 3-46. *Modifying the pie chart source to include colors*

The value of JobColor can be used in the Color property, as shown in Figure 3-47. Note how the reference to JobColor is written as a substitution string.

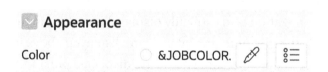

Figure 3-47. *Specifying the pie chart colors*

Another way to customize a chart is to display a *legend*. For example, Figure 3-37 displays a legend underneath the chart. A legend explains the meaning of each color on the chart. Multi-series charts use legends to convey the meaning of each series. Pie charts use legends to identify the segments. Consequently, Figure 3-38 does not need a legend because the label values are displayed directly with each segment.

In APEX, the properties to specify the legend are in the Legend section, which belongs to the region's Attributes node. Figure 3-48 shows the top part of this section.

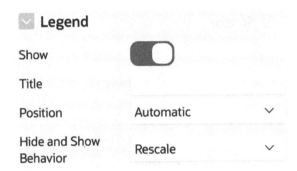

Figure 3-48. *Some chart legend properties*

The most important property is Show, which toggles the visibility of the legend on the page. It usually suffices to use the default value for the other properties, although you should try out the options to see what happens. Especially notable is Hide and Show Behavior. If its value is None, then clicking the legend does nothing. Otherwise, clicking a series name on the legend toggles the visibility of that series in the chart and recomputes the chart accordingly. This behavior is especially interesting for a pie chart, where the legend identifies slices instead of series. As an experiment, enable the legend of the Salary Info chart and set the Hide and Show Behavior value to Rescale. Then run the page, click some legend values, and watch the chart adjust itself.

Another chart customization is to explicitly display data values in the chart. For example, in Figure 3-37, the min and max salaries are displayed above its bar. And in Figure 3-38, the employee count and label name are displayed outside each segment. The relevant properties are in the Label section of the series properties. Figure 3-49 shows how I filled the properties for the pie chart.

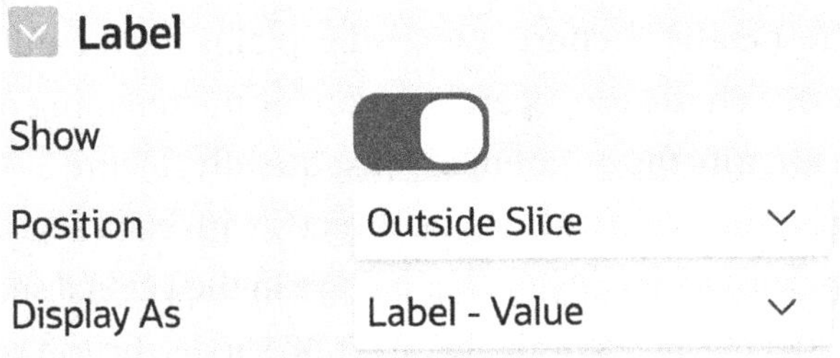

Figure 3-49. *Label properties for the pie chart*

Finally, I would like to briefly mention the properties governing the x and y axes for bar charts. These properties concern how the axes are displayed—how often to display a tick mark, how to format the displayed values, what the range of y values are, and so on. Often, the default values suffice, but occasionally customization is required. One example can be found in the Employee Counts chart from Figure 3-42. Note that its y-axis labels contain duplication. The reason is that the grid markings go up by 0.5, but the labels are displayed as integers only. This situation is depicted in Figures 3-50 and 3-51.

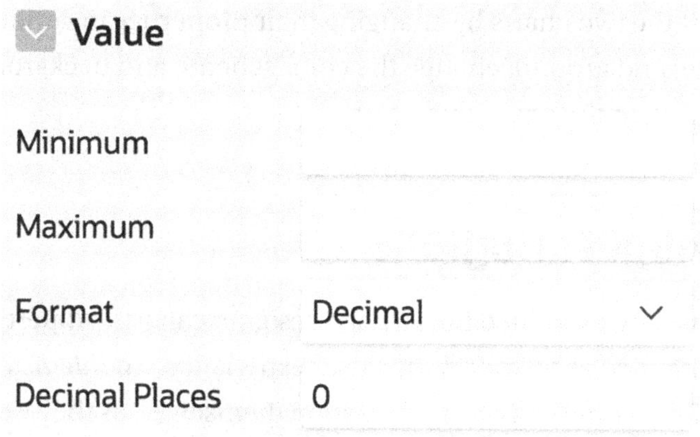

Figure 3-50. *Configuring the values along the y axis*

The Decimal Places property in Figure 3-50 has the value 0, meaning that APEX will display y-axis labels as integers. If you change the value of Decimal Places to 1, then you will see the y-axis labels actually have the value 0.0, 0.5, 1.0, and so on. However, such a chart doesn't make any sense because counts must be integers. A better solution is to change the Minimum Step property in Figure 3-51. This property tells APEX how close the ticks can be. By default, the value is blank, which allows APEX to choose any step value. You need to set the property value to 1, so that the y-axis labels have the values 0, 1, 2, and so on.

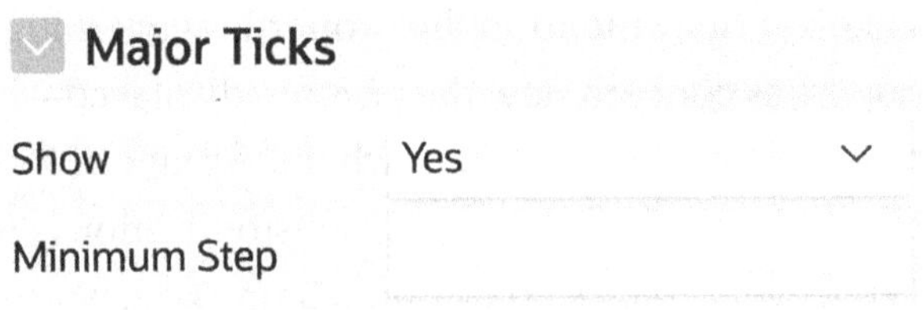

Major Ticks

Show   Yes   ∨

Minimum Step

Figure 3-51. *Configuring when y-axis ticks are displayed*

APEX has many chart-configuration properties. The best way to understand them is to experiment. Edit the two charts by changing their properties in various ways. For example, move the legend around, change the color scheme and background, include or remove labels or values on the chart, and so on.

Interactive Report Regions

The previous sections have examined how a page designer can use properties to customize classic reports and charts so as to improve the user experience. An *interactive report* enables users to perform some of this customization themselves, as they view the page.

Figure 3-52 displays a vanilla, unformatted, interactive report region. To create it, I created a new blank page named `Interactive Reports`, which is page 5 of the `Employee Demo` application. I then created a new region within it named `Employees`, of type `Interactive Report`, and having the source query:

```
select * from EMP
```

Empno	Ename	Job	Mgr	Hiredate	Sal	Comm	Deptno	Offsite
7839	KING	PRESIDENT		11/17/1981	5000		10	N
7698	BLAKE	MANAGER	7839	5/1/1981	2850		30	N
7782	CLARK	MANAGER	7839	6/9/1981	2450		10	N
7566	JONES	MANAGER	7839	4/2/1981	2975		20	N
7788	SCOTT	ANALYST	7566	12/9/1982	3000		20	Y
7902	FORD	ANALYST	7566	12/3/1981	3000		20	N
7369	SMITH	CLERK	7902	12/17/1980	800		20	N
7499	ALLEN	SALESMAN	7698	2/20/1981	1600	300	30	Y
7521	WARD	SALESMAN	7698	2/22/1981	1250	500	30	Y
7654	MARTIN	SALESMAN	7698	9/28/1981	1250	1400	30	N
7844	TURNER	SALESMAN	7698	9/8/1981	1500	0	30	Y
7876	ADAMS	CLERK	7788	1/12/1983	1100		20	N
7900	JAMES	CLERK	7698	12/3/1981	950		30	N
7934	MILLER	CLERK	7782	1/23/1982	1300		10	N

1 - 14

Figure 3-52. *Interactive report region on the EMP table*

An interactive report region has a default template that is different from the other report types you have seen. Those regions used the Standard template, whereas Figure 3-52 uses the Interactive Report template. The most obvious difference is that an Interactive Report template does not display its title across the top.

Note   As always, you can change a region's template from its Appearance section in the property editor.

Apart from its region template, Figure 3-52 looks a lot like a classic report region. In fact, all the properties of classic report regions also apply to interactive report regions—you can specify the region's position on the page, its source query, and the format of each column. If you want, you can configure this region so that it looks exactly like the formatted report of Figure 3-24. However, I would like to keep it unformatted to better focus on the customization that is specific to interactive reports.

The one new feature in Figure 3-52 is the row of items above the report, which is called the *search bar*. The search bar lets users interactively customize the report, by filtering its rows, hiding columns, sorting, creating charts, and performing simple calculations on its values. Although not shown in the figure, an interactive report can also display a *link column* that allows users to examine the report rows individually.

The following sections address issues surrounding the search bar and link column—in particular, how they are used and how an application designer can configure their properties.

Using the Search Bar

The search bar contains four items: the magnifying glass, text box, Go button, and Actions button. The first three items let a user filter the rows of the report. The user enters a search string in the box, clicks the magnifying glass to choose the column to search (All Columns can also be chosen), and clicks Go. The records not containing the search text will be filtered from the report.

For example, entering **82** in the text box and selecting the column Hiredate has the effect of filtering for all employees hired in 1982. Figure 3-53 shows the resulting region.

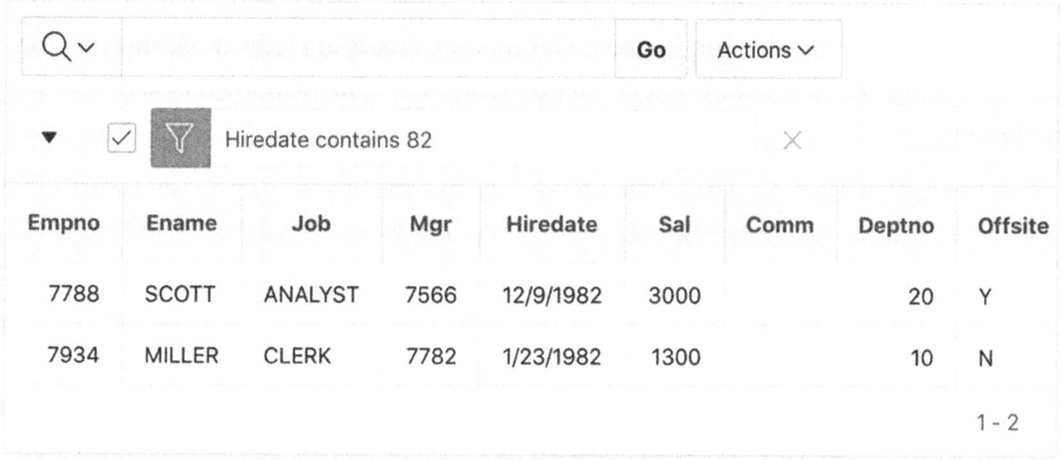

Figure 3-53. *Result of filtering the report of Figure 3-52*

Note that the region now has a row below the search bar that describes the filter. You can click the checkbox on the left to enable/disable it, or you can click the X on the right to permanently remove it.

It is possible to have multiple concurrent filters. For example, to find employees hired in 1982 who work offsite, you would need to add another filter for the Offsite column. The result is shown in Figure 3-54.

In general, a user can explore the contents of a report by creating multiple filters and selectively enabling various subsets of them.

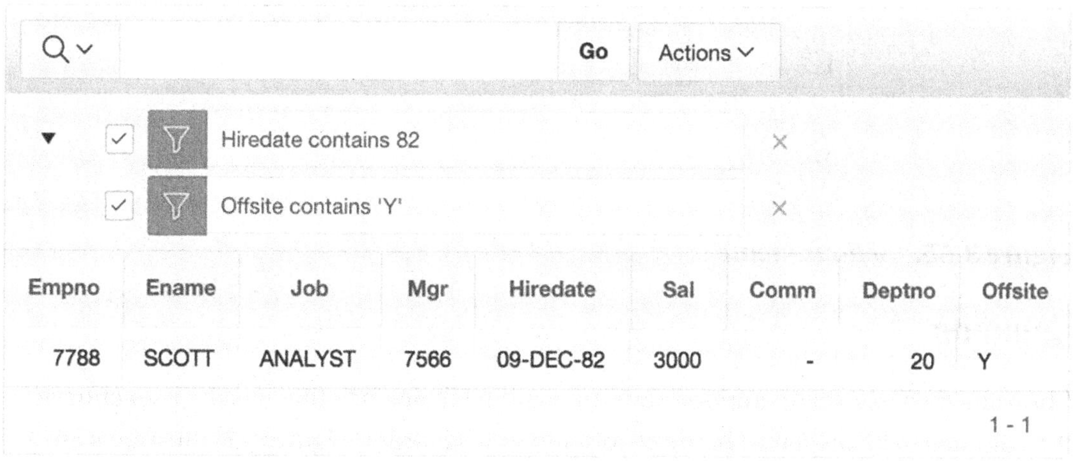

Figure 3-54. *Adding a second filter to the report of Figure 3-53*

The Actions button allows a user to further customize the report. Clicking the button displays its menu of possible operations. This menu appears in Figure 3-55, showing the submenu for the Data action. The following sections describe the more useful of these operations.

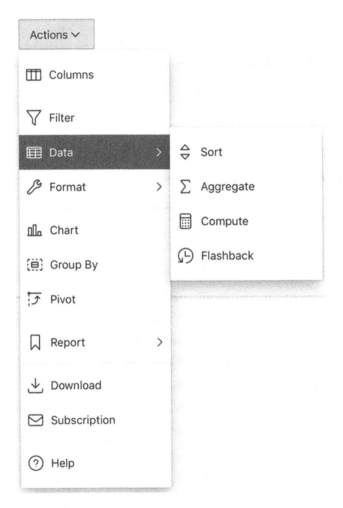

Figure 3-55. *Actions menu*

Columns

Choosing the Columns operation brings up a modal dialog box that lets the user choose the columns to be displayed in the report and in what order; Figure 3-56 illustrates an example that selects the columns Ename, Job, Hiredate, and Sal for display.

Figure 3-56. *Specifying the columns to display*

Filter

Choosing the Filter operation brings up a modal dialog box that lets the user create a
filter; see Figure 3-57. It produces filters similar to the filters you created for Figures 3-53
and 3-54. The difference is that those earlier filters could check only for text
containment, whereas this dialog box allows for many kinds of operations. For example,
the filter specified in Figure 3-57 is Job!='CLERK'.

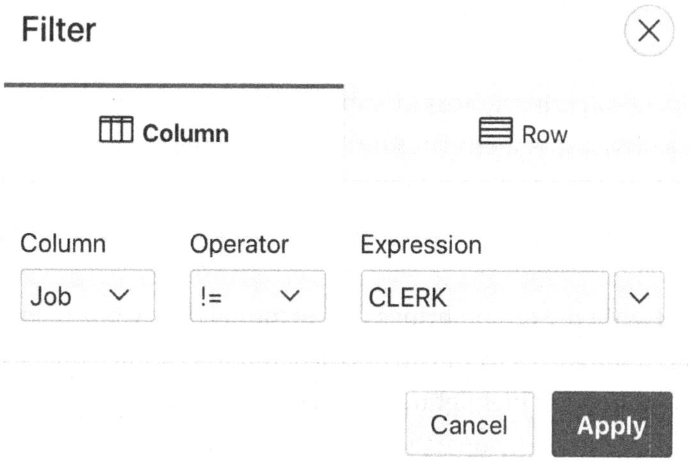

Figure 3-57. *Filter dialog box*

Sort

Choosing the Sort operation brings up a modal dialog box that lets the user choose the desired sort order; see Figure 3-58. The user selects the column(s) to be sorted and whether the sort direction is ascending or descending. The figure shows the menu to select a sort column. Note that the user can sort on both visible and hidden columns.

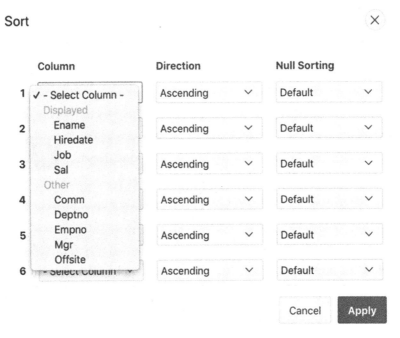

Figure 3-58. *Sort dialog box*

Highlight

The Highlight operation is in the Format submenu. It allows the user to highlight rows or cells that satisfy a specified criterion. Recall that the formatted classic report of Figure 3-24 displayed high salary values in red. This is a form of highlighting. The Highlight operation allows the user to express this and other forms of highlighting easily.

Choosing the Highlight option brings up the modal dialog box of Figure 3-59. The Highlight Condition values specify the values of interest. If the value of Highlight Type is Cell, those values are highlighted; if it is Row, the row containing those values is highlighted. Highlighting can involve the background color, text color, or both. The figure shows the highlighting corresponding to Figure 3-24.

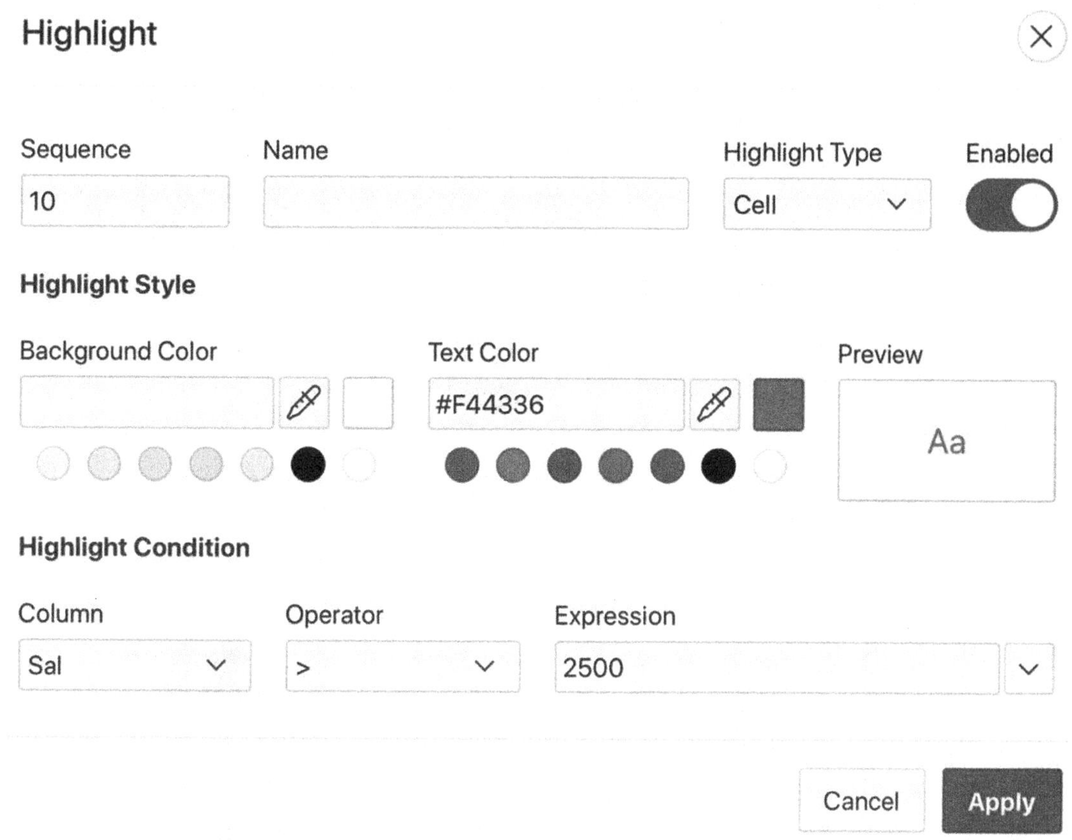

Highlight   ⊗

Sequence	Name		Highlight Type	Enabled
10			Cell ⌄	⬤

Highlight Style

Background Color   Text Color   Preview

	🖊		#F44336	🖊 ◼	

Aa

○ ○ ○ ○ ○ ● ○   ● ● ● ● ● ● ○

Highlight Condition

Column   Operator   Expression

Sal ⌄	> ⌄	2500 ⌄

                                    Cancel   **Apply**

Figure 3-59. *Highlight dialog box*

Rows Per Page

The Rows Per Page operation is also in the Format submeu. It allows the user to change the report pagination at will. Clicking the menu item displays a submenu in which the user can choose from a list of possible rows per page.

Chart

Choosing the Chart operation brings up a modal dialog box that lets the user create charts based on the data in the report; see Figure 3-60.

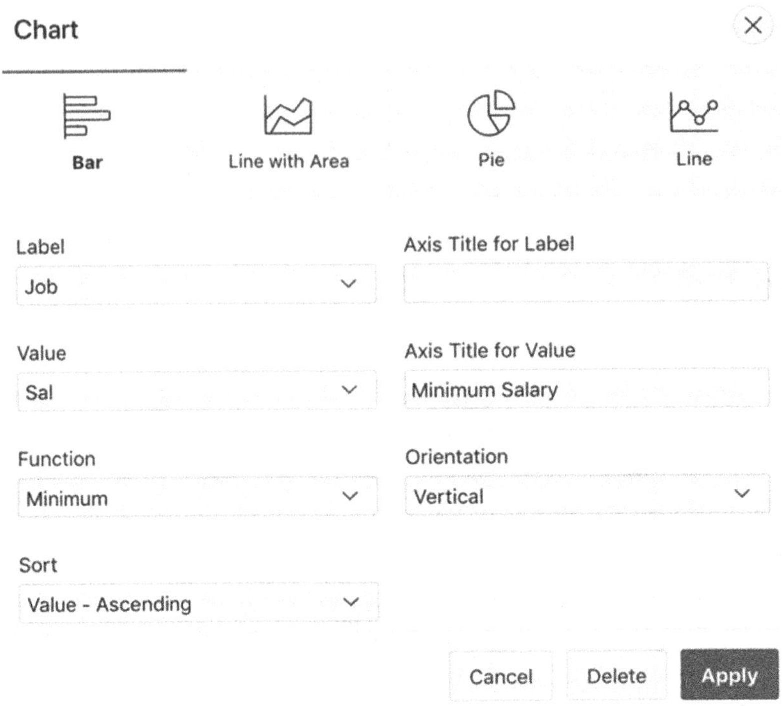

Chart   (×)

| Bar | Line with Area | Pie | Line |

Label
Job   ⌄

Axis Title for Label

Value
Sal   ⌄

Axis Title for Value
Minimum Salary

Function
Minimum   ⌄

Orientation
Vertical   ⌄

Sort
Value - Ascending   ⌄

Cancel   Delete   **Apply**

Figure 3-60. *Chart dialog box*

From this dialog box, a user can create a single-series chart that aggregates over a single column. The figure specifies a bar chart that gives the minimum salary per job, similar to the bar chart shown in Figure 3-37. The resulting chart appears in Figure 3-61.

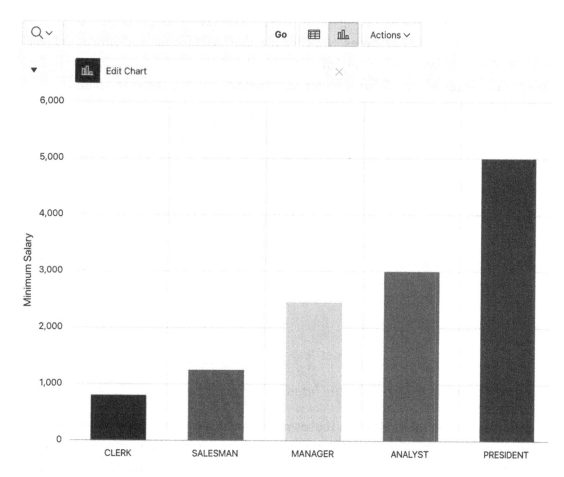

Figure 3-61. *Interactive chart*

There are two things worth noting in this figure. First, many aspects of the chart are not customizable. For example, a chart can have only a single series and the color palette is fixed. Second, the search bar has been extended to include two report/chart buttons to the left of the Action button. The user can use these buttons to toggle between the interactive report and its chart.

Configuring the Search Bar

The search bar has a lot of functionality. However, not all applications need all the functionality. An interactive report region has properties that allow the application developer to limit this functionality. This section examines those properties.

Figure 3-62 shows the rendering tree for the Interactive Reports page and its interactive report region Employees. Note that this tree has the same structure as a classic report (refer to Figure 3-25), namely, that the Attributes component contains the report-specific properties and the Columns folder contains the properties for each column.

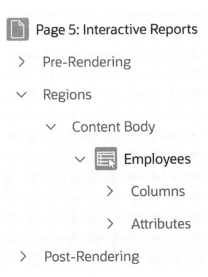

Figure 3-62. *Rendering tree for the Interactive Reports page*

The property editor for the Attributes node contains two relevant sections: Search Bar and Actions Menu. Figure 3-63 shows the properties of the Search Bar section. These properties let you selectively display different portions of the search area. For example, turning off the Include Search Bar property completely disables the bar, turning off the Search Field enables only the Action button, and so on.

Figure 3-63. *Properties to configure the search area*

Figure 3-64 shows the first several properties of the Actions Menu section. These properties let you specify which operations are displayed in the menu. (Not all the properties are shown due to lack of space.)

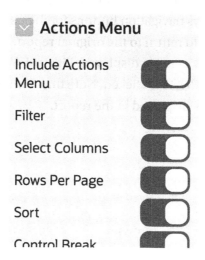

Figure 3-64. *Some properties of the Actions Menu section*

Finally, each column of an interactive report has properties for configuring its specific capabilities. These properties appear in the Enable Users To section of that column and are shown in Figure 3-65. (Again, not all properties are shown because of lack of space.)

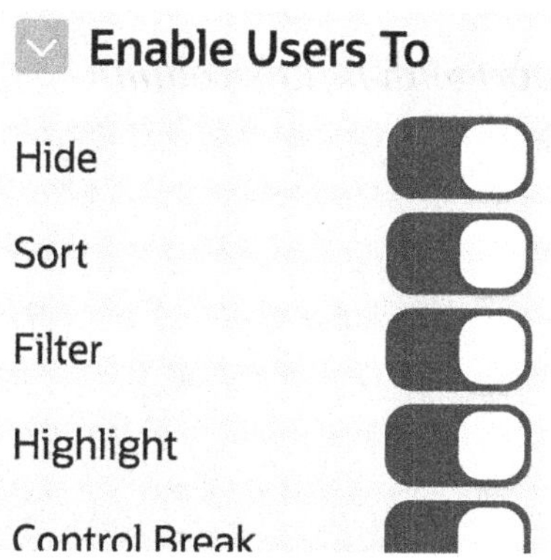

Figure 3-65. *Some properties of a column's Enable Users To section*

Link Column

An interactive report can display a special column, whose value is a link. Clicking this link shows the report in *single row view*. That is, the report changes to show the values of only that row; it also displays navigation buttons for the user to move to the next or previous row and a button to return to the original report. Figure 3-66 shows the interactive report with the link column displayed. Figure 3-67 shows the single row view of the report after the link for BLAKE is clicked. Note that this single row view displays all the columns, not just the ones displayed in the report.

	Ename	Hiredate	Job	Sal
	KING	11/17/1981	PRESIDENT	5000
	BLAKE	5/1/1981	MANAGER	2850
	CLARK	6/9/1981	MANAGER	2450
	JONES	4/2/1981	MANAGER	2975
	SCOTT	12/9/1982	ANALYST	3000

1 - 5 ❯

Figure 3-66. *Interactive report with its link column*

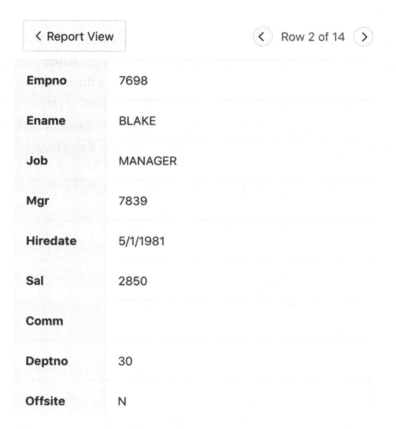

‹ Report View		‹ Row 2 of 14 ›
Empno	7698	
Ename	BLAKE	
Job	MANAGER	
Mgr	7839	
Hiredate	5/1/1981	
Sal	2850	
Comm		
Deptno	30	
Offsite	N	

Figure 3-67. *Interactive report in single row view*

The property editor for the region's `Attributes` component has two sections—`Link` and `Single Row View`—that let you enable the link column and configure its behavior. The properties for the `Link` section appear in Figure 3-68.

☑ Link

Link Column	Link to Single Row View ∨
Uniquely Identify Rows by	ROWID ∨

Figure 3-68. *Properties to enable single-record view*

To enable the link column, set the value of the Link Column property to Link to Single Row View. (You can also set it to link to an arbitrary URL, but this choice is less interesting.) You then have to specify which row is to be selected when the link is clicked. The value ROWID says to use the row that was clicked, which is the most natural.

Figure 3-69 shows the Single Row View section. The interesting property here is Only Displayed Columns: turning it on specifies that the single row view should display the same columns as the report; turning it off specifies that it should display all the columns.

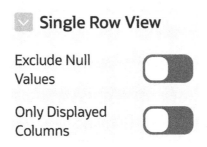

Figure 3-69. *Single Row View properties*

Summary

This chapter focused on the design and use of APEX regions. You began by examining different ways to create a region, the properties needed to specify its location on a page, and its look and feel. You then explored four common region types: Static Content, Classic Report, Chart, and Interactive Report. You looked at how regions of each type are used and how to take advantage of their type-specific properties to format them effectively.

A static content region is used primarily to display HTML code. You examined the APEX-specific nuances associated with relative references—in particular, how to refer to an image stored on the APEX server and how to link to a page of the current application. These relative references relied on the value of certain APEX built-in variables, such as APP_IMAGES and APP_ID. You saw how to use *substitution strings* to access the value of these variables.

A classic report region displays the output of an SQL query. You saw how to use APEX properties to customize the way the region is displayed. Of particular interest is a column's HTML Expression property, which lets you format a column value by wrapping it in an HTML expression. You also saw how to perform conditional formatting by modifying the report's source query.

A chart region displays a chart. You saw how to use an SQL query to specify the content of the chart and how to take advantage of the properties that configure the way the chart looks.

An interactive report region displays a report, similar to a classic report region. The interactive report differs in two ways. First, its search bar enables users to customize the report interactively. Second, its link column allows users to view the report in single-record mode. You examined the functionality provided by these features and compared them with what is possible using classic report and chart regions. You also saw how an application developer can enable only parts of this functionality by setting the properties of the interactive report region, as desired.

CHAPTER 4

Navigation

The user of a web application should be able to easily navigate through its pages. You have already encountered three navigational features in your use of APEX: links, breadcrumbs, and the navigation menu. This chapter examines these features in detail and shows you different ways to use them in your applications.

Lists

In common parlance, a *list* is simply a collection of things. In APEX, however, a list is a collection of links. A list is a useful navigation tool, for the obvious reason that clicking a link takes you to a new page.

For a good example of an APEX list, consider again the SQL Workshop home screen, as shown in Figure 1-3. Its `Create Object` region is a list that enables quick access to the various object–creation wizard pages. That list has an entry for each kind of SQL object, with its link taking you to the creation wizard for that object.

For another example, recall the home page of the `Employee Demo` application, as shown in Figure 3-17. Its `References` region is a list with links that take you to selected web pages.

Perhaps the most notable example of a list is the navigation menu. Each of its entries is a link that takes you to the specified page of the application.

The APEX *list manager* lets you view, edit, and create lists. To get to the list manager, begin at the application's home screen and click the large `Shared Components` button at the top of the page. Search for the `Navigation` section and click `Lists`. You will be taken to the main screen of the list manager, which is shown in Figure 4-1.

© Edward Sciore 2020
E. Sciore, *Understanding Oracle APEX 20 Application Development*,
https://doi.org/10.1007/978-1-4842-6165-1_4

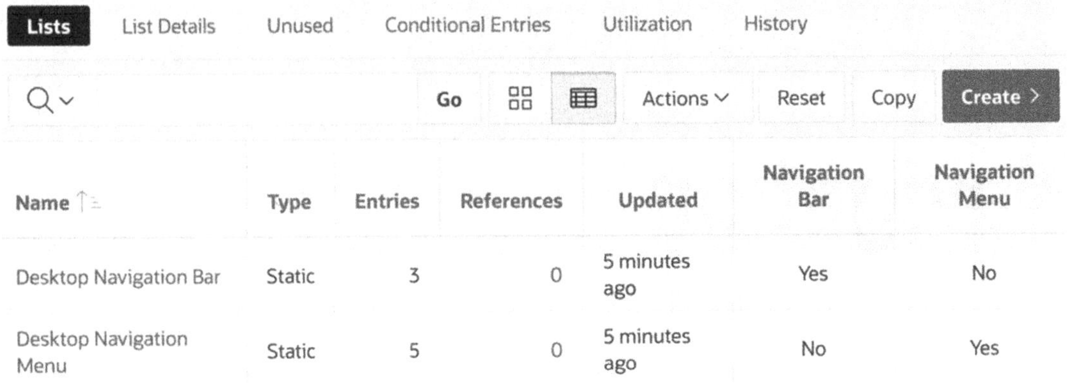

Figure 4-1. *List manager*

The figure shows that the application already has two lists: `Desktop Navigation Bar` and `Desktop Navigation Menu`. APEX treats these lists in a special way—their respective entries are displayed in the navigation bar (which runs across the top of the page) and the navigation menu (which runs down the left side of the page).

Viewing List Details

Clicking the name of a list (or selecting the `List Details` link at the top of the screen) brings you to the `List Details` screen. Figure 4-2 shows this screen for the `Desktop Navigation Menu` list.

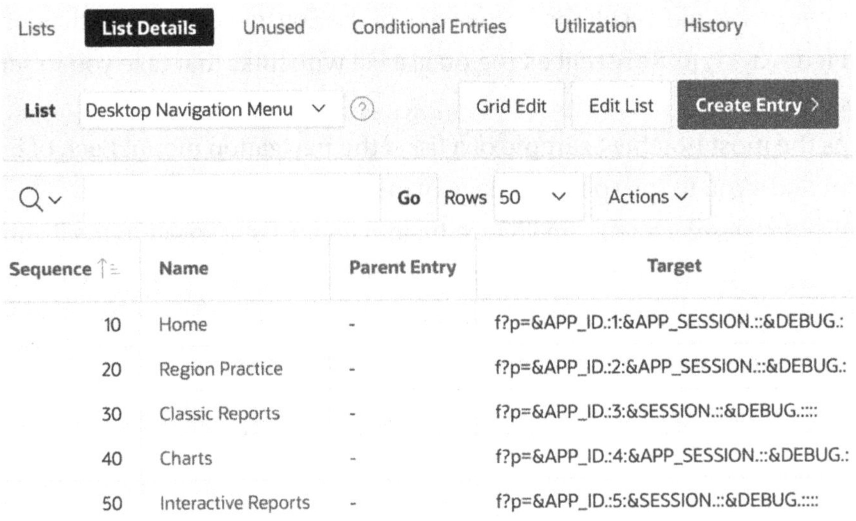

Figure 4-2. *Details of the Desktop Navigation Menu list*

The screen displays information about each entry in the selected list. The most relevant values are `Sequence`, `Name`, and `Target`.

- The sequence numbers determine the order in which the entries appear in the list.

- The name of an entry specifies how it is displayed in the list.

- The target of an entry is the URL that is called when the link is clicked.

Note in the figure that each target URL refers to a page of the current application, using the syntax described in Chapter 2. One new aspect of that syntax is the string "`&DEBUG.`", which appears as the fifth argument to each URL. This portion of the URL specifies that the application should continue to use the current debug mode (which is an issue of minor concern, and is ignored in this book).

Editing List Entries

The name of each entry in the `List Details` screen is a link. Clicking the link for an entry takes you to a `List Entry` screen, in which you can edit the entry's values. Figure 4-3 shows a portion of this screen that results from clicking the `Region Practice` entry.

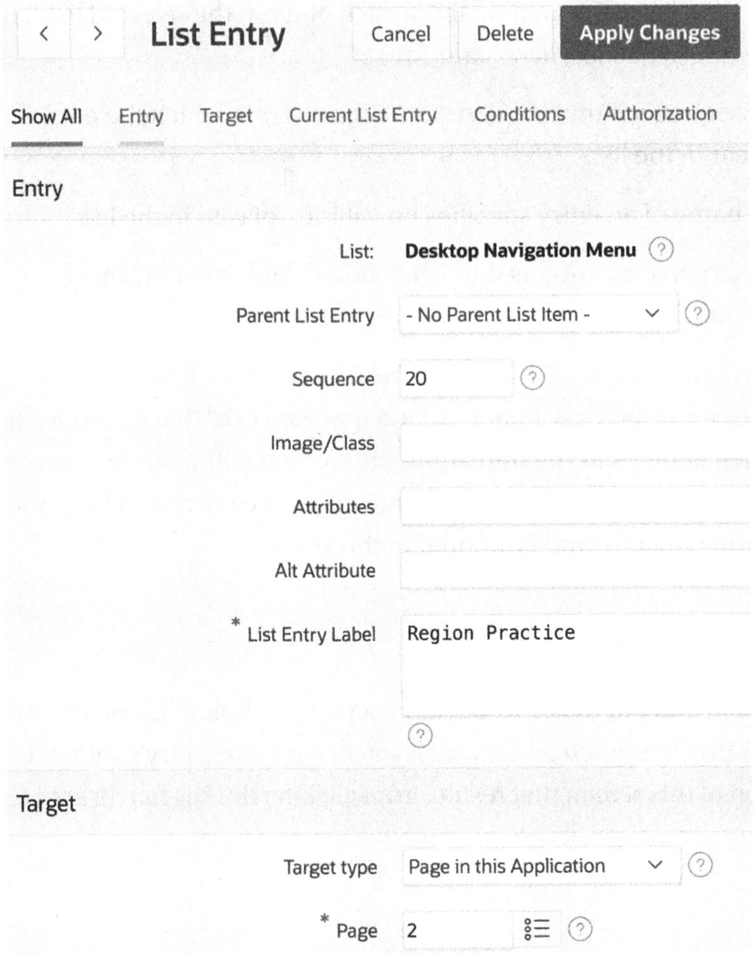

Figure 4-3. *List Entry screen for the Region Practice page*

The relevant properties here are Sequence, List Entry Label, and Page. As an experiment, change the values of these properties—for example, set Sequence to 60 and List Entry Label to Fun with Regions. Then run the application. The navigation menu should now look like Figure 4-4. In particular, the entry formerly titled Region Practice is now titled Fun with Regions and appears last.

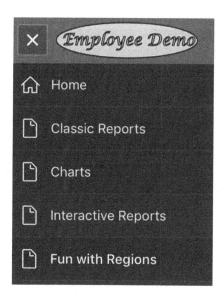

Figure 4-4. *Modified navigation menu*

Creating New List Entries

Now turn your attention to the Desktop Navigation Bar list. The navigation bar in an APEX application runs across the top of each page. By default, the left side of the navigation bar displays the logo, and the right side displays the current user name (as in Figure 2-8 of Chapter 2). The general intent of the navigation bar is to provide quick links to common tasks. For example, the logo is actually a link to the home page, and the username is a menu that has a link to a procedure that logs out the user. Navigation bars typically contain links for displaying a site map, online help, or contact information.

To see how the navigation bar is implemented, go to the List Details screen for the Desktop Navigation Bar list; this screen is shown in Figure 4-5. The list contains three entries. The first entry displays the username, the second is an uninteresting separator, and the third is the link to the logout procedure. These entries are organized hierarchically, which is what creates the menu structure. The username entry is the parent and thus is displayed as a menu. The logout entry is its child and thus is displayed as a menu entry. Hierarchical lists will be discussed in great detail later in this chapter.

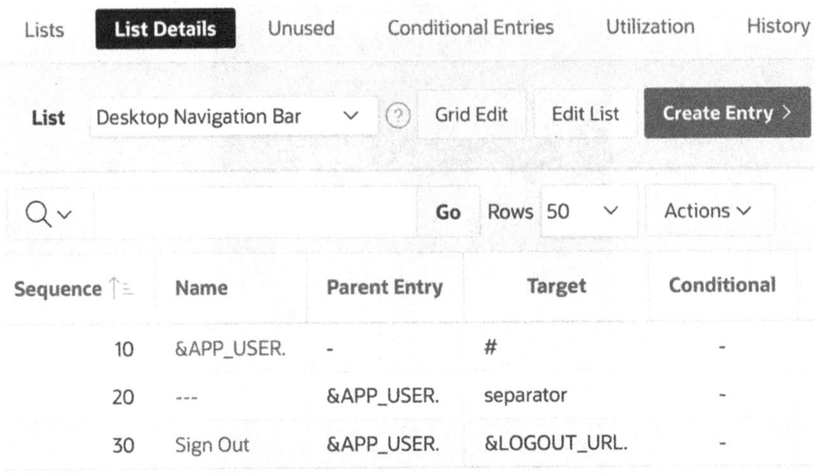

| Lists | **List Details** | Unused | Conditional Entries | Utilization | History |

| **List** | Desktop Navigation Bar | ⌄ | ⑦ | Grid Edit | Edit List | **Create Entry >** |

| Q ⌄ | | | Go | Rows 50 | ⌄ | Actions ⌄ |

Sequence ↑≡	Name	Parent Entry	Target	Conditional
10	&APP_USER.	-	#	-
20	---	&APP_USER.	separator	-
30	Sign Out	&APP_USER.	&LOGOUT_URL.	-

Figure 4-5. *Details of the Desktop Navigation Bar list*

Let's modify the navigation bar to have two new entries: a link to this book's web page and a link to a Contact Info page. To create additional entries, click the Create Entry button. The List Entry screen is then displayed, as shown in Figure 4-6. Note that this screen is essentially the same as Figure 4-3, except that its buttons are for entry creation instead of update.

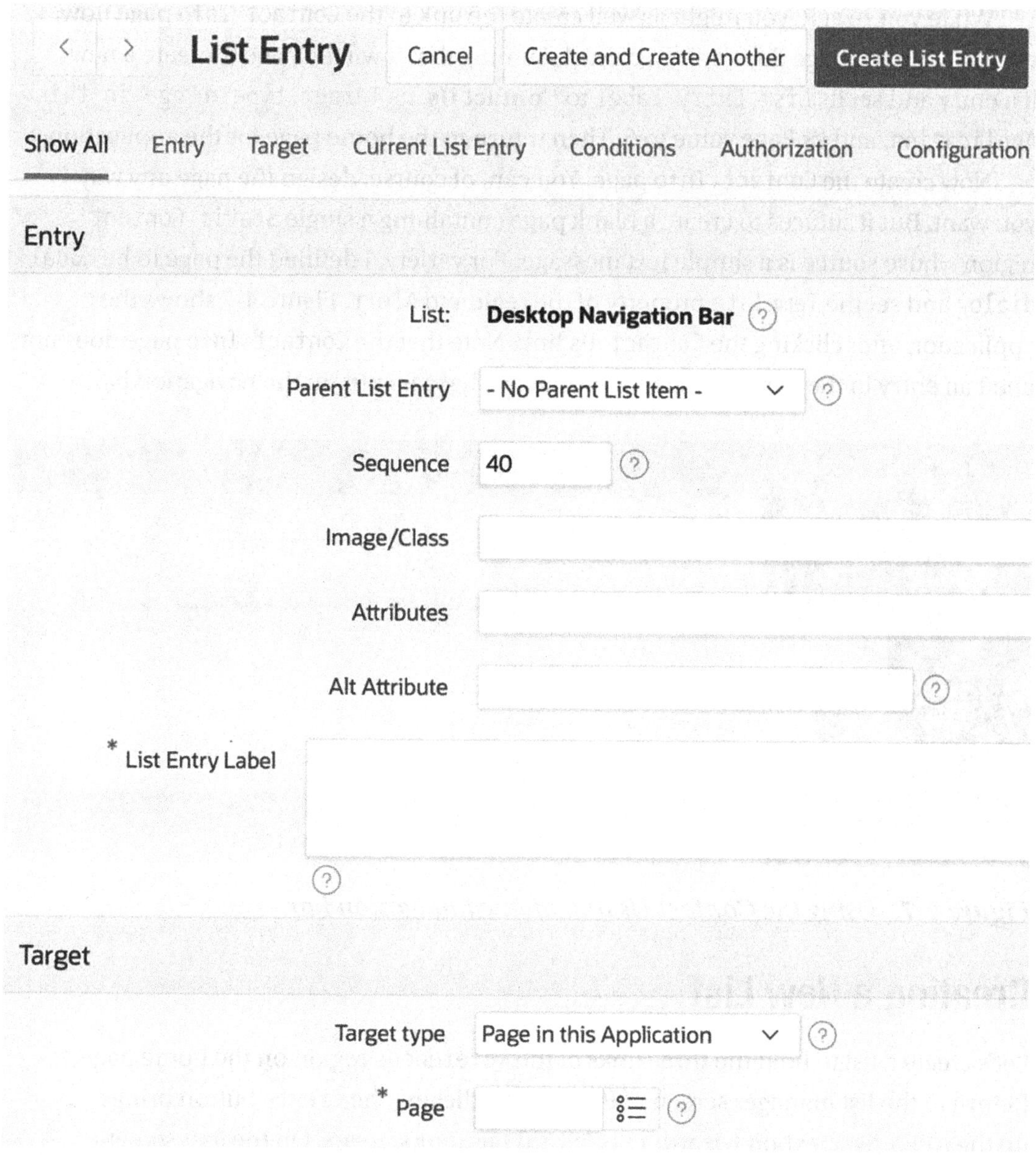

< | >   **List Entry** | Cancel | Create and Create Another | **Create List Entry**

Show All   Entry   Target   Current List Entry   Conditions   Authorization   Configuration

Entry

List: **Desktop Navigation Bar** (?)

Parent List Entry   - No Parent List Item - ⌄ (?)

Sequence   40   (?)

Image/Class

Attributes

Alt Attribute   (?)

* List Entry Label

(?)

Target

Target type   Page in this Application ⌄ (?)

* Page   (?)

Figure 4-6. *List Entry screen for creating a list entry*

To create the link to this book's web page, you only have to enter a value for the property List Entry Label (I entered **Get the Book**) and set the target. Here, the target is a URL, so you set the Target type property to URL and its URL Target property to www.apress.com/9781484261651. Then click Create List Entry.

While you're at it, you might as well create the link to the `Contact Info` page now, even though the page does not yet exist. Assuming that it will be page 6, create a new list entry and set its `List Entry Label` to **Contact Us**, its `Target type` to `Page in this Application`, and its `Page` value to 6. Then return to the home page for the application.

Now create the `Contact Info` page. You can, of course, design the page any way you want. But it suffices to create a blank page containing a single `Static Content` region whose source is a simple text message. For variety, I defined the page to be `modal dialog` and set the `Template` property of the region to `Alert`. Figure 4-7 shows the application after clicking the `Contact Us` link. Note that the `Contact Info` page does not need an entry in the navigation menu because it has an entry in the navigation bar.

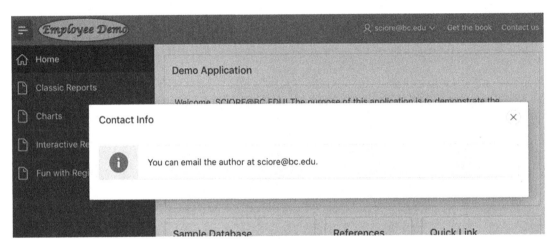

Figure 4-7. *Using the Contact Us link on the navigation bar*

Creating a New List

Let's create a list to hold the three links of the `References` region on the home page. Return to the list manager screen of Figure 4-1. Clicking the `Create` button brings up the APEX list creation wizard. This wizard has four screens. On the first screen, choose to create the list `From Scratch`. On the second screen, give the list a name (say, **References**), and set its type to `Static`.

The third screen gives you the opportunity to create menu entries by entering their label and URL. You can create the entries there, or you can wait and create each entry individually, as shown in the previous section. I find it quicker to create the entries now.

Figure 4-8 shows how I filled in the screen. Note that the figure does not show the entire URLs because they are too long for their text box. For your reference, the complete URLs appeared in Listing 3-3.

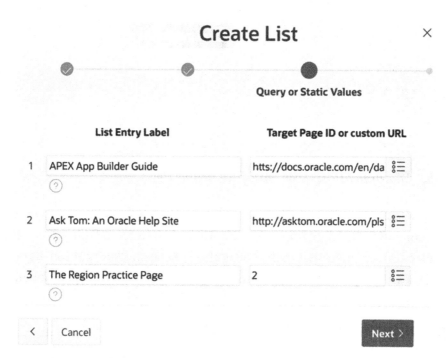

Figure 4-8. *The third Create List screen*

The final screen asks if you want to create a region for the list. Because you have not yet learned about list regions, select No. Then click Create List to create the list. The list manager should now display the entry for your new list.

Modifying the Navigation Interface

By default, the Desktop Navigation Menu list is displayed down the left side of the page, and the Desktop Navigation Bar list is displayed along the top. You can change these defaults by modifying the application's properties.

Chapter 2 discussed how to get at the properties of an application. To review, go to the application's home screen (Figure 2-5) and click the Edit Application Properties button at the top right. You are taken to the application's property screen (Figure 2-6), which has four tabs: Definition, Security, Globalization, and User Interface. Selecting the User Interface tab displays the user interface properties; Figure 4-9 shows the top of that screen.

Figure 4-9. *An application's user interface properties*

Note the selector bar along the bottom of the figure that lists the property sections. You might remember the Logo properties from Chapter 3 (refer to Figure 3-21). Right now, however, you are interested in the Navigation Menu and Navigation Bar sections. Their properties allow you to configure the navigation menu and navigation bar.

Configuring the Navigation Menu

Figure 4-10 shows the Navigation Menu properties.

Figure 4-10. *Application's Navigation Menu properties*

The Navigation Menu List property lets you specify the list that will appear as the navigation menu. You can choose from any existing list. For example, choosing the References list results in the navigation menu shown in Figure 4-11.

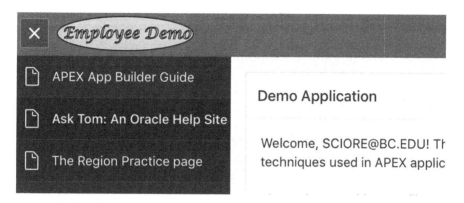

Figure 4-11. *References list is now the navigation menu*

You can also choose the value -Select Navigation Menu List- as the navigation menu. Doing so sets the Navigation Menu List property to null, which causes APEX to not render the navigation menu area at all.

The Position property can have the value Side or Top. Choosing Top tells APEX to render the navigation menu along the top of the page, below the navigation bar. It also causes the value of List Template property to change to Top Navigation Menu. Figure 4-12 shows the result of displaying the Desktop Navigation Menu list along the top.

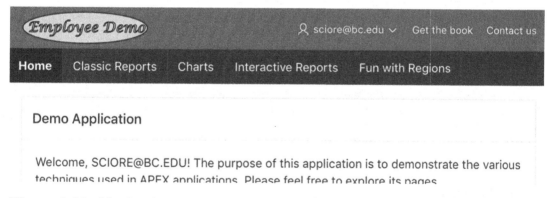

Figure 4-12. *Navigation menu now appears along the top*

Configuring the Navigation Bar

Figure 4-13 shows the `Navigation Bar` properties.

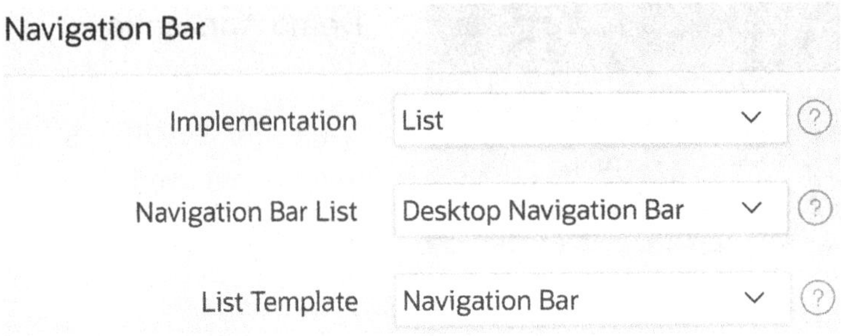

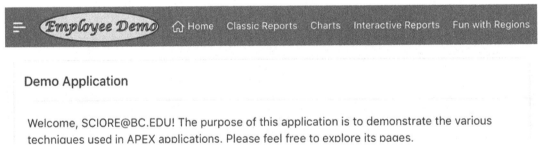

Figure 4-13. *The application's Navigation Bar properties*

The `Navigation Bar List` property lets you specify the list that will appear in the navigation bar. As with the navigation menu, it can be any list, although it cannot be `null`. For example, Figure 4-14 shows the result of placing the `Desktop Navigation Menu` list in the navigation bar.

Figure 4-14. *Navigation menu now appears in the navigation bar*

List Regions

For the contents of a list to be visible on a page, the list must be assigned to a location on that page. The navigation bar and navigation menu locations are predefined. If you want a list to appear anywhere else, you must place it in a region that you create. The region should be of type `List`, and its source should be the name of the list.

As an example, Figure 4-15 shows the List Practice page, which is page 7 of the demo application. This page contains four regions, all of type List. The top three regions display the References list (in three different ways), and the bottom untitled region displays the Desktop Navigation Menu list.

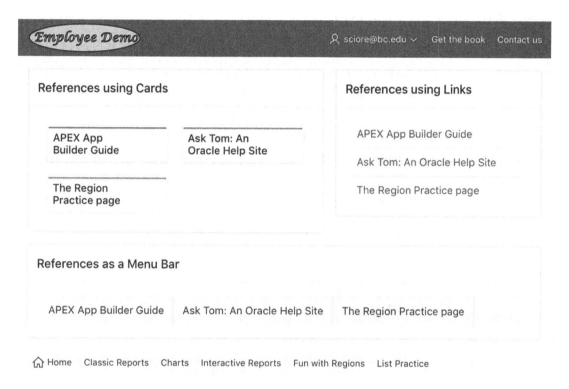

Figure 4-15. *List Practice page*

To build this page, you should create a new page and add four new regions to it. I titled these regions References Using Cards, References Using Links, References as a Navigation Bar, and Navigation Menu. The first region has a column span of 7; the second region begins a new column of the same row; and the other two regions begin new rows.

Set the type of each region to List. The source of a List region must be a list. The property editor lets you choose from the existing lists, as shown in Figure 4-16. Select the list References for the first three regions and Desktop Navigation Menu for the Navigation Menu region.

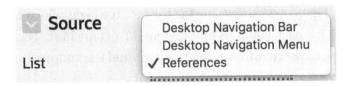

Figure 4-16. *Selecting the source of a list region*

At this point you have the list regions you want, but they are all formatted as links. This is appropriate for the References Using Links region, but the other regions need to be different. To change the way a list is displayed, you must change its template. A region of type List has a property called List Template, which is accessed by selecting its Attributes node in the rendering tree and looking for the Appearance section in the property editor. Figure 4-17 shows the possible values for this property.

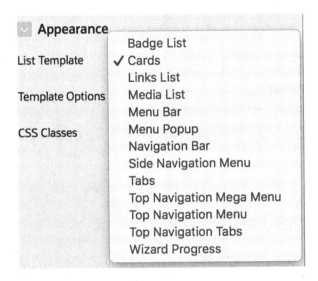

Figure 4-17. *Possible list template values*

To produce the page shown in Figure 4-15, you should set the template of the References Using Cards region to Cards, the template of the References as a Navigation Bar region to Menu Bar, and the template of the Navigation Menu region to Navigation Bar. For fun, you also might want to experiment with assigning other templates to these regions, such as Badge List, Media List, and Tabs.

For further customization, several list templates have options that can be set via the Template Options property. For example, the References Using Cards region uses the options shown in Figure 4-18. In general, the best way to understand the purpose of the various template options is to experiment with them on your regions.

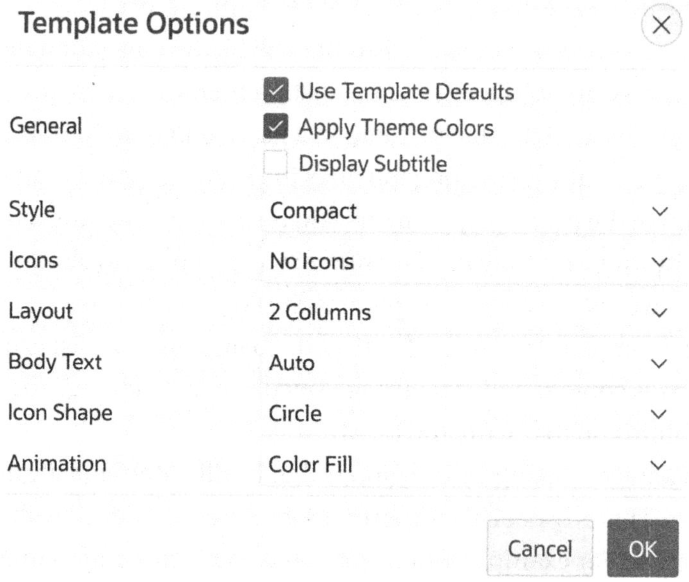

Figure 4-18. *Options for the Cards template*

In addition to choosing a list template, recall that you can also customize a region by choosing a region template. (Figure 3-10 in Chapter 3 showed the possible templates.) The top three regions of Figure 4-15 use the `Standard` template, which displays a header containing the region name. The bottom region uses the `Tabs Container` template. This template displays its contents with no additional border; in fact, it looks a lot like a menu bar. This region demonstrates how you can use a list region to mimic a menu bar that appears somewhere other than the default places on the page.

Another feature of Figure 4-15 is that it does not display the navigation menu area. You saw earlier how to hide the navigation menu on all pages of an application by setting the global property `Navigation Menu List` to `null`. But what if you want the menu hidden on just a single page? The answer is to use the `Navigation Menu` properties of the page, as shown in Figure 4-19.

Figure 4-19. *Configuring the navigation menu for a single page*

Turning on the `Override User Interface Level` property causes the `List` property to be displayed. You can then choose the list that will be the navigation menu for the page, or you can choose to not specify the navigation menu.

Storing links in a list and displaying them in a list region is an important technique; it is far superior to manually formatting the links in HTML, as you did on the `References` region of the home page. One reason is that the template of a list region takes responsibility for formatting the list entries; you just need to choose the template you want. In other words, a list region separates the content (the source list) from the formatting (the list template). Writing HTML code to implement a list is not only tedious, but it also intermixes content and formatting. Any decision to change the format of the entries would require you to rewrite the HTML.

A second advantage of using a list region is that it will automatically be updated as the list changes. This is especially important for regions that display the `Desktop Navigation Menu` list. For example, whenever you create a navigation menu entry for a new page, the `Navigation Menu` region of Figure 4-15 will adjust accordingly.

Hierarchical Lists

The `Employee Demo` application currently has six entries in its `Desktop Navigation Menu` list. Because there are so few entries, it is reasonable to simply display them linearly along the side (or top) of the page. However, as the number of entries grows, a long linear list becomes unwieldy. The common solution is to display the entries *hierarchically*.

The APEX navigation bar (shown in Figure 1-3) is a case in point. Its first tab (containing the logo) corresponds to the APEX home screen; the other tabs correspond to general categories of the APEX site. Each category tab has a primary target page, which acts as the home screen for that category. Clicking the main portion of a category tab takes you to that page. Each category tab also has a down arrow; clicking it displays a menu of secondary tabs for that category. The result is a functional but clean interface, with the secondary tabs hidden until needed.

In a hierarchical list, each list entry can have a *parent* entry. A list entry without a parent defines a hierarchy and is called the *root* of that hierarchy. A hierarchy can have several levels, in the sense that the parent of an entry may also have a parent. For example, Figure 4-20 shows the `App Builder` entry of the APEX navigation bar. One of its children, `Workspace Utilities`, has its own children.

Figure 4-20. *App Builder menu in the APEX navigation bar*

Let's see how to restructure the `Employee Demo` application similarly. Its `Desktop Navigation Menu` list will consist of the home page plus two hierarchies:

- A `Regions` hierarchy that contains the pages `Region Practice`, `Classic Reports`, `Charts`, and `Interactive Reports`

- A `Lists` hierarchy that contains the page `List Practice`

Each hierarchy corresponds to a chapter of the book—the `Regions` hierarchy contains the pages developed in Chapter 3, and the `Lists` hierarchy contains the page from Chapter 4. As the book progresses, I shall keep to this convention, creating a new hierarchy for the pages developed in each chapter.

But before you begin to create the hierarchies, you need to consider how you will configure each root entry. Clearly, the value of its `Parent List Entry` property should be `null`, denoting that it is a root. However, what value should you give to its `Target` properties?

There are three reasonable strategies: you can create a dedicated "home screen" to be the target, or you can set the target to be the same as the target of one of its children, or you can set the target to be null. APEX adopts the first strategy—it has a home screen for the application builder, one for the SQL workshop, and so on. Adopting the second strategy has the effect of making the chosen target be the default page for that section. And adopting the third strategy makes it impossible to choose the parent, thereby forcing the user to select one of the children. This book shall follow the convention that a root having a single child will have that child be its target, whereas a root having several children will have a null target.

To create this hierarchical list, begin at the List Details screen for the Desktop Navigation Menu, which appeared in Figure 4-2. Create two new list entries to be the roots of the two hierarchies, and set their target pages according to the preceding convention: the target of the Regions entry should be null, and the target of the Lists entry should be the List Practice page.

You now need to set the parents of the five child entries. The straightforward way is to go to the List Entry screen for each entry (as shown in Figure 4-3) and modify its Parent List Entry property. However, the List Details screen has a wizard to expedite this process. Click the link titled Reparent List Entries Within this List at the right side of the List Details screen. The link brings you to a Reparent List Entries screen, from which you can quickly specify the children of a given parent entry. Whichever way you do it, the resulting entries for the desktop navigation menu should look like Figure 4-21.

Sequence ↑≣	Name	Parent Entry	Target
10	Home	-	f?p=&APP_ID.:1:&APP_SESSION.::&DEBUG.:
30	Classic Reports	Regions	f?p=&APP_ID.:3:&SESSION.::&DEBUG.::::
40	Charts	Regions	f?p=&APP_ID.:4:&APP_SESSION.::&DEBUG.:::
50	Interactive Reports	Regions	f?p=&APP_ID.:5:&APP_SESSION.::&DEBUG.:::
55	Fun With Regions	Regions	f?p=&APP_ID.:2:&SESSION.::&DEBUG.::::
65	List Practice	Lists	f?p=&APP_ID.:7:&APP_SESSION.::&DEBUG.:::
70	Regions	-	-
80	Lists	-	f?p=&APP_ID.:7:&SESSION.::&DEBUG.::::

Figure 4-21. *Entries for a hierarchical navigation menu*

Figure 4-22 shows a screenshot of the resulting navigation menu, where I clicked the Regions menu to see its children.

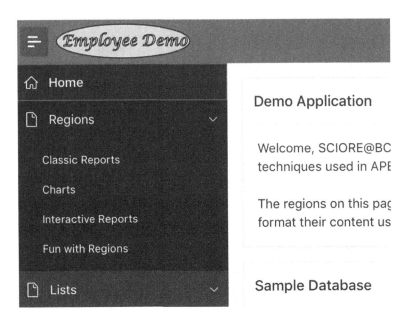

Figure 4-22. *Hierarchical navigation menu*

Each time you create a new page, you could use the preceding techniques to add an entry for it to the Desktop Navigation Menu list. However, it is often more convenient to add a new entry into the list as the page is created. Consider the third screen of the create page wizard, shown in Figure 4-23.

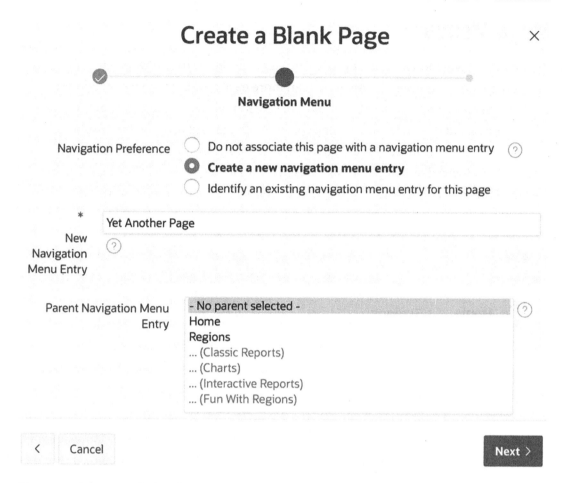

Figure 4-23. *Specifying the menu hierarchy during page creation*

The item labeled `Parent Navigation Menu Entry` displays every entry in the navigation menu list. (You need to scroll through the list to see them all.) The default value is `-No parent selected-`, which causes the new menu entry to be a root. If you want the new entry to be a child of another entry, you must specify a parent. Ideally, you should be able to just select the entry you want from the list. However, some of the entries are grayed out and are not selectable. In particular, the selectable entries are the ones that either are already parents or are "potential parents" in the sense that they have no target. Most of the time, the parent you want will be selectable. But if you want your new entry to be a child of one of the grayed out entries, you must assign its parent via the list manager.

Mega Menus

Hierarchical navigation menus improve the user experience in two ways. First, they structure the menu entries, so that users can more easily understand what actions are available. Second, they reduce the amount of screen real estate that the menu requires.

A more recent design idea is to keep the hierarchical organization but display all menu entries at once, in what is called a *mega menu*. For example, Figure 4-24 shows what the employee demo application looks like with a mega menu. Clicking the icon to the left of the logo toggles the visibility of the menu. Each of the menu entries is a link to its target page.

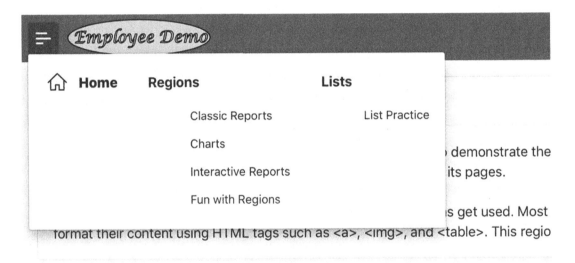

Figure 4-24. *A mega menu*

APEX implements mega menus as just another navigation menu template. To create a mega menu, click the Edit Application Properties button on the application's home page and then the User Interface tab. Find the Navigation Menu section and set its Position property to Top and its List Template property to Top Navigation Mega Menu, as shown in Figure 4-25.

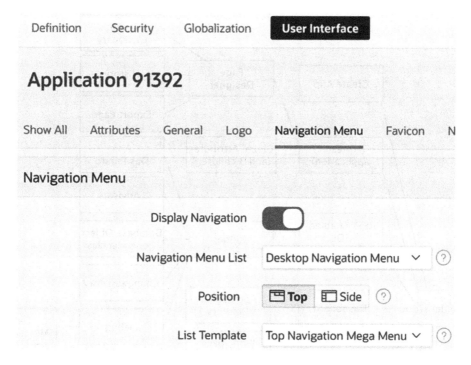

Figure 4-25. *Specifying a mega navigation menu*

Page Hierarchy

A large web application contains too many pages for all of them to be in the navigation menu. Instead, the navigation menu contains the application's *landing pages*—those pages that denote the start of the most prominent tasks.

Typically, the set of all pages in an application also has a hierarchical structure. An explicit rendering of this page hierarchy is called a *site map*. Consider, for example, the pages in an APEX site. Their root in the hierarchy is the APEX home page. The children of the root correspond to the various categories of the application, such as the app builder, the SQL workshop, and the team development tools. Each category has a "home page" that heads a subtree containing the pages of its category.

Figure 4-26 lists a portion of the page hierarchy corresponding to the APEX app builder. Due to space limitations, the figure leaves out many pages.

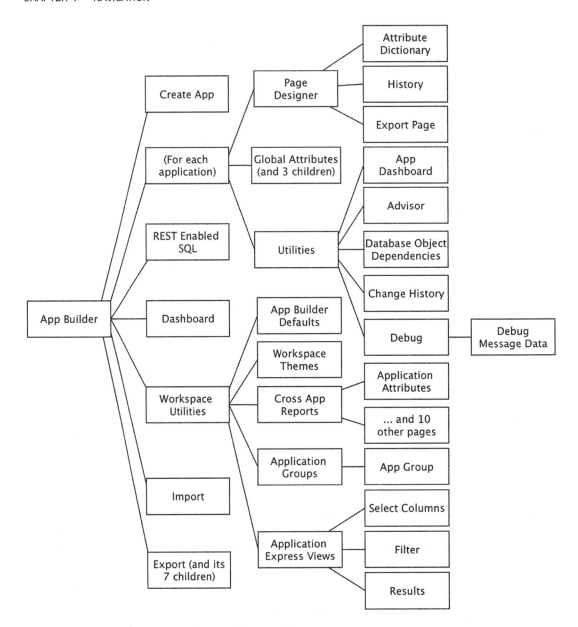

Figure 4-26. *App builder's page hierarchy*

It is worthwhile to compare this page hierarchy with the app builder's navigation menu. The navigation menu covers most (but not all) of the pages at the first three levels of the tree. Prominently missing from the navigation menu are entries corresponding to the subtree for each application; these pages are instead accessed from icons and buttons on the app builder home page.

Breadcrumbs

You can describe the location of any page in an application by giving the sequence of pages in the path of the page hierarchy between it and the home page. For example, the location of the `Application Attributes` page is

`App Builder` > `Workspace Utilities` > `Cross Application Reports` > `Application Attributes`

This path is known as a *breadcrumb*. Not all APEX screens display their breadcrumbs, but if they do, they display them below the navigation bar. Note that the first entry in an APEX breadcrumb is displayed as a circled up arrow, which denotes the root page of the hierarchy.

As an exercise, navigate to other pages on the APEX site and notice their breadcrumbs. In fact, see if you can find all of the pages listed in Figure 4-26. A breadcrumb is clickable. Clicking any portion of its path takes you to that corresponding page.

The navigation menu and breadcrumb are complementary navigation tools. The navigation menu is the same for all pages, and its entries encompass the entire functionality of the application. By looking at the menu, a user can determine the appropriate starting page for any desired action. On the other hand, a page's breadcrumb is specific to that page and provides context about where the page is located within the page hierarchy. For example, suppose that you are looking at the app builder's `Application Attributes` page. Its breadcrumb tells you that the page is one of the cross-application reports. That information might motivate you to click the breadcrumb to explore other cross-application reports.

In APEX, the entire page hierarchy is called a *breadcrumb object*. A breadcrumb object is essentially a hierarchical list—it contains an entry for each page in the hierarchy, with each entry (except the root) having a parent.

APEX automatically creates a breadcrumb object (named `Breadcrumb`) with each application. The APEX *breadcrumb manager* lets you edit this object and create other breadcrumb objects. To get to the breadcrumb manager, begin at the application's home screen and select the `Shared Components` button at the top of the page. Search for the `Navigation` section, click `Breadcrumbs`, and then click the `Breadcrumb` icon. You will be taken to the breadcrumb manager for that breadcrumb object. Figure 4-27 shows the breadcrumb manager for my `Employee Demo` application.

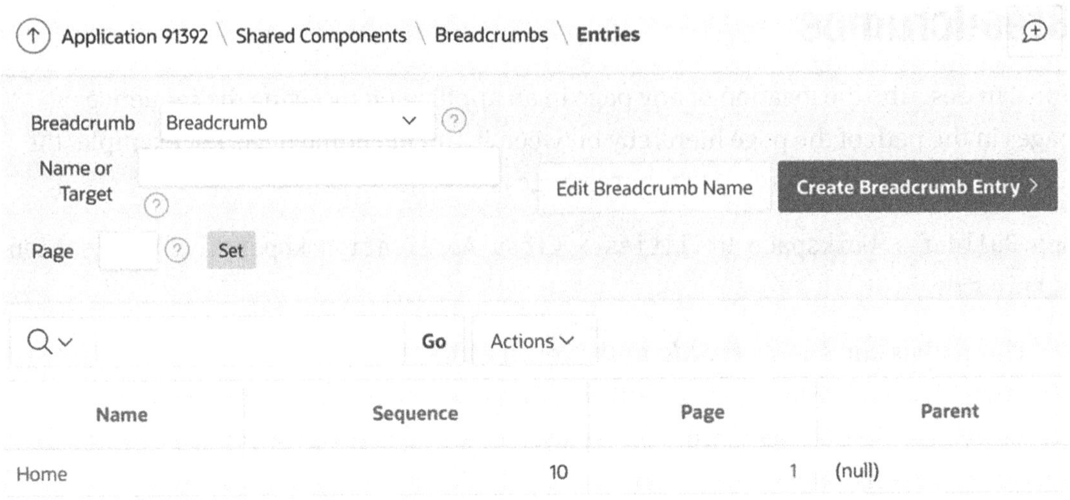

(↑) Application 91392 \ Shared Components \ Breadcrumbs \ **Entries**   ⊕

Breadcrumb   Breadcrumb   ∨   (?)

Name or
Target   (?)   Edit Breadcrumb Name   **Create Breadcrumb Entry >**

Page   (?)   Set

Q ∨   Go   Actions ∨

Name	Sequence	Page	Parent
Home	10	1	(null)

Figure 4-27. Breadcrumb manager

The figure shows that there is only one breadcrumb entry, which corresponds to the home page. This entry was created automatically when I created the application. Note that the entry still exists, even though I deleted its breadcrumb region from the home page.

When I created the other pages, I told the wizard to not create a breadcrumb entry for the new page. Instead, I can use the breadcrumb manager to create the breadcrumb entries now. Click the `Create Breadcrumb Entry` button. Figure 4-28 shows the resulting screen.

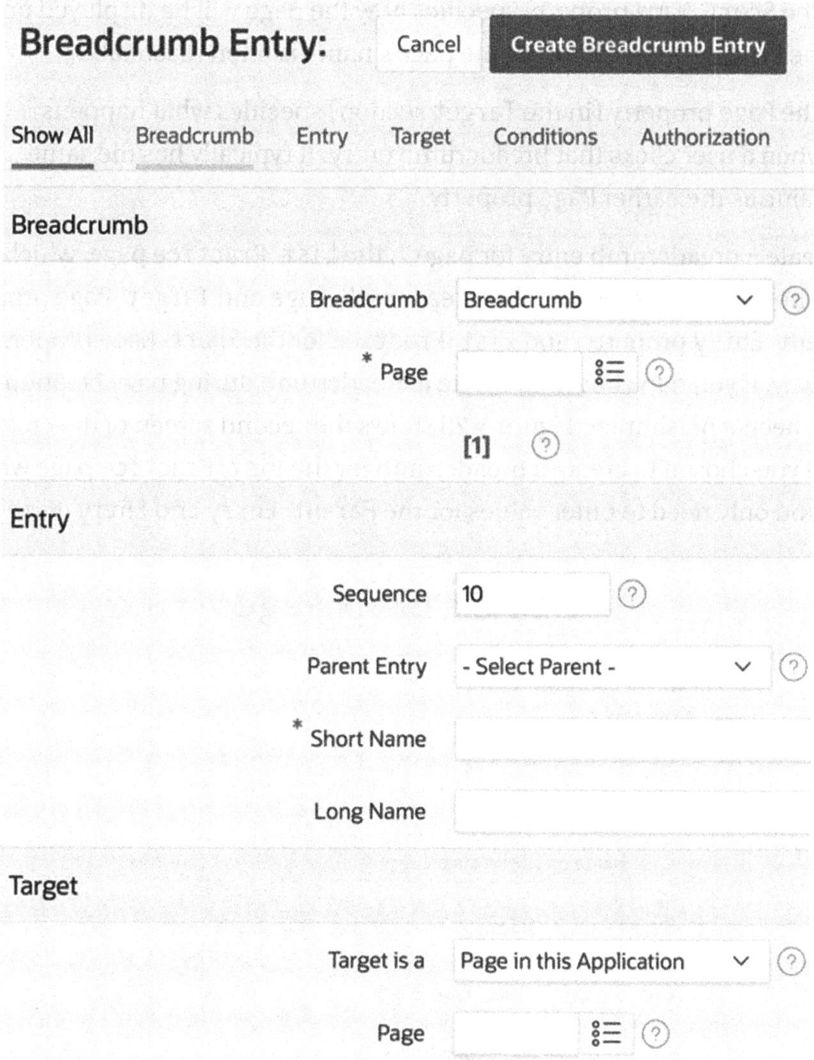

Breadcrumb Entry: Cancel   **Create Breadcrumb Entry**

Show All   Breadcrumb   Entry   Target   Conditions   Authorization

Breadcrumb

Breadcrumb	Breadcrumb ∨ ⑦
* Page	⊟ ⑦
	[1] ⑦

Entry

Sequence	10 ⑦
Parent Entry	- Select Parent - ∨ ⑦
* Short Name	
Long Name	

Target

Target is a	Page in this Application ∨ ⑦
Page	⊟ ⑦

Figure 4-28. *Breadcrumb Entry screen*

This screen lets you specify the page and its parent, as well as information about how the breadcrumb will be displayed on the page. In particular

- The Page property (in the Breadcrumb section) specifies the page.

- The Parent Entry property specifies the parent.

- The Short Name property specifies how the page will be displayed on the breadcrumb. Choosing the page's name is often reasonable.

- The Page property (in the Target section) specifies what happens when a user clicks that breadcrumb entry. It typically has the same value as the earlier Page property.

Let's create a breadcrumb entry for page 7, the List Practice page, which will be a child of the home page. Enter 7 for the Breadcrumb Page and Target Page properties, 1 for the Parent Entry property, and List Practice for the Short Name property.

By the way, if you had chosen to create a breadcrumb during page creation, your task would have been a bit simpler. Figure 4-29 shows the second screen of the create page wizard, had you chosen to create a breadcrumb for the List Practice page when you created it. You only need to enter values for the Parent Entry and Entry Name items.

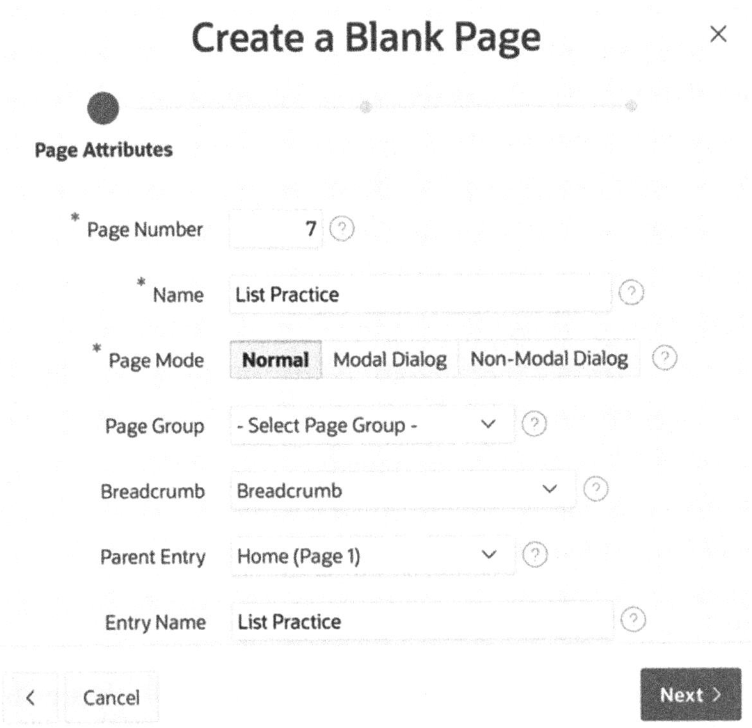

Create a Blank Page   ✕

Page Attributes

* Page Number	7
* Name	List Practice
* Page Mode	**Normal** Modal Dialog Non-Modal Dialog
Page Group	- Select Page Group -
Breadcrumb	Breadcrumb
Parent Entry	Home (Page 1)
Entry Name	List Practice

‹   Cancel   Next ›

Figure 4-29. *Creating a breadcrumb entry during page creation*

Breadcrumb Regions

If you want a page to display a breadcrumb object, you must create a region for it. The `Breadcrumb` region type is designed for this purpose. Although you can place a breadcrumb region anywhere on the page, it naturally goes in the `Breadcrumb Bar` position, which renders immediately below the navigation bar. In general, you need to follow these steps to add a breadcrumb region to a page.

- Add a new region to the page.

- Set the type of the region to be `Breadcrumb`.

- Set the source of the region to be the `Breadcrumb` object.

- Assign the region to the `Breadcrumb Bar` position.

- Set the region template to `Blank with Attributes`, so that it will display without a border or title.

- Set the region template options so that the breadcrumb is displayed with sufficient margins.

In your application, use these steps to add a breadcrumb region to the `List Practice` page. Figure 4-30 shows the navigation bar and breadcrumb region of the resulting page. Note that unlike a list region, a breadcrumb region does not display its entire source object. Instead, it only displays the breadcrumb corresponding to the current page.

Figure 4-30. *Breadcrumb object in a breadcrumb region*

Global Page

The standard way to display a list or a breadcrumb object is by placing it in a region on a page. This technique provides for considerable flexibility—each page can display the list or breadcrumb in a different location and with a different template. However, you often don't want this much flexibility. Suppose instead that you want every page to display a list or breadcrumb exactly the same way. The easiest way to enforce this uniformity is to use the *global page*.

The global page is a special page whose contents are included in every other page of the application. If you place the breadcrumb region of Figure 4-30 or the `Navigation Menu` region of Figure 4-15 in the global page, those regions will appear uniformly on all pages of the application. APEX creates the global page during application creation; by convention, the global page has page number 0.

One of the nice things about a breadcrumb region is that APEX will render it on a page only if the page has a breadcrumb. That is, if you put the breadcrumb region in the global page, it will appear only on those pages that actually have a breadcrumb.

Summary

The dominant navigational tool in APEX is the list of links, otherwise known as a *list*. The entries of the built-in `Desktop Navigation Bar` list are displayed in the application's navigation bar, and the entries of the `Desktop Navigation Menu` list appear in the application's navigation menu. The list manager allows you to edit the contents of these lists, and the application's `User Interface` properties allow you to customize their location and style.

You can also use the list manager to create lists of your own. You can display a list on a page by placing it in a region of type `List`. Each list region has a `Template` property that lets you customize how the list is displayed.

A list can be hierarchical, in the sense that a list entry can be the parent of one or more subentries. This hierarchy provides a structure to the list entries. This structure is especially useful for the navigation menu list because it allows the menu to contain a large number of entries without overwhelming the user.

Another navigational tool is the *breadcrumb*. To define a breadcrumb for a page, you must first understand how the page fits within the hierarchy of all application pages. A page's breadcrumb is the path in the hierarchy from that page to the root. To display a breadcrumb on a page, you must place it in a region of type `Breadcrumb`. It is common to place the breadcrumb region in the application's global page (page 0) so that it appears in the same place on every page.

CHAPTER 5

Items and Buttons

This book has so far focused on how an application can display information to users. In this chapter and the next, you will examine the components that allow users to send information back to the application. These components, which are *items* and *buttons*, are known as *form controls* because they typically appear in web forms.

APEX supports many types of items, which look and behave quite differently from each other. However, they all can be understood as variations of a few basic concepts. The main purpose of this chapter is to explore these concepts and examine how they are embodied in the different item types.

Items

An *item* is an element of a web page that holds a value. Each item has a *type*, such as Text Field, Checkbox, or Select List. Each item type has a specific way of displaying its value and letting users modify that value.

You have already encountered several item types during your use of APEX. For example, Figure 5-1 shows the Object Browser screen for renaming a column of the DEPT table. This figure shows five items: two display-only items (labeled Schema and Table), a select list (Current Column Name), a text box (New Column Name), and a checkbox (Preserve Case). In general, each time you enter a value into an APEX screen, you do so via an item.

© Edward Sciore 2020
E. Sciore, *Understanding Oracle APEX 20 Application Development*,
https://doi.org/10.1007/978-1-4842-6165-1_5

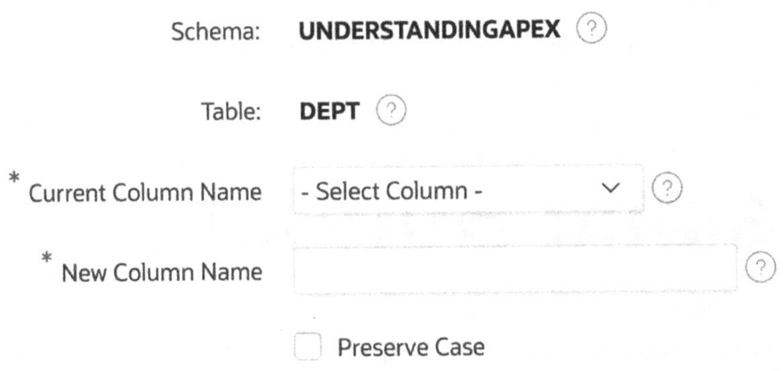

Schema: **UNDERSTANDINGAPEX** ⑦

Table: **DEPT** ⑦

* Current Column Name   - Select Column -   ⌄ ⑦

* New Column Name   ⑦

☐ Preserve Case

Figure 5-1. *Different item types in an APEX screen*

The APEX app builder supports 22 different item types. These item types can be grouped into three categories: *text-based* items let you specify a value by typing it, *list-based* items let you specify a value by choosing it from a list, and *display-based* items prevent you from specifying values. Figure 5-1 contains examples of all three item categories. These categories and their item types will be discussed throughout this chapter.

Item Sampler Page

In this chapter, you will create the page shown in Figure 5-2. This page, named Item Sampler, will be page 8 of the Employee Demo application. The page itself will not do anything interesting; its only purpose is to demonstrate the features of some common item types and show how to configure their properties.

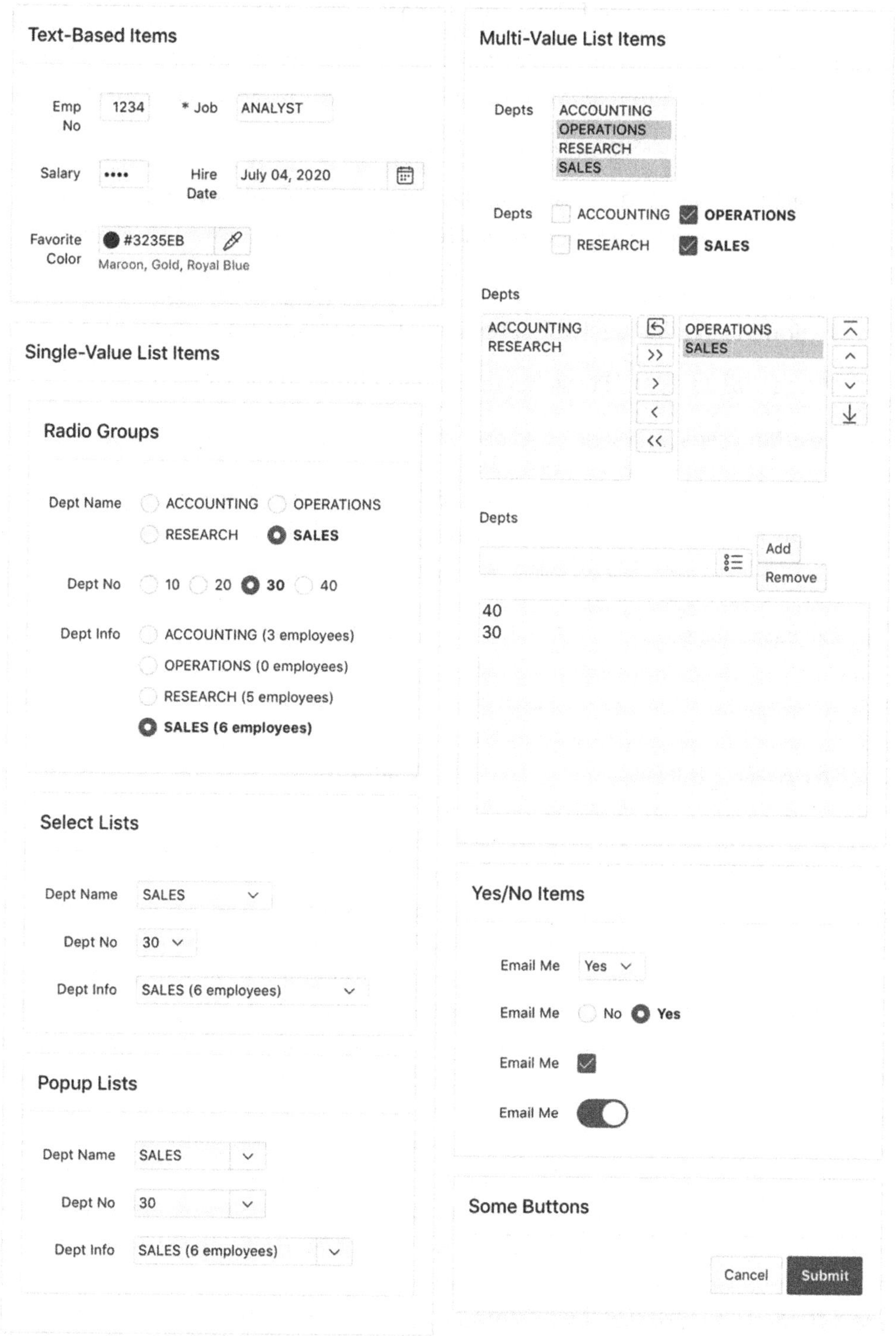

Text-Based Items

| Emp No | 1234 | * Job | ANALYST |

| Salary | •••• | Hire Date | July 04, 2020 🗓 |

Favorite Color ● #3235EB ✎
Maroon, Gold, Royal Blue

Multi-Value List Items

Depts
ACCOUNTING
OPERATIONS
RESEARCH
SALES

Depts ☐ ACCOUNTING ☑ OPERATIONS
       ☐ RESEARCH   ☑ SALES

Depts

ACCOUNTING   ↩   OPERATIONS   ⊼
RESEARCH   ⟩⟩   SALES   ⌃
              ⟩   ⌄
              ⟨   ⤓
              ⟨⟨

Depts

[ ] ⣿≡ Add
        Remove

40
30

Single-Value List Items

Radio Groups

Dept Name ○ ACCOUNTING ○ OPERATIONS
           ○ RESEARCH   ● SALES

Dept No   ○ 10 ○ 20 ● 30 ○ 40

Dept Info ○ ACCOUNTING (3 employees)
           ○ OPERATIONS (0 employees)
           ○ RESEARCH (5 employees)
           ● SALES (6 employees)

Select Lists

Dept Name SALES ⌄

Dept No   30 ⌄

Dept Info SALES (6 employees) ⌄

Yes/No Items

Email Me Yes ⌄

Email Me ○ No ● Yes

Email Me ☑

Email Me ⬤○

Popup Lists

Dept Name SALES ⌄

Dept No   30 ⌄

Dept Info SALES (6 employees) ⌄

Some Buttons

Cancel   Submit

Figure 5-2. *Item Sampler page*

The first step in building the Item Sampler page is for you to create a blank page and eight static content regions. Use the Layout properties of each region to locate them on the page, as described in Chapter 3 (refer to Figures 3-8 and 3-12). In particular

- Text-Based Items begins a new row.

- Single-Value List Items is in the same row and column, which causes it to be placed underneath Text-Based Items.

- Radio Groups, Select Lists, and Popup Lists each have the parent region Single-Value List Items and begin a new row.

- Multi-Value List Items begins a new column of the same row.

- Yes/No Items and Some Buttons are in the same row and column.

As a result, the regions form a single row of two columns. Figure 5-3 shows the resulting empty regions.

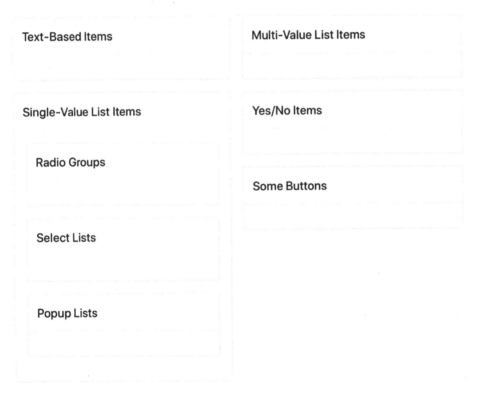

Figure 5-3. *Structure of the Item Sampler page*

Creating and Deleting Items

Each item on a page has a corresponding node in the page's rendering tree, located in the subtree corresponding to the item's region. For example, Figure 5-4 shows the rendering subtree for the completed Text-Based Items region. It has a child named Items, which has a child node for each item in the region.

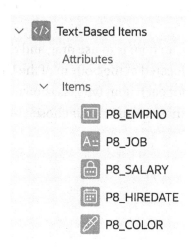

Figure 5-4. *The rendering subtree for the Text-Based Items region*

To create an item for a region, right-click the region's entry in the rendering subtree and select Create Page Item. APEX will then insert a node into the Items subtree for that region. When you click that node, the properties for the item are displayed in the property editor.

APEX assigns default values to a new item's Name and Type properties. These properties appear in the Identification section of the property editor, as shown in Figure 5-5.

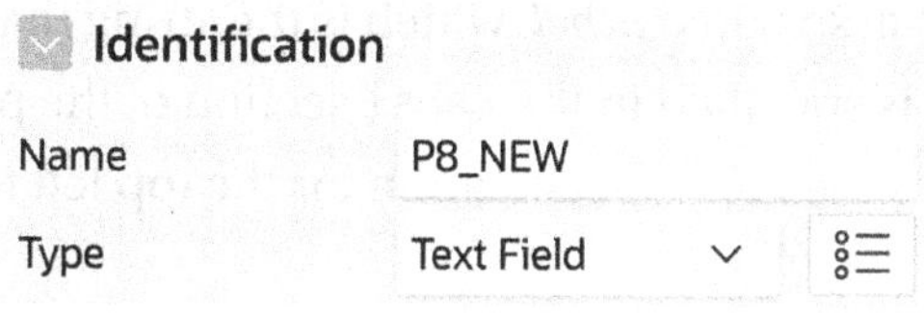

Figure 5-5. *Item's identification section*

The name of this new item is P8_NEW. The prefix denotes the page containing the item, which in this case is page 8. When creating an item, you should rename the suffix from NEW to something more meaningful, but keep the prefix. The APEX community strongly suggests using the page number as the prefix of an item's name, and there is no reason not to follow along.

The Type property specifies the type of the item. By default, the type is Text Field, but you can click the select list to choose from the 22 different item types supported by APEX.

An alternative way to create an item is to use drag and drop. Recall that the page designer has a gallery section, located at the bottom of the Layout tab of its middle panel. The gallery has an icon for each item type, as shown in Figure 5-6. You can create a new item by dragging one of these icons to your chosen region of the page.

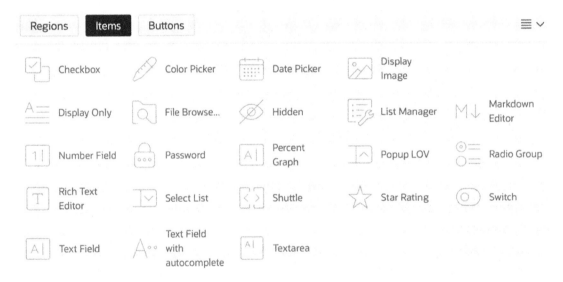

Figure 5-6. *Item gallery*

Each item also has an associated *label*, which is the string that you want displayed with the item. This string is specified in the Label section of the property editor. For example, Figure 5-7 shows the label specification for the top left item of the Item Sampler page.

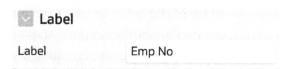

Figure 5-7. *Specifying the label of an item*

Figure 5-8 shows the `Template` property of an item, which is in its `Appearance` section. This property specifies how the label is rendered in relation to its item. There are seven possible values. The value `Hidden` hides the label, the three `Optional` values display the label normally, and the three `Required` values format the label with a red asterisk. The keyword `Above` specifies that the label is placed above the item, and `Floating` specifies that the label appears inside the item with its value. If neither keyword is specified, then the label is placed to the left of the item.

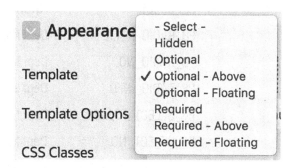

Figure 5-8. *Specifying the appearance of an item*

The items in the `Item Sampler` page mostly use the `Optional` template. The two larger items in the right column use `Optional-Above`, to conserve horizontal space. And the item labeled `Job` at the top of the left column uses the `Required` template. The purpose of the `Required` template is to warn the user that this item value must be filled in. The item's `Value Required` property (which is in its `Validation` section) enforces this restriction and will be discussed in Chapter 8.

To delete an item, right-click its entry in the rendering tree and select the `Delete` option.

You are now ready to create all 22 items of the `Item Sampler` page, placing them in the appropriate regions with appropriate labels. In particular, the `Text-Based Items` region has five items, the `Single-Value Items` regions have three items each, the `Multi-Value Items` region has four items, and the `Yes/No Items` region has four items.

At the moment, you only need to specify the name and label for each item. Table 5-1 lists these values for you. The item types are not yet important; for now, you should leave each item type as Text Field. When you have finished creating the items, feel free to experiment with different label templates.

Table 5-1. *Items in the Item Sampler page*

Region	Name	Label
Text-Based Items	P8_EMPNO	Emp No
	P8_JOB	Job
	P8_SALARY	Salary
	P8_HIREDATE	Hire Date
	P8_COLOR	Favorite Color
Radio Groups	P8_RADIO_NAME	Dept Name
	P8_RADIO_NO	Dept No
	P8_RADIO_INFO	Dept Info
Select Lists	P8_SELECT_NAME	Dept Name
	P8_SELECT_NO	Dept No
	P8_SELECT_INFO	Dept Info
Popup Lists	P8_POPUP_NAME	Dept Name
	P8_POPUP_NO	Dept No
	P8_POPUP_INFO	Dept Info
Multi-Value List Items	P8_M_SELECT	Depts
	P8_CHECKBOX	Depts
	P8_SHUTTLE	Depts
	P8_LIST	Depts
Yes/No Items	P8_YN_SELECT	Email Me
	P8_YN_RADIO	Email Me
	P8_YN_CHECKBOX	Email Me
	P8_YN_SWITCH	Email Me

Positioning an Item

Your next task is to position the items within their region. APEX displays a region's items in rows, either at the top or bottom of the region. The region's `Item Display Position` property (in the region's `Appearance` section) lets you specify whether its items appear above or below its content. This property is irrelevant for the `Item Sampler` page because its regions have no other content, but will become useful for the pages of the next chapter.

An item's `Layout` section determines its position within its region. APEX positions items within a region similar to how it positions regions within a page. Items are placed into rows from left to right according to the value of their `Sequence` property, moving to a new row whenever its `Start New Row` property is selected. The width of the region is divided into 12 grid points. Each item (including its label, if it is displayed to the left of the item) has a starting grid point and a width in grid points.

For example, Figure 5-9 shows the `Layout` section for the item `P8_EMPNO`. These values specify that the item will span the first third of the region (so that `P8_JOB` will have room to span the remaining two thirds).

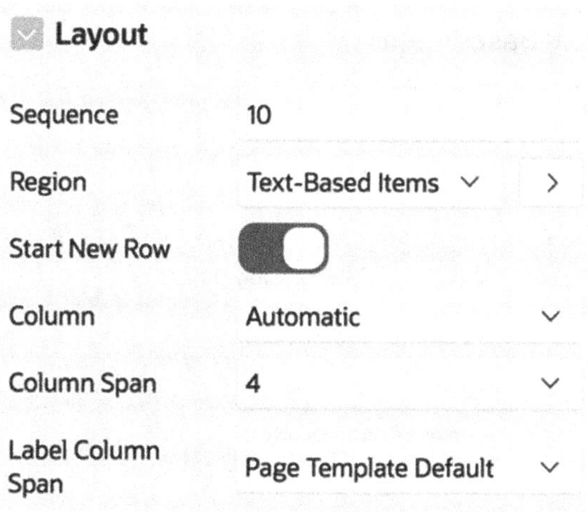

Figure 5-9. *Specifying an item's position in its region*

When an item's label is displayed to its left, APEX needs to decide how much of the item width to devote to the label and how much to the item. The property `Label Column Span`, shown in Figure 5-9, specifies how many grid points to devote to the label.

The default value is usually very good. But if a label is excessively long or requires special treatment, it might be better to specify the label span explicitly (or to specify a Floating or Above label template).

You are now able to position your Item Sampler items in their regions. Most items can use their default layout properties, the only exception being the items in the Text-Based Items region. Items P8_EMPNO and P8_SALARY each begin a new row and have a column span of 4; items P8_JOB and P8_HIREDATE each begin a new column. The item P8_COLOR begins a new row.

The items on your page now have the proper structure, but they still have the default type Text Field. This situation is addressed next.

Text-Based Items

A text-based item is characterized by its input box, into which a user can type a value. APEX supplies several kinds of text-based items, five of which are shown in the Text-Based Items region of Figure 5-2. For readability, this region is reprinted in Figure 5-10.

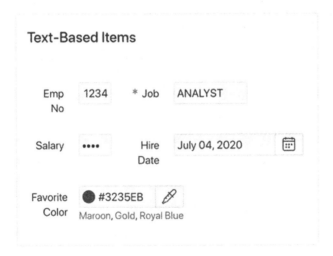

Figure 5-10. *The Text-Based Items region of Figure 5-2*

The following subsections consider the various text-based item types and their properties, followed by a discussion of some properties common to all text-based items.

Text Fields

Text Field is the default item type. It is also the simplest item type, in that there is no restriction on what values you can enter into the input box. The value of the item is whatever you type into the input box.

Number Fields

The item P8_EMPNO is a *number field*; it differs from a text field in that its value can only be numeric. The Settings section of a number field item has several number-specific properties. Figure 5-11 shows these properties for P8_EMPNO. The Minimum Value and Maximum Value properties allow you to restrict the allowable item values in the obvious way. The Number Alignment property allows you to specify the alignment of the number within the input box.

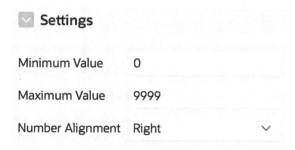

Figure 5-11. *Properties relevant to number fields*

Password Items

The item P8_SALARY is a *password field*, which differs from a text field in that its value is not displayed on the page. Instead, its characters are replaced by circles when the value is being entered and are displayed that way when the page is rendered.

Text Fields with Autocomplete

A *text field with autocomplete* is a text field with an associated list of suggested values. As you type into the input box, the page displays a menu of matching values. If you click a displayed value, then APEX automatically enters that value into the input box. For example, the item P8_JOB is a text field with autocomplete, whose associated list consists of the five current job titles. When I typed **a** into the box, APEX displayed the job title ANALYST (because it was the only job beginning with *a*); I was then able to click that title without the need for further typing.

Autocomplete fields make it easy for users to enter the most common values, but do not require them to pick from those values. Even after selecting a suggested value from the list, a user is free to alter that value via continued typing.

You specify the list of autocompletion values in the item's List of Values section. Figure 5-12 shows this section for P8_JOB.

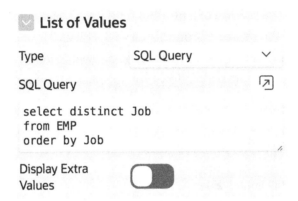

Figure 5-12. *Specifying the autocompletion list*

There are two ways to specify the list. Figure 5-12 demonstrates the first way, which is via an SQL query. The query contains one column, and its output values constitute the list. This method of expressing the list is *dynamic* because the list changes as the job titles in the database change.

An alternative way to specify the list of values is to use *static values*. To do so, set the Type property in Figure 5-12 to Static Values. The property editor will then display a property called Static Values; clicking it brings up a screen where you can enter the values. Figure 5-13 shows what the screen would look like if I specified P8_JOB using static values. The Sort at Runtime property specifies whether APEX should present multiple matching values in sorted order or as listed.

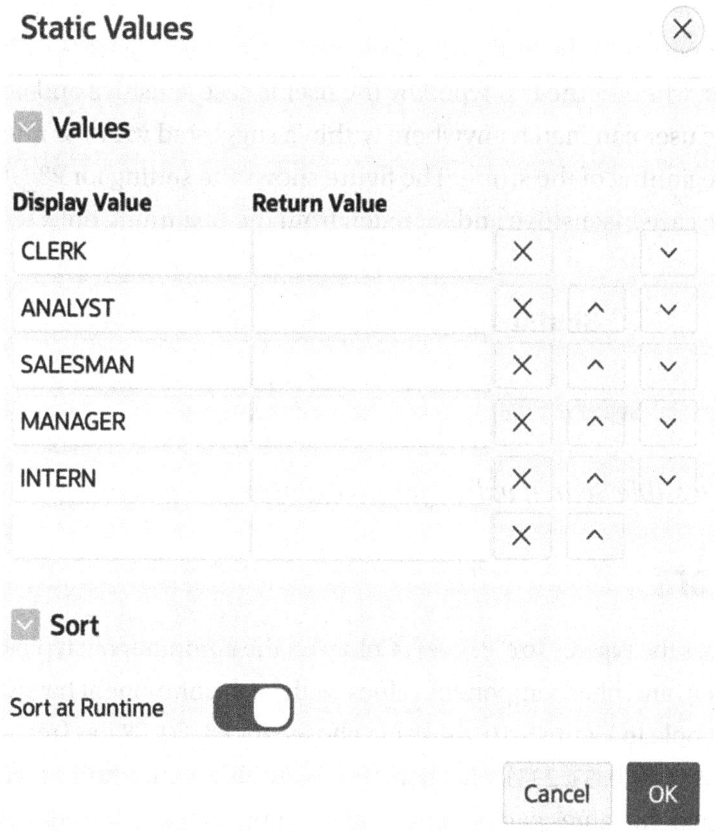

Static Values ⊗

⌄ **Values**

Display Value	Return Value			
CLERK		✕		⌄
ANALYST		✕	⌃	⌄
SALESMAN		✕	⌃	⌄
MANAGER		✕	⌃	⌄
INTERN		✕	⌃	⌄
		✕	⌃	

⌄ **Sort**

Sort at Runtime ⬤

Cancel   OK

Figure 5-13. *Static specification of the autocompletion list*

A static specification is preferable when the value list is fixed and well-known. In Figure 5-13, for example, the static specification enables INTERN to be on the list, even though there are no current employees having that job.

You might recall from Chapter 3 that report columns can have the type Plain Text (based on List of Values), which used a list of values to translate actual column values to their displayed values. That list of values was also specified in a List of Values property section, via an SQL query. The mechanism is similar to how autocompletion values are specified. For example, compare Figure 3-30 with Figure 5-12; the only difference is that an autocompletion SQL query has one output column instead of two.

This similarity explains why the Static Values screen in Figure 5-13 has a column for display values and return values—the screen is also used when defining value lists that perform translation. This latter use of value lists will come up again in this chapter, during the discussion of list-based item types.

Another relevant autocompletion property is Search, which appears in the Settings section. This property has the four possible settings shown in Figure 5-14. These settings cover two issues: whether the text typed by the user is case sensitive and whether the text typed by the user can match anywhere within a suggested value or must it match only from the beginning of the string. The figure shows the setting for P8_JOB, which is configured to be case insensitive and to match from the beginning only.

Figure 5-14. *Possible Search values for an autocomplete item*

Color Pickers

Item P8_COLOR has the type Color Picker. Colors on the computer are typically represented by their red, green, and blue component values, with each component having a value from 0 to 255. For example in Figure 5-10, the value chosen for P8_COLOR has (red, green, blue) component values of (50, 53, 235). That color is mostly blue, with a little green and red.

These component values can be represented compactly as a hexadecimal number. Because a two-digit hexadecimal number can represent 256 different values, a six-digit number can represent every possible color. In Figure 5-10, that color is represented by the number #3235EB. Note that 32 is the hexadecimal value of 50, 35 is the hexadecimal value of 53, and EB is the hexadecimal value of 235.

An APEX color picker item lets you type the value of the color if it is known. Or you can click the eyedropper icon to choose the desired color from a color wheel, and APEX will display the corresponding numeric value in the input box. The links under the color picker are *quick picks*, which will be discussed a bit later.

Date Pickers

The item P8_HIREDATE has the type Date Picker. Date picker items consist of an input box and a calendar icon. As with all text-based items, the user is free to type the desired date into the input box. But the user can also click the icon to bring up a calendar and then navigate the calendar to select a date, which causes the textual representation of the date to appear in the input box.

The properties relevant to a date picker appear in its Settings section. Figure 5-15 shows these values for P8_HIREDATE.

Figure 5-15. *Properties relevant to Date Picker items*

The Highlighted Date property specifies the date that the calendar initially selects; by default, it is the current date. The Minimum Date and Maximum Date property values can be specified in several ways. In Figure 5-15, the values **-5y** and **+5y** specify 5 years ago and 5 years in the future, respectively. The property Show allows you to configure when the calendar is displayed. The calendar can be shown when the icon is clicked (as in Figure 5-10), shown on mouse rollover, or always displayed on the page. The Navigation List for property allows you to configure the calendar for quicker access to dates. By default, the calendar has buttons to navigate only to the previous and next months. You can set the property so that there are also menus for moving directly to a specified month, year, or both. Finally, the Year Range property is an alternative way to specify the maximum and minimum dates, in which you give the allowable range of years. For example, entering the value **2018:2025** would allow only dates between the years 2018–2025.

Properties of All Text-Based Items

Certain properties are common to all text-based items, regardless of their type. Three such properties are Width and Format Mask (both in the Appearance section) and Maximum Length (in the Validation section). Figure 5-16 shows these two sections for the item P8_HIREDATE.

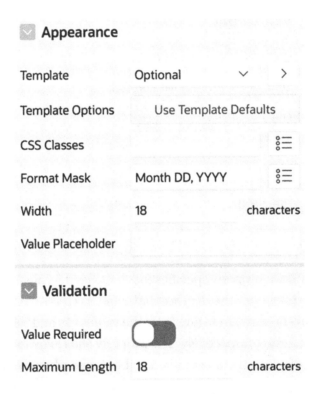

Figure 5-16. *Properties common to all text-based items*

The Format Mask property works the same way as in reports. The value of the property is an expression that describes how the item value gets displayed. In Figure 5-16, the Hire Date item has a format mask of Month DD, YYYY.

The Width property specifies the size of the input box in characters. P8_HIREDATE has a width of 18, as that is large enough to hold all dates. For the other items in Figure 5-10, P8_EMPNO and P8_SALARY have widths of 6, and P8_JOB and P8_COLOR have widths of 10.

The Maximum Length property specifies the maximum number of characters that a user can type into the input box, regardless of its width. The difference between item width and maximum length is as follows. A user can enter a value that is longer than the width of the input box—if so, APEX will scroll the value within the box. But if a user tries to enter a value that is longer than the maximum length, then APEX will refuse to accept the extra characters.

For example, in Figure 5-16, P8_HIREDATE has the same values for Width and Maximum Length, meaning that a user cannot enter a value longer than the size of the input box. For another example, try setting the maximum length of P8_EMPNO to 4; you will discover that you simply cannot enter more than four digits into the input box, even though there is room.

By default, the maximum length is blank, denoting no maximum. A good design rule is to specify a maximum length for all text-based items. In Chapter 13, you will see how an item with no maximum length (or an unreasonably large one) can contribute to serious security loopholes.

Another section common to text-based items is Quick Picks, which enables you to specify commonly used values for the item. For example, the Favorite Color item in Figure 5-10 has three quick-pick values, which display as links below the item. The value shown in its text box is the result of my clicking the link for Royal Blue.

Figure 5-17 shows the Quick Picks section for the Favorite Color item. Enabling the Show Quick Picks property displays the label/value text boxes. Note that you need to specify two values for each pick: the value displayed in the link and the value to be entered into the text box when the link is clicked.

Show Quick Picks	⬤〇
Link Attributes	
Label 1	Maroon
Value 1	MAROON
Label 2	Gold
Value 2	GOLD
Label 3	Royal Blue
Value 3	#3235EB

Figure 5-17. *Specifying an item's quick picks*

Quick picks are useful because they enable users to quickly enter item values. In fact, many items in APEX screens contain quick picks. For example, the properties CSS Classes and Format Mask in Figure 5-16 have a context menu to the right of their text box, as does the Type property in Figure 5-5. Clicking the context menu displays a list of quick-pick values for that item. Sadly, although APEX screens have multiple ways to implement quick picks (such as context menus or links), applications that you can write using APEX are limited to just one way (namely, as links beneath the item).

Items having quick picks are similar in spirit to autocomplete items. Both enable a user to eliminate (or reduce) typing by choosing from suggested values. The difference is that the autocompletion menu gets filtered as the user types, whereas quick picks are presented to the user all at once. Consequently, an item can have arbitrarily many autocompletion values, whereas APEX limits an item to ten quick picks.

List-Based Items

Unlike a text-based item, a list-based item does not have an input box. Instead, a list-based item presents the user with a list of possibilities to choose from. Moreover, the value that a user chooses is not necessarily the value assigned to the item. That is, the item presents a list of *display values* to the user; when the user selects a display value, a corresponding *return value* is assigned to the item.

For example, consider the three subregions of Single-Value List Items in Figure 5-2, which are reprinted in Figure 5-18. Each region is devoted to one of the three common list-based item types—radio groups, select lists, and pop-up lists—and contains three items of that type. Although you cannot tell from the figure, all nine of these items have the same set of possible return values, namely, the set {10, 20, 30, 40} of department numbers. Moreover, the selections shown in the figure are such that every item has the same value, namely, 30.

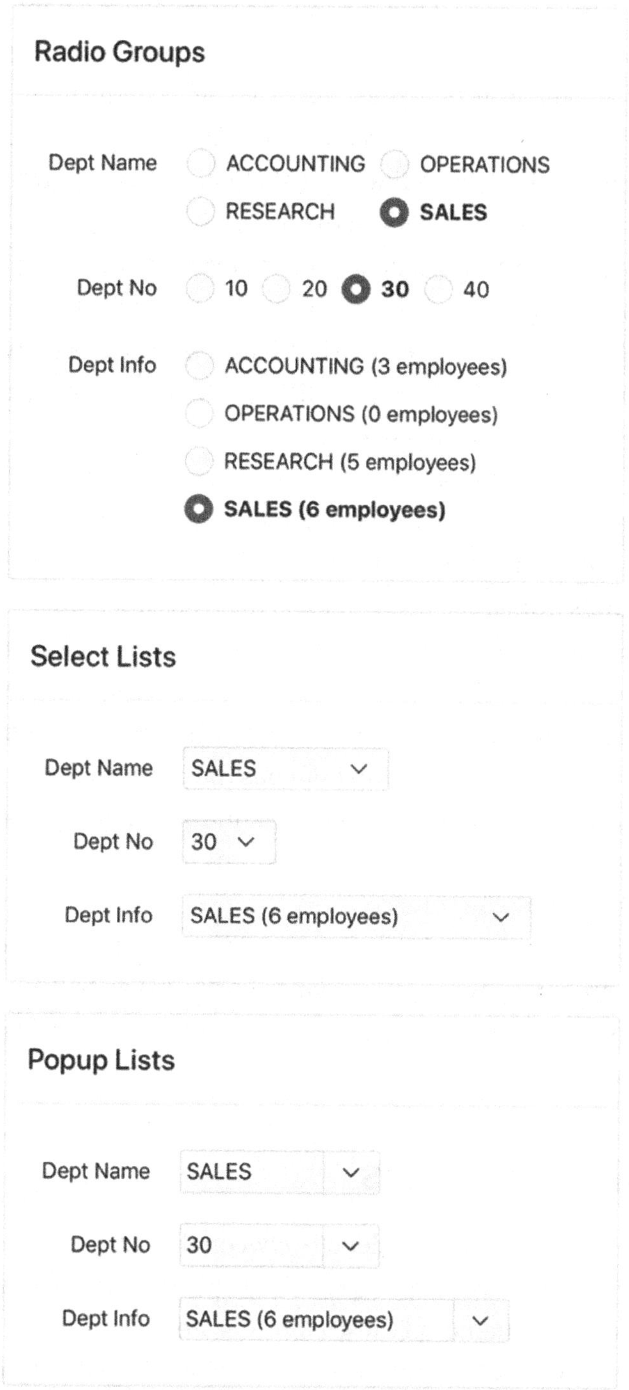

Radio Groups

Dept Name	◯ ACCOUNTING ◯ OPERATIONS
	◯ RESEARCH ● **SALES**
Dept No	◯ 10 ◯ 20 ● **30** ◯ 40
Dept Info	◯ ACCOUNTING (3 employees)
	◯ OPERATIONS (0 employees)
	◯ RESEARCH (5 employees)
	● **SALES (6 employees)**

Select Lists

Dept Name	SALES ⌄
Dept No	30 ⌄
Dept Info	SALES (6 employees) ⌄

Popup Lists

Dept Name	SALES ⌄
Dept No	30 ⌄
Dept Info	SALES (6 employees) ⌄

Figure 5-18. *Single-value list items*

These nine items have identical functionality: a user selects a department, and the corresponding department number is assigned to the item. The items differ only in what their display values are and how they present those values to the user.

Consider first the radio groups. In a radio group, all the display values appear on the page, and the user selects a desired value by clicking it. Each radio group in the Radio Groups region has different display values: the first group displays the list of department names, the second displays the list of department numbers, and the third displays each department name with the count of its employees in parentheses.

Now consider the select lists. When a user clicks a select list, a menu of display values appears. The display values in the first select list are identical to those of the first radio group, and similarly for the other two select lists.

Finally, consider the pop-up lists. When a user clicks the arrow to the right of the item, a menu of display values appears for the user to pick from. The display values of the three pop-up lists are the same as the corresponding display values of the other two regions.

A pop-up list differs from a select list in that it also has a search box. The user can type a prefix of the desired value into the search box and click the magnifying glass; the displayed list of values will be filtered to include only the values having that prefix. Pop-up lists make it possible to select from a lengthy value list without a lot of scrolling.

The Settings section of a radio group item has the property Number of Columns. This property specifies the placement of the radio buttons on the page. In Figure 5-18, you can see that the first radio group has two columns, the second group has four columns, and the third group has one column.

The most important issue for a list-based item is how to specify its display values and return values. You can specify these values dynamically, via an SQL query, or statically, via explicit values. All nine items in Figure 5-18 are specified dynamically, so I shall begin the discussion there.

Dynamic List–Based Items

An SQL query to specify the correspondence between display values and return values will have two columns: the first column gives the display values, and the second column gives the return values. The names of these columns are not important.

For an example, consider the radio group item P8_RADIO_NAME. Its query should have department names in its first column and department numbers in its second column. Moreover, the items P8_SELECT_NAME and P8_POPUP_NAME will also have these same display and return values. Thus, the values for all three items can be specified by the following query:

```
select DName, DeptNo
from DEPT
order by DName
```

This query is specified in the item's List of Values section. This is the same section as in Figure 5-12, which specified the value list for autocomplete text items; the only difference is that list-based items require a two-column query.

You are now ready to configure the items P8_RADIO_NAME, P8_SELECT_NAME, and P8_POPUP_NAME. Set their Type property to Radio Group, Select List, and Popup List, respectively, and set their List of Values properties to the preceding SQL query. You should also set the Number of Columns property for P8_RADIO_NAME to 2.

Now consider the items P8_RADIO_NO, P8_SELECT_NO, and P8_POPUP_NO—that is, the second items of each region of Figure 5-12. Each of these items has the same display and return values. The interesting situation here is that the display and return values are both department numbers. If you wrote their SQL query in a straightforward way, then the names of the two output columns would be identical, which is illegal in SQL. To make the query legal, you need to rename at least one of its columns. The query should look something like this:

```
select DeptNo as DisplayVal, DeptNo as ReturnVal
from DEPT
order by DisplayVal
```

Note   The names of the columns can be anything; SQL requires only that they be different from each other.

You should configure the items P8_RADIO_NO, P8_SELECT_NO, and P8_POPUP_NO analogously to the preceding three items. Set their Type property to Radio Group, Select List, and Popup List, respectively, and their List of Values properties to the preceding SQL query. You should also set the Number of Columns property for P8_RADIO_NO to 4.

The treatment of the items P8_RADIO_INFO, P8_SELECT_INFO, and P8_POPUP_INFO is similar. Their property values are the same as for the previous items, except that they have a different query. Here is the query, which shows how to create complex display values:

```
select d.DName || ' (' || count(e.EmpNo) || ' employees)' as Display,
       d.DeptNo as ReturnVal
from DEPT d left join EMP e on d.DeptNo = e.DeptNo
group by d.DeptNo, d.DName
order by Display
```

The left join in the query ensures that all departments are included, even those with no employees.

Static List–Based Items

When you use a query to specify the values of a list-based item, APEX will execute that query each time it renders the page. If the output of the query will never change, then you can use a static expression to avoid the call to the database.

You specify a static expression the same as you would for an item of type Text Value with Autocomplete: First, set the Type property in the List of Values section to Static Values; then click the Static Values property to bring up the Static Values screen. You can then enter the display and return values for each member of the list. Figure 5-19 shows how I could have filled in the values for P8_RADIO_NAME, P8_SELECT_NAME, and P8_POPUP_NAME.

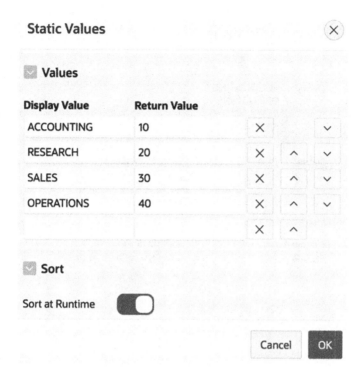

Figure 5-19. *Static values for a list-based item*

Multi-Value List Items

A list-based item allows a user to choose only one value from its list. A *multi-value list item* lets a user choose multiple values from its list. The Multi-Value List Items region of Figure 5-2 contains four types of multi-value item, and is reprinted for clarity in Figure 5-20. Each of the items in this region has its operations and sales departments chosen.

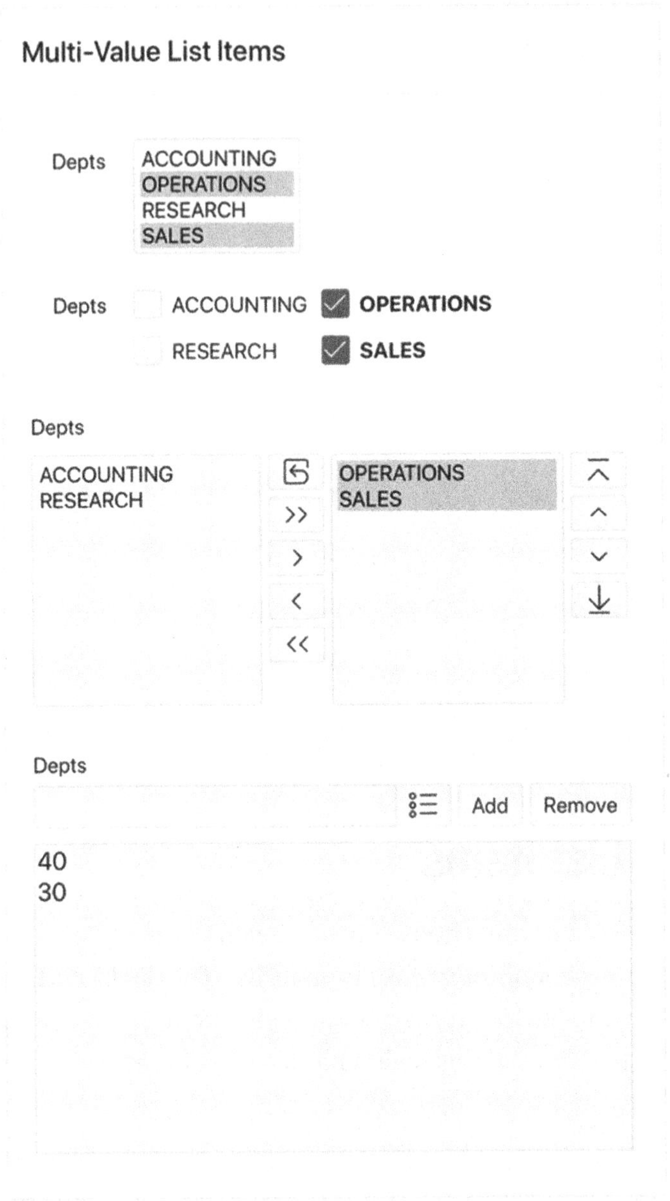

Multi-Value List Items

Depts
ACCOUNTING
OPERATIONS
RESEARCH
SALES

Depts   ☐ ACCOUNTING ☑ **OPERATIONS**

☐ RESEARCH ☑ **SALES**

Depts

ACCOUNTING RESEARCH	↩	OPERATIONS SALES	⊼
	››		^
	›		∨
	‹		⊻
	‹‹		

Depts

| | ☰ | Add | Remove |

40
30

Figure 5-20. *Multi-value list items*

Multi-value list items are configured the same way as single-value items. In particular, they use an SQL query or static expression to indicate their display values and return values. For example, the SQL query for each of the four items in the region is this:

```
select DName, DeptNo
from DEPT
order by DName
```

The main issue is how to assign a single return value to an item that has multiple display values selected. APEX uses the convention that the value of a multi-value item is a string consisting of the selected return values separated by colons. If no display values are selected, then the item's value is null. For example, the items in Figure 5-20 all have the value 40:30.

Let's examine these four item types. The first item, P8_M_SELECT, is a select list; that is, the same item type as in the Single-Value List region. To specify that the item is to be a multi-value select list, you set its Allow Multi Selection property (in the Settings section) to Yes. The value of its Height property (in the Appearance section) determines how many menu rows to display. All other properties are configured the same.

Note that the multi-value select list P8_M_SELECT looks and behaves differently from the single-value select list P8_SELECT_NAME. The multi-value list displays the menu on the page at all times, instead of on demand. (And if the list has more items than can be displayed on the page, a scrollbar appears so that the user can scroll through the values.) A user can choose additional menu items from the multi-value list by holding the control or command key while clicking, depending on the operating system.

The second item in the region, P8_CHECKBOX, is a checkbox group. Checkbox groups are configured exactly the same as radio groups. Checkbox groups behave differently from radio groups in that multiple checkboxes can be selected, and clicking a box toggles its value.

The third item, P8_SHUTTLE, is a shuttle list, which is very similar to a multi-value select list and is configured the same way. The difference between them is that a multi-value select list denotes selected values by highlighting them, whereas a shuttle has separate menus for displaying the selected and unselected values.

The fourth item, P8_LIST, is a list manager, which is a cross between an autocompletion text box and a pop-up list. Similar to autocompletion, a user can enter any value into the input box and click the Add button to add it to the selected value list. Alternatively, the user can click the pop-up arrow to bring up a menu of values to choose from, with the selected value getting added to the input box. It is important to note, however, that although the pop-up list shows display values, it places return values in the input box. Thus, Figure 5-20 shows that the department numbers 30 and 40 are selected, even though the pop-up list displays department names.

Yes/No Items

A web page often needs to request yes/no information from users. The Yes/No Items region of Figure 5-2 illustrates four different ways to perform this task, and is reprinted for clarity in Figure 5-21. The region contains four list-based items, each denoting that the user wants to be contacted.

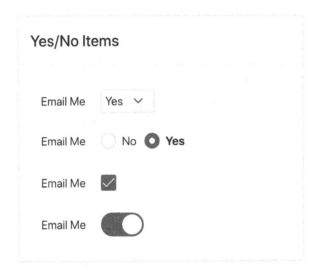

Figure 5-21. *Yes/No items*

The first item, named P8_YN_SELECT, has the type Select List, and the second, named P8_YN_RADIO, has type Radio Group. They both have the same list of values, namely, {No, Yes}, and their display values are the same as the return values. Figure 5-22 shows their Static Values screen. Note that you need not specify the return value when it is the same as the display value.

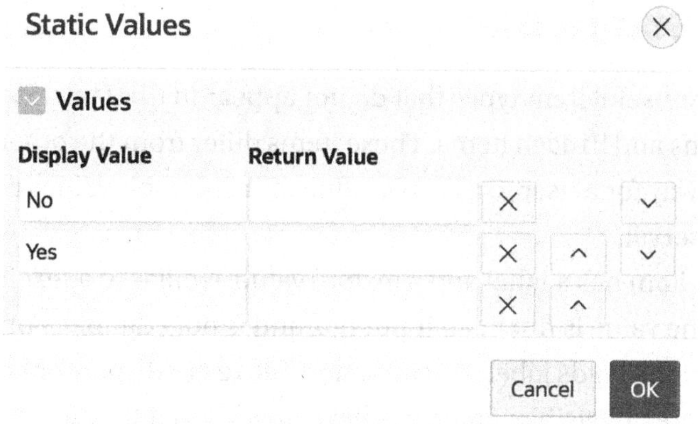

Figure 5-22. *Static values for the yes/no select list and radio buttons*

The third item, P8_YN_CHECKBOX, has the type Checkbox. Figure 5-23 shows its Static Values screen. It has one entry, whose display value is a space and return value is Yes. The value of the item is thus Yes if the box is selected and (as with all multi-value items) it is null if not selected.

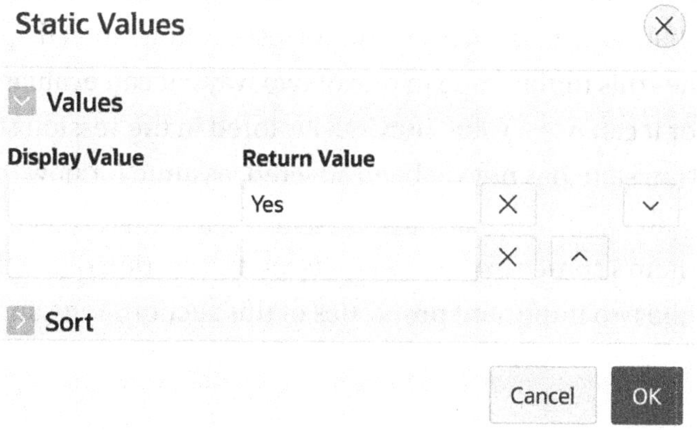

Figure 5-23. *Static values for the Yes/No checkbox*

The fourth item, P8_YN_SWITCH, has the type Switch. It does not need configuration. By default, it has no display values and two predefined return values: Y if the switch is on and N if it is off.

Display-Based Items

There are two other useful item types that do not appear in the Item Sampler page: Display Only items and Hidden items. These items differ from the others you have seen in that there is no way for a user to assign a value to them; their values can be assigned only by the APEX server.

A display-only item has a label and a textual value, similar to a text field; the difference is that the value is not in an input box and is not editable. For example, refer again to Figure 5-1; the fields labeled Schema and Table are display only.

Hidden items are not visible, and users have no idea that they exist. They are typically used to hold the value of an operation so that another operation can use it. You will see examples of this technique in Chapter 6.

Initial Item Values

When APEX renders a page, it assigns an initial value to each item on the page. If the item is text based, APEX places that value inside that item's input box; if the item is list based, APEX uses that value to determine the corresponding initial display value.

APEX determines this initial value in one of two ways: it can evaluate the item's *source expression*, or it can use a value previously stored in the session state. Because the concept of session state has not yet been covered, assume for now that session state values are always null.

You specify an item's source expression in its Source section of the property editor. Figure 5-24 shows the two important properties of this section, Type and Used, with their default values.

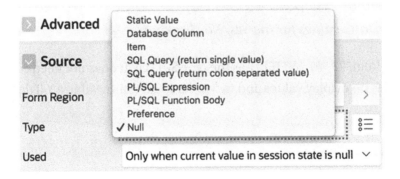

Figure 5-24. *Item's source properties*

The Type property specifies the type of the source expression; Figure 5-24 shows all possible source types. Three common choices are Null (which is the default), Static Value, and SQL Query (return single value). Choosing a type other than Null will cause the property editor to display an area for entering the source expression.

The Used property specifies when the source expression is applicable. The default choice, shown in Figure 5-24, is to use the session state if it is not null, and the source expression otherwise. The other choice, not shown in the figure, is to always use the source expression. These choices will be discussed in Chapter 6.

If you use an SQL query as the source type, then that query must return a single row and column; the initial value of the item is the value returned by the query. For example, consider again the text-based items of the Item Sampler page, as shown in Figure 5-10. Suppose that you want the initial value of P8_EMPNO to be the employee number of the president. You would set its source type to be SQL Query (return single value) and its source query to be the following query:

```
select EmpNo
from EMP
where Job = 'PRESIDENT'
```

For another example, suppose that you want the initial value of each item in Figure 5-18 to be the department that is first alphabetically (with the lowest department number breaking the tie if there are multiple departments having the same name). You · can assign the following source expression to each item:

```
select min(DeptNo)
from DEPT
where DName in (select min(DName) from DEPT)
```

A source expression whose type is Static Value is typically a constant. For example, suppose instead that you want the initial value of the items in Figure 5-18 to be the sales department. Simply set the source expression for each item to be 30. If you want the initial value of the multi-value list items in Figure 5-20 to be both the operations and sales departments, set the source expression of those items to be 30:40.

One issue that arises with list-based items is how they should respond to an initial value that is not one of their specified return values. For example, suppose that you assign the static value 85 to be the source of the list-valued items. What should the items display, given that there is no department numbered 85? There are two options: accept the value and add it (temporarily) to the list, or reject the value and display an arbitrary value from the list. This choice is specified by the Display Extra Values property in the List of Values section, as shown in Figure 5-12. In most cases, it makes no sense to display a value that is not a valid selection option, so Display Extra Values should usually be turned off.

Buttons

A button performs an *action* when clicked. An APEX button has two fundamental actions: it can redirect or it can submit. The term *redirect* simply means to move to another web page. In this respect, the button acts like an HTML link. The term *submit* means to have the web server process the current page. This processing can involve setting the session state and performing operations on the database, as well as moving to another page. Chapters 6 through 10 will cover in detail the uses of redirect and submit actions.

As an example, let's see how to add two buttons to the Some Buttons region of the Item Sampler page: a Cancel button with the action Redirect to page 8 and a Submit button with the action Submit.

There are two ways to create a button in a region. The first way is to right-click the region's node in the rendering tree and select the Create Button operation. Alternatively, you can drag a button icon from the page designer gallery to the region (in a way similar to dragging items). In either case, APEX will create a node for the button in a subtree of its region node named Region Buttons. Figure 5-25 shows the rendering tree of Item Sampler after the two buttons have been created.

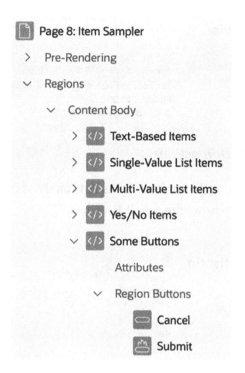

Figure 5-25. *Adding buttons to the rendering tree*

To configure a button, you need to specify four things: its name, label, action, and position. The button's name and label are specified in the Identification section; see Figure 5-26. The name of the button is an internal value that APEX uses to identify the button and cannot have spaces. The button's label is an arbitrary HTML string that is displayed with the button when the page is rendered.

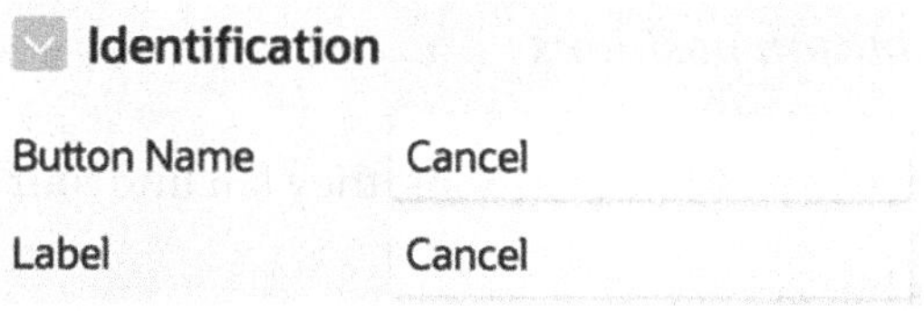

Identification

Button Name	Cancel
Label	Cancel

Figure 5-26. *Identifying a button*

The button's action is specified in its Behavior section. The Action property has the five possible values shown in Figure 5-27. The most common options are Submit Page and Redirect to Page in this Application. The Target property, which is applicable to redirect actions, lets you specify the target page.

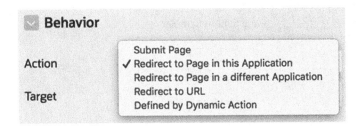

Figure 5-27. *Possible button actions*

The position of a button is determined by its `Button Position` property in the Layout section. Figure 5-28 shows the possible values.

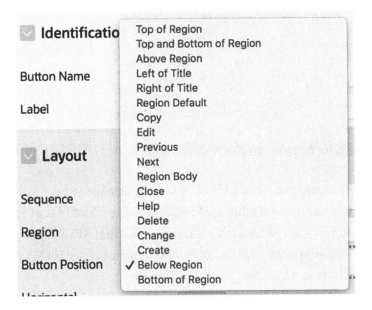

Figure 5-28. *Possible button positions*

Although there are many possible positions, they fall into four basic categories:

- In the region's header

- At the top or bottom of the region

- At predefined locations in the region

- In the region body

164

The values `Left of Title` and `Right of Title` place the button in the region's header, to the left or right of the title. If several buttons are in the same position, their relative position is determined by their sequence numbers.

The values `Top of Region`, `Top and Bottom of Region`, `Above Region`, `Below Region`, and `Bottom of Region` display buttons at the top or bottom of the region. When you choose one of these values, the property editor displays the `Horizontal Alignment` property, which lets you specify whether the button should appear at the left or right side of the region. The buttons in Figure 5-2 are positioned at the top of the region, aligned to the right.

Many page templates have specially designated positions for certain buttons. Their purpose is to ensure that buttons common to multiple regions are located in the same place in those regions. The button positions `Copy`, `Edit`, `Previous`, `Next`, `Close`, `Help`, `Delete`, `Change`, and `Create` correspond to these special-purpose buttons, although you are free to use them for any button. Of particular note are the positions `Copy` and `Edit`, which display the button at the far right of the header.

The `Region Body` position is different from the others because it places the button among the region's items. When you choose this value, a `Layout` section appears for you to specify the position of the button relative to the other items in the region. Moreover, the button's node in the rendering tree shows up in the subtree for the region's items.

The two buttons in Figure 5-2 are colored differently: the `Cancel` button has the same color scheme as the page items, whereas the `Submit` button is blue. The color of the `Submit` button is intended to draw the user's attention to it; APEX calls it a *hot button*. A button's Appearance section has a property named Hot, which enables you to specify whether the button is hot or not. Figure 5-29 shows this section for the `Submit` button.

Figure 5-29. *Specifying a hot button*

Summary

An item is a page element that holds a value. There are many item types, which differ in the way in which they display their value on the page and how they help users specify that value. Of primary importance is the distinction between text-based items and list-based items.

A text-based item displays its value in an input box, and users can specify a value by typing it into the input box. The text-based item types support the entry of unusual values (such as colors and dates), aid in data entry (such as autocompletion), and restrict allowable values (such as number fields).

A list-based item forces a user to choose from a given list of values. This list can be defined dynamically, via an SQL query, or statically via explicit values. In every case, there is a distinction between the display values (the values presented to the user) and the return values (the value that is actually held by the item). The various list-based item types differ primarily in how they present the display values on the page.

The purpose of an item is to allow a user to send a value to the server. Chapter 6 examines this issue and provides examples that show typical uses of items in web applications.

CHAPTER 6

Session State

A user's interaction with an application is called a *session*. A session can encompass several page requests. For example, in an ecommerce application, a session can involve browsing the products for sale, adding some of them to a shopping cart, entering payment and shipping information, and finalizing the transaction.

During a session, the user assigns values to page items, encompassing perhaps several pages, and sends these values to the server for processing. The item values for a given session comprise what is called its *session state*. In this chapter, you will examine the various ways that an application can modify and access the session state and look at some common page design techniques that make use of this state.

Session IDs

Building session capability into a web application is problematic because browser requests are anonymous. There is no built-in way for a server to know whether two browser requests are part of the same session. APEX solves this problem by assigning an identifier to each session. A browser request indicates its session by adding the session's ID to the request.

Recall that an APEX URL consists of the f?p= string followed by a colon-delimited string of values. The first two values are the application ID and page ID; the third value is the session ID. To see session IDs in action, log in to APEX and browse its screens. Look at the URL associated with each screen you visit. You should discover that every URL has the same session ID value. Now log out of APEX. When you log back in, APEX will assign a new session ID to the interaction. The URL of each screen you visit will now have this new session ID.

You can also observe the session IDs in your own applications. Log out of APEX and run your Employee Demo application. APEX will assign a session ID that will appear in

© Edward Sciore 2020
E. Sciore, *Understanding Oracle APEX 20 Application Development*,
https://doi.org/10.1007/978-1-4842-6165-1_6

the URL of each page. You can request a new session by submitting a request having a session ID of 0. (Actually, any random ID value will do.) For example, I can view the home page of my application in a new session by submitting the following URL:

```
apex.oracle.com/pls/apex/f?p=91392:1:0
```

When the page loads, the URL will contain a new session ID.

Submit vs. Redirect

Suppose that you modify the value of an item on a web page, perhaps by selecting a radio button or typing into a text field. Your browser knows how to display this change directly, without having to ask the server to re-render the page. Consequently, the server will know nothing about the change you made to the item and thus cannot use the new value.

If you want your application to know about the values of the items on a page, you must first upload those values to the server. This action is called *submit*. The server holds a variable for each item of your application. When you submit a page, the value of each item on that page is saved in its corresponding variable. In effect, the submit action synchronizes the session state with the current page.

Recall that the action of a button is either `submit` or `redirect`. Both actions cause the APEX server to render a target page and send it to the browser. For redirect, you specify the target page as part of the redirect action. For submit, you specify the target page via a separate *branch* component—if no branches are specified, the current page is reloaded. Branches are discussed in Chapter 9, so for now you can assume that a submit operation always reloads the current page.

The primary difference between submit and redirect is that submit uploads the page's item values to the server, whereas redirect does not. If a user changes the value of some items on a page and then does a redirect, those changes will be lost—even if the redirect is to the same page.

To see an example of this difference, consider the `Item Sampler` demo page from Chapter 5, as shown in Figure 5-2. Recall from Chapter 5 that the initial value of an item is determined by its `Source` properties. The default is to use the session state value if it is not null. This means that if you assign a non-null value to an item and submit, then that value will become the item's initial value when the page is reloaded. You can verify this fact by changing some of the values on the page and clicking the `Cancel` button. Because that button does a redirect, your changes are lost. Now modify those values again and click the Submit button. The item values remain as chosen because the submit operation wrote those changes to the session state and then retrieved them when the page was reloaded. If you navigate to a different page and come back, the values will still be there.

Recall that when you run a page from within APEX, the developer toolbar appears on the bottom of the screen. The toolbar button labeled Session shows you the current session state. Clicking it opens a window that displays all items and their current session values. This window is very useful when debugging pages. In the example, open the session window and look at the session state. Then change some items and submit. Open the session window again, and verify that the item values have changed.

It is important to understand that specifying an initial value of an item will affect the value of the item in the browser, but will never, ever change its value in the session state. You can run some experiments on the Item Sampler page to verify this fact. Go to the property editor, set the source of the item P8_JOB to be the static expression CLERK, and have it be used Always, replacing any existing value in session state. Run the page, change the item's value to ANALYST, and click the Submit button, checking the session state at each step. The session state value stays blank until the page is submitted, at which point it becomes ANALYST. The browser, however, will show CLERK when the page is rendered. Now go back to the property editor and change the Source Used property of the item to be Only when current value in session state is null and repeat the experiment. (Start by setting the value of the item to blank and clicking the Submit button to clear the session state.) You should observe that the session state values behave the same as before. The browser, however, will display CLERK until you submit a new value, after which it will display that value.

Using an Item to Submit a Page

The primary way to submit a page is to use a button. However, certain item types can also perform a submit. The Settings section of a text field or password field has the property Submit when Enter pressed. Turning on this property causes the item to submit the page when the user presses the Enter key.

The Settings section of a select list or radio group has the property Page Action on Selection. This property is shown in Figure 6-1 for a select list. The default value of the property is None. If you set it to Submit Page, then the page will be submitted each time a user changes the value of the item.

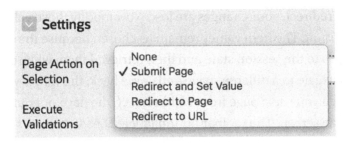

Figure 6-1. *Possible actions for a select list*

The figure also shows three other values for this property. These values correspond to different forms of redirect. The `Redirect and Set Value` option saves the value of that item in the session state and then redirects to the same page. That is, it behaves like submit, but for just one item instead of all items on the page.

The `Redirect to Page` and `Redirect to URL` options have different intents. The `Redirect to Page` action causes the item to act as a navigation list—its values are interpreted as page numbers, and selecting a value causes APEX to redirect to that page. For example, consider a select list having the static values of Figure 6-2 and whose action is `Redirect to Page`. This item displays the three options (`Home`, `Employee Reports`, `Charts`); choosing an option redirects to the corresponding page number.

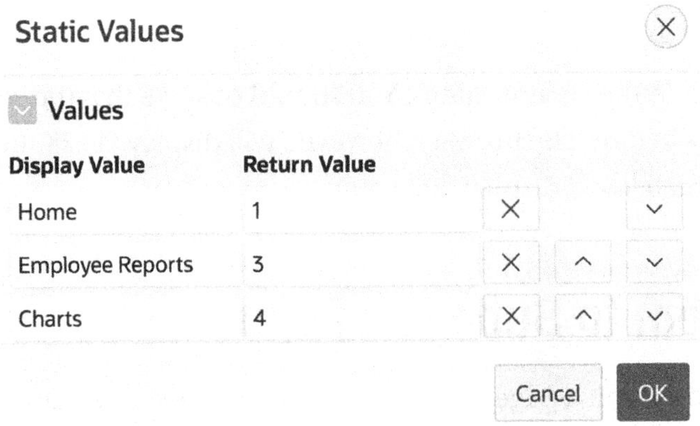

Figure 6-2. *Static values for a Redirect to Page action*

The `Redirect to URL` option is similar, except that the item values are assumed to be URLs. Neither of these two options changes the session state.

Redirect Can Set Session State

Consider the redirect action of a button. Even though that action does not submit the page, it nevertheless can modify the session state.

When you set the action of a button to Redirect to Page in this Application, the Target property appears in the property editor. Clicking the property's input box brings up the Link Builder wizard page shown in Figure 6-3.

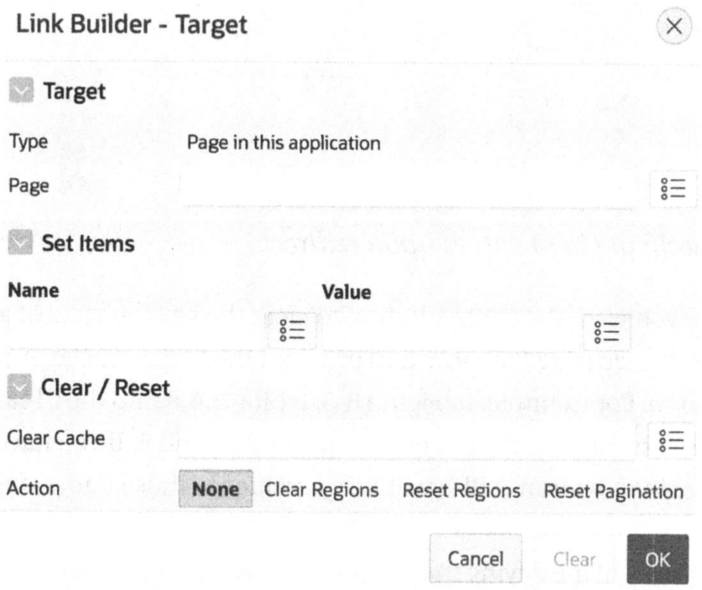

Figure 6-3. *Link Builder wizard page*

In addition to setting the Page property to the desired target, you can use the Set Items section to set the value of as many items as you want. Enter the item name in the Name box and its desired session state value in the Value box. Each time you fill up a row, another row appears, thus allowing you to enter arbitrarily many name/value pairs.

For example, consider again the Item Sampler page of Figure 5-2. Suppose that you want the Cancel button to set the value of the items P8_EMPNO to 9999 and P8_JOB to CLERK and to clear the value in P8_SALARY. Then the Set Items section of the link builder would look like Figure 6-4.

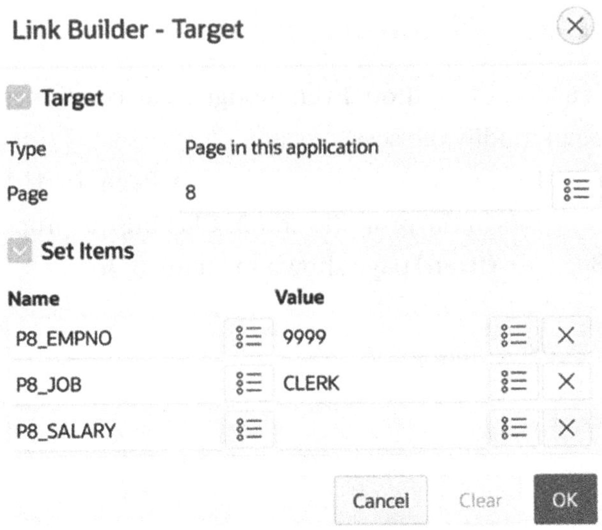

Link Builder - Target   ⊗

☑ **Target**

Type   Page in this application

Page   8   ⦀≡

☑ **Set Items**

Name   **Value**

P8_EMPNO   ⦀≡ 9999   ⦀≡ ✕

P8_JOB   ⦀≡ CLERK   ⦀≡ ✕

P8_SALARY   ⦀≡   ⦀≡ ✕

                              Cancel   Clear   OK

Figure 6-4. *Specifying item values upon redirect*

Suppose that you want the Cancel button to clear the session state of all items in the page. APEX calls this *clearing the cache* and provides the Clear Cache property in the link builder to do so. For example, in Figure 6-3, typing **3,4,8** into the Clear Cache input box will clear the session state for all items on pages 3, 4, and 8. If you have also specified items in the Set Items section, APEX will assign values to those items after clearing the cache.

Note that this way of modifying the session state is totally unlike the submit action, because it does not (and cannot) use values displayed in the browser. That is, a redirect from a button can set the session state value of an item to a constant or computed value, but it cannot set it to a browser value entered by the user.

Referring to Session State Variables

Now that you know how to set the value of a session state variable, you need to know how to get a page to access that value. There are two primary techniques. If you want to reference the variable from within SQL code, prepend a colon in front of the item name. Such a reference is called a *bind variable*. If you want to reference an item from within an HTML expression, prepend an ampersand in front of the item name and append a period at its end. This latter reference, which is called a *substitution string*, was introduced in Chapter 3.

For example, consider the item P8_EMPNO on the Item Sampler page. To refer to it as a substitution string, write "&P8_EMPNO.". To refer to it as a bind variable, write ":P8_EMPNO".

In this book, you have seen several uses for SQL queries, such as the source of a report or chart, the initial value of an item, and the definition of the values of a list-based item. You have also seen several uses for HTML expressions, such as the title of a page or region and the label of an item. The remaining sections of this chapter give examples of how you can greatly increase the functionality of your pages by using item references within these SQL queries and HTML expressions.

Before building any of the pages in this chapter, you might want to go to the List Details page for the DeskTop Navigation Menu (as shown in Figure 4-21), and add a root entry named Session State. Then, each time you create a page, you can assign the parent of its navigation menu entry to be Session State.

Customized Reports

A *customized report* is a report whose contents are affected by the values of one or more items. A user enters values for some items on the page and clicks a Submit button. The page then displays a report based on those input values. In this section, you will build three customized report pages to illustrate this technique.

Filter by Job and Department Page

The first page, which is titled Filter by Job and Department, is page 9 of the demo and appears in Figure 6-5. The idea is that a user chooses values for the Job and Dept items and clicks the Submit button. The report then shows the employees who have the selected job and are in the selected department. For example, Figure 6-5 shows the clerks who work in the research department.

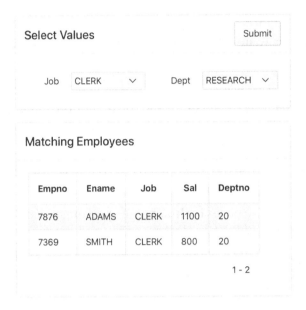

Figure 6-5. *Filter by Job and Department page*

This page has two regions: `Select Values` and `Matching Employees`. The `Select Values` region is a static content region that contains two select lists, `P9_JOB` and `P9_DEPTNO`, both of whose values are defined by SQL queries. The list-of-values query for `P9_JOB` is as follows:

```
select distinct Job as DisplayVal, Job as ResultVal
from EMP
order by DisplayVal
```

The list-of-values query for `P9_DEPTNO` is as follows:

```
select DName, DeptNo
from DEPT
order by DName
```

The action of the button is `Submit` and its position is `Edit`.

The `Matching Employees` region is a report region. For the report to display the `EMP` records having the selected job and department number, its source query needs to reference the value of the two items. The following query does the trick; note how it uses bind variable syntax to refer to the two items.

```
select EmpNo, EName, Job, Sal, DeptNo
from EMP
where Job = :P9_JOB  and  DeptNo = :P9_DEPTNO
order by EName
```

You can improve the functionality of this region by allowing a user to select a null value for P9_JOB or P9_DEPTNO. The intent is that a null value for P9_JOB (or P9_DEPTNO) should mean that the query will not use that item for filtering. For example, if both items were null, the report would display all employees. To enable this functionality, revise the source query to explicitly test for null item values, as follows:

```
select EmpNo, EName, Job, Sal, DeptNo
from EMP
where (:P9_JOB is null  or  Job = :P9_JOB)
and   (:P9_DEPTNO is null  or  DeptNo = :P9_DEPTNO)
order by EName
```

I would like to point out that there was no particular need to use two regions on this page. In fact, it is easy to modify this page to use a single region. First, go to the Layout section for the item P9_JOB and change its Region property to Matching Employees. Then do the same thing for P9_DEPTNO and the Submit button. Finally, go to the Appearance section of Matching Employees and set its Item Display Position property to Above Content, so that the two items appear above the report. (You can also delete the Select Values region if you like.) Now run the page. You should discover that its behavior has not changed. That is, the decision to use one or two (or even three!) regions is based purely on aesthetics.

Filter by Possible Department Page

The second custom report page, titled Filter by Possible Department, is page 10 of the demo and appears in Figure 6-6. This page has a structure similar to the previous one. The top region is used for input—the user selects departments from a checkbox item and clicks the Submit button. The bottom region displays a report of the employees in the selected departments. For example, the ACCOUNTING and RESEARCH boxes are checked in Figure 6-6, which means that the report lists those employees in either the accounting or research departments. If no boxes are checked, the report will display no records.

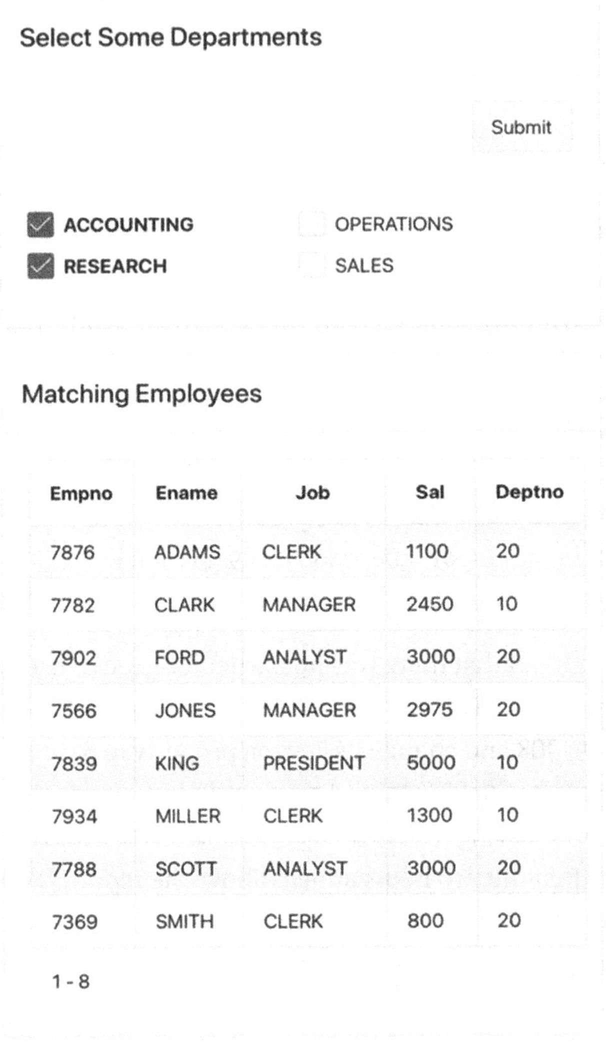

Select Some Departments

Submit

☑ **ACCOUNTING**   ☐ OPERATIONS
☑ **RESEARCH**   ☐ SALES

Matching Employees

Empno	Ename	Job	Sal	Deptno
7876	ADAMS	CLERK	1100	20
7782	CLARK	MANAGER	2450	10
7902	FORD	ANALYST	3000	20
7566	JONES	MANAGER	2975	20
7839	KING	PRESIDENT	5000	10
7934	MILLER	CLERK	1300	10
7788	SCOTT	ANALYST	3000	20
7369	SMITH	CLERK	800	20

1 - 8

Figure 6-6. *Filter by Possible Department page*

The Select Some Departments region is a static content region containing a checkbox item and a button. The checkbox item is named P10_DEPTNO, its template is Hidden, and its values are defined by the query

```
select DName, DeptNo
from DEPT
order by DName
```

Recall that the value of a multi-value item is a string containing the selected checkbox values separated by colons. For example, the value of P10_DEPTNO in Figure 6-5 is 10:30. If all four departments were checked, the value would be 10:40:20:30. (The order of the selected values in the string is based on the sort order of the item's list-of-values query, which in this case is by department name.)

The Matching Employees region is a classic report. The task is to come up with a source query for the report that will filter the records based on this item value. One approach is to test each EMP record to see if its DeptNo value is a substring of P10_DEPTNO. This approach leads to the following query, which almost works:

```
select EmpNo, EName, Job, Sal, DeptNo
from EMP
where InStr(:P10_DEPTNO,  DeptNo) > 0
order by EName
```

The InStr function tests whether the second argument is a substring of the first one. If so, it returns the character position of the match; otherwise, it returns 0. Thus, the query returns those EMP records whose DeptNo value appears somewhere in the item. This query is almost what you want, but not quite. For example, suppose that the value of the item is 10:30. The EMP records having a DeptNo value of 10 and 30 will match, and those having a value of 20 and 40 will not match. This is correct, but look at what happens if a new department is created with the department number 3. The employees in this department will match, which is incorrect.

The solution is to not only test for the DeptNo value but to also test for the colons on either side of it. You should add a colon to each end of the item value, so that all components of the value are surrounded by colons. The query thus becomes this:

```
select EmpNo, EName, Job, Sal, DeptNo
from EMP
where InStr(':' || :P10_DEPTNO || ':',':' || DeptNo || ':') > 0
order by EName
```

Note   Many people (including me) have difficulty coming to terms with this query; if you feel the same, try working out an example. In particular, note the two different uses of the colon: the colon outside of quotes denotes a bind variable, whereas a colon inside the quotes is a delimiter character.

Filter by Salary Range Page

The third customized report page, titled `Filter by Salary Range`, is page 11 of the demo and appears in Figure 6-7. A user enters the minimum and maximum salary values and clicks the `Submit` button. The page then customizes an employees-per-job chart for those employees in the specified salary range.

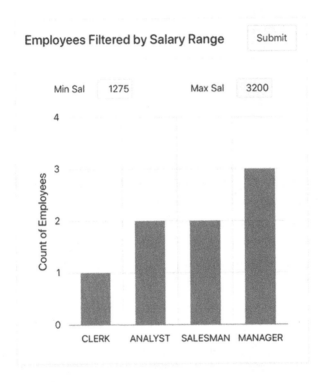

Figure 6-7. *Filter by Salary Range page*

This page contains a single region, which is of type `chart`. The region's `Item Display Position` property (in its `Appearance` section) has the value `Above Contents`, which is why the two items and `Submit` button are located above the chart. The two items, named `P11_MINSAL` and `P11_MAXSAL`, are number fields having a `Width` value of 5. The button's position is `Edit`.

Of course, this page customizes a chart, not a report, but the technique is exactly the same. Recall from Chapter 3 that the source query for this chart will have two output columns: a label, which here is the value of `Job`, and the series value, which here is the count of records for that job. To customize the chart to consider only employees in the specified salary range, simply add that restriction to the where clause of the query. The source query becomes this:

```
select Job, count(*) as EmpCount
from EMP
where (:P11_MINSAL is null  or  :P11_MINSAL <= Sal)
and   (:P11_MAXSAL is null  or  :P11_MAXSAL >= Sal)
group by Job
order by EmpCount
```

As with the Filter by Job and Department page, this query ensures that a null item value will not contribute to the filter.

It should also be clear to you that the chart's source query would be the same if you decided to move the two items and button to a separate region. If not, try it and see.

Master-Detail Reports

A *master-detail report* is a set of two reports. These reports are *linked*, in the sense that each row of the detail report has an associated row in the master report. A user interacts with the reports by choosing one of the master rows; the detail report responds by displaying just the detail rows associated with the chosen master record.

In this section, you will build a master-detail page titled Employees by Department, which is page 12 of the Employee Demo application. Its master report contains one row for each department. Clicking a department row causes the detail report to display the list of employees in that department. Figure 6-8 shows the page after clicking the link for the accounting department.

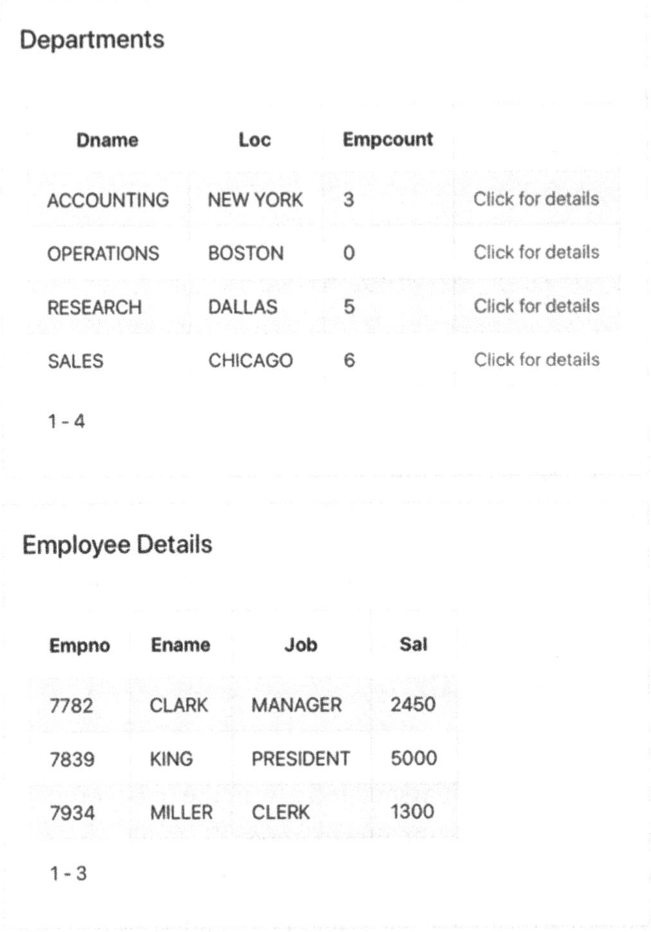

Departments

Dname	Loc	Empcount	
ACCOUNTING	NEW YORK	3	Click for details
OPERATIONS	BOSTON	0	Click for details
RESEARCH	DALLAS	5	Click for details
SALES	CHICAGO	6	Click for details

1 - 4

Employee Details

Empno	Ename	Job	Sal
7782	CLARK	MANAGER	2450
7839	KING	PRESIDENT	5000
7934	MILLER	CLERK	1300

1 - 3

Figure 6-8. *Employees by Department page*

Consider how to implement this page. The main issue is that the master report needs to let the detail report know which row was selected. The standard technique is to use a hidden item, whose value is the key of the selected row. Let's name this item P12_DEPTNO. The master report will assign to P12_DEPTNO the DeptNo value of the selected row. The detail report will then use this value to customize itself.

Implementing the customized detail report is straightforward and has the following source query:

```
select EmpNo, EName, Job, Sal
from EMP
where DeptNo = :P12_DEPTNO
order by EName
```

The hard part is implementing the master report. You have three questions to answer: What is the source query of the report? How do you get its fourth column to display a link? And how do you assign the appropriate value to P12_DEPTNO?

The master report has four columns. The first three are the department name, location, and employee count; the fourth contains the link to the detail table. Because the purpose of the link is to select a department number, it makes sense for the value of that column to be DeptNo. You therefore have the following source query (which is a right join so that the master report can display departments having no employees):

```
select d.DName, d.Loc, count(e.EmpNo) as EmpCount, d.DeptNo
from EMP e right join DEPT d
on  e.DeptNo = d.DeptNo
group by d.DeptNo, d.DName, d.Loc
order by DName
```

Chapter 3 described how to specify a link for a report column. To review, go to the page designer and click the DEPTNO column in the rendering tree. Set the type of the column to Link. Find the Link section in the property editor (refer to Figure 3-35 in Chapter 3) and set the link text to Click for details. Clicking the Target box will take you to the Link Builder page, in which you can set the target to page 12 (the current page).

Wait a minute. A redirect to the current page doesn't do anything, so what is the point of the link? Its real purpose is to change the session state. Recall that the Link Builder page also has a Set Items section, in which you can set the hidden item P12_DEPTNO to the selected department number. Recall from Chapter 3 that you refer to the value of column X in the current row by writing #X#. Thus, you should set P12_DEPTNO to #DEPTNO#, as shown in Figure 6-9.

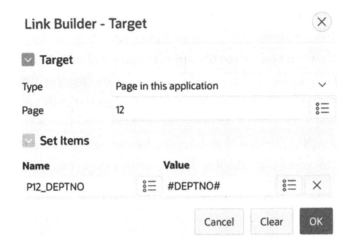

Figure 6-9. *Configuring the master report's column link*

Finally, you have to actually create the item P12_DEPTNO. You know that it should be a hidden type, but where should it be placed? Because the item is hidden, it doesn't really matter which region on the page it goes in. I chose to place it in the master region because that is where its value is assigned.

Chart Drill Down

The next page, Employees by Job, is page 13 of the Employee Demo application and is shown in Figure 6-10. The page has two regions: a pie chart and an employee report. The chart gives the employee count per job. Clicking a pie segment customizes the report so that it displays the employees having that job. Figure 6-10 shows the page after clicking the MANAGER slice.

Employee Count by Job

Employee Details

Empno	Ename	Dname	Sal
7698	BLAKE	SALES	2850
7782	CLARK	ACCOUNTING	2450
7566	JONES	RESEARCH	2975

1 - 3

Figure 6-10. *Employees by Job page*

This technique of clicking a chart to see more detail is called *chart drill down*. Here, clicking the chart selects a category value, which is then used to customize the report.

Chart drill down is very similar to master detail. The chart is the master, and the report is the detail. In fact, the implementation strategy is essentially the same as for master-detail reports:

1. Create a hidden item, here called P13_JOB.

2. Create the detail report customized by that item.

3. Create the chart, configuring it to assign the selected job to the hidden item when clicked.

The source query for the detail report is essentially the same as in `Employees` by `Department`. The only difference is that the query does a join so that the report can display the department name. The SQL code is as follows:

```
select e.EmpNo, e.EName, d.DName, e.Sal
from EMP e join DEPT d
on     e.DeptNo = d.DeptNo
where e.Job = :P13_JOB
order by EName
```

The source code for a pie chart is an SQL query having two output columns. The following query creates a pie section for each job, whose value is the number of employees having that job:

```
select Job, count(*) as EmpCount
from EMP
group by Job
order by EmpCount desc
```

The only remaining issue is how to specify the chart's behavior when it is clicked. This behavior is determined by the `Link` properties of the chart's series; see Figure 6-11.

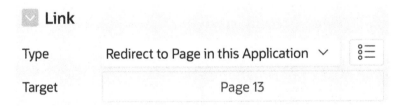

Figure 6-11. *Link properties for a chart series*

The `Type` property has the value `Link to Page in this Application`. Choosing it exposes the Target property, from which you can use the `Link Builder` screen to specify the target page. Figure 6-12 shows that screen as it was configured for the chart. You use the same technique that you used for the master report of Figure 6-9: choose the target to be the current page, and set the value of the hidden item. The only difference is how you refer to the selected value. When that value comes from column X of a report, you write **#X#**. When it comes from column X of a chart, you write **&X.**—that is, you reference the column name as a substitution string.

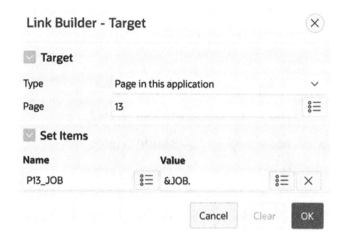

Figure 6-12. *Configuring a chart for drill down*

Customized Titles and Labels

In Chapter 3, you saw how to use HTML tags to format a region title. In fact, you can use HTML tags to format any property whose value is displayed on the page, such as page and region titles, item labels, and button text. Moreover, these properties can also be customized by item values.

For example, looking back at the master-detail and chart drill-down pages, I can see a small problem: the detail reports do not indicate which master record (or chart slice) was selected. A good solution to this problem is to customize the title of the detail region. For example, Figure 6-13 shows the revised detail region for the Employees by Department page. Note that the region title contains the selected department name.

Employee Details: ACCOUNTING department

Empno	Ename	Job	Sal
7782	CLARK	MANAGER	2450
7839	KING	PRESIDENT	5000
7934	MILLER	CLERK	1300

1 - 3

Figure 6-13. Employee detail report with a customized title bar

Similarly, Figure 6-14 shows the revised detail region for the Employees by Job page. Its title bar shows the selected job.

Employee Details: MANAGER

Empno	Ename	Dname	Sal
7698	BLAKE	SALES	2850
7782	CLARK	ACCOUNTING	2450
7566	JONES	RESEARCH	2975

1 - 3

Figure 6-14. Another customized title bar

The technique for implementing these title bars is relatively straightforward. Let's begin with Figure 6-14, which involves changes to the Employee Count by Job page. The region's Title property simply needs to be changed to have the following expression:

Employee Details: &P13_JOB.

That's it! You're done. Note that you use the substitution string notation because the title is an HTML expression.

Now consider Figure 6-13, which is part of the Employees by Department page. The region's Title property has the following expression:

Employee Details: &P12_DNAME. department

There is just one glitch to this expression: the page currently has no item named P12_DNAME. For this expression to make sense, you have to create the item and assign the selected department name to it. Fortunately, you already know how to do these things. First, create P12_DNAME as a hidden item. Then, go back to the master report, enter the link builder for the DeptNo column, and add a row to the Set Items property. See Figure 6-15.

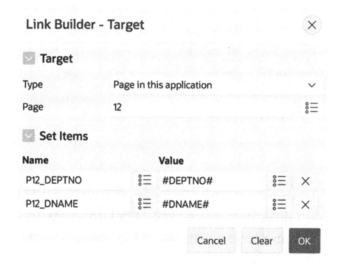

Figure 6-15. *Setting two hidden item values in the link builder*

Cascading Lists

The next task is to build a page that enables a user to choose an employee name from a select list and then displays a report containing information about that employee. This page, titled Cascading Lists, is page 14 of the Employee Demo application and appears in Figure 6-16. The page has two regions, each of which gives a solution to this task.

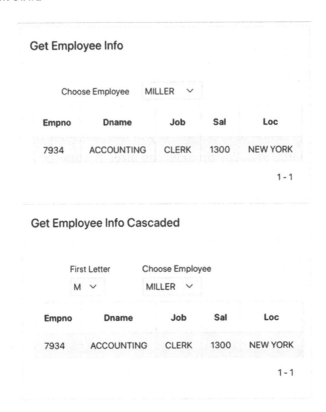

Figure 6-16. *Cascading lists*

The top region has a single item, named P14_EMPNO. This item is a select list that displays the names of all employees and has employee numbers as the result values. That is, its list-of-values query is this:

```
select EName, EmpNo
from EMP
order by EName
```

The top region has no button. Instead, the select list has the action Redirect and Set Value, which means that choosing an employee name from the select list causes the item's value to be changed in the session state.

The type of the top region is Classic Report. Its source query is customized by the value of P14_EMPNO, as follows:

```
select e.EmpNo, d.DName, e.Job, e.Sal, d.Loc
from EMP e join DEPT d
on    e.DeptNo = d.DeptNo
where e.EmpNo = :P14_EMPNO
order by EmpNo
```

If you try out this region, you should discover that it is easy to scan through the list of names, due to the small number of employees. Suppose, however, that the EMP table were large, with thousands of employees to pick from. Scrolling through the select list would be awkward and time-consuming, even if the names were sorted. A common solution to this problem is to let the user choose the name in steps, via a series of select lists.

The bottom region of Figure 6-16 uses two select lists to choose an employee. The first select list displays the first letter of each employee name, and the second one displays the names of employees whose names begin with that letter.

This technique is called a *cascading list*, in which the display values of the second select list change according to the value selected for the first one. This technique can be extended to multiple select lists—the values of each select list except the first change according to the values chosen for the select lists previous to it. The advantage of this approach is that a user can scroll through several small select lists instead of one large one.

The two select lists in the bottom region are named P14_FIRST_LETTER and P14_EMPNO_CASCADE. They are defined as follows.

The select list P14_FIRST_LETTER is not dependent on any other items, so its query is straightforward:

```
select FirstLetter as DisplayVal, FirstLetter as ResultVal
from  (select distinct substr(EName, 1, 1) as FirstLetter
        from EMP)
order by DisplayVal
```

The list P14_EMPNO_CASCADE is dependent on the value of P14_FIRST_LETTER, resulting in the following query:

```
select EName, EmpNo
from EMP
where substr(EName, 1, 1) = :P14_FIRST_LETTER
order by EName
```

The source of the bottom report is exactly the same as the top report, except that P14_EMPNO is replaced by P14_EMPNO_CASCADE.

If you set the action of both these select lists to Redirect and Set Value, then choosing a first letter causes the list of names to be updated, and choosing a name causes the report to be updated.

The concept of a cascaded list is common enough that APEX has a specific property to handle it, called Parent Item(s), which is in the Cascading List of Values section of a select list. Figure 6-17 shows the specification for the P14_EMPNO_CASCADE list.

Figure 6-17. *Specifying the cascading parent item*

This figure specifies that P14_EMPNO_CASCADE depends on the value of P14_FIRST_LETTER; that is, it monitors the behavior of P14_FIRST_LETTER and refreshes itself when the value of P14_FIRST_LETTER changes. Consequently, the action of P14_FIRST_LETTER should now be None. The action of P14_EMPNO_CASCADE should be Redirect and Set Value, as before. The Cascading List of Values property enables APEX to use JavaScript and Ajax to refresh the select list without having the re-render the entire page. It is the most efficient way to implement cascading.

Conditional Rendering

Throughout your use of the app builder, you have come across numerous situations in which choosing a particular value in the property editor caused the editor to suddenly display other properties. The Link Builder page shown in Figure 6-15 is such an example—if you choose the target type URL, then the Set Items properties suddenly disappear, and if you change its value back to Page in this application, then those items reappear. What's going on here?

Although it looks like the items are getting created and deleted on the spot, they are not; instead, those items always exist. When you are in the link builder and select the value Page in this application, APEX displays the additional items; when you select the value URL, APEX hides them. This ability to dynamically show or hide an item is called *conditional rendering*.

Conditional rendering can be defined for items, buttons, and regions. Each one has a `Server-side Condition` section in its property editor, which lets you choose a condition type from a select list. Although there are many condition types, the focus here is on the type `SQL expression`. The value of this type is an SQL expression that returns `true/false`. The value of the expression determines whether the item, button, or region is rendered.

For an example, let's return to the `Employees by Department` page shown in Figure 6-8. Note that the detail report region will be empty until a value from the master report has been chosen. If you don't want the page to display an empty report region, then you can use conditional rendering, displaying the region only when the item `P12_DEPTNO` is not `null`. The region's conditional SQL expression is shown in Figure 6-18.

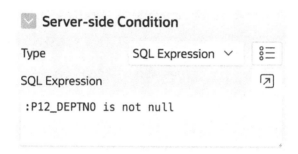

Figure 6-18. *Conditionally displaying the Employee Details region*

For another example, consider the `Display Table` page shown in Figure 6-19, which will be page 15 of the `Employee Demo` application. The `Select Table` region contains two checkboxes and a button. Clicking the button causes the checked tables to be displayed.

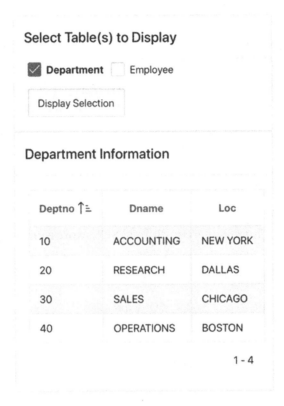

Figure 6-19. *Conditional region rendering*

Implementing the Select Table region is straightforward. Its checkbox item is named P15_CHOICE, and it contains the two static values shown in Figure 6-20. The button performs a Submit action.

Figure 6-20. *The static values for P15_CHOICE*

```
select * from EMP
```

And the `Department Info` region has the following source:

```
select * from DEPT
```

Both of these regions are displayed conditionally, depending on the value of `P15_CHOICE`. The condition for `Employee Info` is the following SQL expression:

```
InStr(:P15_CHOICE, 'Employee') > 0
```

And the condition for `Department Info` is the following SQL expression:

```
InStr(:P15_CHOICE, 'Department') > 0
```

When the button is clicked, APEX creates a colon-delimited string containing the values of the checked boxes and saves it in the session state. When the page is then re-rendered, APEX uses the session state value to initialize `P15_CHOICE` and evaluates each conditional expression to determine which regions to display. Consequently, it is important that the `Source` properties of `P15_CHOICE` be specified as in Figure 6-21.

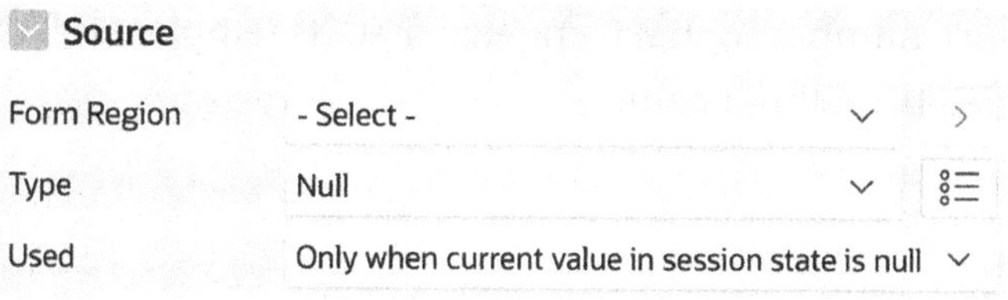

Figure 6-21. *Source properties of P15_CHOICE*

Region Display Selectors

Recall from Chapter 2 (and Figure 2-6) that the `Application Properties` screen lets you manage application-wide properties, such as the application logo and the location of the navigation menu. Figure 6-22 shows the top part of that screen.

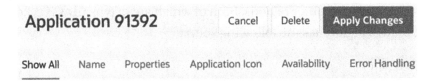

Figure 6-22. *Part of the Application Properties screen*

Note in particular the tab bar under the title, with tabs labeled Show All, Name, Properties, and so on. This bar is a *region display selector*. If you click the Show All tab, the page displays all its regions; if you click any of the other tabs, the page displays only the chosen region.

You can add a region display selector to your application. Let's build a page similar to the Display Table page of Figure 6-19, but using a region display selector instead of a radio group. This page, titled Select Region, will be page 16 of the Employee Demo application. Figure 6-23 shows the page with the Department Information tab selected.

This page consists of two classic report regions, one for each of the EMP and DEPT tables. Above it is a Region Display Selector region. To create the display selector region, create a region in the page designer and then change its type to Region Display Selector. Unlike every other region you have encountered, this region has no source; its sole purpose is to display a tab bar for the regions of the page.

The region display selector in Figure 6-23 is placed in the Content Body position with a small sequence number so that it appears first. Its template is Buttons Container, which formats the region without a title.

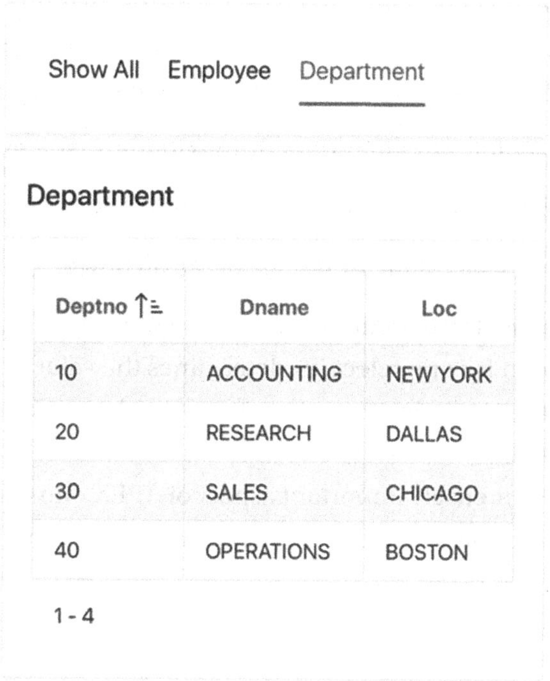

| Show All | Employee | Department |

Department

Deptno ↑≞	Dname	Loc
10	ACCOUNTING	NEW YORK
20	RESEARCH	DALLAS
30	SALES	CHICAGO
40	OPERATIONS	BOSTON

1 - 4

Figure 6-23. *Using a region display selector region*

By default, the region display selector displays a tab for every region on the page (provided that there is more than one region to display). If you want to exclude a region, use its property Region Display Selector, which is a switch in the Advanced section. Turning the property off excludes that region from having a tab in the display selector.

Summary

The APEX server maintains data about each user session; this data is called the *session state*. In this chapter, you saw how the session state gets modified and examined ways that an application developer can make use of it.

The session state has a variable for each item in the application. These variable values can get modified as the result of a submit or redirect action. When a page is submitted, the values of all items on the page will be updated in the session state. When a page redirects to a target page, the redirect operation can assign values to specific items. In particular, when you configure a button, report link, or chart to redirect, the property editor will display the Link Builder wizard, which has a section for specifying session state values.

One common use of session state is to enable users to customize reports. The idea is that a user specifies some values, and those values affect which of the report records are displayed. You saw examples of several ways that a user could specify those values:

- The user can enter the values directly into items on the page.

- The user can select a row from a master report.

- The user can select a value by doing chart drill down.

This chapter also considered additional uses of session state, such as *cascading lists*, in which the value chosen for one select list determines the values displayed by another, and *conditional rendering*, in which the value of an item determines whether a region should be visible or hidden.

Session state is an immensely important aspect of APEX. Most of the examples in the rest of the book will make use of the techniques mentioned in this chapter.

CHAPTER 7

Processes

As you have seen, it is possible to write highly functional web pages using only items, reports, and charts. But to implement anything more complex, you have to be able to perform calculations and interact with the database more generally. The notion of a *process* addresses both issues. This chapter examines some typical situations that require the use of processes and introduces the basics of PL/SQL so that you can write your own code to implement these processes. It also examines the pitfalls you might encounter when writing PL/SQL code, such as the possibility of lost updates.

Stages of a Submit Action

Recall that the left panel of the page designer contains four tabs. This book so far has focused on the Rendering tab; it is now time to move to the Processing tab. To get to this tab, click the circular-arrows icon, third from the left at the top of the panel. Figure 7-1 shows the resulting screen.

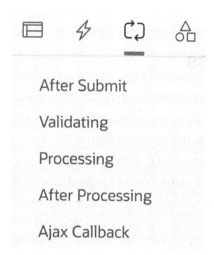

Figure 7-1. *Processing tab of the page designer*

© Edward Sciore 2020
E. Sciore, *Understanding Oracle APEX 20 Application Development*,
https://doi.org/10.1007/978-1-4842-6165-1_7

The figure shows five nodes. The first four correspond to the four stages of activity that can occur during a submit action; APEX calls these stages *execution points*. These stages have the following purposes:

- During the *After Submit* stage, the server computes additional session state values in preparation for the main processing activity. Such computations are occasionally useful and are briefly discussed in Chapter 10.

- During the *Validation* stage, the server runs validation checks to ensure that the submit request has been called with appropriate data. The server will abort further processing if it detects a problem. Validation is the subject of Chapter 8.

- During the *Processing* stage, the server executes the processes that have been associated with the submit request. The definition and use of these processes is the subject of this chapter and Chapter 10.

- During the *After Processing* stage, the server uses branches to decide which page to send to the browser. Branching is the subject of Chapter 9.

The fifth node in Figure 7-1, named `Ajax Callback`, is not an execution point; instead, its purpose is to hold code that can be called from JavaScript functions. As the use of JavaScript in APEX is beyond the scope of this book, I shall not mention this node further.

Creating a Process

This section provides a quick introduction to APEX processes, using the `Item Sampler` page (page 8) of your employee demo application. Go to its page editor and click the `Processing` tab; you should see the screen of Figure 7-1. To create a new process, right-click the `Processing` node and select `Create Process`. The app builder will create a process, titled New, and add a node for it to the `Processing` subtree as shown in Figure 7-2. Note that the parent of the new node is the node `Processes`, which in turn is a child of `Processing`. The purpose of the `Processes` node is to group together all process components associated with the `Processing` execution point.

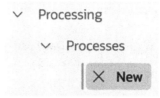

Figure 7-2. *The Processing component tree*

Click the node for your new process and look at its properties. The Identification section specifies the name and type of the process. By default, a newly created process has the name New and the type PL/SQL Code. Figure 7-3 shows that I renamed my process SampleProcess and kept the default type value.

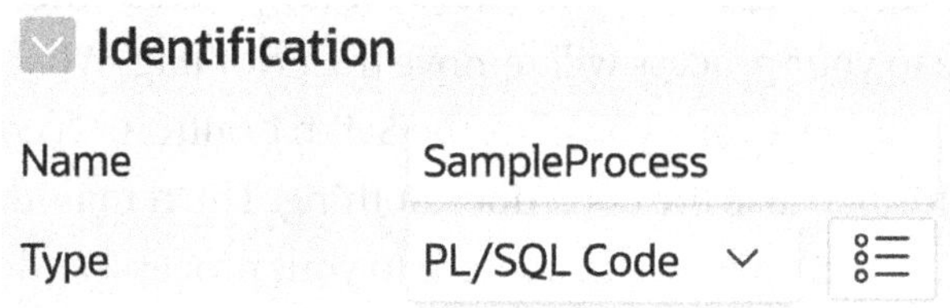

Identification

Name	SampleProcess
Type	PL/SQL Code ∨

Figure 7-3. *Specifying the name and type of a process*

Click the select list for the Type property and look at the other process types that are available. These types facilitate special purpose actions, such as modifying a table, sending email, or clearing the session state, and are the subject of Chapter 10. This chapter focuses exclusively on the PL/SQL Code process type, which enables you to write your own general-purpose actions.

The code for a PL/SQL process is specified in its Source section by the property PL/SQL Code. Look at the Source section for your new process—you will see that it has no code, which is why the node in Figure 7-2 is flagged as having an error. Let's fix that.

In its most basic form, a PL/SQL code block consists of one or more statements surrounded by the keywords begin and end. For example, Figure 7-4 shows the Source section containing the simplest possible PL/SQL block. Performing it executes the null statement, which (as you might imagine) does absolutely nothing.

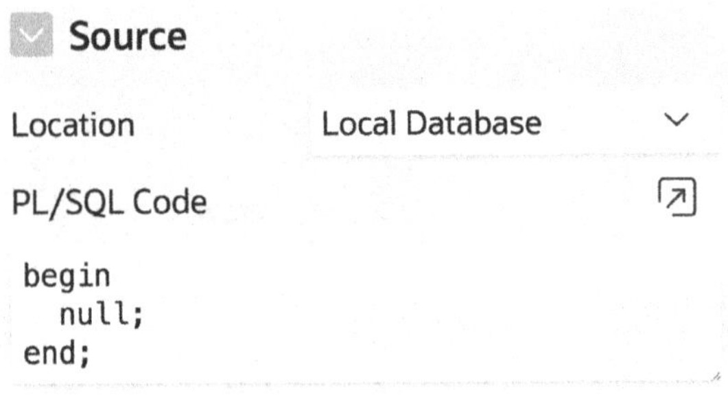

Source

Location	Local Database	⌄
PL/SQL Code		↗

```
begin
  null;
end;
```

Figure 7-4. *A PL/SQL code block to do nothing*

Note the semicolons. Each statement must be followed by a semicolon, as must the end keyword. If you forget to do this (and you probably will at some point), APEX will display an error message. When in doubt, check for forgotten semicolons.

Adding this code to your process will remove the error flag. When you run the page, the process will execute every time you click the Submit button. Of course, you have no way of knowing this because the code does nothing. The remainder of this chapter examines how you can add meaningful content to your processes.

PL/SQL to Access the Database

PL/SQL processes are commonly used to access the database. An SQL data modification command can be used as a PL/SQL statement, which means that a process that modifies the database can consist of just that one statement. For example, the following PL/SQL block increases the salary of everyone in department 10.

```
begin
  update EMP
  set Sal = Sal + 100
  where DeptNo = 10;
end;
```

For a more comprehensive example, consider the Employee Data Entry page shown in Figure 7-5, which is page 17 of the Employee Demo application. This page illustrates the ability of PL/SQL to modify the database. It has regions to delete a specified employee, insert a new employee, and update the columns of a specified employee. Above these regions is a report region that displays the employee table, so you can see the effect of your modifications.

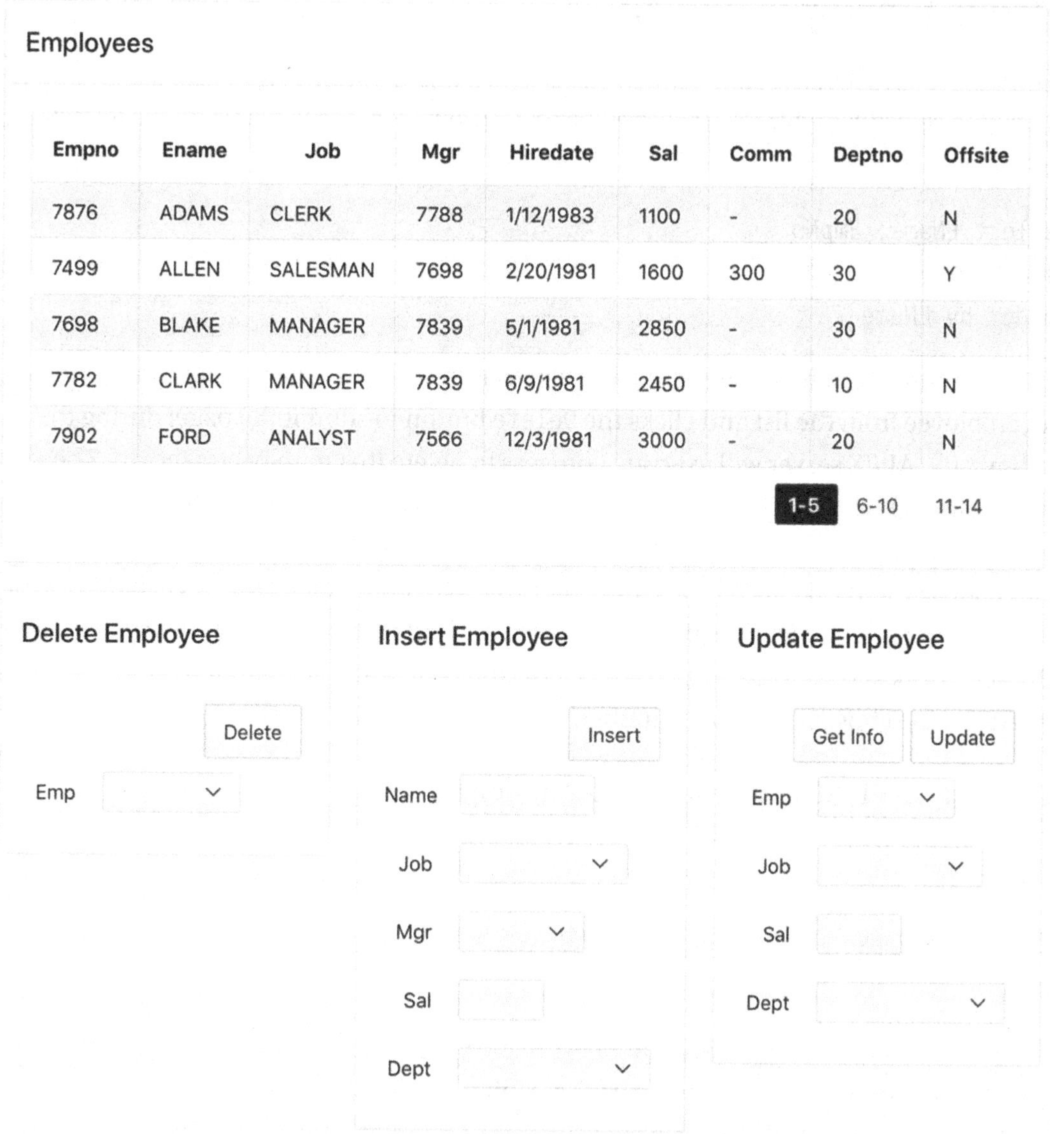

Employees

Empno	Ename	Job	Mgr	Hiredate	Sal	Comm	Deptno	Offsite
7876	ADAMS	CLERK	7788	1/12/1983	1100	-	20	N
7499	ALLEN	SALESMAN	7698	2/20/1981	1600	300	30	Y
7698	BLAKE	MANAGER	7839	5/1/1981	2850	-	30	N
7782	CLARK	MANAGER	7839	6/9/1981	2450	-	10	N
7902	FORD	ANALYST	7566	12/3/1981	3000	-	20	N

1-5   6-10   11-14

Delete Employee

Delete

Emp ⌄

Insert Employee

Insert

Name

Job ⌄

Mgr ⌄

Sal

Dept ⌄

Update Employee

Get Info   Update

Emp ⌄

Job ⌄

Sal

Dept ⌄

Figure 7-5. *The Employee Data Entry page*

To create this page, begin by creating a blank page and four regions. The Employees region is a classic report region whose source is the entire EMP table. The other three regions are static content regions, positioned as follows: Delete Employee begins a new row, and the remaining two regions begin a new column of that row. The following subsections discuss the content of these three regions.

Delete Employee Region

The Delete Employee region contains a select list and a button. The select list is named P17_DELETE_EMPNO, which performs no action on selection and whose values are defined by the query:

```
select EName, EmpNo
from EMP
order by EName
```

The button is named Delete, and its action is Submit. The idea is that a user chooses an employee from the list and clicks the Delete button to submit the page; during the submit, the APEX server will execute a process to delete that employee's record. The following steps explain how to create this process and associate it with the button.

First, go to the Processing tab of the page designer, right-click the Processes node, and choose Create Process. Give the new process a name, such as DeleteEmp.

Second, go to the Source property section, and enter into its PL/SQL Code area the PL/SQL block shown in Listing 7-1. Note how the code uses bind variable syntax to reference the chosen employee number.

Listing 7-1. PL/SQL Code for the DeleteEmp Process

```
begin
    delete from EMP
    where EmpNo = :P17_DELETE_EMPNO;
end;
```

Third, change the When Button Pressed property in the process's Server-side Condition section, as shown in Figure 7-6. Doing so specifies that the process will execute only when the Delete button is pressed. Otherwise, the process would execute each time a submit action occurs, regardless of how the submit occurred. This would be a problem for the Employee Data Entry page because it has four buttons, all doing a submit. You want the DeleteEmp process to execute only when the Delete button is pressed, which is the purpose of the When Button Pressed property.

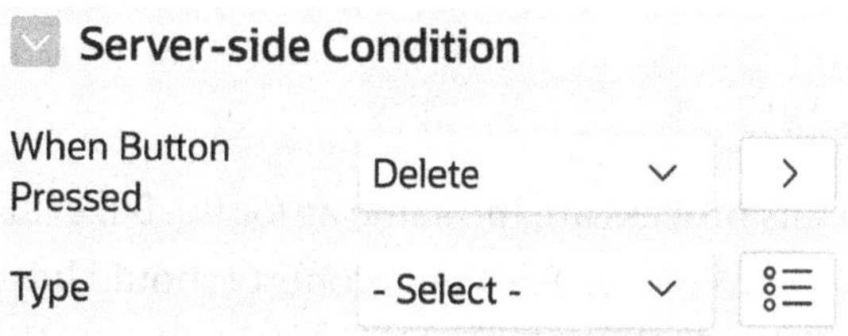

Server-side Condition

| When Button Pressed | Delete | ∨ | > |
| Type | - Select - | ∨ | ≡ |

Figure 7-6. *Setting the When Button Pressed property*

Insert Employee Region

The Insert Employee region contains five items and a button. The items correspond to columns of the EMP table and have the names P17_INSERT_ENAME, P17_INSERT_JOB, and so on. Item P17_INSERT_ENAME is a text field and P17_INSERT_SAL is a number field. The other three items are select lists, whose values are defined via the following list-of-values queries.

The values of P17_INSERT_JOB are defined by the query:

```
select distinct Job as DisplayVal, Job as ResultVal
from EMP
```

The values of P17_INSERT_MGR are defined by the query:

```
select EName, EmpNo
from EMP
where Job = 'MANAGER'
```

The values of P17_INSERT_DEPTNO are defined by the query:

```
select DName, DeptNo
from DEPT
```

The button is named Insert, and its action is Submit. A user enters values for the items and clicks the Insert button. The process associated with the button will then insert a new record into the EMP table, using the specified item values for five of the columns and computing the following values for the other four columns:

- EmpNo automatically gets the next value in the sequence determined by EMP's built-in insertion trigger.

- HireDate gets the current date.

- Comm gets 0.

- Offsite gets 'N'.

The steps to create this process are the same as for the DeleteEmp process. Call the process InsertEmp. Its When Button Pressed property should have the value Insert. Its PL/SQL code consists of the single SQL command shown in Listing 7-2.

Listing 7-2. PL/SQL Code for the InsertEmp Process

```
begin
    insert into EMP (EName, Job, Mgr, Sal, DeptNo,
                    HireDate, Comm, Offsite)
    values (:P17_INSERT_ENAME,
            :P17_INSERT_JOB,
            :P17_INSERT_MGR,
            :P17_INSERT_SAL,
            :P17_INSERT_DEPTNO,
            current_date,  0,  'N');
end;
```

At this point, you might want to test your page as it stands. Insert a record and make sure it appears correctly in the report. Then delete it, and watch the report return to its original state.

Update Employee Region

The Update Employee region has four items and two buttons. The items are named P17_UPDATE_EMPNO, P17_UPDATE_JOB, and so on. The select list values are defined the same as in the other regions. The buttons are named GetInfo and Update, and both have the action Submit.

Two steps are required to use this region. First, a user selects the desired employee from P17_UPDATE_EMPNO and clicks the GetInfo button. The process associated with this button populates the items P17_UPDATE_JOB, P17_UPDATE_SAL, and P17_UPDATE_DEPTNO with the corresponding values from that employee's EMP record. The user then changes those items as desired. When the user clicks the Update button, the process associated with that button updates the record with the new values.

Each button will have its own process. The process for the Update button is called UpdateEmp. Its PL/SQL code is as shown in Listing 7-3, and its When Button Pressed property has the value Update.

Listing 7-3. PL/SQL Code for the UpdateEmp Process

```
begin
    update EMP
      set Job    =  :P17_UPDATE_JOB,
          Sal    =  :P17_UPDATE_SAL,
          DeptNo =  :P17_UPDATE_DEPTNO
    where EmpNo  =  :P17_UPDATE_EMPNO;
end;
```

The process for the GetInfo button is named GetEmpInfo. It differs from the other processes on the page in that it reads from the database instead of writing to it. The technique is to write an SQL query that places its output directly into items on the page. The PL/SQL code in Listing 7-4 does just that.

Listing 7-4. PL/SQL Code for the GetEmpInfo Process

```
begin
    select Job, Sal, DeptNo
    into :P17_UPDATE_JOB, :P17_UPDATE_SAL, :P17_UPDATE_DEPTNO
    from EMP
    where EmpNo = :P17_UPDATE_EMPNO;
end;
```

The critical part of the query is the clause beginning with the keyword into. This clause indicates that the query's three output values will be placed into the three specified items. In other words, the into clause turns an SQL query into a PL/SQL statement that extracts values from the database and assigns them to items. Note that the into clause makes sense only if the SQL query returns exactly one row. A process that executes a multi-row SQL query needs to do something totally different with the query output, as you will see later in the next section.

PL/SQL to Compute Values

This section considers the programming-language aspects of PL/SQL. At its heart, PL/SQL is a traditional programming language with variables, assignment statements, conditionals, and loops. In this regard, it is not much different from C, Java, Python, and similar languages. If you have experience with any of these languages, then the most difficult part of writing PL/SQL code will probably be figuring out the appropriate syntax.

As an example, let's build the Sales Commission page shown in Figure 7-7, which will be page 18 of the Employee Demo application.

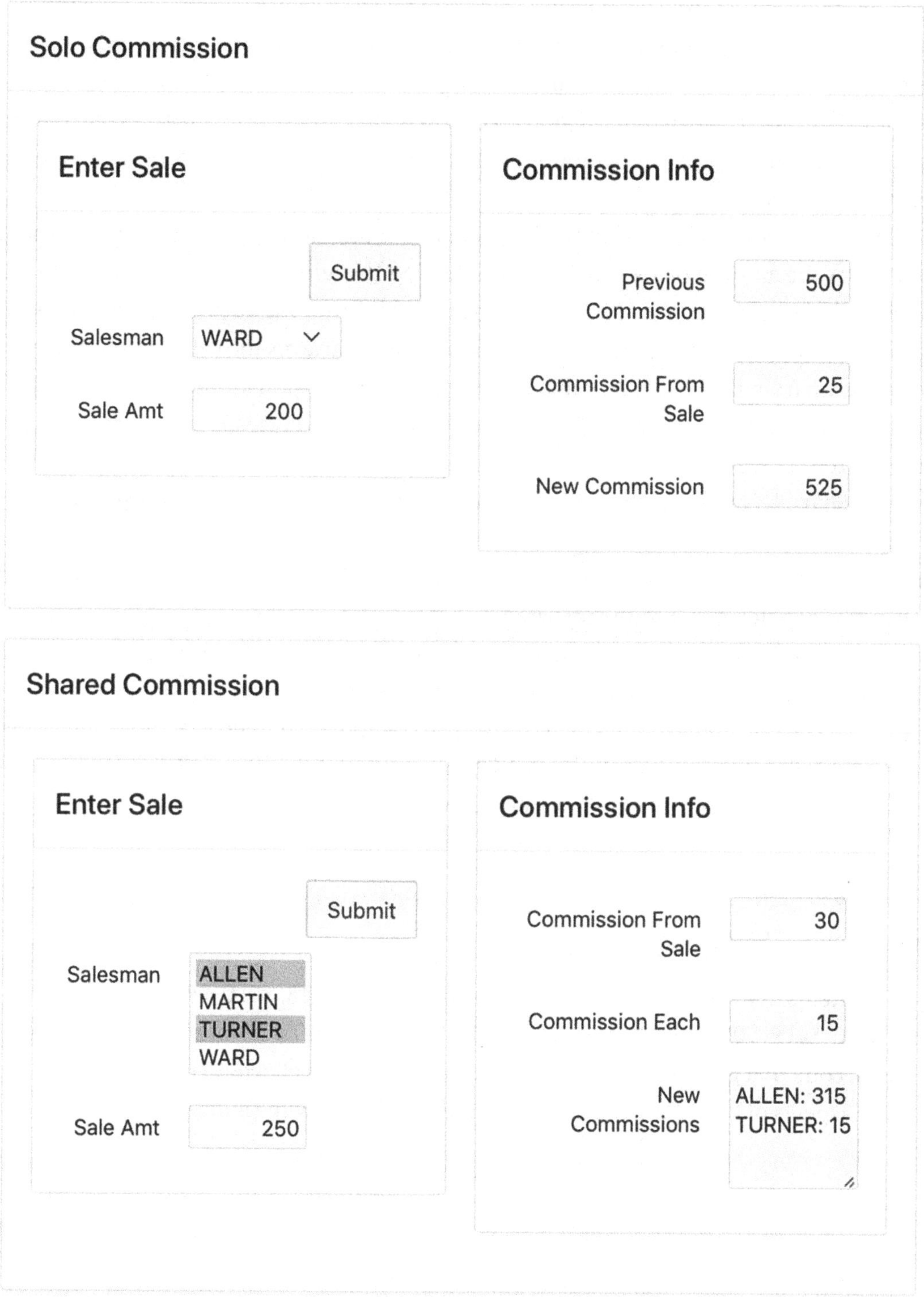

Solo Commission

Enter Sale

Submit

Salesman   WARD ∨

Sale Amt   200

Commission Info

Previous Commission   500

Commission From Sale   25

New Commission   525

Shared Commission

Enter Sale

Submit

Salesman   ALLEN
MARTIN
TURNER
WARD

Sale Amt   250

Commission Info

Commission From Sale   30

Commission Each   15

New Commissions   ALLEN: 315
TURNER: 15

Figure 7-7. *Page to calculate sales commissions*

This page will get used each time a salesman makes a sale. Assume that salesmen receive 15 percent commission on the first $100 of a sale and 10 percent on the remaining amount; if several salesmen collaborate on a sale, they split the commission equally. The page has two outer regions. The top region, titled Solo Commission, is for entering an individual sale. The bottom region, titled Shared Commission, is for entering a collaborative sale.

The Solo Commission region works as follows. A user selects the salesman's name and enters the amount of the sale into the Enter Sale region. Clicking the Submit button submits the page and causes a process to execute. This process does several things: It calculates the commission based on the sale amount, retrieves the salesman's previous commission from the EMP table, calculates the new commission amount by summing the two values, and places those three values into the three corresponding items of the Commission Info region. It also updates the EMP table with the new commission value.

The Shared Commission region works similarly, except that several salesmen can be chosen from the select list. Its process calculates the total commission on the sale and the prorated amount, updates the EMP table, and writes the new commissions of the collaborating salesmen into the text area.

This section considers the implementation of the Solo Commission region. (The Shared Commission region will be examined in the section "Handling Multi-Row SQL Queries".) The two items in the Enter Sale Info region are named P18_SOLO_SALESMAN and P18_SOLO_AMOUNT. Item P18_SOLO_AMOUNT is a number field, and P18_SOLO_SALESMAN is a select list with values defined by the following SQL query:

```
select EName, EmpNo
from EMP
where Job = 'SALESMAN'
```

The items in the Commission Info region are named P18_SOLO_PREV_COMMISSION, P18_SOLO_SALE_COMMISSION, and P18_SOLO_NEW_COMMISSION. Listing 7-5 contains the PL/SQL code that gets executed when the Submit button is clicked. This code illustrates several aspects of PL/SQL, which are described in the following subsections.

Listing 7-5. PL/SQL Code to Handle a Solo Commission

```
declare
    v_amount int := :P18_SOLO_AMOUNT;
    v_saleCommission number(7,2);
    v_prevCommission number(7,2);
    v_newCommission  number(7,2);
begin
    -- Step 1: Calculate the new commission as 15% of the first $100
    -- and then 10% of the remaining sale price.

    if v_amount > 100 then
            v_amount := v_amount - 100;
            v_saleCommission := 15 + (v_amount * 0.1);
    else
            v_saleCommission := v_amount * 0.15;
    end if;

    -- Step 2: Retrieve the previous commission from EMP
    -- and calculate the new commission.

    select Comm into v_prevCommission
    from EMP
    where EmpNo = :P18_SOLO_SALESMAN;

    v_newCommission := v_prevCommission + v_saleCommission;

    -- Step 3: Update the employee's record.

    update EMP
    set Comm = v_newCommission
    where EmpNo = :P18_SOLO_SALESMAN;

    -- Step 4: Compute the item values.

    :P18_SOLO_SALE_COMMISSION := v_saleCommission;
    :P18_SOLO_PREV_COMMISSION := v_prevCommission;
    :P18_SOLO_NEW_COMMISSION  := v_newCommission;
end;
```

Local Variables

A PL/SQL block can have a *variable declaration section* prior to the begin keyword. The declaration section starts with the keyword declare and is followed by a series of variable declarations. The code of Listing 7-5 declares four local variables: v_amount, v_saleCommission, v_prevCommission, and v_newCommission. The syntax for each declaration is similar to the syntax for declaring table columns in SQL, and the possible variable types are also the same. For example, the last three variables have the type number(7,2), which is the same type as the column Comm in the EMP table.

Local variables and item references can be used interchangeably in a PL/SQL block. The difference is that local variables are referenced as is, whereas an item reference requires a prepended colon. For example, the SQL update command in step 3 references both the local variable v_newCommission and the item P18_SOLO_SALESMAN. Because items are referenced using bind variable syntax, they are easy to spot. However, local variable references in SQL commands are hard to distinguish from column names or function calls. To avoid confusion, you should always name local variables so that people know they are variables. A common convention, which is adopted here, is to begin each local variable name with v_.

Comments

As in SQL, PL/SQL denotes comments with two consecutive minus signs. All characters following the two minus signs are ignored until the end of the line.

Assignment Statements

Assignment statements in PL/SQL use := as the assignment operator. Assignment can also be used in the declare section to assign an initial value to a local variable.

Conditional Statements

PL/SQL supports several forms of a conditional statement; the form appearing in step 1 of Listing 7-5 is good for general-purpose use. Note that the keywords act as section boundaries: the conditional expression appears between if and then, the statements to be executed when the condition is true appear between then and else, and the statements to be executed when the condition is false appear between else and end if. As usual, if there are no statements between the else and end if keywords, the else keyword can be omitted.

Handling Multi-Row SQL Queries

Now let's see how to build the Shared Commission region of Figure 7-7. Its Enter Sale region is essentially the same as in the Solo Commission region. Its item names are P18_SHARED_SALESMAN and P18_SHARED_AMOUNT. The items in the Commission Info region are named P18_SHARED_SALE_COMMISSION, P18_SHARED_COMMISSION_EACH, and P18_SHARED_NEW_COMMISSIONS.

The select list P18_SHARED_SALESMAN has the same property values as P18_SOLO_SALESMAN; the difference is that its Allow Multi Selection property is set to Yes, with a Height value of 4. Recall from Chapter 5 that the value of such an item is a string containing the return values separated by colons. For example, in Figure 7-7, ALLEN and TURNER are chosen from the multi-value select list P18_SHARED_SALESMAN. Because their corresponding employee numbers are 7499 and 7844, the value of this item is the string "7499:7844".

It is not especially easy to extract the information you need from this string, so some fancy footwork is required. You will need to do two things: determine the number of selected employees, and extract their records from the EMP table.

Note that the number of selected employees is one more than the number of colons in the string. You can determine the number of colons by using the SQL replace function to create a new string in which the colons are replaced by the empty string (effectively removing the colons) and then comparing the lengths of the two strings. That is, if P18_SHARED_SALESMAN contains the string, the number of employees is given by this expression:

```
1 + length(:P18_SHARED_SALESMAN)
  - length(replace(:P18_SHARED_SALESMAN, ':', ''))
```

To extract the records for each selected employee, use the instr function, just as you did for the Filter by Possible Department page of Figure 6-6. As in that page, the following query will retrieve the EMP record of all selected employees:

```
select *
from EMP
where instr( ':'|| :P18_SHARED_SALESMAN||':',  ':'||EmpNo||':' ) > 0
```

With these issues taken care of, you can now write the process for the region's Submit button. The PL/SQL code appears in Listing 7-6.

Listing 7-6. PL/SQL Code to Handle Shared Commissions

```
declare
    v_saleCommission number(7,2);
    v_amount         int := :P18_SHARED_AMOUNT;
    v_empCount       int;
    v_commissionEach number(7,2);
    v_empInfo        varchar2(25);
    v_output         varchar2(250) := '';
begin
    -- Step 1: Calculate the new commission as 15% of the first $100
    -- and then 10% of the remaining sale price.
    if v_amount > 100 then
        v_amount := v_amount - 100;
        v_saleCommission := 15 + (v_amount * 0.1);
    else
        v_saleCommission := v_amount * 0.15;
    end if;

    -- Step 2: Determine the shared commission.
    v_empcount := 1 + length(:P18_SHARED_SALESMAN)
                    - length(replace(:P18_SHARED_SALESMAN, ':', '' ));
    v_commissionEach := v_saleCommission / v_empcount;

    -- Step 3: Update the EMP table.
    update EMP
    set Comm = Comm + v_commissionEach
    where instr( ':'||:P18_SHARED_SALESMAN||':',  ':'||EmpNo||':' ) > 0;

    -- Step 4: Use a loop to collect employee info.
    for row in (
        select EName, Comm
        from EMP
        where instr( ':'||:P18_EMPNO_SHARED||':',  ':'||EmpNo||':' ) > 0 )
    loop
        v_empInfo := row.EName || ': ' || row.Comm || chr(13);
        v_output  := v_output || v_empInfo;
    end loop;
```

```
-- Step 5: Write the item values.
:P18_SHARED_SALE_COMMISSION   := v_saleCommission;
:P18_SHARED_COMMISSION_EACH   := v_commissionEach;
:P18_SHARED_NEW_COMMISSIONS   := v_output;
end;
```

Step 1, which calculates the commission on the sale, is the same as before. Step 2 calculates the prorated commission for each employee, which you get from dividing the commission by the employee count. Step 3 updates the records for the selected employees. Step 5 writes a value to each item in the Commission region.

The most interesting code appears in step 4, in which you handle each selected employee. The issue is that the SQL query to retrieve the employee information returns multiple rows, so you cannot use the into clause the way that you did earlier. Instead, the technique is to loop through the records in the query, processing one row each time through the loop.

The loop has the following basic structure:

```
for r in ( <SQL query> )
loop
    -- statements to process row r
end loop;
```

Variable r need not be declared. Each time through the loop it will hold the next row of the query. If C is an output column of the query, the expression r.C will return the C-value of the current row. For example, in Listing 7-6, the row variable is named row, and the two output columns of the query are EName and Comm. The loop code therefore makes reference to row.EName and row.Comm.

The body of the loop processes each selected employee. Its task is to construct the string that summarizes the new commission of that employee. The code creates the summary string by concatenating the employee's name with the new commission value. The expression chr(13) denotes a newline character.

Concurrent Database Updates

At any point in time, a web server such as APEX may be executing requests from multiple users concurrently. The users are not aware of this concurrency because the server gives each user the illusion that their application is the only one running on the system. However, application developers must see beyond the illusion. Applications that are unaware of this illusion can unintentionally interfere with each other, with disastrous consequences. This section discusses these issues.

Lost Update Problem

One frequently encountered situation is called the *lost update problem*. It arises when two users update the same database record at approximately the same time, and the timing of the updates is such that the database system loses one of them. Here are two scenarios that illustrate the problem.

For the first scenario, consider the Employee Data Entry page of Figure 7-5. Assume that two users use the Update Employee region to update Allen's record—user A wants to change the salary to 1800, and user B wants to change the job to ANALYST. If both users click the GetInfo button at approximately the same time, then they both will retrieve the same record from the EMP table, which says that Allen is a salesman who has a salary of 1600. When user A changes the salary and clicks the Update button, that record will be replaced by one saying that Allen is a salesman who has a salary of 1800. User B, however, doesn't see the updated salary. When user B changes the job and clicks the Update button, the record will be replaced by one saying that Allen is an analyst making 1600.

This scenario is problematic, regardless of who writes first. If user A modifies first, user B will overwrite the new salary with its previous value; if user B modifies first, user A will overwrite the new job with its previous value. No matter what happens, the database system will lose one of the updates.

You can verify this scenario for yourself. Open the Employee Data Entry page in two private browser windows (using private windows keeps APEX from realizing that they both belong to you). Select the same employee in each window and click the GetInfo button. Then do an update in each window and click their Update button. Now look at the modified record in the report—you will see that your first update was lost.

For the second scenario, consider the Sales Commission page of Figure 7-7. Suppose that Allen made solo sales of $100 and $200, earning commissions of $15 and $25, respectively. Users A and B each enter one of the sales into the Solo Commission region of the page and click its Submit button concurrently. Suppose that the execution of their PL/SQL processes both hit step 2 of Listing 7-5 at roughly the same time, meaning that both processes would see a current commission of $300. User A's process would then calculate a new commission of $315 in step 3, and user B's process would calculate a new commission of $325. Whichever process updates last would overwrite the commission of the process updating first. The overwritten update would be lost.

You can also verify this scenario for yourself. This time, open the Sales Commission page in your two private browser windows. In each window, select the same salesman, pick different sale amounts, and click the Submit button. Most likely, neither update will be lost. The reason is that the lost update scenario will only occur when the APEX server happens to postpone its execution of the first process immediately after step 2, which is possible but unlikely. You can improve the odds considerably by introducing a *sleep* statement into the process immediately after step 2, as follows:

```
...
v_newCommission := v_prevCommission + v_saleCommission;
dbms_session.sleep(10);
-- Step 3: Update the employee's record.
...
```

This statement causes the process to sleep for 10 seconds before beginning step 3. Now repeat the experiment. If you click the two Submit buttons within 10 seconds of each other, the problem scenario will occur and the first commission you submitted will be lost.

In both of these scenarios, the occurrence of a lost update depends entirely on the timing of the user requests. This dependence on timing means that lost updates tend to occur at seemingly random times. For example, it is quite possible for an application to run for months (or years) without a lost update and then have several in short succession.

Lost updates are clearly a very bad thing. A lost update might not be detected until long after it occurred, at which point it might be too late. The application developer must ensure that they never occur. Their unpredictable nature makes it hard to discover the problem via testing. Consequently, any PL/SQL process that updates the database must be written specifically to avoid lost updates.

Avoiding Lost Updates

Lost updates occur when two concurrent processes read the same data and then make conflicting updates to it. The way to avoid this problem is to force the conflicting processes to interact sequentially, so that the second process reads the data written by the first one.

The Oracle database system uses *write locks* to ensure this sequentiality. You specify write locks by adding the clause for update to an SQL query. When your process executes a query having that clause, the database system locks the query's output records so that they cannot be read or modified by any other process. Your process can then modify these records without fear of conflict. The database system releases the locks when your process completes.

For example, consider the second scenario earlier, in which two users concurrently update the Solo Commission region. Step 2 of Listing 7-5 contains the problematic SQL query:

```
select Comm into v_prevCommission
from EMP
where EmpNo = :P18_EMPNO;
```

The output of this query is the Comm value of the specified EMP record, which will be modified later in step 3. To keep other processes from accessing this record, you lock it by changing the query to the following:

```
select Comm into v_prevCommission
from EMP
where EmpNo = :P18_EMPNO for update;
```

If another process tries to access this record while it is locked, the database system will delay that process until your process completes. Consequently, step 3 of your process can modify the record, secure in the knowledge that it will not overwrite the modification of another process.

Go to page 18 of your Employee Demo application and make this modification to the process for the Solo Commission region. Then use two private browser windows to verify that it works, as described in the previous section. The page should never lose an updated commission, even if you add the *sleep* statement before step 3 of the process.

Now consider the first scenario, in which two users concurrently update an employee record. In this scenario, the activity of updating a record requires two processes: the GetEmpInfo process reads values from a specified record, and the UpdateEmp process modifies that record. It is not sufficient for GetEmpInfo to lock its records, because the locks will be released when GetEmpInfo finishes (and therefore, before UpdateEmp begins). Instead, explicit cooperation between these two processes is needed. Here is a good strategy.

The GetEmpInfo process reads the values of the selected record, displays them on the page, and saves the original values for future reference. The UpdateEmp process rereads the values from the database and compares them with the saved values. If they match, then the process can perform the update. If not, then another process must have updated the record, which means that UpdateEmp must refuse to perform the update.

Page 19 of the Employee Demo application, named Revised Employee Data Entry, contains the implementation of this strategy. It looks the same as page 17 and has the same behavior. The only difference (for the moment) is that its GetEmpInfo and UpdateEmp processes have been revised so that they cannot lose updates.

Because this page is substantially the same as page 17, the best way to implement it is to begin with a copy of page 17. To do so, go to the page designer for any page and find the insert icon along its top row (the icon labeled +). Then choose its Page as Copy menu item as shown in Figure 7-8.

Figure 7-8. *Selecting the Page as Copy wizard*

This item will bring up the APEX page copy wizard. Its first screen asks you where the to-be-copied page is; select Page in this application. The second screen asks you to specify the source and destination pages; Figure 7-9 shows how I filled it in. On the third screen, you should set up a navigation menu entry, in the usual way. The fourth screen tells you whether there were difficulties copying the page components; ignore that screen and click the Create button.

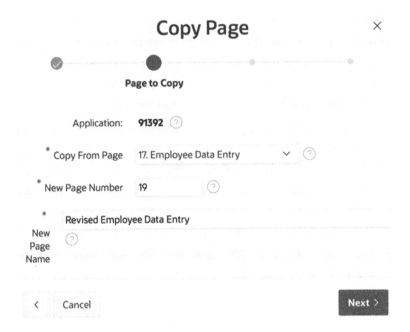

Figure 7-9. *Copying a page*

Listing 7-7 shows a revision of the `GetEmpInfo` process of Listing 7-4 (bold lines are new). After retrieving the values for the specified employee, it saves them in the new hidden items `P19_ORIGINAL_JOB`, `P19_ORIGINAL_SAL`, and `P19_ORIGINAL_DEPTNO` (which you should create).

Listing 7-7. Revising the GetEmpInfo Code of Listing 7-4

```
begin
    -- First retrieve the data.
    select Job, Sal, DeptNo
    into :P19_UPDATE_JOB, :P19_UPDATE_SAL, :P19_UPDATE_DEPTNO
    from EMP
    where EmpNo = :P19_UPDATE_EMPNO;

    -- Then use hidden items to save a copy of the data.
    :P19_ORIGINAL_JOB    := :P19_UPDATE_JOB;
    :P19_ORIGINAL_SAL    := :P19_UPDATE_SAL;
    :P19_ORIGINAL_DEPTNO := :P19_UPDATE_DEPTNO;
end;
```

Listing 7-8 shows the corresponding revision of the UpdateEmp process of Listing 7-3 (bold lines are new). The code rereads the values from the database and compares them against the original values in the hidden items.

Listing 7-8. Revising the UpdateEmp Code of Listing 7-3

```
declare
    v_newjob  varchar2(9);
    v_newsal  number(7,2);
    v_newdept number(4,0);
begin
    -- First re-read the data.
    select Job, Sal, DeptNo
    into v_newjob, v_newsal, v_newdept
    from EMP
    where EmpNo = :P19_UPDATE_EMPNO for update;

    -- Then compare it with the original data.
    if :P19_ORIGINAL_JOB = v_newjob and
       :P19_ORIGINAL_SAL  = v_newsal and
       :P19_ORIGINAL_DEPTNO = v_newdept
    then
        -- The record hasn't changed, so update it.
        update EMP
        set Job    = :P19_UPDATE_JOB,
            Sal    = :P19_UPDATE_SAL,
            DeptNo = :P19_UPDATE_DEPTNO
        where EmpNo = :P19_UPDATE_EMPNO;

    else
        -- The record has changed, so abort.
        raise_application_error(-20000,
                    'The record is out of date. Get it again.');
    end if;
end;
```

The code to abort the process requires explanation. The `raise_application_error` function causes APEX to abort the process and display an error message on the page. The function takes two arguments: the first argument is the error code, which can be any number between –20,000 and –20,999; the second argument is the error message.

Note that the query contains the `for update` clause. The process needs to lock the specified EMP record until it can execute the update statement, to ensure that the record cannot be modified in the meantime.

You can test this code as you did in the previous section, by running the page from two private browser windows. In each window, select the same employee and click the `GetInfo` button. Then modify the item values in each and click the `Update` buttons. The second update operation will not work; instead, APEX will display the error message shown in Figure 7-10.

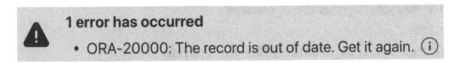

Figure 7-10. *Error message arising from an avoided lost update*

Using a Hash Function

Although this revised code works, the technique does not scale well. The need to save and compare all the original values is tedious and will become more so as the number of saved values increases. An easier approach is to combine all the original values into a single value; you can then save and compare that one value. The preferred technique is to use a *hash function*, which transforms a collection of values into a single fixed-length value, called a *checksum*. A hash function also obfuscates its input, which makes it useful for encoding user passwords—as will be seen in Chapter 13.

APEX has a built-in hash function, named `apex_util.get_hash`. The input to this function is a collection that contains the values you want hashed. You should use the APEX built-in type `apex_t_varchar2` to hold this collection. For an illustrative example, consider the following code:

```
v_vals   apex_t_varchar2 := apex_t_varchar2('CLERK', 20);
v_result varchar2(1000)  := apex_util.get_hash(v_vals);
```

The first line of the code declares a variable `v_vals` of type `apex_t_varchar2` and assigns it the collection that gets created by the type's constructor function (which is also called `apex_t_varchar2`). The arguments to the constructor function are the values 'CLERK' and 20. The second line of the code declares a variable v_result of type varchar2(1000) and assigns it the result of the apex_util.get_hash function. In other words, the variable v_result will contain the hash of the values ['CLERK', 20].

You should use this hash function to revise the code for the GetEmpInfo process so that the three updatable values are encoded into a single hash value. This hash value is then saved in the hidden item P19_HASH (which you will need to create). This code appears in Listing 7-9 (bold lines are new).

Listing 7-9. Second Revision of the GetEmpInfo Process of Listing 7-4

```
declare
    v_valuesToHash apex_t_varchar2;
begin
    -- First retrieve the data.
    select Job, Sal, DeptNo
    into :P19_UPDATE_JOB,
         :P19_UPDATE_SAL,
         :P19_UPDATE_DEPTNO
    from EMP
    where EmpNo = :P19_UPDATE_EMPNO;

    -- Then save the hash of these values.
    v_valuesToHash := apex_t_varchar2(:P19_UPDATE_JOB,
                                      :P19_UPDATE_SAL,  :P19_UPDATE_DEPTNO);
    :P19_HASH := apex_util.get_hash(v_valuesToHash);
end;
```

The code for the UpdateEmp process should also be re-revised so that it rereads the updatable values from the database, hashes them, and compares that hash value with the saved hash value. The code appears in Listing 7-10 (bold lines are new).

Listing 7-10. Second Revision of the Update Code of Listing 7-3

```
declare
    v_valuesToHash apex_t_varchar2;
begin
    -- First re-read the data.
    select apex_t_varchar2(Job, Sal, DeptNo)
```

```
into v_valuesToHash
from EMP
where EmpNo = :P19_UPDATE_EMPNO for update;

-- Then compare it with the original data.
if :P19_HASH = apex_util.get_hash(v_valuesToHash)
then
    -- The record hasn't changed, so update it.
    update EMP
    set Job    = :P19_UPDATE_JOB,
        Sal    = :P19_UPDATE_SAL,
        DeptNo = :P19_UPDATE_DEPTNO
    where EmpNo = :P19_UPDATE_EMPNO;
else
    -- The record has changed, so abort.
    raise_application_error(-20000,
                'The record is out of date. Get it again.');
end if;
end;
```

Although this code does what you want, it is somewhat clunky. This code will be revisited at the end of Chapter 8, where you will see how to improve it using validations.

Success and Error Messages

A process that changes the database should display a message indicating what happened. Consider again the Revised Employee Data Entry page. If the employee report contains only a few records, a user can verify that the update was successful by seeing how the report changed. However, if the report contained thousands of records, it would be far more difficult to determine what happened. It would be better if the deletion process displayed a success message such as **Your record was deleted**. APEX processes have the Success Message and Error Message properties for exactly this purpose. Figure 7-11 shows these property values for the Delete process.

Figure 7-11. *Success and error message properties*

Go to the property editor and add success and error messages to the processes in your Sales Commission and Revised Employee Data Entry pages. Run a page and make some changes. Your specified success messages will be displayed when the page is re-rendered. (If you are interested in seeing the error message in action, modify the process's PL/SQL code so that it refers to a nonexistent table.)

Success and error messages can contain HTML code and item references. For example, suppose that you want the success message in Figure 7-11 to indicate the number of records affected, the way the SQL command window in the APEX SQL Workshop does. How do you get the number of affected records into the process' success message?

The solution is to use the built-in PL/SQL function SQL%RowCount. If you call this function after executing an SQL command, it will return the number of affected records. Thus, you should modify the DeleteEmp process to assign that value to a hidden item (call it P19_DELETE_COUNT) and then refer to that item within the message body. The revised PL/SQL code for the DeleteEmp process is shown in Listing 7-11 (the bold line is new).

Listing 7-11. Revising the DeleteEmp Process of Listing 7-1

```
begin
    delete from EMP
    where EmpNo = :P19_DELETE_EMPNO;

    :P19_DELETE_COUNT := SQL%RowCount;
end;
```

You can then change the text of the success message in Figure 7-11 to this:

```
There were &P19_DELETE_COUNT. record(s) deleted.
```

Note that the reference to `P19_DELETE_COUNT` uses bind variable syntax in the PL/SQL process and substitution string syntax in the HTML message.

Conditional Processes

So far, each process you have written has had an associated button, and you used its When Button Pressed property to specify the association between the process and its button. This is a natural and typical way to use processes and usually all you need.

There are two situations in which the When Button Pressed property is not sufficient: when the submit action was not caused by a button and when the process is relevant to multiple buttons. The following subsections consider these situations.

Submitting via Items

Recall that items of certain types (i.e., radio groups, select lists, text fields, and password fields) can be configured to perform a submit action. Such items should be able to have an associated process. The problem is that the When Button Pressed property doesn't give you the option of picking an item.

The solution to this conundrum is to forego the When Button Pressed property in the Server-side Condition section and instead use the property below it named Type (refer back to Figure 7-6). That property lets you explicitly specify a condition for when the process should execute. Its options are the same as for conditional rendering, described in Chapter 6.

For example, let's change the Update Employee region of the Revised Employee Data Entry page so that it doesn't use the GetInfo button. Figure 7-12 shows what the new region looks like. Now, simply choosing an employee from the select list is sufficient to cause the job, salary, and department of the selected employee to appear automatically.

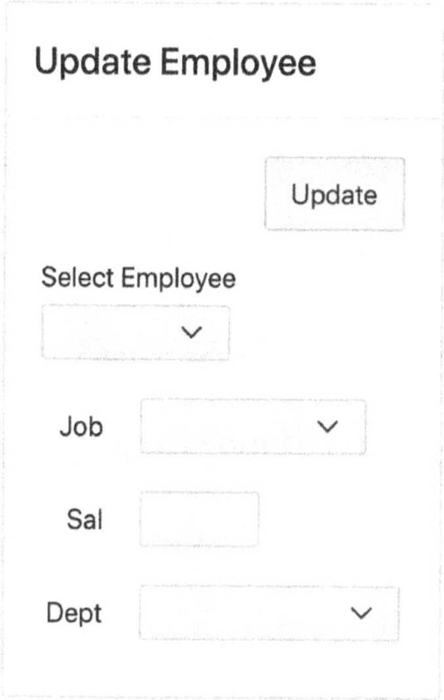

Update Employee

Update

Select Employee

Job

Sal

Dept

Figure 7-12. *Using a select list to invoke the GetEmpInfo process*

The way to implement this behavior is to first modify the select list so that it submits the page when changed and then modify the GetEmpInfo process to execute when that submit occurs. For the first task, modify the action of select list P19_UPDATE_EMPNO to be Submit Page, as shown in Figure 7-13.

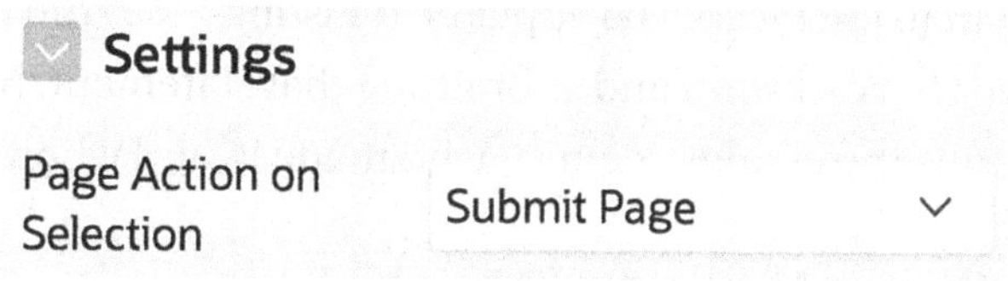

Settings

Page Action on Selection   Submit Page   ⌄

Figure 7-13. *The select list now submits when changed*

For the second task, change the Server-side Condition properties of the GetEmpInfo process as shown in Figure 7-14. Note that its SQL expression makes use of the APEX variable REQUEST, which holds the name of the item that performed the submit action. Because the expression is an SQL expression, it references the variable using bind variable notation. The expression compares the variable value to the string 'P19_UPDATE_EMPNO' (without a colon) because the expression is interested in the *name* of that item, not the *value* it holds.

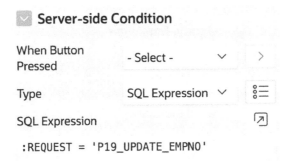

Figure 7-14. *The revised condition for the GetEmpInfo process*

When you are done, you can delete the GetInfo button from the page.

Multiple-Use Processes

Another situation that cannot make use of the When Button Pressed property is when a process is applicable to more than one button. This section contains two examples related to the Revised Employee Data Entry page.

For the first example, suppose that you want to log all changes made to the EMP table. In particular, each click of the Delete, Insert, or Update button should cause an appropriate record to be inserted into a table named EMPLOG.

The SQL statement to create EMPLOG appears in Listing 7-12. You should create this table by going to the SQL Workshop and submitting that statement. Note that the records in the table will describe the change request, who made it, and when.

Listing 7-12. SQL Code to Create the EMPLOG Table

```
create table EMPLOG(Request varchar2(20),
                    UserName varchar2(20),
                    RequestDate Date)
```

Let LogChanges be the name of the process that inserts records into EMPLOG. You should create this process in the Revised Employee Data Entry page, giving it the PL/SQL code of Listing 7-13.

Listing 7-13. PL/SQL Code for the LogChanges Process

```
begin
    insert into EMPLOG (Request, UserName, RequestDate)
    values (:REQUEST, :APP_USER, sysdate);
end;
```

This code refers to the built-in variables APP_USER and REQUEST, both of which you have seen before. The variable APP_USER holds the name of the logged in user, and REQUEST holds the name of the button or item that performed the submit action. Thus, the LogChanges process inserts a record into the EMPLOG table containing the source of the submit action, the user who performed it, and the date it occurred.

This process needs to execute each time the Insert, Delete, or Update button is clicked, but not when a value is chosen from the item P19_UPDATE_EMPNO. Clearly, the When Button Pressed property is of no use here because it lets you choose only a single button.

The solution is to set the server-side condition of the process to be the SQL expression shown in Figure 7-15. This expression ensures that the process will fire only when the button named Insert, Delete, or Update is clicked. Because each of these buttons also has its own dedicated process, clicking any of these buttons will cause two processes to execute. The processes will execute in order of their sequence number.

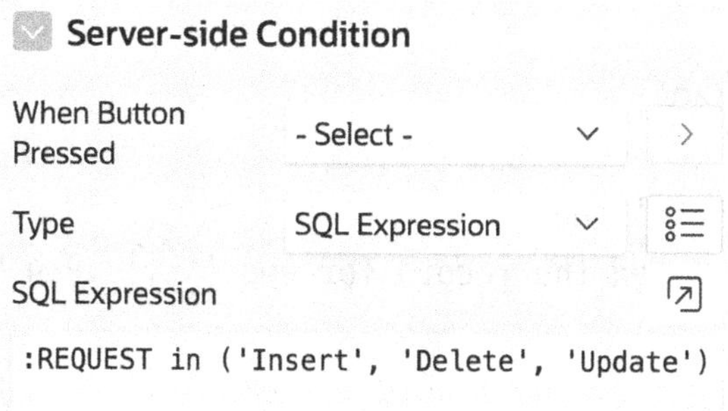

Figure 7-15. *Condition section for the LogChanges process*

You might be thinking that you don't need a separate process to do the logging; instead, you could append the logging code to each of the button-specific processes for these buttons. This strategy works, but is not advisable. The problem is that doing so would duplicate the logging code, which means that if you want to change the way the logging works (such as by adding a new column to the EMPLOG table or changing the RequestDate column to hold the time as well as the date), you will need to update it in three places. Moreover, if you decide to add a new button to the page, you must remember to extract this logging code from an existing button and add it to the process for the new button. It is much more elegant and practical to have a separate process that can be called by multiple buttons.

A second example of a process that cannot make use of the When Button Pressed property involves the sending of email. In particular, suppose that you want the Revised Employee Data Entry page to send an email to the database administrator when it detects a suspicious modification. Let's define a suspicious modification as a deletion or update that occurs outside of normal 9 a.m. to 5 p.m. working hours. To implement this feature, you will need to do two things: create a process (call it SendSuspiciousEmail) to send the email, and specify a condition for when it will fire.

To create the process, you can use the APEX email-sending function called apex_mail.send. This function can take several arguments, denoting (among others) the sender and recipient addresses, the subject, and the message body. The code for the process simply has to calculate these argument values and call the function. Listing 7-14 shows my code. (Of course, if you want to try this code for yourself, you should change the recipient to be your own email address.)

Listing 7-14. Code for the SendSuspiciousEmail process

```
declare
  v_action varchar2(40);
begin
  if :REQUEST = 'Delete' then
    v_action := ' deleted the record for emp '  || :P19_DELETE_EMPNO;
  else
    v_action := ' modified the record for emp ' || :P19_UPDATE_EMPNO;
  end if;
  apex_mail.send(
      p_from => 'EmployeeDemo@MyCompany.com',
      p_to   => 'dba@MyCompany.com',
      p_subj => 'Suspicious changes to EMP',
      p_body => :APP_USER || v_action);
end;
```

The only notable part of this code is its use of the REQUEST variable to customize the message body so that it mentions the operation performed and the affected employee record. For example if the user boris@secret.org modified the contents of president KING's record, the body of the email would say:

```
boris@secret.org modified the record for emp 7839
```

This code should execute when the Delete or Update button is pressed and the current time (as determined by the current_timestamp function) is earlier than 9 a.m. or later than 5 p.m. Figure 7-16 shows the SQL expression for this condition.

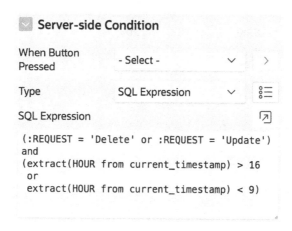

Figure 7-16. *Condition for the SendSuspiciousEmail process*

Page Rendering Processes

So far, all the processes in this chapter have executed during submit. The remainder of the chapter considers processes that execute during page rendering. This situation often arises when a page uses redirection instead of submit, such as when linking from a row of a report.

For an example, recall from Chapter 3 how an interactive report can have a link column, such that clicking a row's link column displays the values for that row in *single row view* (refer to Figures 3-66 and 3-67). The single row view has buttons to move to the previous and next rows of the table and another button to move back to report view.

Page 20 of the employee demo application is called Single Row View, and is shown in Figure 7-17. The page contains two regions that work similar to the single row view of an interactive report. The Employees region is a classic report of EMP records. A user can select a row by clicking the link in its first column; APEX responds by placing that row's values into the items of the Emp Info region. The Emp Info region has three buttons: the arrow buttons at the bottom select the previous or next record, and the Report View button at the top transfers control back to the report.

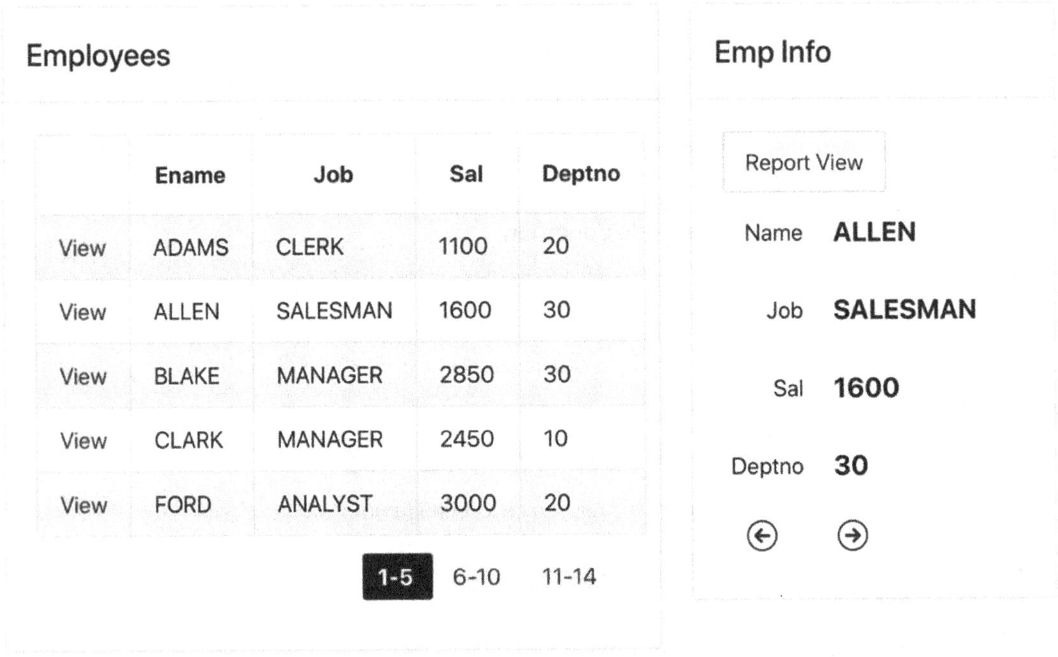

Figure 7-17. *Single Row View page*

Although Figure 7-17 shows the Employees and Emp Info regions together, they actually are never displayed this way. The Employees region is displayed only when there is no selected record, and the Emp Info region is displayed only when there is a selected record.

Several issues arise when you try to implement this page. How and when do the items in the Emp Info region get their values? How does the page know whether to display the Employees region or the Emp Info region? How are the arrow buttons implemented? These issues are discussed in the following sections.

Executing a Process Without a Submit

Let's first consider how to build the Employees region. It is a classic report region having the following source query:

```
select EmpNo, EName, Job, Sal, DeptNo
from EMP
order by EName
```

You should set the type of the EmpNo column to be Link. To configure this link, click the column's Target property to bring up the Link Builder wizard screen. Figure 7-18 shows the screen as I filled it in. It specifies that when a link is chosen, APEX will set an item named P20_EMPNO to the selected employee number and redirect to the same page. For this to be meaningful, you will of course need to create P20_EMPNO as a hidden item.

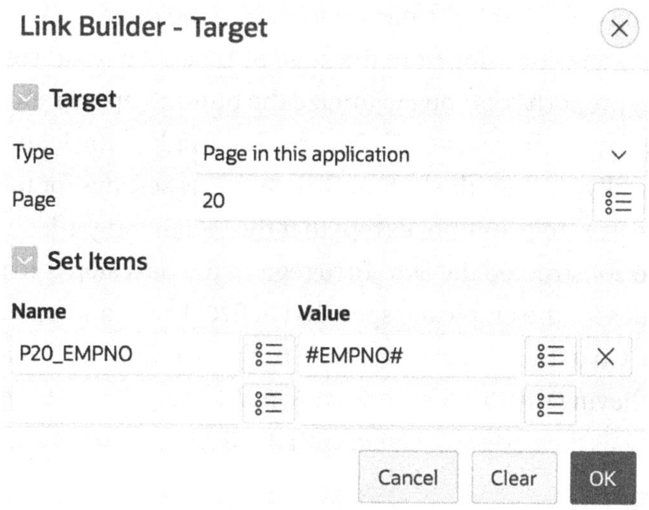

Figure 7-18. *Configuring the link for the EmpNo column*

Now consider the Emp Info region. It should have four items and three buttons. The items are named P20_ENAME, P20_JOB, P20_SAL, and P20_DEPTNO. They all have the type Display Only so that they cannot be modified. The buttons are named ReportView, Previous, and Next. ReportView is positioned Above Region, and Previous and Next are positioned Below Region; all three buttons are aligned left.

The Previous and Next buttons use the same icons as the buttons used in the single row mode of an interactive report. I chose to use them in this region just to illustrate how it's done. Figure 7-19 shows the Appearance properties for the Previous button.

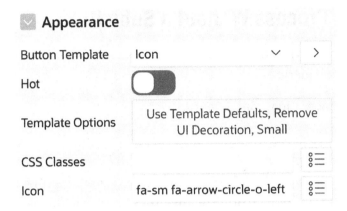

Figure 7-19. *Appearance section for the previous button*

To specify that the button should be displayed as an icon, you set the value of the Button Template property to Icon and the value of the Icon property to the name of the desired icon file. You can get this file name by clicking the quick-pick symbol to the right of the Icon property and choosing from the large number of icons displayed. Clicking the Template Options property lets you customize the button's appearance. In particular, setting the Style property to Remove UI Decoration displays the icon without the rectangle that typically outlines the button. The property settings for the Next button are the same as for the Previous button, except that the icon is a right-facing arrow.

Once you have constructed the Emp Info region, the next step is to write a process to retrieve the values for the employee specified in P20_EMPNO and place them into the items of Emp Info. Go to the Processing tab of the page editor and create a process named FetchRow, having the PL/SQL code shown in Listing 7-15. This code is similar to Listing 7-4, which was the code associated with the GetEmpInfo button on the Employee Data Entry page.

Listing 7-15. PL/SQL Code for the FetchRow Process

```
begin
  if :P20_EMPNO is not null then
    select EName, Job, Sal, DeptNo
    into :P20_ENAME, :P20_JOB, :P20_SAL, :P20_DEPTNO
    from EMP
    where EmpNo = :P20_EMPNO;
  end if;
end;
```

Although this process has the correct code, it has the wrong execution point. The Processing execution point means that the process executes when a submit action occurs. But the Employees region does not perform a submit; instead, it invokes a link, and links perform a redirect. What you need is for the process to execute after the redirection occurs—that is, during page rendering.

Click the node for FetchRow in the page designer and look at its Execution Options section. The Point property specifies the execution point of the process. Figure 7-20 shows you the possible values.

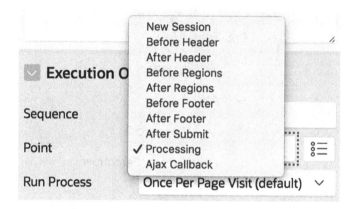

Figure 7-20. *Possible process execution points*

If a process has the execution point New Session, it will execute only when a session begins. The execution points from Before Header to After Footer denote the six stages of page rendering; a process assigned to one of these points will execute during the specified rendering stage. The execution points After Submit and Processing are two stages of a submit action. You assign the process to the After Submit point if you want it to execute before the validation stage and to Processing if you want it to execute after validation.

Although these options can be useful for advanced applications, the differences between many of the execution points are subtle and in most cases irrelevant. For our purposes, the only interesting distinction is between processes that execute during submit and those that execute during rendering. In particular, all processes in this book have the execution point After Header when they execute during page rendering, and Processing when they execute during submit.

Turn your attention back to the FetchRow process, and change its execution point to After Header. You should observe that the node for the process will vanish from the processing tree and reappear in the rendering tree, as shown in Figure 7-21. This makes sense, because the rendering tree contains everything that occurs during page rendering, which includes processes. This figure also shows that the After Header execution point is a *pre-rendering* point—that is, it occurs before the regions are rendered. This is important, as it ensures that FetchRow will assign values to the page items before they are rendered.

Figure 7-21. *FetchRow is now a rendering process*

FetchRow will get called each time the page is rendered. But it doesn't make sense for it to go to the database unless the user has selected a row—that is, it should execute its SQL statement only when P20_EMPNO is non-null. That is the purpose of the if-statement in Listing 7-15. (An equally good equivalent solution is to remove the if-statement and change the Server-side Condition properties of the process so that it executes only when P20_EMPNO is not null.)

Instead of creating FetchRow as a submit process and then changing its execution point, it is easier to create it directly as a rendering process. You simply need to right-click the After Header node in the rendering tree and select Create Process.

Moving Between Regions

At this point in your application, you should verify that clicking a link on the Employees report will correctly place the values for the selected employee into the items of Emp Info. The next issue is to work out a plan for how the regions can "take turns" rendering themselves.

The key idea is to realize that a non-null value for P20_EMPNO indicates that a row has been selected. So to "un-select" a row, it follows that you should put a null value into P20_EMPNO. The two regions can thus use the value of that item to determine their conditional rendering—the Employees region should be visible when the item value is null, and the Emp Info region should be visible when the value is not null. In other words, the value of P20_EMPNO determines whether the page is in *report mode* or *single row mode*.

This reasoning also leads to a natural way to implement the ReportView button. It should simply redirect to the same page, setting P20_EMPNO to null. Make these changes, and test your page again. Clicking a row of the report should display the Emp Info region for that employee, and clicking the Report View button should display the report again.

Finding Previous and Next Rows

The final issue is how to implement the Previous and Next buttons so that clicking them causes the region to display the previous (or next) row of the report. This section considers two different ways to implement this functionality. The first approach is easier to understand, but it has some limitations. The second approach is a bit harder to understand but is much more elegant.

Approach 1: Different Processes for Previous and Next

Consider the Previous button, which needs to select the previous row. Assume for the moment that "previous row" means the row having the next-lowest employee number. The PL/SQL code in Listing 7-16 does the job.

Listing 7-16. Simplified Code for the Previous Button, Approach 1

```
declare
    v_prevEmp number(4,0);
begin
    select max(EmpNo) into v_prevEmp
    from EMP
    where EmpNo < :P20_EMPNO;

    if v_prevEmp is not null then
        :P20_EMPNO := v_prevEmp;
    end if;
end;
```

The if-statement is necessary to handle the case when you try to get the previous row of the first employee. In this case, the query would return a null value. Without the if-statement, the button would put that null into P20_EMPNO, effectively deselecting the row and returning to report mode. By using the if-statement, clicking the Previous button from the first row will have no effect.

Now suppose that you want to use a different column to determine the previous row, such as EName. The preceding query does not extend easily to this case. Instead, you should use the SQL analytic function lag, which finds the previous value based on a specified sort order. Listing 7-17 gives the resulting PL/SQL code.

Listing 7-17. PL/SQL Code for the Previous Button, Approach 1

```
declare
    v_prevEmp number(4,0);
begin
    select PrevEmp into v_prevEmp
    from (select EmpNo, lag(EmpNo) over (order by EName) as PrevEmp
        from EMP)
    where EmpNo = :P20_EMPNO;

    if v_prevEmp is not null then
        :P20_EMPNO := v_prevEmp;
    end if;
end;
```

The inner query creates a two-column table of employee numbers, in which each employee is paired with the employee appearing immediately before in the sort order. The outer query then selects the row from that table whose EmpNo value equals P20_EMPNO and returns the PrevEmp value of that record.

In addition to the lag function, SQL also has the lead function that behaves the same way, except that it returns the next-highest value in the sort order. This function can be used in the implementation of the Next button, and its PL/SQL code is similar to Listing 7-17 (and thus is omitted).

Because the Previous and Next buttons each have their own process, you should set their actions to submit. You should also configure each process to execute conditionally on its button. Although this is not the best solution to the problem, it works well and is worth implementing just to see it in action.

Approach 2: A Unified Previous/Next Process

Approach 1 suffers from the fact the Previous and Next buttons don't have any visible effect when they get to the first or last record; to the user, they seem to have stopped working. An alternative idea is to hide the buttons when they are not applicable. To do this, the page needs to "read ahead." That is, in addition to keeping track of the current employee number, the page also needs to keep track of the previous and next values. This way, it can hide the Previous button if the previous value is null and similarly for the Next button.

To implement this approach, create the hidden items P20_PREV and P20_NEXT to hold the previous and next employee numbers. Then, whenever a record is selected, a process can "read ahead" and assign the appropriate values to these items. This process, called FindPreviousNext, appears in Listing 7-18.

Listing 7-18. PL/SQL Code to Find Previous and Next Values

```
begin
  if :P20_EMPNO is not null then
    select PrevEmp, NextEmp
    into :P20_PREV, :P20_NEXT
    from (select EmpNo, lag(EmpNo)  over (order by EName) as PrevEmp,
                        lead(EmpNo) over (order by EName) as NextEmp
          from EMP)
```

```
    where EmpNo = :P20_EMPNO;
  end if;
end;
```

This code is similar to the code in Listing 7-17, but differs in that it is not specific to any particular button. In fact, it must execute whenever a row gets selected, regardless of whether the selection is via a link from the report or via one of the Previous or Next buttons. In other words, the FindPreviousNext process should execute during page rendering, just like the FetchRow process.

As a consequence, the Previous and Next buttons can be configured much more simply. Consider the Previous button (the Next button is similar). Because P20_PREV holds the EmpNo of the previous row, you can configure the button to redirect when clicked, placing the value of P20_PREV into P20_EMPNO. See Figure 7-22.

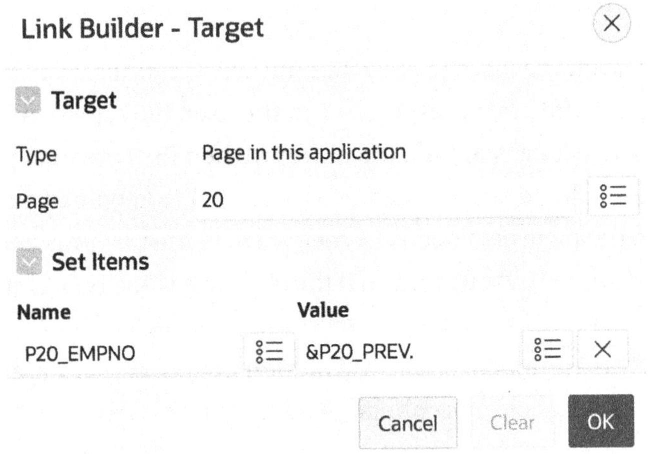

Figure 7-22. Configuring the action of the Previous button

You can also use P20_PREV and P20_NEXT to customize when the Previous and Next buttons get displayed. In particular, the Previous button should be displayed when P20_PREV is not null, and the Next button should be displayed when P20_NEXT is not null. These conditions can be expressed using conditional rendering. For example, Figure 7-23 shows the Server-side Condition section for the Previous button.

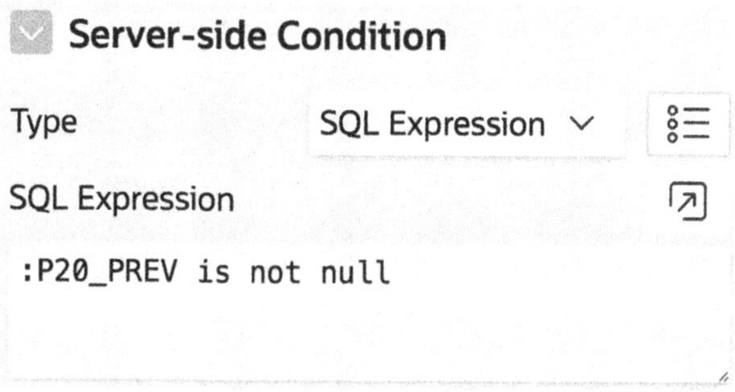

Figure 7-23. *Customizing when the Previous button is displayed*

To summarize, approach 2 implements previous/next functionality as follows. You first create hidden items P20_PREV and P20_NEXT. You then create the process FindPreviousNext, which calculates the value of these two items using the code of Listing 7-18 and executes during page rendering.

Finally, you configure the Previous and Next buttons to redirect to the current page, assigning a value to P20_EMPNO. The Previous button uses the value of P20_PREV, and the Next button uses the value of P20_NEXT. Each button uses conditional rendering, so that it displays only when its associated item value is not null.

As a result, the entire page consists of two relatively small processes: one that fetches the values of the selected row and one that calculates the employee number of the previous and next records. Both processes execute during page rendering. A user will select a row by clicking either a report link or a Previous/Next button. In each case, the page will determine the employee number of the selected record, save it to the item P20_EMPNO, and redirect, thereby causing the two processes to execute. Everything works without any submit operations.

Single Row Update

Another use for the report mode/single row mode idea is to support data entry. The Single Row Update page illustrates this idea. It is page 21 of the demo application and appears in Figure 7-24. The three regions of the page are shown together in the figure, but in actuality only one region is visible at a time. The page will be in report mode, update mode, or insert mode, depending on which region is visible.

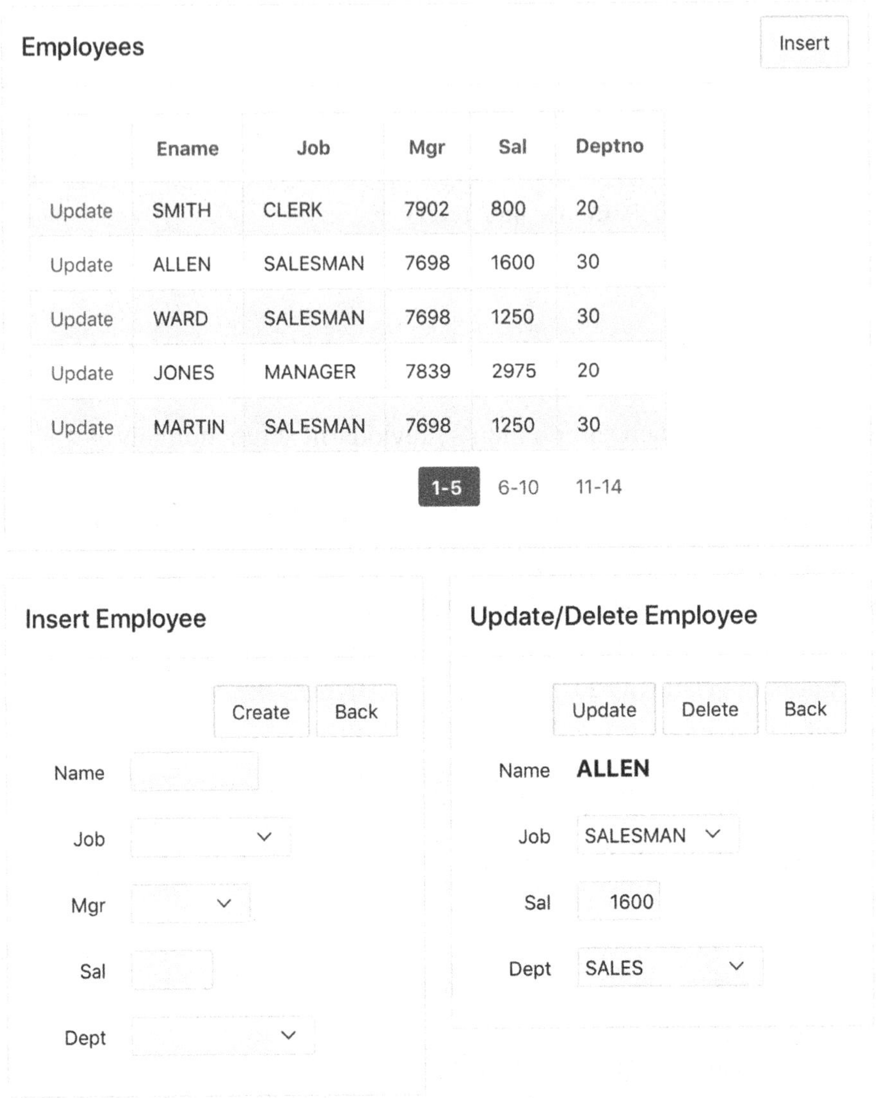

Figure 7-24. *Single Row Update page*

Initially, the page displays the Employees region in report mode. From there, the user can click the Insert button to move to insert mode or click one of the Edit links to move to update mode.

The page displays the Insert Employee region when in insert mode. This region is essentially the same as the corresponding region in the Employee Data Entry page. Its Create button creates a new EMP record having the specified values and then clears the items in anticipation of another insertion. The Cancel button returns to report mode.

The page displays the Update/Delete Employee region when in update mode. The region's items are initially populated with the chosen employee's information. The user can change item values in the region and click the Update button, which updates the database. Alternatively, clicking the Delete button deletes the chosen record. Deleting a record also returns to report mode because there is no longer a record to display. Clicking the Cancel button simply returns to report mode.

Now that you know how the page should work, you can consider how to implement each region. The following subsections examine these issues.

Implementing the Report Region

The implementation of the report region is essentially the same as in the Single Row View page of Figure 7-17. One difference is that it also has a hidden item, called P21_ MODE, to distinguish between the three modes. The item will have the values Report, Insert, and Update, as appropriate, with a null value indicating report mode.

The EmpNo column is implemented as a link. The link redirects to page 21 and sets values for two items when it redirects: P21_EMPNO is set to the chosen employee number, and P21_MODE is set to Update. The Insert button also redirects, setting P21_MODE to Insert. The region is conditionally rendered according to this SQL expression:

```
:P21_MODE = 'Report' or :P21_MODE is null
```

Implementing the Insert Region

A new EMP record has nine values, but only five need be specified by the user. The Insert Employee region has an item for each of these five values. The items are named P21_ INSERT_ENAME, P21_INSERT_JOB, and so on. The region also has two buttons, named Create and CancelInsert. The region is conditionally rendered according to this SQL expression:

```
:P21_MODE = 'Insert'
```

The Create button performs a submit action. It has an associated process named InsertEmp that does two things: execute an SQL insert command and set its items to null. It uses default values for HireDate, Comm, and Office. Its code appears in Listing 7-19.

Listing 7-19. PL/SQL Code for the InsertEmp Process

```
begin
    insert into EMP(EName, Job, Mgr, Sal, DeptNo, HireDate, Comm, Offsite)
    values (:P21_INSERT_ENAME,
            :P21_INSERT_JOB,
            :P21_INSERT_MGR,
            :P21_INSERT_SAL,
            :P21_INSERT_DEPTNO,
            current_date,  0,  'N');

    -- Clear the region's visible items.
    :P21_INSERT_ENAME   := null;
    :P21_INSERT_JOB     := null;
    :P21_INSERT_MGR     := null;
    :P21_INSERT_SAL     := null;
    :P21_INSERT_DEPTNO  := null;
    -- But do not change the mode.
end;
```

The CancelInsert button redirects, setting P21_MODE to Report.

Implementing the Update/Delete Region

The items in the Update/Delete Employee region get populated by a process named
FetchRowForUpdate, which executes during page rendering and is conditional on the
SQL expression

```
:P21_MODE = 'Update'
```

The code for this process appears in Listing 7-20. The code is essentially the same
as the FetchRow process in Listing 7-15, except that it also deals with the lost update
problem. (This issue was not relevant with the Single Row View page because that page
performed no updates.) It calculates the hash value of the three modifiable items and
saves it in the hidden item P21_HASH.

Listing 7-20. PL/SQL Code for the FetchRowForUpdate Process

```
declare
    v_valuesToHash apex_t_varchar2;
begin
  if :P21_EMPNO is not null then
    -- First, fetch the employee record and save its values.
    select EName, Job, Sal, DeptNo
    into :P21_UPDATE_ENAME,
         :P21_UPDATE_JOB,
         :P21_UPDATE_SAL,
         :P21_UPDATE_DEPTNO
    from EMP
    where EmpNo = :P21_EMPNO;
    -- Then save the hash of the updatable values.
    v_valuesToHash := apex_t_varchar2(:P21_UPDATE_JOB,
                        :P21_UPDATE_SAL, :P21_UPDATE_DEPTNO);
    :P21_HASH := apex_util.get_hash(v_valuesToHash);
  end if;
end;
```

The PL/SQL code for the region's Delete button is named DeleteEmp. It executes an SQL delete command, similar to Listing 7-1, and then returns to report mode. Its code appears in Listing 7-21.

Listing 7-21. Code for the DeleteEmp Process

```
begin
    -- First, delete the record.
    delete from EMP
    where EmpNo = :P21_EMPNO;
    -- Then return to report mode.
    :P21_EMPNO := null;
    :P21_MODE  := 'Report';
end;
```

The code for the Update button is named UpdateEmp. It executes an SQL update command after ensuring that there is no lost update. The code is essentially the same as the update code for the Revised Employee Data Entry page (refer to Listing 7-10). The code appears in Listing 7-22.

Listing 7-22. Code for the UpdateEmp Process

```
declare
    v_valuesToHash apex_t_varchar2;
begin
    -- First re-read the data.
    select apex_t_varchar2(Job, Sal, DeptNo)
    into v_valuesToHash
    from EMP
    where EmpNo = :P21_EMPNO for update;
    -- Then compare it with the original data.
    if :P21_HASH = apex_util.get_hash(v_valuesToHash) then
        -- The record hasn't changed, so update it.
        update EMP
        set Job    = :P21_UPDATE_JOB,
            Sal    = :P21_UPDATE_SAL,
            DeptNo = :P21_UPDATE_DEPTNO
        where EmpNo = :P21_EMPNO;
    else
        -- The record has changed, so abort.
        raise_application_error(-20000,
                    'The record is out of date. Get it again.');
    end if;
end;
```

To summarize, the Single Row Update page has four processes. Three of the processes execute during submit; their responsibilities are to run their respective insert, delete, and update SQL statements. The fourth process is responsible for running an SQL query to initialize a region's items; it executes during page rendering.

Summary

A process is a page component that lets you access the database and perform calculations. This chapter examined the role that processes play in an application. For example, a button that performs a submit action typically has an associated process that will execute when the button is clicked. A process can also be configured to execute during page rendering and calculate initial values for items.

This chapter focused entirely on PL/SQL processes. To specify the behavior of a PL/SQL process, you write PL/SQL code. PL/SQL integrates SQL commands directly into a general-purpose programming language, which makes it easy to write database-aware code. Chapter 10 examines other process types.

Although PL/SQL processes can be very useful, they require careful coding. This chapter examined one common pitfall, known as the lost update problem. You learned how to recognize the problem and how to write the necessary PL/SQL code to avoid it.

CHAPTER 8

Data Validation

When a process writes to the database, it typically takes its values from the session state. Consequently, an application developer must verify that the session state values are *valid*, to ensure that the process was used appropriately and to preserve the integrity of the database. This chapter examines three aspects of a valid session state—constraint preservation, input validation, and process validation—and shows you how to implement them in an APEX application.

Constraint Preservation

The integrity of a database is important. The presence of an incorrect record not only reduces the value of any query involving that record; it also reduces the value of the entire database—because if one record is wrong, users will suspect that other records might also be wrong. Such databases can quickly become useless.

The primary mechanism that a database system uses to protect itself is the *constraint*. A database administrator typically specifies constraints when the tables are created. For example, the EMP table has the following four constraints defined for it:

- The column EmpNo is a *key*, which ensures that no two employees have the same EmpNo value.

- The column DeptNo is a *foreign key* of DEPT, which ensures that every non-null value of DeptNo corresponds to an existing DEPT record.

- The column Mgr is a *foreign key* of EMP, which ensures that every non-null value of Mgr corresponds to an existing EMP record.

- An EmpNo value *cannot be null*, which ensures that every employee has a number.

© Edward Sciore 2020
E. Sciore, *Understanding Oracle APEX 20 Application Development*,
https://doi.org/10.1007/978-1-4842-6165-1_8

Let's add two more constraints to the database:

- An ENAME value *cannot be null,* which ensures that every employee has a name.

- A Sal value *must be at least 0,* which ensures against meaningless salaries.

You can define these constraints by separately executing the two SQL commands of Listing 8-1 in the APEX SQL workshop.

Listing 8-1. Two Additional Constraints for the EMP Table

```
alter table EMP
    add constraint ValidName
    check (EName is not null)

alter table EMP
    add constraint ValidSalary
    check (Sal >= 0)
```

Whenever you write an APEX page that updates the database, you must be aware of its constraints. To investigate these issues, this chapter will use the Revised Employee Data Entry page as a running example. This page was discussed in Chapter 7 and is page 19 of the Employee Demo application.

Using this page, try to insert a new employee that does not have a value for EName. You won't be able to do it—the database will reject the insertion because the new record would violate the null value constraint. APEX displays the error message shown in Figure 8-1.

Figure 8-1. *Result of attempting to violate a constraint*

Although the database was able to enforce the constraint, its error message is not particularly satisfactory. The message is unhelpful, giving obscure, system-level details about what went wrong. It also does not tell you what caused the mistake or how to fix it. In fact, the message leaves open the possibility that the problem is due to a bug in the system over which you have no control.

Consequently, APEX pages should always anticipate attempted constraint violations and handle them itself. Ideally, the database will never need to throw one of its obscure constraint violation messages, because APEX would have detected and handled the violation first. APEX has several features that can help you in this regard. Let's examine how they apply to each of the preceding constraints.

A violation of the key constraint could occur if a user is allowed to choose the EmpNo value for a new employee. The best way to handle this constraint is to not give the user that choice. For example, the Revised Employee Data Entry page does not have a place for a user to enter an employee number. Instead, the SQL insertion command obtains the new EmpNo value automatically from an insertion trigger, thereby guaranteeing that a unique value will be chosen.

A violation of a foreign key constraint could occur if a user is able to enter an inappropriate value for DeptNo or Mgr. The solution adopted by the Revised Employee Data Entry page is to use list-based items. The advantage of a list-based item is that you can populate it with exactly the values you want, which means that there is no way that the user can pick an improper value. (Caveat: this statement is true for a properly secured application. Chapter 13 discusses how a malicious user can select arbitrary values from an unsecured list-based item.)

A violation of a null value constraint on EName could occur if a user does not enter a value into the item P19_INSERT_ENAME. The solution to this problem is to use the item's Value Required property, which is in its Validation section. If you set the property to On, then APEX will refuse to submit the page as long as that item value is null. Instead, APEX will redisplay the page with an error message under the item, as shown in Figure 8-2. This error message is far better than the one in Figure 8-1.

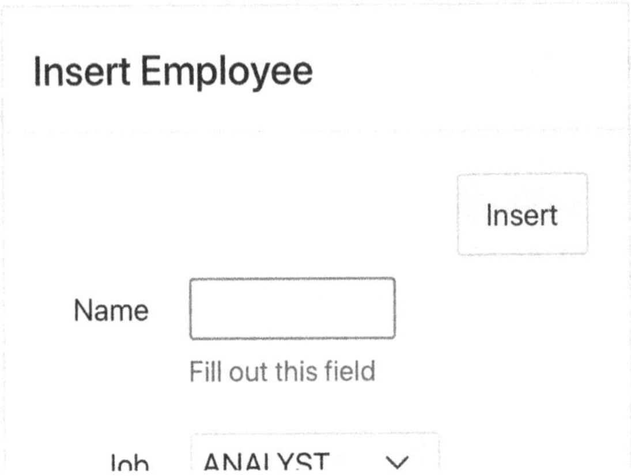

Insert Employee

Insert

Name

Fill out this field

Job   ANALYST

Figure 8-2. *A better way to handle an attempted constraint violation*

Finally, consider the constraint on Sal. The item P19_INSERT_SAL is a number field, which has the properties Minimum Value and Maximum Value in its Settings section. Set the minimum value to 0, and try to insert a record having a negative salary. APEX will display the error message shown in Figure 8-3.

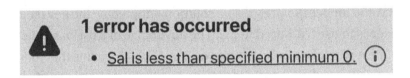

Figure 8-3. *Result of attempting to violate a numeric constraint*

Note that the application developer cannot specify these error messages. Instead, APEX uses a stock message that references the problematic item by its label. To specify your own error message, you can use a validation, as discussed in the next section.

In addition to having explicit constraints, a database also has implicit constraints that arise from the type of each column. For example, the column EName is of type varchar2(50), which means that a constraint violation would occur if a user tried to store a name containing more than 50 characters. Figure 8-4 shows the error message that results from trying to insert a new employee having a 52-character name.

1 error has occurred

- ORA-12899: value too large for column
  "UNDERSTANDINGAPEX"."EMP"."ENAME"
  (actual: 52, maximum: 50) ⓘ

Figure 8-4. *Result of stuffing too many chars into a column value*

Again, such error messages are an unsatisfactory way to give feedback to the user. Hackers often try to generate constraint violations, not because they expect them to work, but because they are interested in the error message. The message in Figure 8-4 divulges that there is an EMP table having an ENAME column of type varchar2(50).

Fortunately, there is a simple way to avoid this problem. By setting the text field's Maximum Length property to 50, you guarantee that the text field cannot hold more than 50 characters. If a user tries to enter too many characters into a text field, APEX will ignore the extra characters.

Similarly, a constraint violation would occur if a user tried to insert a non-numeric value for Sal or Comm. This problem can be avoided by implementing their items as number fields. If the number field contains a non-numeric value when the page is submitted, APEX will catch the error and generate the error message instead of the database. Figures 8-5 and 8-6 show error messages that result from trying to insert a new record having a non-numeric salary. In Figure 8-5, I changed the item P19_INSERT_SAL to be a text field, so the constraint error is caught by the database. In Figure 8-6, the item is a number field, which allows APEX to catch the error. Note that APEX generates a much better error message.

Figure 8-5. *Error message generated by the database for invalid numeric input*

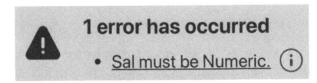

Figure 8-6. *Error message generated by APEX for invalid numeric input*

Although a number field can check for non-numeric input, it cannot check for specific kinds of numbers. The reason is that SQL is very forgiving about inaccurate numeric input. For example, the SQL command of Listing 8-2 is completely legal.

Listing 8-2. Inappropriate but Legal SQL Command

```
insert into EMP (EmpNo, DeptNo, Sal,
                EName, Job, Mgr, HireDate, Comm,  Offsite)
values (8090.4, 29.6, 130.678,
        'FRANK', 'SALES', 7839, current_date, 0, 'N')
```

The specified values for EmpNo, DeptNo, and Sal (in bold) are problematic because the columns EmpNo and DeptNo are defined as integers, and Sal is defined to have at most two numbers to the right of the decimal point. However, when Oracle is asked to store a value into a numeric column that exceeds the column's precision, it automatically rounds the value to the nearest legal value before saving it. (Some database systems truncate the value instead.) The previous insertion command therefore creates a new employee having employee number 8090 in department 30 and having a salary of 130.68. Similarly in the Revised Employee Data Entry page, if a user enters 130.678 as the salary value of a new record, APEX will process the input smoothly, without generating a constraint error.

Input Validation

Let's rethink the way APEX handles numeric input. Its behavior is technically correct, but rather misleading. It is likely that a user entering a salary with more than two numbers to the right of the decimal point has either made a typo (such as typing 130.678 instead of 1306.78) or doesn't understand the purpose of the field. In either case, it would be better if APEX informed the user of the problem instead of making a possibly incorrect assumption.

In general, you want APEX to stop users from entering inappropriate values, even if they are legal. Here are three more examples for the Revised Employee Data Entry page:

- A user should not be able to delete or modify the record for an employee having the job PRESIDENT. (Assume that this functionality is performed some other way.)

- A user should not be able to enter a salary that is higher than the president's.

- Changes to the database should only be made between the hours of 9 a.m. and 5 p.m.

APEX should reject a request that violates these conditions and inform the user why the request is inappropriate.

The way to enforce these validity checks is to create a *validation* in APEX. A validation is code that gets executed when the page is submitted. If a validation fails, submit processing stops, and the page is redisplayed with an error message for each failed validation. If all validations succeed, the submit processing continues normally.

To create a validation, go to the Processing tab of the page designer, right-click the Validating node, and select Create Validation. APEX will create a default validation named New, having the type PL/SQL Expression.

Figure 8-7 shows some of the possible validation types. A PL/SQL Expression validation succeeds if the specified PL/SQL expression returns true, and similarly for an SQL Expression validation. Two other useful validation types are Rows returned and No Rows returned. You specify these validations by an SQL query. A Rows returned validation succeeds if the query returns at least one row; a No Rows returned validation succeeds if the query returns no rows.

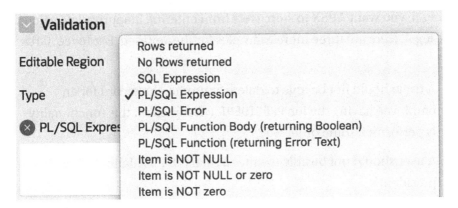

Figure 8-7. *Some validation types*

Whichever validation type you select, the property editor will display the needed properties for specifying the validation. For example, the PL/SQL Expression type has a corresponding text area for entering the expression, which can be partially seen in Figure 8-7. A Rows returned or No Rows returned validation has a text area for specifying the query.

Validations can execute conditionally, as determined by their Server-side Condition properties. Typically, a validation is conditional on a button, and you can thus use the When Button Pressed property, but you can also specify an arbitrary condition by selecting the Type property.

Each validation must have a specified error message. The Error section contains the relevant properties. The Error Message property contains the text of the error message. The Display Location specifies where the message will be displayed: within the error notification, beneath a specified item, or both.

To illustrate these concepts, let's write validations for the issues mentioned at the beginning of this section. Figure 8-8 displays the properties for the validation named DontDeleteThePresident, which verifies that the president's record is not deleted. This validation has the type No Rows returned, with the query

```
select * from EMP
where EmpNo = :P19_DELETE_EMPNO
and Job = 'PRESIDENT'
```

This query will return a record only if the chosen employee has the job PRESIDENT, which means that the validation will succeed if the chosen employee does not have the job PRESIDENT.

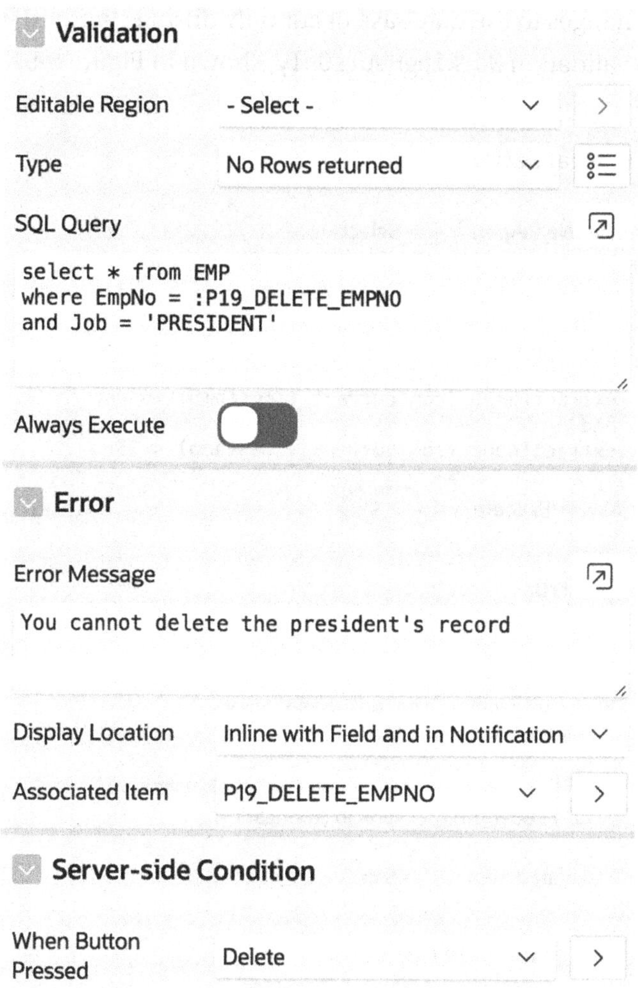

Figure 8-8. *DontDeleteThePresident validation*

Similarly, you can use the following No Rows returned query to write the validation InsertedSalaryNotTooLarge, which ensures that the value in P19_INSERT_SAL is not larger than that of the president's:

```
select * from EMP
where Job = 'PRESIDENT' and :P19_INSERT_SAL > Sal
```

The DontDeleteThePresident validation applies to the DELETE request, and InsertedSalaryNotTooLarge applies to the INSERT request. You should also create two similar validations for the UPDATE request, called DontUpdateThePresident and UpdatedSalaryNotTooLarge. The code for these validations is omitted.

To verify that changes to the database occur only during standard working hours, you can create the validation WorkingHoursOnly, shown in Figure 8-9.

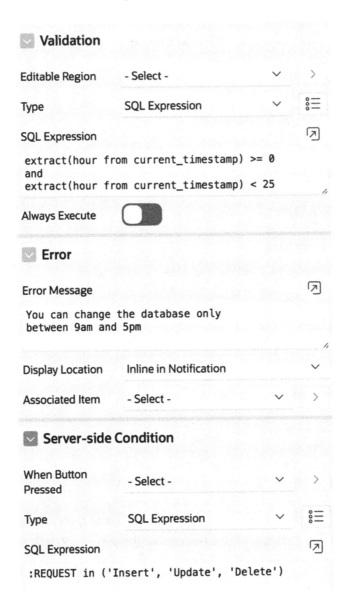

Figure 8-9. *WorkingHoursOnly validation*

This validation uses an SQL expression to calculate the desired time interval. Note that this expression is independent of the session state, so the error message will appear only with the notification. The validation is conditional on the Insert, Delete, and Update buttons.

The final example of this section concerns how to enforce specific numeric formats. For example, the column Sal is defined as the type NUMBER(7,2), which means that a salary value has no more than seven total digits, with no more than two digits to the right of the decimal place. The best way to verify this condition is to use a *regular expression*, which is a pattern that denotes a set of legal values. In this case, the following regular expression will work:

```
^\d{0,5}\.{0,1}\d{0,2}$
```

Without delving too deeply into regular expressions here, you should know that the character ^ matches the beginning of the string, \d matches any digit character, \. matches the decimal point, and $ matches the end of the string. The notation {m,n} matches at least *m* and at most *n* occurrences of the previous pattern. Therefore, the regular expression matches up to 5 digits, followed by 0 or 1 decimal point, followed by 0 to 2 more digits.

Oracle SQL has the built-in function regexp_like, which returns true if a value matches a regular expression. The validation could therefore be defined by the SQL expression shown in Figure 8-10.

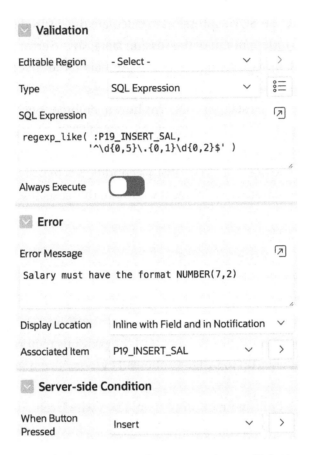

Figure 8-10. *One way to express a regular expression validation*

APEX also has the validation type `regular expression`, which provides a place to enter the regular expression directly. Figure 8-11 shows its use.

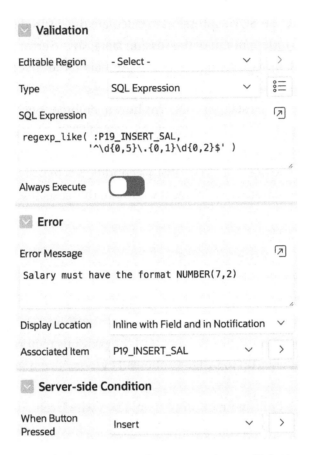

Figure 8-11. *Another way to express a regular expression validation*

Constraint Validations

The beginning of this chapter discussed how some APEX properties help to enforce constraints. However, there are situations where these properties are not sufficient. For example, Figure 8-2 illustrated how an item's Value Required property can be used to enforce a null value constraint. However, this technique will not work properly if the page contains multiple regions, each with its own submit button. The Revised Employee Data Entry page is a case in point. If P19_INSERT_ENAME has a Value Required value of Yes, that restriction will be enforced even when the Delete or Update buttons are clicked. Consequently, you would not be able to delete or update a record without entering a dummy value into P19_INSERT_ENAME.

This problem can be fixed by using a validation to enforce the null value constraint. The validation will be conditional on the Insert button and have the following SQL expression:

```
:P19_INSERT_ENAME is not null
```

You can also use a validation to verify a foreign-key constraint. For example, the Revised Employee Data Entry page uses a select list to restrict the possible departments of a new employee. Suppose instead that you want users to enter the department number into a number field. To enforce the foreign-key constraint, you simply have to ensure that the specified number is in the DEPT table. The solution is to create a validation having the following Rows returned query, conditional on the Insert button:

```
select * from DEPTNO
where DeptNo = :P19_INSERT_DEPTNO
```

Finally, you should use a validation whenever you want APEX to display a customized error message. For example, APEX displays the stock error message "Fill out this field" when you attempt to insert a null value for EName, as shown in Figure 8-2. If you use a validation to test for the constraint, it can display any error message you want, such as "An employee must have a name".

Process Validation

Chapter 7 examined the following algorithm for avoiding lost database updates: before an update operation changes the database, it first checks to see whether the relevant values have already changed; if so, the operation aborts. The code developed in that section aborted the operation by calling the function `raise_application_error`, which displayed the error message shown in Figure 7-10. Given that validations provide a cleaner way to handle error scenarios, it is natural to wonder whether a validation can be used in this situation as well. The answer is yes.

Recall the code for the Update button in Listing 7-10. That code can be divided into two parts: the first part re-reads the data and compares it with the original values, and the second part either performs the update or aborts, depending on the result of the comparison. The first part is essentially a validation. The update in the second part is a process that is conditional on the success of the validation.

Thus, you can rewrite the code for the Update process so that the first part is moved to a validation. The code for the process becomes just a simple update, the way it was originally written in Listing 7-3:

```
begin
     update EMP
     set Job    = :P19_UPDATE_JOB,
         Sal    = :P19_UPDATE_SAL,
         DeptNo = :P19_UPDATE_DEPTNO
     where EmpNo = :P19_UPDATE_EMPNO;
end;
```

You then create a validation to embody the first half of the code. Because the validation will need to execute PL/SQL code, its type needs to be PL/SQL Function Body (returning Boolean)—that is, PL/SQL code that returns either TRUE or FALSE. This code appears in Listing 8-3.

Listing 8-3. Validation Code for Detecting a Lost Update

```
declare
      v_valuesToHash apex_t_varchar2;
begin
      -- first re-read the data
      select apex_t_varchar2(Job, Sal, DeptNo)
      into v_valuesToHash
      from EMP
      where EmpNo = :P19_UPDATE_EMPNO for update;

      -- then compare it with the original data
      if :P19_HASH = apex_util.get_hash(v_valuesToHash) then
          return TRUE;
      else
          return FALSE;
      end if;
end;
```

The validation is conditional on the Update button, and its error message is "The record is out of date. Please get it again". The result is that the Update process is executed only when the validation succeeds. If the validation fails, the error message will be displayed on the Employee Data Entry page.

Summary

This chapter explored ways to stop users from inadvertently misusing a web application. It first considered database constraints. You saw how a properly chosen item type can avoid potential problems. For example, list-based item types can avoid foreign-key constraint violations. You also looked at item properties such as required values and min/max numeric values that can avoid or detect constraint violations.

The chapter then considered the use of APEX validations. A validation is an APEX component whose purpose is to abort inappropriate submit operations. Validations provide a flexible, general-purpose way to handle constraints. They can display customized error messages for constraint violations and can be used to selectively check for constraint violations. They can also be used to check for inappropriate user activity, apart from constraint violations.

Finally, the chapter reconsidered the Chapter 7 code to check for potential lost updates. You saw how to use validations to separate the code for lost-update testing from the code to update the database, which leads to a cleaner design with better error handling.

Branches

When the APEX server receives a submit request from a browser, it performs the validations and processes associated with that request. Its final task is to choose a target page to send to the browser. By default, APEX chooses the page that was submitted, but it is possible to specify another page by creating a *branch*.

You have been able to get this far through the book without needing to use branches because of the ease in which multiple regions can be created on a page and the way that these regions can be conditionally rendered to give the effect of multiple pages. But there are many situations in which an application will use multiple pages to implement a user activity. This chapter investigates the use of branches to support these situations.

Separating Input from Output

A common application design technique is to use separate pages for input and output. A user enters input on a page and clicks a button; the application then branches to another page that displays the output.

As an example of this technique, consider the two pages shown in Figures 9-1 and 9-2. The pages have a single region each and work similar to the two-region `Filter by Job and Department` page of Chapter 6. In particular, a user begins on the `Filter and Branch` page shown in Figure 9-1, choosing a job and department from the select lists and then clicking a button. The system then branches to the `Filtered Employees` page of Figure 9-2, which displays a report of employees who have that job and are in that department.

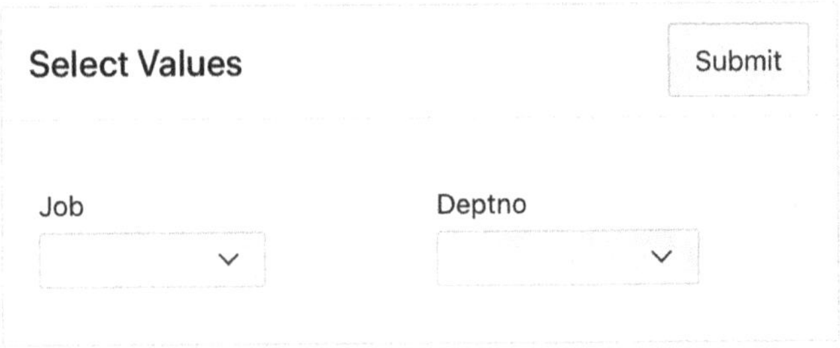

Figure 9-1. *Filter and Branch page*

Figure 9-2. *Filtered Employees page*

Let's examine how to implement these pages. The Filter and Branch page will be page 22 of the Employee Demo application. Its region is titled Select Values and has the type Static Content. It has two select lists named P22_JOB and P22_DEPTNO. The list of values for these select lists are specified by the same SQL queries as in Chapter 6. In particular, the query for P22_JOB is

```
select distinct Job as DisplayVal, Job as ResultVal
from EMP
order by DisplayVal
```

And the query for P22_DEPTNO is

```
select DName, DeptNo
from DEPT
order by DName
```

The Filtered Employees page is page 23 of the demo and its region is a classic report. Its source query, which is also similar to what you saw in Chapter 6, is the following:

```
select EmpNo, EName, Job, Sal, DeptNo
from EMP
where (:P22_JOB is null  or  Job = :P22_JOB)
and   (:P22_DEPTNO is null  or  DeptNo = :P22_DEPTNO)
order by EName
```

Each page has a button. The Submit button on the Filter and Branch page will perform a submit action to save its two item values in the session state. The Back button on the Filtered Employees page can simply redirect back to page 22 because it has no need to submit.

The Filter and Branch page will have an entry in the navigation menu. The Filtered Employees page will not, however, because the only way to access the page should be through the Filter and Branch page. This situation is true in general—when an interaction is broken up among several pages, usually only the first page of the interaction is accessible from the navigation menu.

There are two implementation issues that have not been discussed: how do you customize the region title of the Filtered Employee page, and how do you get page 22 to redirect to page 23 upon submit? Each issue will be discussed in turn.

Consider first the Filtered Employees region. One downside of using a separate page for output is that the input is no longer visible. The design strategy in Figure 9-2 is to recapitulate the input within the region's title bar. Let's examine how to implement this feature.

Recall that a region's Title property is HTML code. Although HTML code cannot perform computation, it can reference the value of an item. Thus, the technique is to write a process to compute the title of the region and save it in a hidden item. Listing 9-1 gives the code for this process. This code considers the four cases in which the two items are empty or not, computes the region title appropriately, and saves it in the hidden item P23_REGION_TITLE.

Listing 9-1. Customizing the Title of the Filtered Employees Region

```
declare
    v_title varchar(100);
begin
    if :P22_JOB is not null and :P22_DEPTNO is not null
    then
            v_title := 'Job=' || :P22_JOB  || ' and Dept=' || :P22_DEPTNO;
    elsif :P22_JOB is not null then
            v_title := 'Job=' || :P22_JOB;
    elsif :P22_DEPTNO is not null then
            v_title := 'Dept=' || :P22_DEPTNO;
    else
            v_title := 'All Employees';
    end if;
    :P23_REGION_TITLE := 'Filter by ' ||  v_title;
end;
```

This process belongs to page 22 and is conditional on the Submit button. The HTML expression for the Filtered Employees region title then becomes a reference to that hidden item. In particular, the region title is the HTML expression "&P23_REGION_TITLE.". Note that the expression uses substitution string syntax to refer to the item.

Creating a Branch

To get page 22 to redirect to page 23, you need to create a *branch* object. A branch object is similar to a process, in the sense that it performs an action in response to a submit. The difference is that a process executes code, whereas a branch redirects to a page. A branch typically executes last, after all processes have finished.

Creating a branch is similar to creating a process. Begin by going to the Processing tab of the page designer. Right-click the node labeled After Processing and choose Create Branch. APEX will create an unnamed branch that has the properties shown in Figure 9-3.

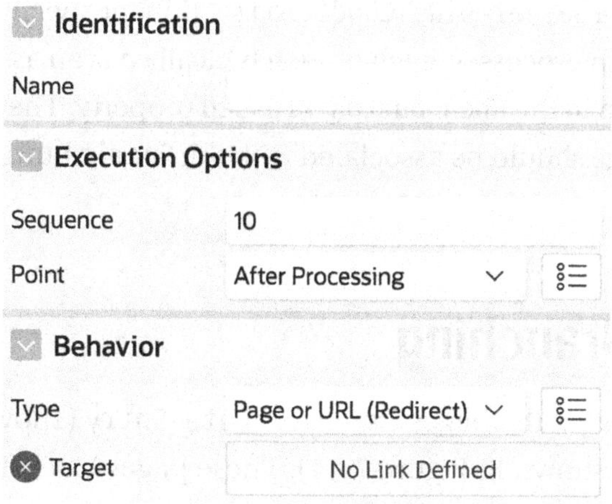

> **Identification**

Name

> **Execution Options**

Sequence   10

Point   After Processing   ∨

> **Behavior**

Type   Page or URL (Redirect) ∨

⊗ Target   No Link Defined

Figure 9-3. *Properties of a newly created branch*

You should give the branch a name. But what else must you do? Two important properties shown in Figure 9-3 are Point and Type; their default values specify that the branch will execute after all processes and will redirect to a specified page or URL. These default values are almost always what you want, and you should leave them as is.

The one property that requires your attention is Target. This property shows an error, indicating that you need to specify the target of the branch. Clicking the property's Target property brings up the Link Builder wizard. Figure 9-4 shows the builder, configured to redirect to page 23.

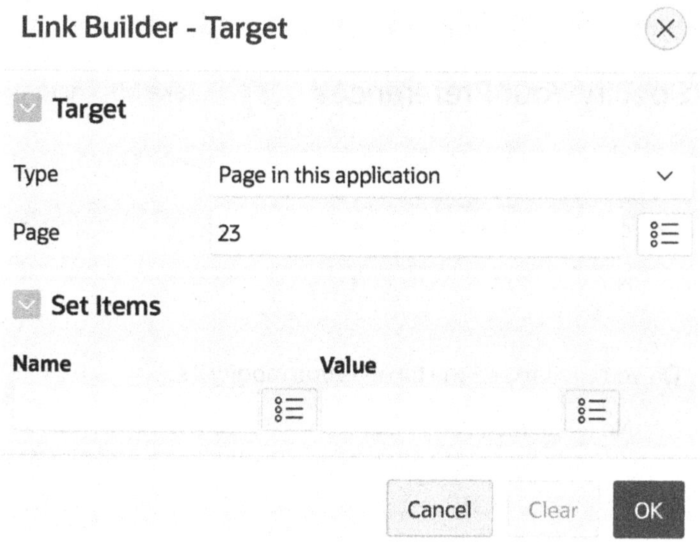

Link Builder - Target   ⊗

> **Target**

Type   Page in this application   ∨

Page   23

> **Set Items**

Name   **Value**

                                                  Cancel   Clear   OK

Figure 9-4. *Using the link builder to specify a branch target*

A branch also has a `Server-side Condition` section for specifying when the branch should execute. As with processes, each branch typically has an associated button, and you specify that button in the `When Button Pressed` property. The branch in the `Filter and Branch` demo page should be associated with the `Submit` button and have no other condition.

Conditional Branching

In Chapter 7, you created the pages `Employee Data Entry` (shown in Figure 7-5) and `Single Row Update` (shown in Figure 7-24). These pages have similar functionality—they both allow a user to insert, delete, and update the `EMP` table—but they use very different interfaces to do so. In particular, the `Employee Data Entry` page is very expansive; it displays all the report and update regions at the same time. On the other hand, the `Single Row Update` page is compact, always displaying a single region at a time.

Let's build a page that helps a user decide which page to use. This page, called `Preference Chooser`, is page 24 of the demo application and appears in Figure 9-5. The page has a single region that asks the user two questions. A user answers these questions and clicks the button; the button will then branch to page 17 (the `Employee Data Entry` page) if the first answer is `No` or the second answer is `Yes` or to page 21 (the `Single Row Update` page) otherwise.

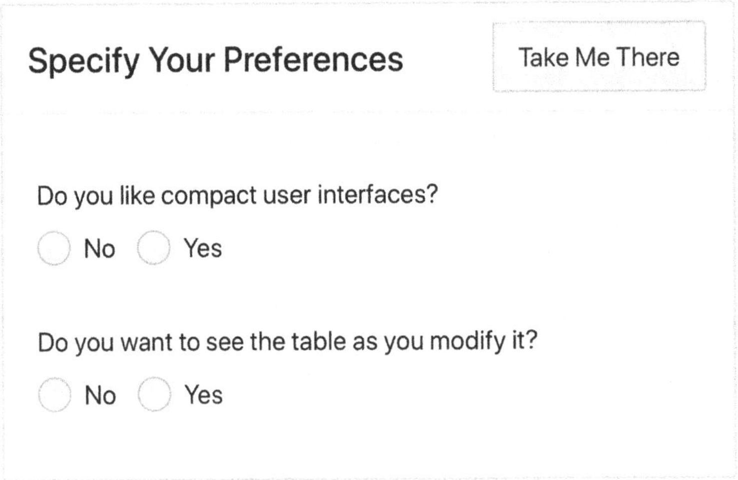

Figure 9-5. *Page with conditional branching*

You can implement this page as follows: the two radio groups are named P24_COMPACT and P24_SEE_TABLE, having the static list of values {No, Yes}.

The button performs a submit action. Intuitively, you might imagine that the button makes the decision about which page to branch to. But that is not how branching works; instead, you need to create two branch objects, each of which is conditional on the button. Each branch will also have an extra condition. The branch object that redirects to page 17 has this condition:

```
:P24_COMPACT = 'No' or :P24_SEE_TABLE = 'Yes'
```

The branch object that redirects to page 21 has this condition:

```
:P24_COMPACT = 'Yes' and :P24_SEE_TABLE = 'No'
```

When the button performs the submit, only one of these conditions will be satisfied. The branch having the satisfied condition will perform its redirection.

Wizard-Like Interfaces

The final example of branching is also related to the problem of data entry. In each of the data entry pages of Chapter 7, a user creates a new record by entering the desired values into some items and then clicking an insert button. Such a design presupposes that the user has these values at hand. An alternative design is to create a series of pages that leads the user through the data entry process, much as a wizard does in APEX. The design will have four pages.

A user will begin on the Basic Info page (see Figure 9-6) by entering the name, job, department, and salary of the new employee. The most common situation is for the employee to have been hired that day, so there is a checkbox for that case. The user then clicks the Continue button to submit the page.

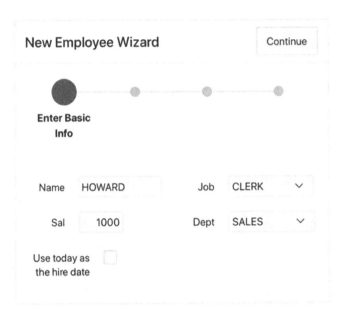

Figure 9-6. *Entering the basic info*

The next step is to determine the employee's manager. Assume that the company assigns managers to employees as follows: the president has no manager, employees with the job MANAGER report to the president, and other employees (except clerks) report to the manager of their department. The exceptions are clerks. The manager of a clerk can be any employee (except another clerk) in the same department as the clerk, so the user will need to specify the manager of a new clerk explicitly.

If the new employee is a clerk, clicking the Continue button will branch to the Manager Info page (see Figure 9-7), in which the user chooses the employee's manager from a select list.

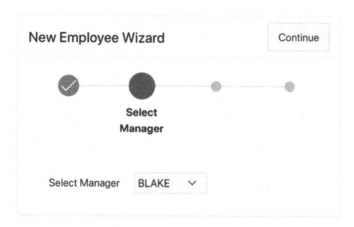

Figure 9-7. *Selecting the manager*

If the hiredate checkbox on the Basic Info page is unselected, the application will branch to the Hiredate Info page (see Figure 9-8), to let the user select a date. This branch will happen either from the Manager Info page or the Basic Info page, depending on whether the employee is a clerk. After selecting a date, the user clicks the Continue button.

Figure 9-8. *Choosing the employee's hire date*

The final page of the wizard is the Confirm Employee Info page (see Figure 9-9), which displays the selected values for the new employee. The wizard branches to this page when all the necessary values are known. This branch can occur from any of the three earlier wizard pages. The Basic Info page can branch directly to the confirmation page when the new employee is not a clerk and the hiredate checkbox is selected, the Manager Info page can branch directly to the confirmation page when the checkbox was selected, and the Hiredate Info page always branches to the confirmation page.

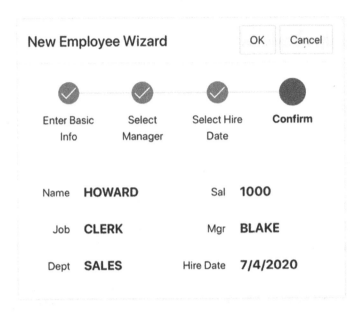

Figure 9-9. *Confirming the employee's information*

The Confirm Employee Info page has buttons labeled OK and Cancel. Clicking the Cancel button redirects to the Basic Info page and clears the session state of each wizard page. Clicking the OK button inserts the new record into the EMP table, clears the session state of each page, and branches to the Basic Info page.

Now that you understand the flow of control through the wizard, let's examine how to implement its pages. The following subsections address the issues.

Implementing the Progress Bar

The region containing the colored circles along the top of the wizard pages is called a *progress bar*. A progress bar region is simply a fancy way to display a list of page numbers. The progress bar in each of these wizard pages displays the same list, namely, a list containing the page numbers [25, 26, 27, 28]. The step names in the progress bar are the labels associated with these page numbers.

To create the progress bars in the New Employee Wizard pages, you first need to create their common list. Then you can create a progress bar region on each page. Call the list New Employee Wizard; to create it, use the techniques you learned in Chapter 4. The list will have an entry for each of the four (not yet created) wizard pages, as shown in Figure 9-10.

	List Entry Label	Target Page ID or custom URL	
1	Enter Basic Info	25	
2	Select Manager	26	
3	Select Hire Date	27	
4	Confirm	28	

Figure 9-10. *Entries for the New Employee Wizard list*

Then create the wizard pages. Start by creating four blank pages, numbered 25–28. Then create a region for each page, of type List, whose source is the list New Employee Wizard. Figure 9-11 shows the Attribute properties for the region. In particular, to display a list region as a progress bar, you only need to set its List Template property to be Wizard Progress.

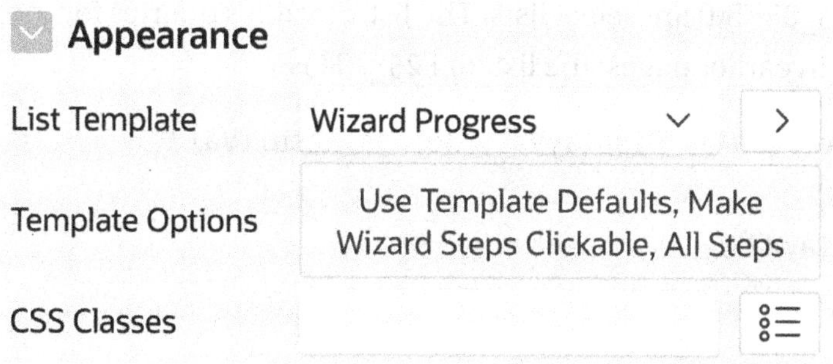

Appearance

List Template	Wizard Progress
Template Options	Use Template Defaults, Make Wizard Steps Clickable, All Steps
CSS Classes	

Figure 9-11. *List region properties*

When you have added the list region to all four pages, run each page individually from the page editor. You should observe that the pages display the progress bar differently, based on the location of the page in the list.

You can customize the look and feel of the wizard progress bar by clicking the Template Options property in Figure 9-11. Figure 9-12 shows the resulting dialog box. The Make Wizard Steps Clickable checkbox configures the progress bar so that each of its circles is a link—clicking a circle branches to the page corresponding to its step. Another option is Label Display, which lets you specify whether the progress bar should display labels for all steps or just the current one (or no labels). For example, the progress bar in Figures 9-6 through 9-8 show only the current step, whereas Figure 9-9 shows all steps. By default, the progress bar displays all steps, as shown in Figure 9-12.

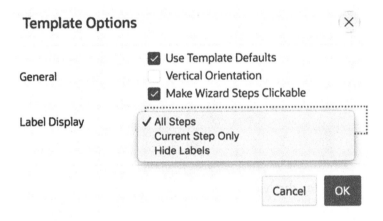

Figure 9-12. *Template options for a progress list*

Basic Info Page

The Basic Info page has five items: P25_NAME is a text field, P25_SAL is a number field, P25_JOB and P25_DEPTNO are select lists. The list-of-values queries for these select lists are the same as in earlier pages: the list for P25_JOB is

```
select distinct Job as DisplayVal, Job as ResultVal
from EMP
order by DisplayVal
```

And the list for P25_DEPTNO is

```
select DName, DeptNo
from DEPT
order by DName
```

The item P25_HIRED_TODAY is a checkbox group having the single static value [,Yes]. That is, the display value is a space and the return value is Yes. Recall that a checkbox group is a multi-value item, so its value will be Yes if checked and null otherwise.

The Continue button performs a submit operation. During this submit, several things need to happen:

- If the new employee is not a clerk, the page needs to calculate the employee's manager.

- If the hiredate box is checked, the page needs to set the employee's hire date to be today.

- The page needs to determine which of the other three wizard pages it should branch to.

The first bullet point requires that you write a process to calculate the manager of a non-clerk. Call this process ComputeManager. Its PL/SQL code appears in Listing 9-2.

Listing 9-2. PL/SQL Code for the ComputeManager Process

```
begin
  case :P25_JOB
  when 'PRESIDENT' then   -- the president has no manager
        :P26_MGR := null;
  when 'MANAGER' then   -- a manager's manager is the president
        select EmpNo into :P26_MGR
        from EMP
        where Job = 'PRESIDENT';
  else   -- the employee's manager is the manager of the dept
        select EmpNo into :P26_MGR
        from EMP
        where DeptNo = :P25_DEPTNO and Job = 'MANAGER';
  end case;
end;
```

The `ComputeManager` process calculates its value in one of three ways, depending on the value of P25_JOB. In each case, it assigns the computed value to P26_MGR, which will be an item on the `Manager Info` page. In other words, this process assigns a value to the item on the `Manager Info` page so that the user doesn't have to. (It is ok to write code that references a not-yet-existing item; you will just not be able to run it until the item exists.)

The `ComputeManager` process is associated with the `Continue` button and should execute only when the new employee is not a clerk. That is, the process is conditional on the following SQL expression:

```
:P25_JOB <> 'CLERK'
```

The second bullet point also requires you to write a process; call it `ComputeHiredate`. This process needs to calculate the current date and assign it to the item P27_HIREDATE, which will be on the `Hiredate Info` page. Its PL/SQL code uses Oracle's built-in function `sysdate` and appears in Listing 9-3.

Listing 9-3. PL/SQL Code for the ComputeHiredate Process

```
begin
    :P27_HIREDATE := sysdate;
end;
```

The `ComputeHiredate` process is also associated with the `Continue` button. It should execute only when the P25_HIRED_TODAY box has been checked. That is, it is conditional on this SQL expression:

```
:P25_HIRED_TODAY = 'Yes'
```

The third bullet point requires you to create three branch objects, one for each possible target. Call these branches `GoToPage26`, `GoToPage27`, and `GoToPage28`. The target specification for each branch is straightforward: the targets are pages 26, 27, and 28, respectively. Each branch is also associated with the `Continue` button. The only difficult issue is to specify their respective conditions.

The `GoToPage26` branch should fire when the user has to choose a manager, so its condition is this SQL expression:

```
:P25_JOB = 'CLERK'
```

The GoToPage27 branch should fire when the user does not need to choose a manager, but does need to choose the hire date; thus, its condition is this SQL expression:

```
:P25_JOB <> 'CLERK' and :P25_HIRED_TODAY is null
```

Finally, the GoToPage28 branch should fire when neither the manager nor the hire date need to be chosen; thus, its condition is this SQL expression:

```
:P25_JOB <> 'CLERK' and :P25_HIRED_TODAY = 'Yes'
```

Manager Info Page

Now consider the Manager Info page, which has the single item P26_MGR. This item is a select list with values that denote all employees who are allowed to manage clerks. Assuming that a clerk's manager must be in the same department and cannot be another clerk, the item's list of values would be defined by the following query:

```
select EName, EmpNo
from EMP
where DeptNo = :P25_DEPTNO and Job <> 'CLERK'
```

The page also has a Continue button whose action is submit. The page does not need to compute any values, so no processes are needed. But it does need to decide whether to branch to the Hiredate Info page or the confirmation page. Thus, you need two branch objects, called GoToPage27 and GoToPage28. These branches are both associated with the Continue button.

The GoToPage27 branch should fire when P25_HIREDATE is not checked; thus, its condition is this SQL expression:

```
:P25_HIRED_TODAY is null
```

Conversely, the GoToPage28 branch should fire when P25_HIREDATE is checked; thus, its condition is this SQL expression:

```
:P25_HIRED_TODAY = 'Yes'
```

Hiredate Info Page

Now consider the Hiredate Info page. It has a single Date-Picker item named P27_
HIREDATE to hold the hire date, a Continue button whose action is submit, and a branch
to the Confirm Employee Info page that is conditional on the button. Submitting the
page causes APEX to save the selected date in the session state and execute the branch.

Confirm Employee Info Page

Finally, consider the Confirm Employee Info page. Its six items are all of type Display
Only, and their values are simply copied from the items on the other pages. For example,
consider the employee's name, which is in the item P28_NAME. Its source type is PL/SQL
Expression and has the following value:

```
:P25_NAME
```

The source expressions for the items P28_SAL and P28_JOB are similar. The source
expression for P28_HIREDATE is

```
:P27_HIREDATE
```

Specifying the source expressions for P28_MGR and P28_DEPTNO requires a little
more work. Consider P28_MGR. If its source were simply the value of P26_MGR, the page
would display the manager's employee number. Looking back at Figure 9-9, however,
you can see that the page displays the name of the manager, which is easier for a user to
understand. Similarly, P28_DEPTNO displays the name of the department, even though
the value of P25_DEPTNO is the department number.

To get P28_MGR to display the manager's name, set its source to be SQL query
(return single value), having the following query:

```
select EName
from EMP
where EmpNo = :P26_MGR
```

Similarly, the source of P28_DEPTNO is this SQL query:

```
select DName
from DEPT
where DeptNo = :P25_DEPTNO
```

The `Confirm Employee Info` page has two buttons. The `Cancel` button redirects to the `Basic Info` page and clears the cache of the four wizard pages. Clicking the button's Target property brings up the link builder, where you can specify the details of the redirection. Figure 9-13 shows the link builder values for my `Cancel` button. The `Clear Cache` property contains the page numbers of those pages whose item values should be cleared.

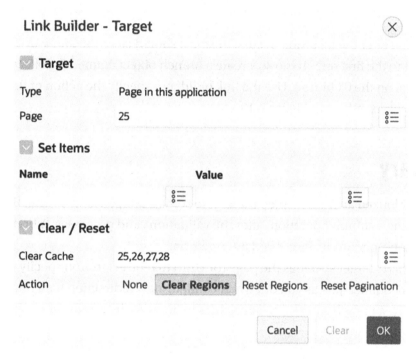

Figure 9-13. *Link builder values for the Cancel button*

The `Continue` button performs a submit action. The button has an associated process, called `InsertRecord`, which will insert the new employee record into the `EMP` table. The code for this process is similar to the code from Chapter 7 and appears in Listing 9-4.

Listing 9-4. PL/SQL Code for the InsertRecord Process

```
begin
    insert into EMP (EName, Job, Sal, DeptNo,
                     Mgr, HireDate, Comm, Offsite)
    values (:P25_NAME, :P25_JOB, :P25_SAL, :P25_DEPTNO,
            :P26_MGR, :P27_HIREDATE, 0, 'N');
end;
```

Recall that after the insertion occurs, the page should clear the four wizard pages and redirect to the first one. To do so, create a branch object, named GoToPage25, which is conditional on the OK button. Use the link builder to specify the action of the branch, which will look exactly as in Figure 9-13.

Summary

This chapter looked at branch objects and gave some examples of their use. Branches execute during a submit operation, after the validations and processes. A branch has two important components: its target and its condition.

The branch's target specifies the page (or URL) to redirect to. You specify the target using the link builder, just as you did when configuring a redirection for a button or link. Consequently, a branch can also assign values to items in the session state or clear item values on a page.

The branch's condition specifies when the branch is relevant. A page might have several target pages, depending on its session state. You address this situation by creating a branch for each target page and assigning a condition to each branch. The branch conditions should be non-overlapping so that at most one branch will be able to fire during any submit operation.

CHAPTER 10

Forms

Many of the processes from Chapter 7 involve certain basic tasks, such as retrieving the values of a record given its key, finding the previous and next records of a given record, updating records in a table, and modifying the session state.

APEX has a region type, called `Form`, which makes it possible to perform these tasks without any PL/SQL programming whatsoever. A form region contains two generic processes—one that executes during rendering and one that executes during processing—which you can configure to meet many of your needs.

This chapter examines the use of form regions, their processes, and some related processes built into APEX. It also evaluates some of the APEX wizards for creating form-based pages. Knowing how and when to use the APEX form regions and wizards can relieve you of the need to write PL/SQL code for the more common page development tasks.

Form Regions

A form region is similar to a report region, in that both have a source query. Their difference is in how they display their output records. A report displays several output records at a time tabularly, whereas a form displays one record at a time, with each value in an item. Reports are read-only, but forms can modify the database.

Looking back at Chapter 7, the `Emp Info` region of the `Single Row View` page (refer to Figure 7-17) is used as a form, as are the `Insert Employee` and `Update/Delete Employee` regions of the `Single Row Update` page (refer to Figure 7-24). Those regions had the type `static content` and used PL/SQL code to implement their functionality. This section introduces the `Form` region type and shows how the same functionality can be obtained without any PL/SQL coding.

© Edward Sciore 2020
E. Sciore, *Understanding Oracle APEX 20 Application Development*,
https://doi.org/10.1007/978-1-4842-6165-1_10

Figure 10-1 shows page 29 of the Employee Demo application, titled Form View. This page has a single region, called Browse Employees, that lets a user browse the EMP table one record at a time. The region has five items. The first four items display the values of four fields of an EMP record. Selecting an employee name populates the other three items with values from the selected record. Clicking the Previous (or Next) button moves to the previous (or next) record in the table. The fifth item displays the string **6 of 14**, indicating the record's position in the table.

Figure 10-1. *The Form View page*

To build this page, create a new blank page titled Form View. Then create a region named Browse Employees, assign it the type Form, and give it the source query shown in Figure 10-2.

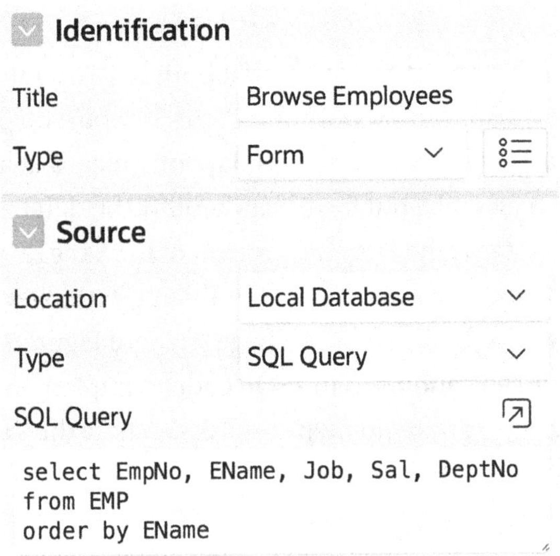

Figure 10-2. *Source of the Browse Employees region*

When you create a Form region, APEX will automatically create an associated rendering process for it, plus an item for each column in the source query. Figure 10-3 shows the rendering tree immediately after creating the Browse Employees region and setting its source.

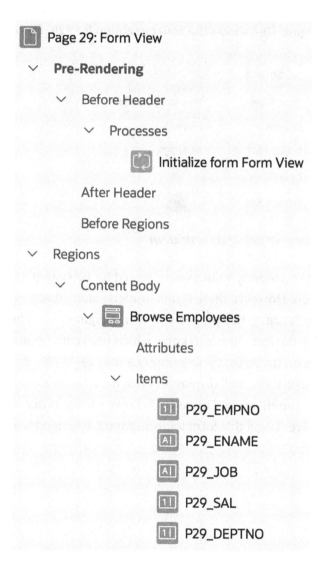

Figure 10-3. *The rendering tree for a form region*

The name and type of each item are taken from the corresponding column definitions. For example, the item corresponding to the column EmpNo is named P29_EMPNO, and its type is Number Field. The item type for a character field is Text Field, the type for a date field is Date Picker, and so on.

An item's Source section has properties that specify the correspondence between the item and its column. Figure 10-4 shows the Source section for P29_EMPNO.

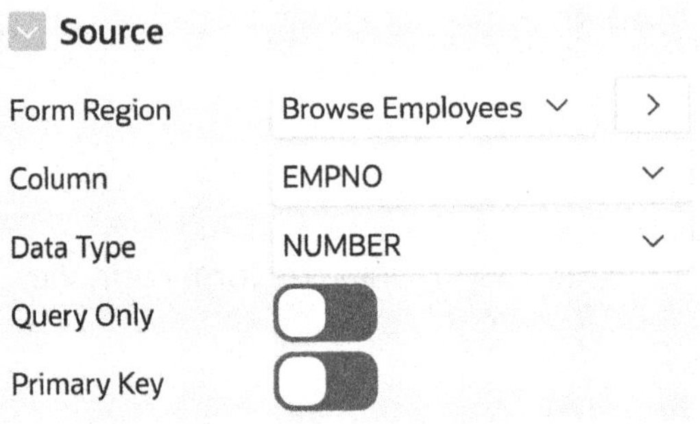

Figure 10-4. *Source properties of a form item*

These items and their property values were created for you when you specified the source of the form region. However, there is one property value that you must specify yourself, and that is the Primary Key property shown in Figure 10-4. The rendering process that comes with the form needs to know which item corresponds to the primary key. So you should turn on the Primary Key property for P29_EMPNO. If you forget to specify a primary key item, APEX will display an error message to remind you.

You are now able to run the page. Figure 10-5 shows what gets displayed. Admittedly, this is not very impressive. To get this form to do anything, you need to make use of its rendering process.

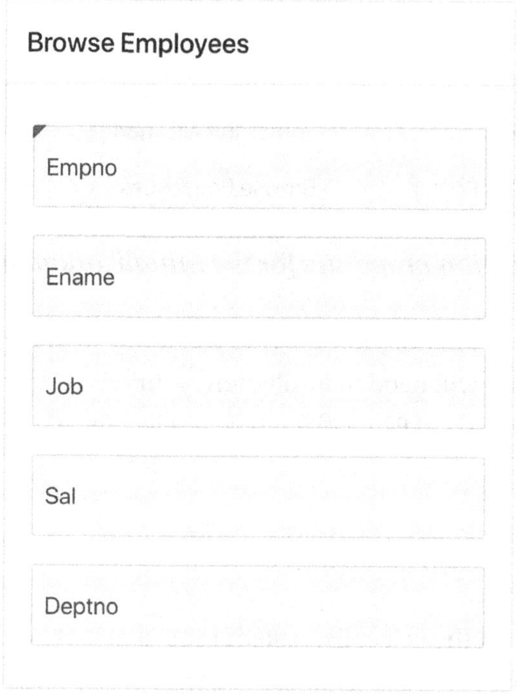

Browse Employees

Empno

Ename

Job

Sal

Deptno

Figure 10-5. *The default form region*

Figure 10-6 shows the Identification section for the rendering process. The default name for the process is Initialize form P, where P is the name of the page. The type of the process is Form-Initialization, which suggests that its purpose is to initialize the form's items. In fact, the initialization process has similar functionality to the GetEmpInfo process of Listing 7-9. If the session state value for P29_EMPNO is not null when the page is rendered, then the process will fetch the EMP record having that employee number and use it to initialize the other items.

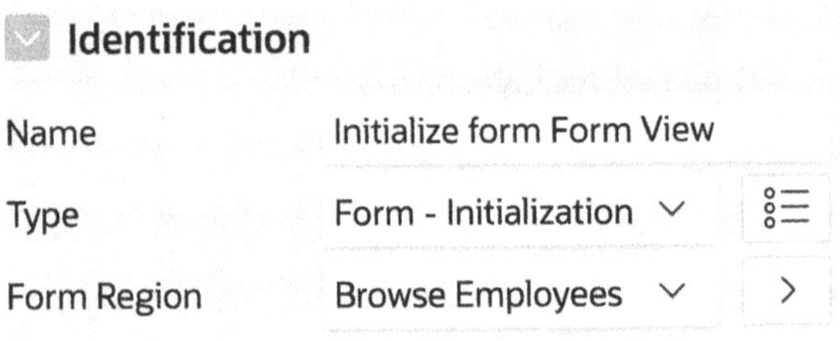

Identification

Name	Initialize form Form View
Type	Form - Initialization ∨
Form Region	Browse Employees ∨

Figure 10-6. *Identification properties for the initialization process*

However, the form region does not provide you a way to place a value for P29_EMPNO into the session state; you will need to implement your own way to do that. The approach I took was to change the type of P29_EMPNO to be a select list whose list-of-values query is

```
select EName, EmpNo
from EMP
order by EName
```

I then set the action of the select list to Redirect and Set Value. Consequently, when an employee name is chosen from the list, the corresponding employee number will be assigned to the item P29_EMPNO. You should verify this in your page. Select an employee name from the list and watch the corresponding employee values appear in the items.

The initialization process also contains previous/next functionality. It works the same as the FindPreviousNext process of Figure 7-18, with the added feature that it also keeps track of the record's position in the table. To configure it, you need to perform the following steps:

- Create two hidden items to hold the previous and next employee numbers. I called these items P29_PREV and P29_NEXT.

- Create a text field item to hold the string that displays the position of the current record. I called this item P29_COUNT.

- Go to the Settings section for the initialization process, and set its Next Primary Key Item, Previous Primary Key Item, and Current Row/Total Item properties as shown in Figure 10-7.

- Create two buttons, called Previous and Next. The Previous button should redirect, setting the value of P29_EMPNO to &P29_PREV., as shown in Figure 10-8. Configure the Next button similarly.

- Optionally, go to the Server-side Condition section for the
  Previous button, and set its condition to the SQL expression **:P29_**
  PREV is not null. Configure the Next button similarly. This causes
  the buttons to be rendered only when appropriate.

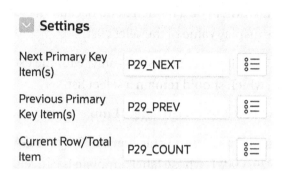

Figure 10-7. *Configuring the form's initialization process*

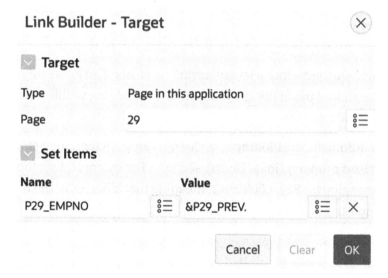

Figure 10-8. *Configuring the action of the Previous button*

At this point, your page should be fully functional. If you are like me, however, you will want to change how it looks. This is where the techniques of Chapter 5 become useful. I invite you to explore different item type, layout, and appearance properties. Here is what I did to get to Figure 10-1:

- Change P29_ENAME to be a hidden item, because its value duplicates the display value of the select list.

- Change the visible items to be display-only, with the exception of P29_EMPNO, which should remain a select list.

- Set the label of P29_EMPNO to **Select Emp**.

- Set the label template of the visible items to Optional-Above. The exception is P29_COUNT, whose label template is Hidden.

- Set the position of the Previous and Next buttons to be Region Body, so that they are displayed with the items.

- Set the sequence numbers of the items and buttons so that the three highest are Next, P29_COUNT, and Previous in that order.

- Position the items into a layout having two rows. The Previous button should begin the second row. The remaining visible items begin new columns.

- If the automatic positioning of an item is not sufficient, then change its Column property (in its Layout section). For example, I set the Column value for P29_COUNT to 3, meaning that it begins at the third grid point.

Form Update

A form can also use its item values to change the database. Page 30 of the Employee Demo application will illustrate the issues. This page is named Form Update and appears in Figure 10-9. The page has two form regions: one to delete/modify an existing record and one to insert a new record. The following subsections discuss each region.

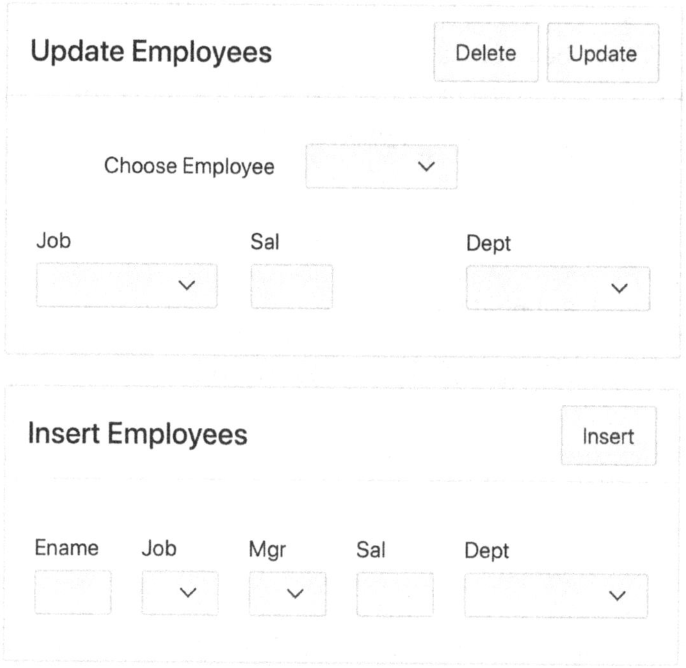

Figure 10-9. *The Form Update page*

Updating Records

The Update Employees region works as follows: a user chooses an employee from the select list. The EMP record for that employee will then be fetched and its values used to initialize the region's items. The user can then modify the item values, as desired. Clicking the Update button will modify that record to have those values. Clicking the Delete button will delete the record.

To create this region, begin by creating a new blank page, named Form Update and having page number 30. Then create a new region of type Form and name it Update Employees. Set the source to the SQL query

```
select EmpNo, Job, Sal, DeptNo
from EMP
```

Look at the resulting rendering tree. APEX has created an item for each of the fields in the query, as well as an initialization process. This is the same situation that you encountered in the Form View page. Before you forget, go to the Source properties for P30_EMPNO (as in Figure 10-4) and turn on its Primary Key property.

You should now customize the form to match Figure 10-9. In particular, change the template of P30_EMPNO to be Optional and the template of the other three items to be Optional-Above. Change the type of P30_EMPNO, P30_JOB, and P30_DEPTNO to be Select List. The list-of-values query for P30_EMPNO should be

```
select EName, EmpNo
from EMP
```

The query for P30_JOB should be

```
select distinct Job as DisplayVal, Job as ResultVal
from EMP
```

And the query for P30_DEPTNO should be

```
select DName, DeptNo
from DEPT
```

You should also create two buttons, named Delete and Update. Their position is Edit, and their action is Submit.

Your form should now be able to successfully retrieve the information for a selected employee. Your remaining task is to get the buttons to perform their intended database modifications. This turns out to be surprisingly easy.

A form region's ability to modify the database is disabled by default. To enable it, go to the rendering tree for the form region, click its Attributes node, and look at the Enabled property in the Edit section. By default, this property is turned off. When you turn it on, additional properties will be displayed, as shown in Figure 10-10. The checkboxes allow you to specify which editing operations the region should allow. The Update Employees region performs updates and deletes, so you should ensure that only Update Row and Delete Row are checked.

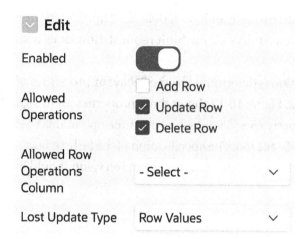

Figure 10-10. *A form region's edit properties*

As an aside, note the `Lost Update Type` property at the bottom of Figure 10-10. This property lets you specify how the process should implement lost update detection. Its default value is `Row Values`, which corresponds to the lost update detection algorithm of Listing 7-10.

When you enable editing in a form region, APEX adds a process to the `Processing` tab. This process has the type `Form-Automatic Row Processing (DML)` and is known as an *ARP process*. The default name of the process is `Process form R`, where R is the name of the form region. Figure 10-11 shows the `Identification` properties for the `Update Employees` process.

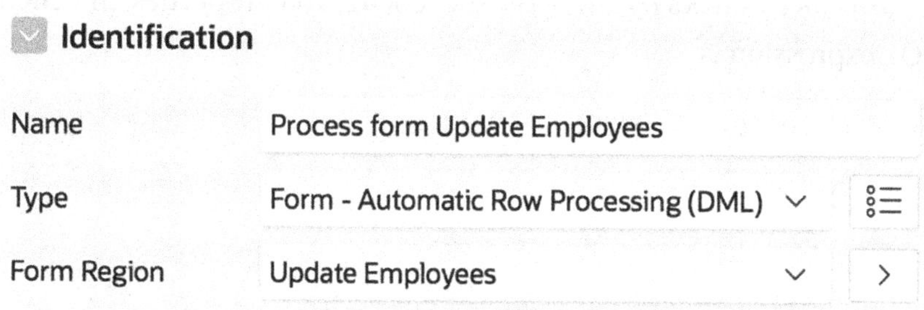

> ### Identification
>
> | | |
> |---|---|
> | Name | Process form Update Employees |
> | Type | Form - Automatic Row Processing (DML) ∨ |
> | Form Region | Update Employees ∨ |

Figure 10-11. *ARP process properties*

An ARP process can execute an insert, delete, or update operation in response to a submit action. But given a particular submit request, how does it know which operation to execute?

The desired operation is determined by the Behavior properties of the button performing the request. Figure 10-12 shows these properties for the Update button. The Database Action property specifies which of the three operations to execute. In the figure, this value is SQL UPDATE action. The specification of the Delete button is similar—its Action value should be Submit Page and its Database Action value should be SQL DELETE action.

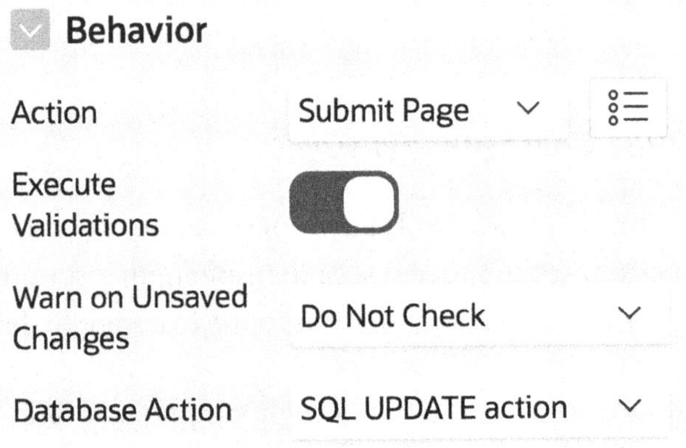

Figure 10-12. *Configuring the behavior of the Update button*

An ARP process can be conditionally executed, just like any other process. The ARP process for the Update Employees region should fire when the Update or Delete button is clicked. Figure 10-13 shows its Server-side Condition properties, in which the specified SQL expression is

```
:REQUEST = 'Update' or :REQUEST = 'Delete'
```

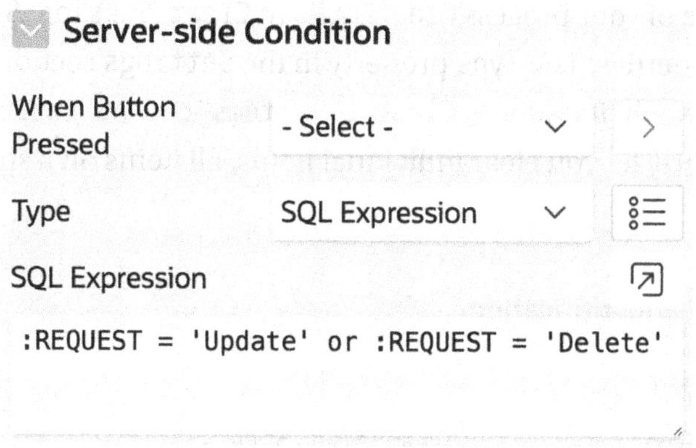

Figure 10-13. *Specifying the condition for a process*

Clearing Session State

Take some time to run your Form Update page. Choose a record, modify its values, and click the Update button. Everything should work. However, you will discover a problem with the Delete button. When you click it, APEX will display an error message.

The problem is that after the deletion, the item P30_EMPNO still contains the deleted employee number. So during page rendering, the initialization process will attempt to fetch values from this nonexistent record, thereby generating the error. The solution is to set P30_EMPNO to null after the deletion occurs. In fact, this is exactly what you did in the PL/SQL code for the DeleteEmp process shown in Listing 7-21.

But how to get the Delete button on page 30 to set the value of an item? Since you cannot touch the built-in ARP process, your only option is to create another process that will execute after the deletion occurs. Let's call this process ClearEmpNo.

One way to implement ClearEmpNo is as a PL/SQL process having the following code:

```
begin
    :P30_EMPNO := null;
end;
```

Those of us familiar with PL/SQL coding realize that this is a straightforward, simple solution. But APEX has another solution for those unfamiliar with PL/SQL, namely, the Clear Session State process type. Here is how to use it.

Change the type of your process ClearEmpNo to Clear Session State. Figure 10-14 shows its initial properties. The Type property in the Settings section specifies which items to clear. By default, its value is Clear all items on the Current Page. Other values for the property let you clear individual items, all items on a specified page, or all items on all pages.

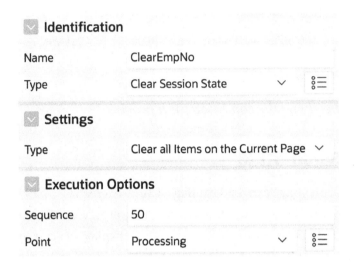

Figure 10-14. *Properties of a Clear Session State process*

Although the default value is perfectly fine, it is also reasonable to change the type to Clear Items. If you do, then you will be able to enter explicit item names for the Item(s) property, as shown in Figure 10-15.

Settings

Type	Clear Items	∨
Item(s)	P30_EMPNO	

Figure 10-15. *Configuring a process to clear P30_EMPNO*

No matter how you create the `ClearEmpNo` process, you must perform the following two steps to ensure that it only executes after a delete operation:

- You must set the value of its `When Button Pressed` property to `Delete`.

- You must set its sequence value (shown in Figure 10-14) to be larger than that of the ARP process.

Inserting Records

The second region of the `Form Update` page of Figure 10-9 is called `Insert Employees`. It works as follows: A user enters values into the five items of the region and clicks the `Insert` button. APEX will then insert a record into the EMP table, using default values for the unmentioned fields.

An ARP process can only insert values appearing in page items. Thus, it is important that the `Insert Employees` region have an item for each field of EMP. In other words, the source of the form should be the query `select * from EMP`. You can then hide the items that are to receive default values.

When you create a form region having the preceding source, APEX will immediately inform you of a problem. The issue is that several of its generated items have duplicate names. The name of a generated item is based entirely on the name of its corresponding field, so a field name that appears in multiple forms on the page will have multiple items with the same name.

Fortunately, the solution is simple; just rename the problematic items. Figure 10-16 shows my strategy, which was to add "`INSERT`" to all items in the `Insert Employees` region, duplicate or not.

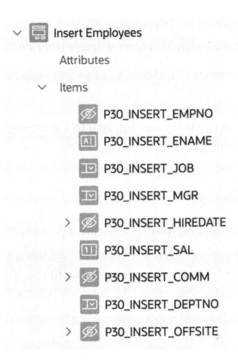

Figure 10-16. *Renaming duplicate items*

The two initialization processes also have duplicate names. To resolve the problem, I renamed each one to have the name of their region, as shown in Figure 10-17.

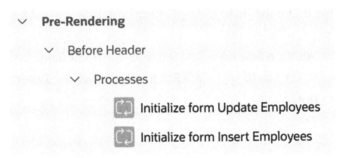

Figure 10-17. *Renaming duplicate initialization processes*

You have now resolved all of the issues with the region, so APEX will finally let you save your changes. Your remaining tasks are similar to what you did for the Update Employees form:

- Turn on the Primary Key property for P30_INSERT_EMPNO in its Source section.

- Turn on the Enabled property in the Edit section of the Insert Employee Attributes. Then ensure that only the Add Row operation is checked.

- Create a button named Insert. Configure its Action property to be Submit Page and its Database Action property to be SQL INSERT action.

- Go to the property editor for the ARP process named Process form Insert Employees, and give its When Button Pressed property the value Insert.

- Format the type and layout of the items according to your taste.

If you try out your new region, you will discover one further problem, namely, that the form expects you to always have values for P30_EMPNO and P30_INSERT_EMPNO. This requirement was appropriate when Update Employees was the only region, because the Delete and Update operations make no sense without an employee number. But P30_EMPNO can (and should) be null when the Insert button is pressed. Similarly, P30_INSERT_EMPNO should be null when the Delete and Update buttons are pressed. Thus, you need to disable the Value Required property in the Validation section of both items.

The Insert operation places the new employee number into P30_INSERT_EMPNO. Although the item is hidden, its value can be part of the Success Message property of the ARP process, as shown in Figure 10-18.

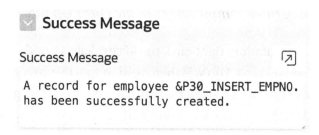

Figure 10-18. Improving the Insert button's success message

Computations

The Insert Employees region shown in Figure 10-9 only displays items for the columns ENAme, Job, Salary, and DeptNo; the items for HireDate, Comm, and Offsite are hidden. The idea is these hidden items will contain default values—in particular, P30_INSERT_HIREDATE will contain the current day, P30_INSERT_COMM will be 0, and P30_INSERT_OFFSITE will be 'N'. The ARP process will use the values of these items when it performs its insertion operation.

The question, then, is how to get default values into the hidden items. The answer is to use an APEX *computation*. A computation is a page component that assigns a value to one item. The idea is to create a computation for each item that needs a default value and to arrange for these computations to be executed before the ARP process executes. In that way, the computed values will wind up as part of the session state, and the ARP process will use them when it creates a new record.

The Form Update page has a computation for each of the three items that needs a default value. Figure 10-19 shows the Processing tab of the page designer with the three computations listed. Note that the execution point of the computations is After Submit, which means that they will execute before any of the processes.

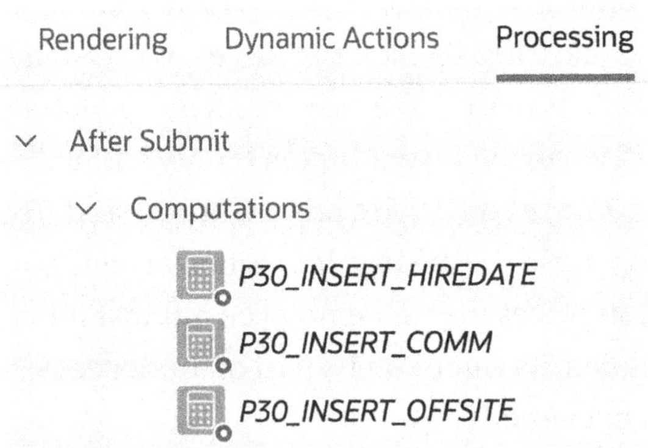

Figure 10-19. *Adding three computations to the Form Update page*

To create a new computation, right-click the After Submit node of Figure 10-19 and select Create Computation. You will then need to specify properties for its Identification and Computation sections. Figure 10-20 shows the property values for the P30_INSERT_HIREDATE computation. The Identification section has the property

Item Name, in which you specify the target item. The Computation section has the property Type, in which you specify how the item's value is computed. In Figure 10-20, the type is SQL Expression, and the expression is simply a call to the SQL function current_date.

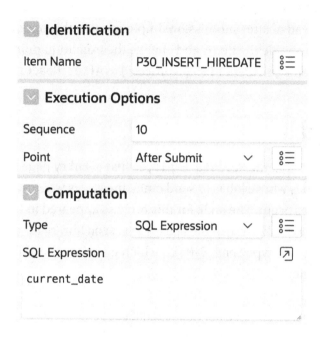

Figure 10-20. *Properties for the HireDate computation*

The other two computations are created similarly. The simplest way to specify a constant is to use the type Static Value, but you can also specify it using an SQL expression.

Instead of creating three computations, you could achieve the same effect using a single PL/SQL process, as shown in Listing 10-1. The execution point of the process would be After Submit, the same as the computations.

Listing 10-1. PL/SQL Code Equivalent to Three Computations

```
begin
    P30_INSERT_HIREDATE := current_date;
    P30_INSERT_COMM := 0;
    P30_INSERT_OFFSITE := 'N';
end;
```

I intentionally hid the items P30_INSERT_HIREDATE, P30_INSERT_COMM, and P30_INSERT_OFFSITE in Figure 10-9 to keep users from changing their default values. Another design option is to display these items with their default values already filled in. The user can then treat these values as suggestions and modify them if desired.

This option implies that the computed values should be assigned to the items during page rendering, instead of after submission. Implementing this option is straightforward. All you need to do is unhide the items and change the execution point of the three computations (or their equivalent PL/SQL process) to After Header.

Sending Email

Recall from Chapter 7 that the Revised Employee Data Entry page has a process SendSuspiciousEmail, whose job is to send email messages when suspicious database deletions and updates occur. The code for this process appeared in Listing 7-14. It is written in PL/SQL and makes use of the apex_mail.send library function.

APEX has the process type Send E-Mail, which gives you the ability to send email without having to write PL/SQL code. This section will show how to use this process to achieve the same functionality as in Listing 7-14.

Create a new process for page 30. Call it SendSuspiciousEmail, and give it the type Send E-Mail. In the property editor, look for the Settings section. You will need to specify values for the properties From, To, Subject, and Body Plain Text. Figure 10-21 shows how I entered these values. (If you want to test the process, be sure to use your own email address as the recipient.)

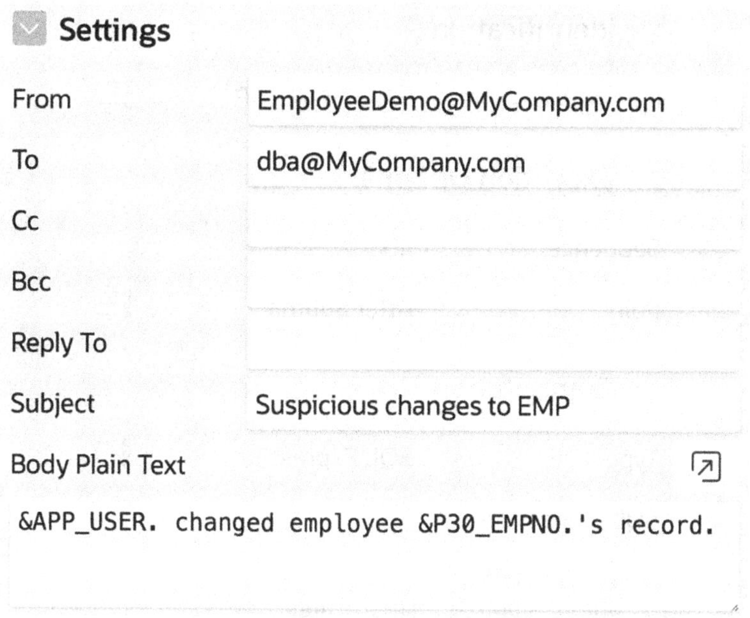

Settings

From	EmployeeDemo@MyCompany.com
To	dba@MyCompany.com
Cc	
Bcc	
Reply To	
Subject	Suspicious changes to EMP
Body Plain Text	↗

```
&APP_USER. changed employee &P30_EMPNO.'s record.
```

Figure 10-21. *Properties for a Send E-Mail process*

The body text makes use of the APP_USER variable and the item P30_EMPNO to identify the user and the affected employee number. This behavior is the same as in Listing 7-14, except for one feature—the body of the email does not indicate whether the operation was a delete or an update. Listing 7-14 implemented this feature by an if-statement inside the PL/SQL code. How can you do the same thing when you use a process of type Send E-Mail?

The trick is to first create a hidden item to hold the value you need to compute and then create a computation for it. For example, my hidden item is called P30_EMAIL_OP. Figure 10-22 shows the relevant properties of its computation. I then changed the value of the Body Plain Text property in the SendSuspiciousEmail process to be the following expression:

```
&APP_EMP. &P30_EMAIL_OP. employee &P30_EMPNO.'s record.
```

For example, a possible email message arising from this expression could be

```
boris@secret.org deleted employee 7839's record.
```

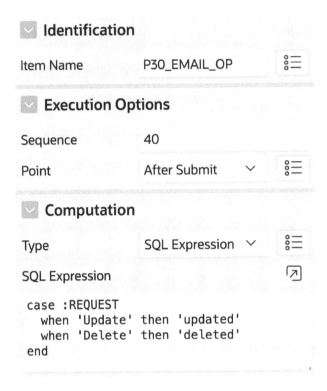

Figure 10-22. *A computation to identify the request*

Finally, you need to specify when the SendSuspiciousEmail process executes. Its server-side condition should specify what is meant by a "suspicious" change to the database. I chose to use the same condition shown in Figure 7-16. In addition, the sequence number of the process must be chosen such that it executes after the database operation but before the ClearEmpNo process clears the deleted employee number from P30_EMPNO.

Report with Form Pages

An APEX Form region automatically generates items for you and provides two powerful built-in processes, which save you time over having to write comparable items and PL/SQL processes. However, you still need to create and configure additional buttons and items. To simplify your work further, APEX provides wizards for creating prebuilt form pages. You enter your information into the wizard and it creates the necessary regions, items, buttons, and processes. Such wizards can be effective shortcuts if you want what they produce.

A list of these wizards can be found starting from the initial Create Page screen of Figure 2-9. Instead of clicking the usual Blank Page icon, select the Form icon. APEX will display the screen shown in Figure 10-23, which contains icons for the form-related wizards. The Report with Form wizard is a good illustrative example, so let's begin with that.

A Report with Form page is actually two pages—a report page and a form page. It works similarly to the Single Row Update page in Figure 7-24, but the report and form are on two separate pages instead of being on separate regions of the same page.

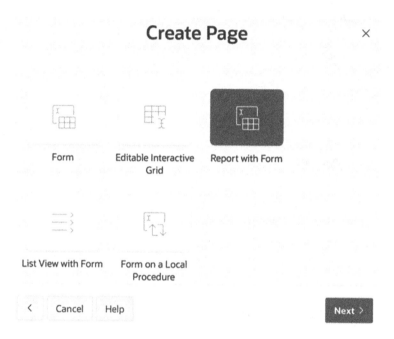

Figure 10-23. *APEX wizards to create form pages*

Clicking the Next button in Figure 10-23 displays the first Report with Form wizard screen, shown in Figure 10-24. The Report Type property asks you to specify whether the report should be an interactive report, an interactive grid (to be discussed in Chapter 11), or a classic report; I chose Classic Report. The next four properties ask you to provide a page number and name for the report and form pages. In my application, the report is on page 31 and the form is on page 32. Finally, you are asked to specify whether the form page should display normally or as a modal dialog box. (Modal pages were discussed at the end of Chapter 2; see Figure 2-15.) I chose Normal in the figure, but Modal Dialog is also interesting and worthwhile.

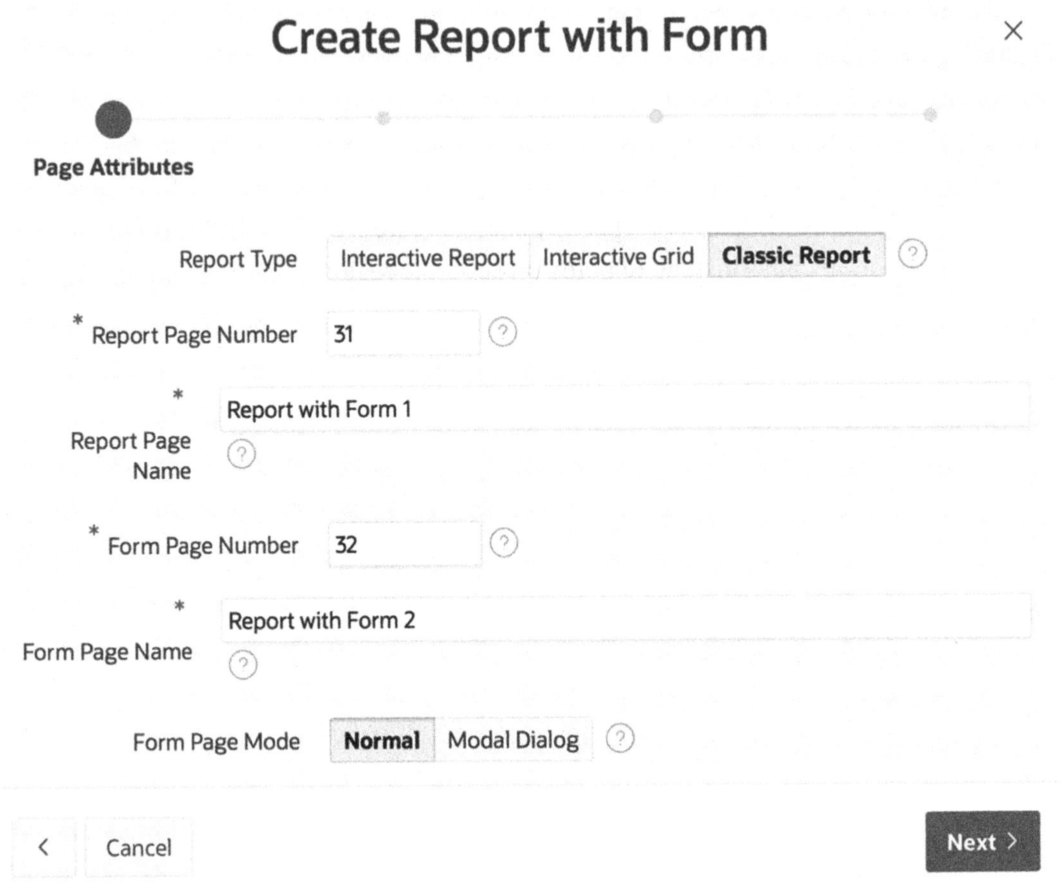

Create Report with Form   ✕

Page Attributes

Report Type	Interactive Report Interactive Grid **Classic Report** ⓘ
* Report Page Number	31 ⓘ
* Report Page Name ⓘ	Report with Form 1
* Form Page Number	32 ⓘ
* Form Page Name ⓘ	Report with Form 2
Form Page Mode	**Normal** Modal Dialog ⓘ

‹   Cancel   Next ›

Figure 10-24. *Creating report with form pages*

Clicking the Next button brings you to the second wizard screen, shown in Figure 10-25. This screen asks you to supply a data source to be used for both the report and the form. If you are planning to use the form for insertion then the source will need to contain the entire table, as shown in the figure. In this case, the wizard screen also lets you specify the columns that you want displayed in the report.

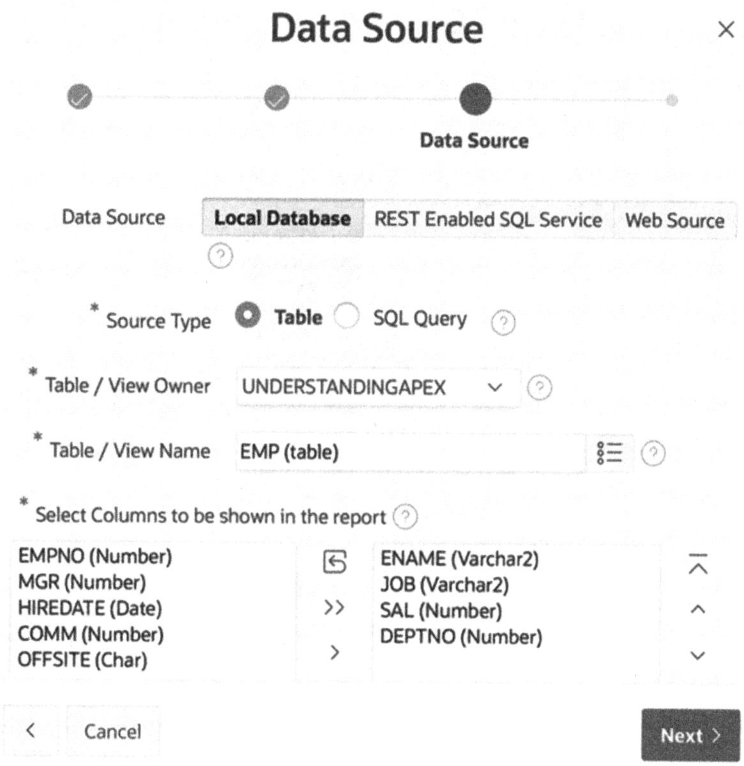

Data Source   ×

Data Source

| Data Source | **Local Database** | REST Enabled SQL Service | Web Source |

* Source Type   ◉ **Table** ◯ SQL Query ⓘ

* Table / View Owner   UNDERSTANDINGAPEX   ∨ ⓘ

* Table / View Name   EMP (table)   ☰ ⓘ

* Select Columns to be shown in the report ⓘ

EMPNO (Number)	↰	ENAME (Varchar2)	⌃̅
MGR (Number)		JOB (Varchar2)	
HIREDATE (Date)	≫	SAL (Number)	⌃
COMM (Number)		DEPTNO (Number)	
OFFSITE (Char)	›		⌄

‹   Cancel   Next ›

Figure 10-25. *Entering the source query for the report and form*

The third screen (not shown) is where you specify the navigation menu entry for the report page. Note that the form page does not get a menu entry because it should only be accessed via its report page.

The fourth screen, shown in Figure 10-26, lets you specify the source columns you want displayed in the form. It also forces you to specify the primary key column.

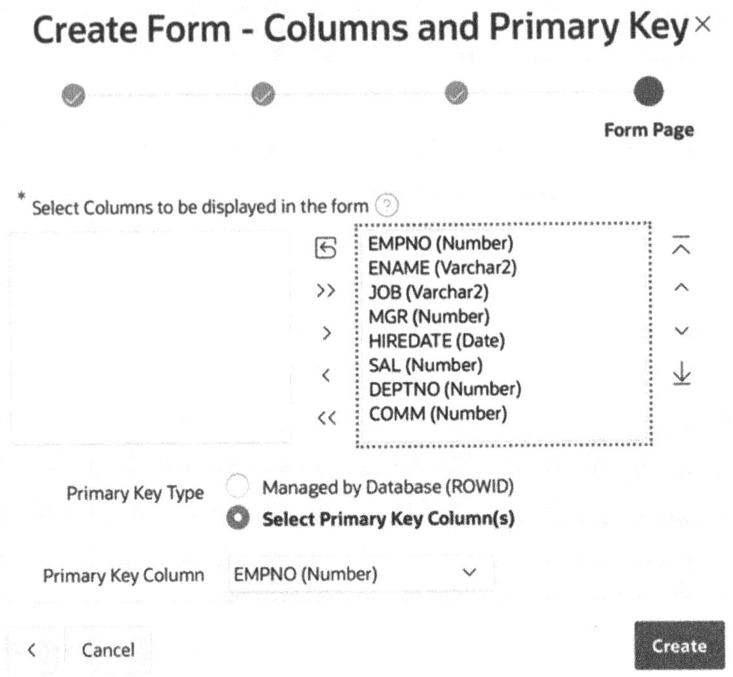

Figure 10-26. *Specifying the primary key column*

When at last you click the Create button, APEX will create two fully functional pages. Figure 10-27 shows the result of running the report page. (I chopped off the bottom to save space.)

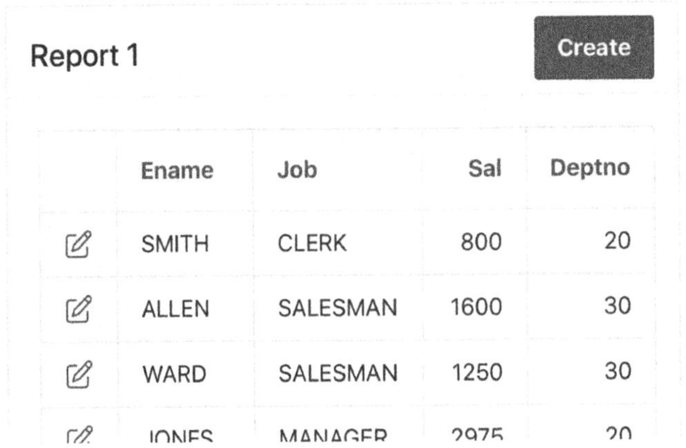

Figure 10-27. *The Report with Form report page*

There are two ways to get from the report page to the form page. Clicking the CREATE button brings up the form page in insert mode, as shown in Figure 10-28. Alternatively, clicking the link at the beginning of a row brings up the form page in update/delete mode, populated with the values for the selected employee. Figure 10-29 shows the form page after clicking the link for WARD.

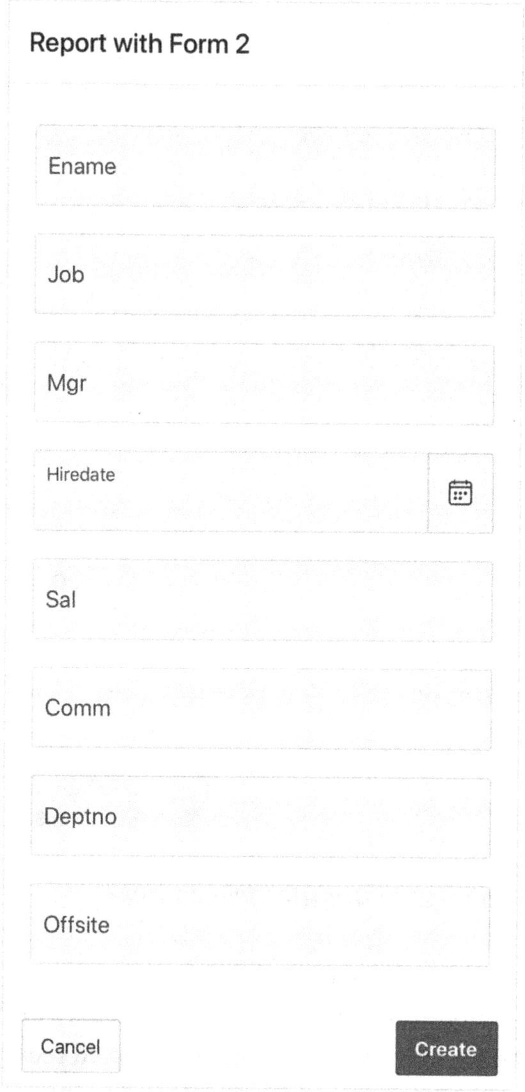

Figure 10-28. *The form page in insert mode*

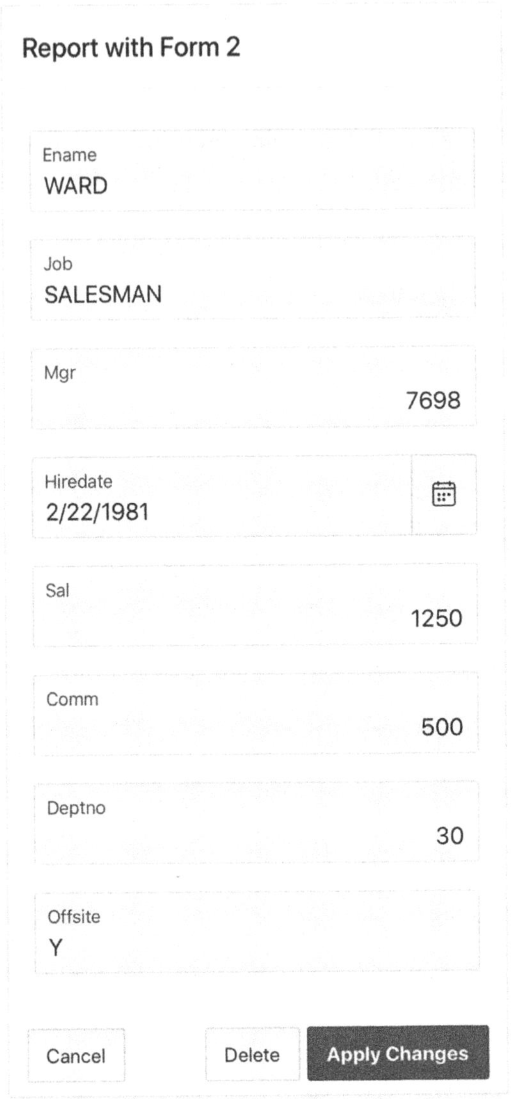

Report with Form 2

Ename
WARD

Job
SALESMAN

Mgr
7698

Hiredate   📅
2/22/1981

Sal
1250

Comm
500

Deptno
30

Offsite
Y

Cancel   Delete   **Apply Changes**

Figure 10-29. *The form page in update/delete mode*

Note that the buttons on the form page differ according to its mode. In insert mode, the page displays a Create button, which inserts a new record into the EMP table. In update/delete mode, the Delete button deletes the selected record and the Apply Changes button updates it. All three buttons return to the report page after changing the table. The Cancel button is common to both modes; it simply returns to the report page without changing the table.

The following subsections investigate how the wizard implemented these pages.

The Report Page

The report page (Figure 10-27) has one region, which I chose to be a classic report. Its implementation is completely straightforward. The only interesting feature is the EMPNO column, which has the type Link (as described in Chapter 3). Figure 10-30 shows its Link Builder screen. It specifies that the link will redirect to page 32 (the form page) and will set the item P32_EMPNO to the employee number of the selected row.

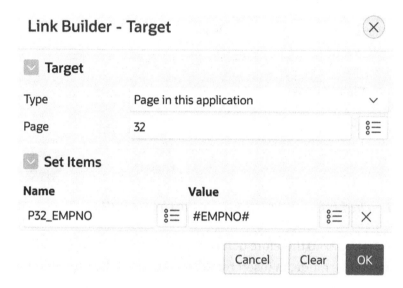

Figure 10-30. *The Link Builder screen for the EMPNO column*

The action of the Create button is to redirect to the form page and clear its session state, as shown by the Link Builder screen of Figure 10-31. Compare these two figures. They both redirect to the form page; their difference is that a row link assigns a value to P32_EMPNO, whereas the Create button clears the value of P32_EMPNO (as well as all other items on the page).

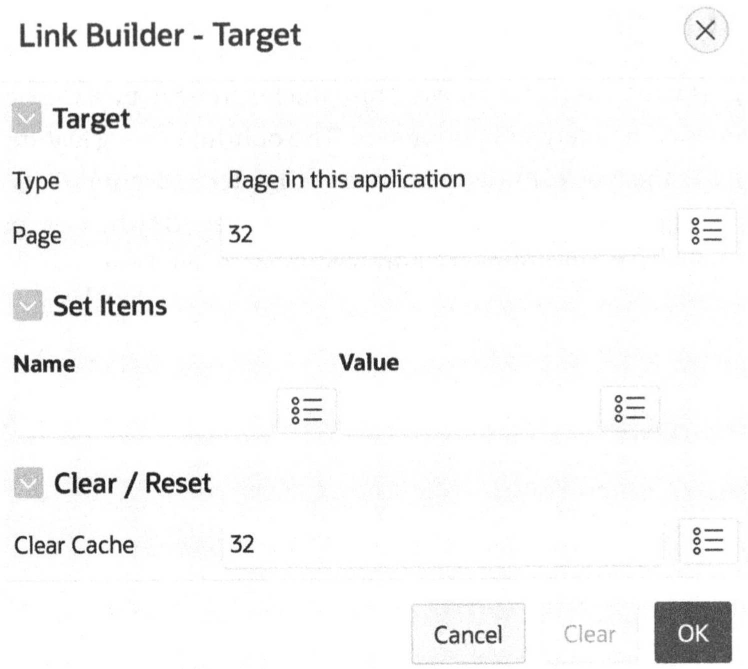

Link Builder - Target   ⊗

⌄ Target

Type   Page in this application

Page   32   ≡

⌄ Set Items

Name   **Value**

                          ≡   ≡

⌄ Clear / Reset

Clear Cache   32   ≡

                                            Cancel   Clear   OK

Figure 10-31. *The Link Builder screen for the Create button.*

The value of P32_EMPNO therefore determines whether the form page is in insert mode or update/delete mode. In insert mode, the values of the page items will all be null because the Create button cleared them. In delete mode, the values of the page items will all have a value, due to the action of the initialization process.

The Create button is rendered in blue to indicate that it is a "hot" button. The relevant property is named Hot and is in the button's Appearance section, as shown in Figure 5-29.

The Form Page

The form page (Figures 10-28 and 10-29) has a single region, of type Form. Figure 10-32 shows its rendering tree. As with all form regions, it has an initialization process, as well as an item for each source value. (Those items are not shown in the figure to save space.) The main difference from a standard form region is that it also has four buttons. The CANCEL button redirects to the report page. The other three buttons are configured to have a Database Action value of SQL INSERT action, SQL DELETE action, and SQL UPDATE action.

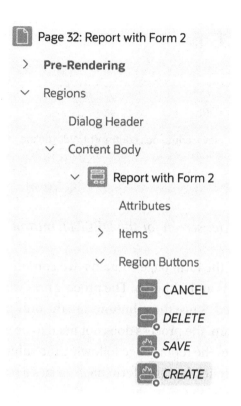

Figure 10-32. *The rendering tree for the form page*

Recall that the DELETE and SAVE buttons are rendered only when the page is in update/delete mode and the CREATE button is rendered only in insert mode. The form uses the value of P32_EMPNO to determine the conditional rendering. If it is null, then CREATE is rendered; otherwise, DELETE and SAVE are rendered. The form page also contains a branch that redirects to the report page after the submit processing has finished.

The action of the CREATE and SAVE buttons is Submit Page. Interestingly, the action of the DELETE button is Redirect to URL, where the URL is

```
javascript:apex.confirm(htmldb_delete_message,'DELETE');
```

Figure 10-33 shows the Link Builder screen for this action. The JavaScript function apex.confirm displays a confirmation window; clicking Yes causes the page to submit using the request named DELETE. In other words, the DELETE button actually does perform a submit, albeit indirectly through JavaScript.

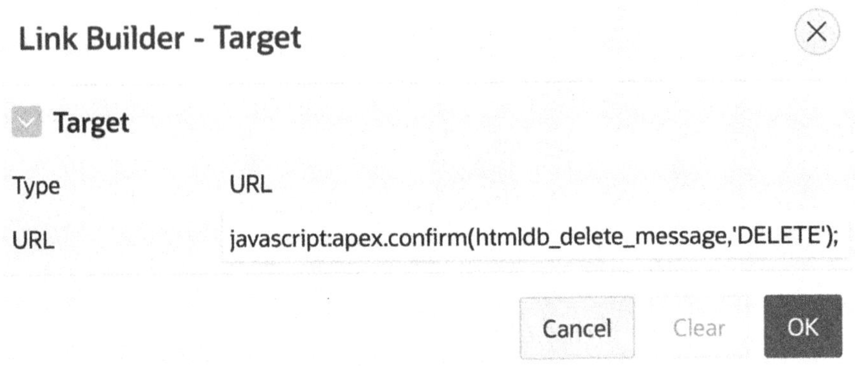

Link Builder - Target   ⊗

☑ **Target**

Type	URL
URL	javascript:apex.confirm(htmldb_delete_message,'DELETE');

[Cancel] [Clear] [**OK**]

Figure 10-33. *Link Builder screen for the DELETE button*

The `Processing` tab of the form page contains two components: the ARP process common to all form regions and a branch. The process fires when the CREATE, SAVE, or DELETE button is clicked. Since these buttons are the only components on the page that perform a submit action, the process does not need to be conditional. The branch unconditionally redirects to the report page following the submit processing, which explains why every button click from the form page causes a return to the report page.

Customizing the Report and Form

Although the `Report with Form` wizard produces fully functional pages, they are raw and unpolished. It is unlikely that you would want to use them as is in any real application. Instead, you ought to think of them as the foundation of a more expansive, customized application. These customizations fall into three basic categories: aesthetic, functional, and organizational.

The aesthetic customizations improve the look and feel of the application. For example, you can use the techniques of Chapter 3 to improve the format of the report and its columns and the techniques of Chapter 5 to improve the appearance and layout of the buttons and items. You can change the default region titles, button text, and item labels.

Another aesthetic issue concerns the visibility of form items. Recall from Figure 10-25 that the `Report with Form` wizard asked you to specify the items that should appear in the form page. The problem is that the form page gets used for both insert and update, and these two operations have different requirements. For example, the insert operation needs to have items for all columns, but you might want to hide the items for columns that receive default values. Moreover, the update operation should only show items for updatable columns. Therefore, it would be a good idea to provide a Server-side Condition expression for each item, specifying when that item should be visible.

Alternatively, you could choose to disable an item instead of hiding it. Each item has a property section Read Only, which lets you specify a condition, much like the Server-side Condition section does. Whereas Server-side Condition hides an item, Read Only makes it unmodifiable. So, for example, in update mode, it might be a good idea to display the entire record, but format the unmodifiable ones (such as EName) as read-only.

Functional customizations add features to the pages generated by the wizard. For example, you could add Previous and Next buttons to the form page. You could also modify the insert and update operations so that they remain on the form page after changing the database, as in the Single Row Update page of Figure 7-24.

Organization-related customizations involve adding or deleting pages and regions and moving existing page components among them. For example, the report and form regions could be moved to the same page. Or you could split the form region into two regions— one for insertion and one for update/delete—as in the Single Row Update page. Or you could even have three form regions, as in the Employee Data Entry page of Figure 7-5.

Form Pages

The two pages created by the Report with Form wizard are very loosely connected. Their only interaction is when a link on the report page or its Create button is clicked, both of which set the value of the item P32_EMPNO on the form page. Consequently, the form page can be used in conjunction with other kinds of page, the only requirement being that the other page provides the form page with an employee number.

In this section, instead of connecting a report with a form, I want to connect a *tree* with a form. A tree depicts a table's records hierarchically, which is possible when the table has a field that can be the basis of the hierarchy. For example, the Mgr field of EMP determines a hierarchy, known in business as the *management hierarchy*. The president, who has no manager, is the root of the hierarchy. Every other employee is the child of its manager.

Page 33 of the Employee Demo application displays the employee records as a tree. This page is named Management Hierarchy Tree and appears in Figure 10-34. Each node of the tree displays an employee name. Clicking a name redirects to a form page, named Management Hierarchy Form, that displays additional values for that employee and gives you the opportunity to update them or to delete the employee's record. Figure 10-35 shows the form page that results from clicking ADAMS.

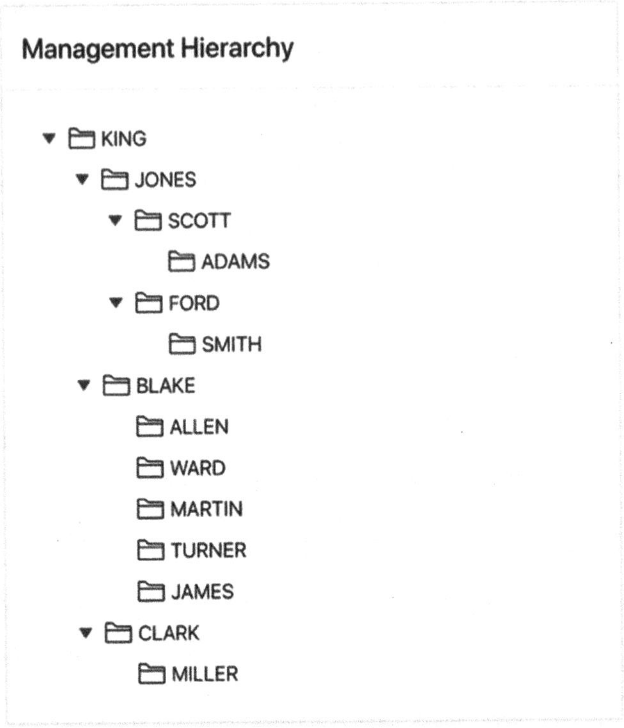

Figure 10-34. *The Management Hierarchy tree page*

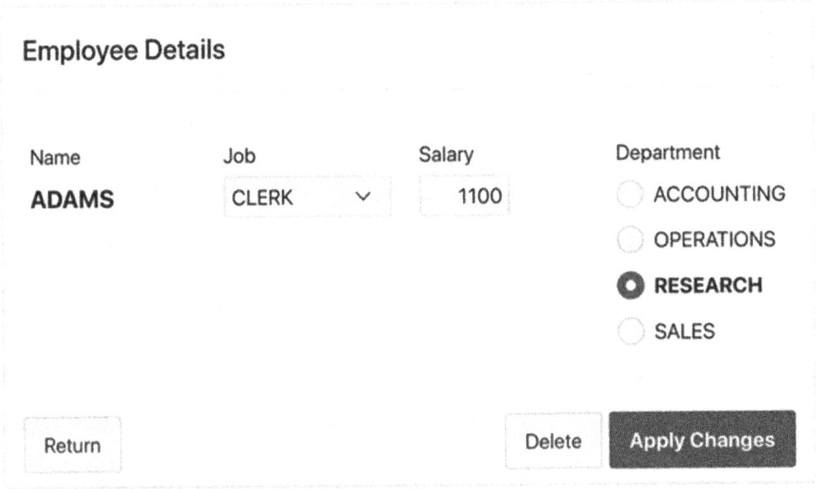

Figure 10-35. *The Management Hierarchy form page*

Implementing the Tree Page

Although APEX has a page wizard to create trees, it is more instructive (and simpler!) to create the page yourself. So create page 33 as a blank page named Management Hierarchy Tree, and create a region of type Tree. Its source should be the EMP table.

The properties to configure the tree are in the region's Setting section, which you get to from the Attributes node in the rendering tree. Figure 10-36 shows the Settings properties for the tree of Figure 10-34.

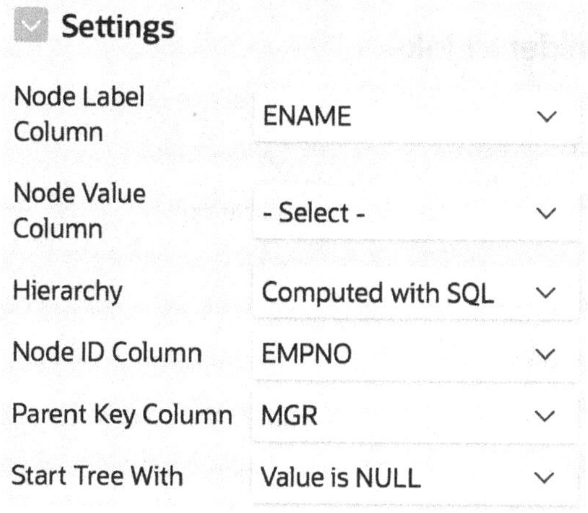

Settings

Node Label Column	ENAME
Node Value Column	- Select -
Hierarchy	Computed with SQL
Node ID Column	EMPNO
Parent Key Column	MGR
Start Tree With	Value is NULL

Figure 10-36. *Tree region settings*

The property named Hierarchy should have the value Computed with SQL, which tells APEX to compute the hierarchy from the following settings:

- Node Label Column is the field whose values are the labels of the tree nodes.

- Node Id Column is the primary key field.

- Parent Key Column is the field that defines the hierarchy. A record's value for this field specifies the primary key of its parent.

- Start Tree With specifies the root of the hierarchy. The setting Value is NULL asserts that the root of the hierarchy is the record whose parent key column value is null.

Run your page at this point, and explore the tree. If a node has children, there will be an arrow to its left. Clicking on these arrows will expand or contract their list of children.

The final configuration step is to specify what happens when a user clicks a node in the tree. The property you need is Link, which is further down the Settings section. Clicking its box brings up the Link Builder wizard. Figure 10-37 shows how I configured the link. It specifies that clicking the node redirects to page 34 and sets the value of P34_EMPNO to the node's EMPNO value. Note that substitution string syntax is used to reference the value of a node's field.

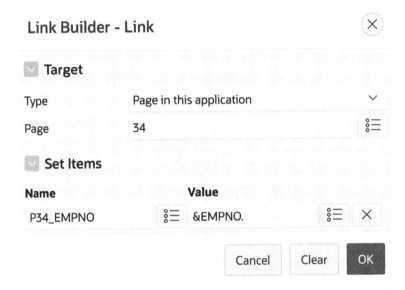

Figure 10-37. Specifying the link to the form page

Implementing the Form Page

Page 34 of the Employee Demo application is the form page shown in Figure 10-35. It is easy enough to implement it by creating a blank page and adding a Form region to it. However, it is even easier to use a wizard to create the form page itself.

Looking back at the Create Page screen of Figure 10-23, you can see an icon for a wizard named Form. Clicking it brings up the Create Form screen of Figure 10-38.

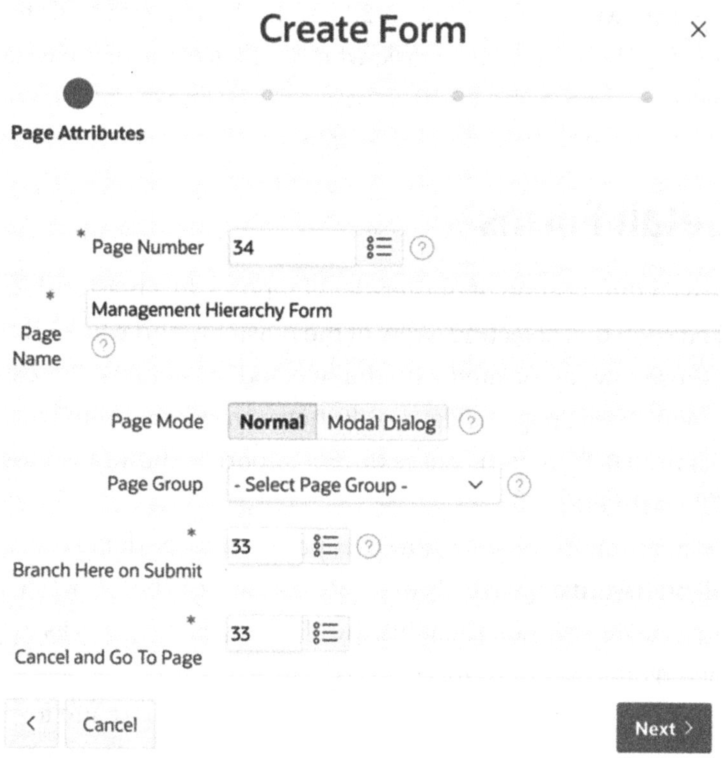

Create Form   ✕

Page Attributes

* Page Number   34   ⦀ ⓘ

*
Management Hierarchy Form

Page ⓘ
Name

Page Mode   **Normal**   Modal Dialog   ⓘ

Page Group   - Select Page Group -   ⌄   ⓘ

*
33   ⦀ ⓘ

Branch Here on Submit

*
33   ⦀

Cancel and Go To Page

‹   Cancel   Next ›

Figure 10-38. *The first screen of the Create Form wizard*

After asking for the page number and name, the wizard requests two things: the page that the form should branch to after a submit (i.e., the Delete and Apply Changes buttons) and after a redirect (i.e., the Cancel button). The remaining screens are similar to what you've seen before—a screen asking about the navigation menu, a screen requesting the source, and a final screen requesting the primary key.

The form page generated by the wizard should work seamlessly with the tree page, without any additional configuration on your part—the tree redirects to the form when a tree node is clicked, and the form redirects to the tree when a button is clicked. My form page in Figure 10-35 is the result of simply changing the type and layout of the items generated by the wizard.

I want to stress that the form page generated by the Form wizard is exactly the same as the form page generated by the Report with Form wizard—the only difference between the two wizards is that Report with Form also generates a page containing a Create button and a report. Moreover, the page generated by the Form wizard is exactly the same as a blank page with a Form region, plus a few buttons and property settings.

The other form-based wizards in Figure 10-23 are similar to `Report with Form`. Knowing this can help you decide, for any given task, whether to use one of the wizards or to write the pages yourself.

Master-Detail Forms

Chapter 6 discussed the creation of master-detail reports. In a master-detail report, two reports are linked such that selecting a row of the master report causes the detail report to display only those rows associated with the selected master row. For example, the `Employees by Department` page in Figure 6-8 shows an `EMP` report linked to the master `DEPT` report; clicking a `DEPT` record causes the `EMP` report to show only those employees in the selected department.

In this section, I want to consider how to expand a master-detail report to include updates. A straightforward approach is to create two sets of `Report with Form` pages, one for `DEPT` and one for `EMP`, and then link the `DEPT` and `EMP` reports as in Chapter 6. Let's see how much effort this requires.

Begin by using the `Report with Form` wizard to create report and form pages for `DEPT`. The report page is named `Master Report` and is page 35; the form page is named `Master Form` and is page 36. The page source is `select * from DEPT`.

Then use the wizard to create report and form pages for `EMP`. The pages are numbered 37 and 38; the report page is named `Detail Report` and the form page is named `Detail Form`. Their source is `select * from EMP`.

At this point, you have two unrelated sets of pages. Their report pages need to be related as follows:

- The master report needs a link column that takes you to the detail report.

- The detail report needs to display only the records associated with the selected detail row.

- The detail report needs a button that returns you to the master report.

Figures 10-39 and 10-40 show these two reports. Figure 10-40 shows the result of clicking "view emps" for the `ACCOUNTING` department. Note that I changed the region titles on both pages from what the wizard generated. In particular, the title of the detail region is customized with the department name.

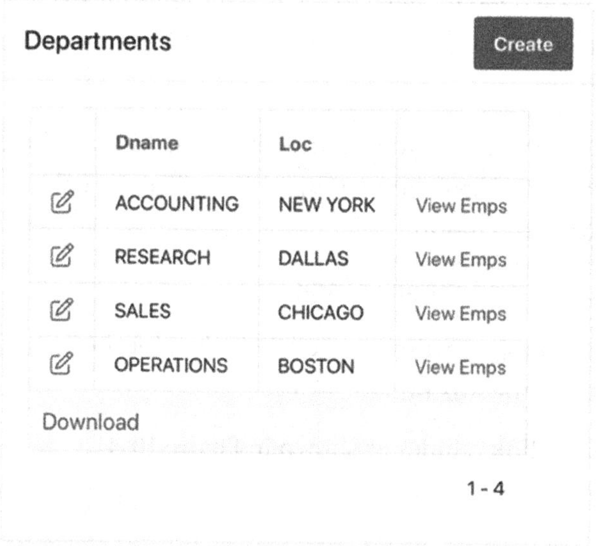

Figure 10-39. *The master report*

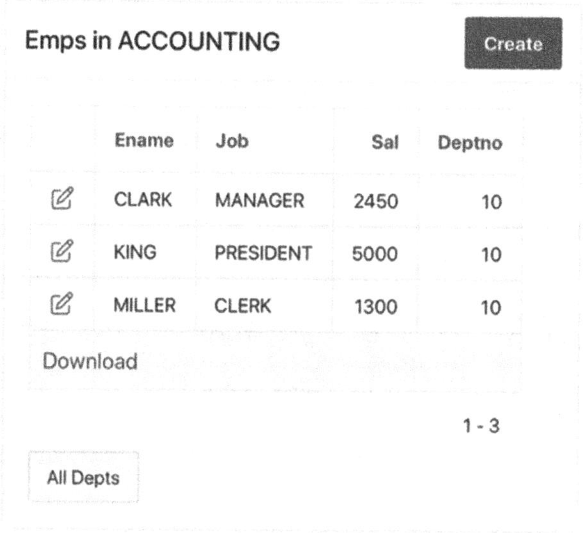

Figure 10-40. *The detail report*

The only change you need to make to the master report is to create the additional "view emps" column. To do that, you should create and configure a *virtual column* for the report, as follows:

- Right-click the Columns node of the rendering tree, and select the *Create Virtual Column* menu item. APEX will add a column named DERIVED$01 to the report.

- Set the type of this column to Link.

- Go to the Settings section, and click the box for the Target property. This brings up the link builder.

- Configure the link builder as shown in Figure 10-41.

- Set the Link Text property for the column to be **View Emps**.

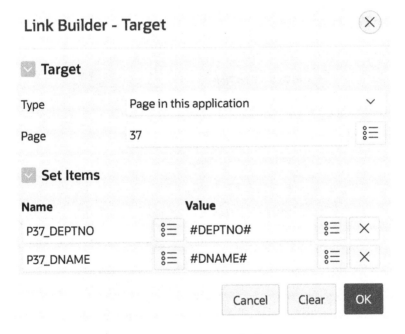

Figure 10-41. *Link builder for the View Emps link*

You will then need to make the following changes to the Detail Report page.

- Create hidden items P37_DEPTNO and P37_DNAME.

- Change the source of the region to

  ```
  select * from EMP
  where DeptNo = :P37_DEPTNO
  ```

- Change the title of the region to

  ```
  Emps in &P37_DNAME.
  ```

- Create a button that has the label All Depts and redirects to page 35.

That's it! The advantage of using the page wizard is that you can quickly construct fully functional web pages. You will probably want to configure the look and feel of the regions, but that shouldn't be too onerous.

The only problem with using the page wizard is that it forces you into a particular page architecture—in this case, the use of four single-region pages. There are many other possible designs. In fact, APEX has a Create Page wizard that constructs master-detail forms quite differently. Figure 10-42 shows its primary page.

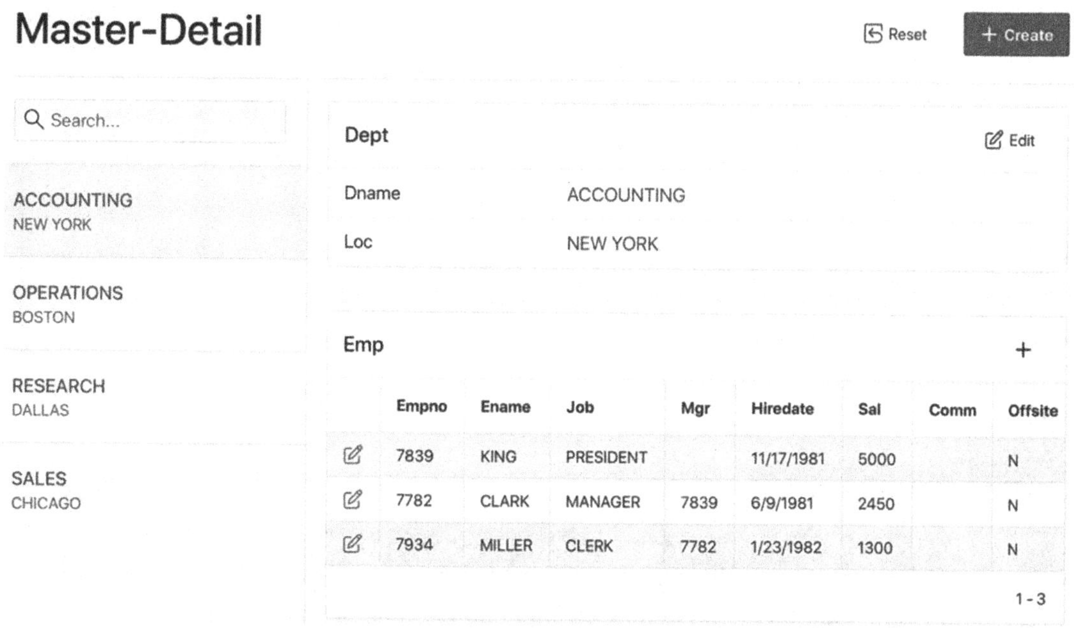

Figure 10-42. *A combined master-detail page*

The page has five regions: a region across the very top, named `Master-Detail` and having two buttons; a region in the left column containing the search bar; a report region down the left column listing the master rows; a report region (named `Dept`) at the top, listing the selected master row; and a report region (named `Emp`) at the bottom, listing the associated detail rows.

The rows of the master region in the left column are links. When you click a row, it becomes the selected row and the two regions to its right adjust themselves accordingly.

A user can edit this page in four ways:

- The `Create` button in the Master-Detail region inserts a new row into the master table.

- The `Edit` button in the `Dept` region edits the current master row.

- The "+" button in the `Emp` region inserts a new row into the detail table.

- The edit links in the detail report edit the selected detail row.

Clicking a button or link displays a form in a modal dialog page. For example, Figure 10-43 shows the result of clicking the `Edit` button. The user can modify the master record, delete it, or return to the master-detail page without doing anything.

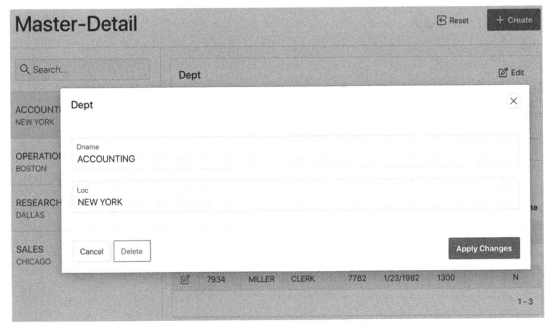

Figure 10-43. *Editing the current master record*

From a design point of view, it is worth comparing this master-detail page with the previous solution. This page displays the master and detail reports on the same page, similar to the Employees by Department page of Figure 6-8. This page is primary, and the user never loses contact with it. When an edit is required, the appropriate form is displayed modally and then disappears when the edit is complete. In comparison, the previous solution consisted of four pages. The user switches from one page to the other according to the task at hand ("view the master report," "edit a master row," "view the detail report," or "edit a detail row"), and no page is more important than any other page.

The point is not that one approach is better than the other, but that there are many ways to approach a problem. You need to be facile enough with APEX to produce the pages you envision, instead of being forced into a design based on the pages that the wizards produce.

With that in mind, let's use the wizard to create these master-detail pages and then examine their implementation. Start from the initial Create Page screen of Figure 2-9. When you click the Master Detail icon, APEX displays the screen shown in Figure 10-44. From there, clicking the Side by Side icon results in the screen of Figure 10-45.

Figure 10-44. *Selecting the desired master-detail wizard*

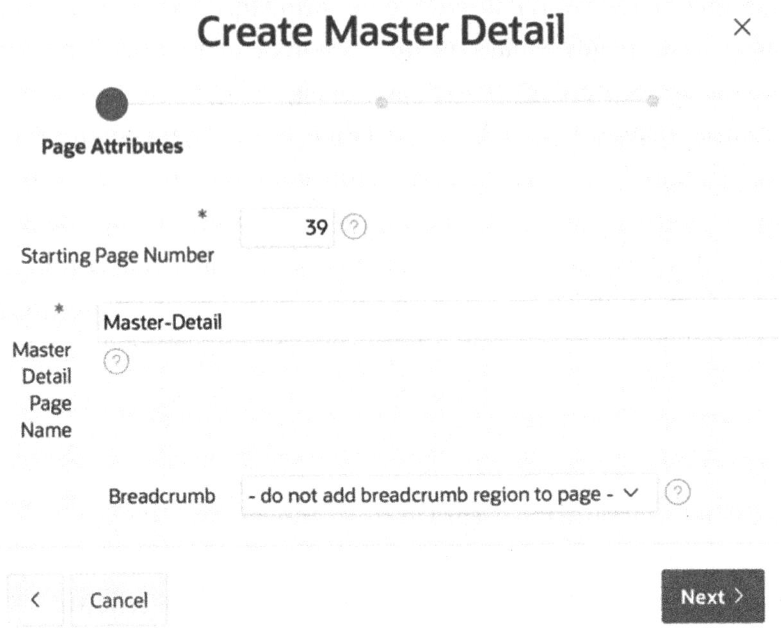

Figure 10-45. *The first master-detail screen*

This screen asks you for the name and page number of the primary page (i.e., the page shown in Figure 10-42). The wizard will also create two more pages to hold the master and detail forms, but you don't get to choose their numbers. Clicking the Next button takes you to the screen where you specify the navigation menu entry. You've seen this screen before, so I am omitting it here. The final screen, shown in Figure 10-46, asks you for the master and detail tables. The properties for Primary Display Column and Secondary Display Column denote the two values to be displayed in the master records. Clicking the Create button produces the three fully functioning pages. In my application, those pages are 39, 40, and 41.

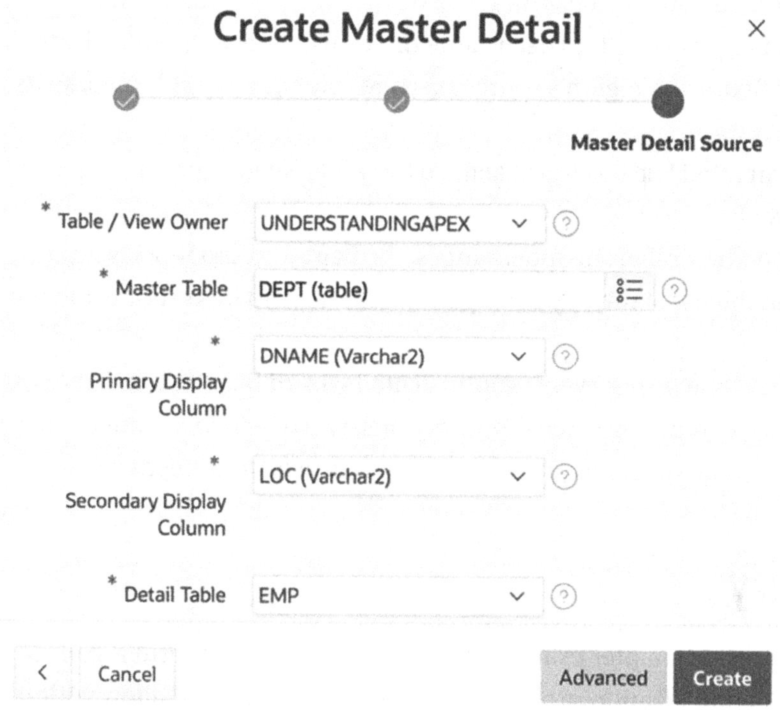

Create Master Detail ✕

Master Detail Source

* Table / View Owner	UNDERSTANDINGAPEX ⌄ ⊙
* Master Table	DEPT (table) ☰ ⊙
* Primary Display Column	DNAME (Varchar2) ⌄ ⊙
* Secondary Display Column	LOC (Varchar2) ⌄ ⊙
* Detail Table	EMP ⌄ ⊙

‹ Cancel   Advanced **Create**

Figure 10-46. *The third master-detail screen*

Pages 40 and 41 are form pages and are the same as what you would get by calling the Create Form wizard. So the main issue is how the report page is implemented.

The three report regions are, perhaps surprisingly, Classic Report regions. Their different appearance is due to their region templates. The master report template is Media List. This template displays two values, which it calls List_Title and List_Text. If you want the report rows to be links, then the source query must also have a field Link, whose value is the URL to redirect to. The source query generated by the wizard is complex, but it essentially is this:

```
select DeptNo, DName as List_Title, Loc as List_Text,
    apex_page.get_url(p_items  => 'P39_DEPTNO',
                      p_values => DEPTNO) as Link
from DEPT
```

The function apex_page.get_url returns a URL to an APEX page. By default, the URL redirects to the current page. The parameters p_items and p_values specify how the session state should be changed.

The region titled Dept in Figure 10-42 has the template Value Attribute Pairs – Column. This template displays each value on its own line, prepended by the column name. In the figure, the region's source has one row with two columns, so its report displays two rows.

The region titled Emp has the Standard template, so its report is displayed in the standard way.

Apart from their different appearances, the Dept and Emp reports interact with their form pages in the usual way, by having their buttons and links redirect to the appropriate form page.

The bottom line is that even a sophisticated wizard like Master-Detail is just creating a page containing three report regions, two of which are linked to form pages. If you wish, you can then customize those regions to fit your needs.

Summary

The first part of this chapter examined APEX form regions. A form region contains two processes—an initialization process and an ARP process—that allow your pages to access the database without having to write PL/SQL code. APEX also provides built-in processes for some common tasks, which work smoothly with the two form processes. Several examples demonstrated both the advantages and limitations that these processes have over corresponding PL/SQL processes.

The second part of the chapter examined some APEX page-creation wizards that create forms. These varied from the single-page Form wizard, which creates a page that is intended to be used in conjunction with other pages, to the Report with Form wizard, which pairs the Form page with a simple report page, to the sophisticated Master-Detail wizard, which matches two Form pages with a page containing three report regions. In each case, the focus was to uncover the mystery of these wizards, so that you feel empowered to create the pages you need, with or without them.

Interactive Grids

Reports are read-only. If you are looking at a report and want to change its contents, then you must use a form. For example, consider the `Report with Form 1` page of Figure 10-27. Suppose a user wants to modify a row of the employee report. The following steps occur:

- The user clicks the link of the desired row, which redirects to the `Report with Form 2` page (Figure 10-29) and places the selected employee number into an item on that page.

- The initialization process for the form then retrieves that employee's information from the database and stores it in the appropriate items.

- The user then modifies the content of those items and clicks the `Apply Changes` button to perform the update.

The peculiar thing about these steps is that the second step doesn't make use of the employee report. Instead, the initialization process re-retrieves the desired employee record from the database, even though its values are right there in the report.

The concept of an *interactive grid* addresses this situation by allowing users to update report values directly. An interactive grid is essentially an "updatable report," combining the features of a report and a form in a single region. This chapter examines the techniques needed to build and customize interactive grids.

Read-Only Interactive Grids

An APEX interactive grid is essentially an interactive report that can be edited like a form. This section examines the report-like features of interactive grids; the remainder of the chapter will cover the form-related issues. Page 42 of the `Employee Demo` application is called `Interactive Grids` and will be used as a running example throughout the chapter.

© Edward Sciore 2020
E. Sciore, *Understanding Oracle APEX 20 Application Development*,
https://doi.org/10.1007/978-1-4842-6165-1_11

To create this page, begin by creating a blank page. Add a region named `Departments`, and give it the type `Interactive Grid`. You will be asked for a source, which should be the query `select * from DEPT`. Figure 11-1 shows the rendering tree generated by APEX and its relevant properties. You should note that it looks no different from any report region.

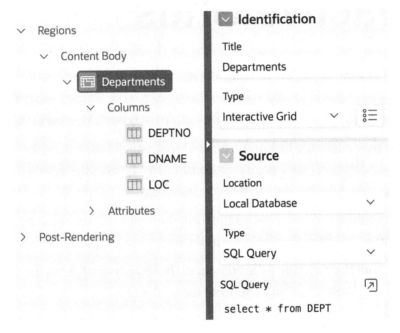

Figure 11-1. *Creating an interactive grid region*

Figure 11-2 shows the resulting region. Note the toolbar above the report, containing the search field and action menu. This bar looks the same as in an interactive report and has nearly the same functionality. For example, the action menu of an interactive grid lets you hide and reorder columns, create charts, filter records, and so on, just like an interactive report. An interactive grid also provides operations such as resizing and freezing columns and reorganizes the action menu somewhat. The `Reset` button restores the report to its default settings.

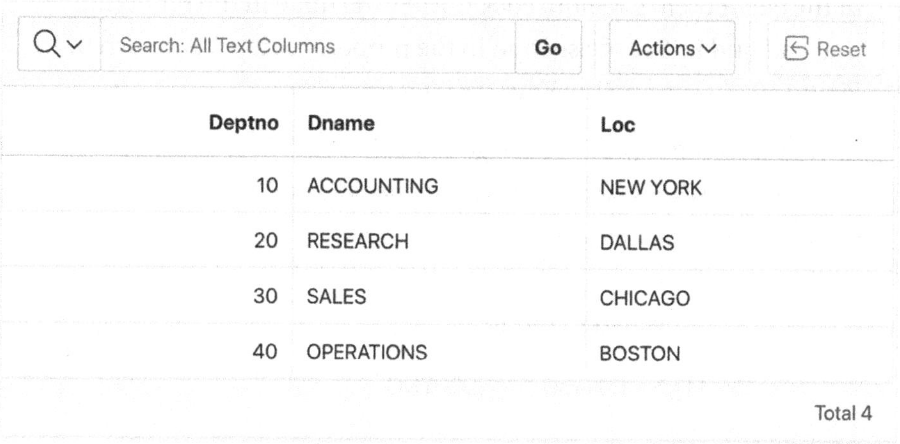

Search: All Text Columns
Go
Actions
Reset
Deptno
Dname
Loc
10
ACCOUNTING
NEW YORK
20
RESEARCH
DALLAS
30
SALES
CHICAGO
40
OPERATIONS
BOSTON
Total 4

***Figure 11-2.** An interactive grid region*

To customize the toolbar of an interactive grid, you use the same properties you would use to customize an interactive report; see Figure 11-3. One difference is that interactive grids do not have properties to customize the action menu.

Toolbar
Show
Controls
Search Column Selection
Search Field
Actions Menu
Reset Button
Save Button

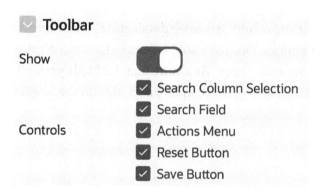

***Figure 11-3.** Properties to customize the toolbar*

Unlike interactive reports, interactive grids have properties to create a master-detail relationship between two grids. To implement this feature in your `Interactive Grids` page, follow these steps:

- Create a new interactive grid region named `Employees`, having the source `select * from EMP`.

- In the Departments region, click the DEPTNO node in the rendering tree and find its Source section in the property editor (as shown in Figure 10-4). Turn on the Primary Key property.

- In your new Employees region, go to the Master Detail property section of the DEPTNO column, and set its Master Column property to DEPTNO, as shown in Figure 11-4.

Figure 11-4. *The Master Detail property section*

These last two steps establish the key-foreign key relationship between the two grids. The column DEPTNO in the Departments grid is the key, and the column DEPTNO in the Employees grid is the foreign key. APEX will ensure that whenever a user selects a row from the Departments grid, the Employees grid will show only the rows having corresponding DEPTNO values.

Figure 11-5 shows the resulting master-detail grids. Take some time to explore how they behave in your application. You should observe how the detail grid changes each time you select another master row. Also note that the Employees grid no longer shows the DeptNo column because its value can be inferred from the selected Departments row.

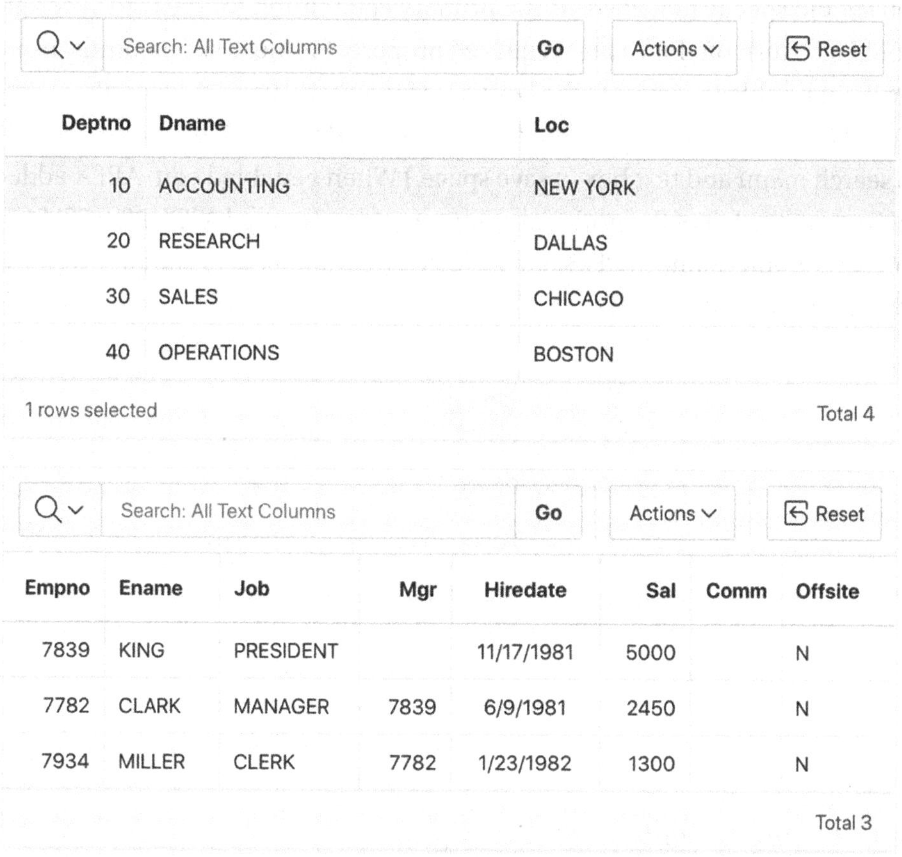
Search: All Text Columns
Go
Actions
Reset
Deptno
Dname
Loc
10 ACCOUNTING NEW YORK
20 RESEARCH DALLAS
30 SALES CHICAGO
40 OPERATIONS BOSTON
1 rows selected
Total 4
Search: All Text Columns
Go
Actions
Reset
Empno Ename Job Mgr Hiredate Sal Comm Offsite
7839 KING PRESIDENT 11/17/1981 5000 N
7782 CLARK MANAGER 7839 6/9/1981 2450 N
7934 MILLER CLERK 7782 1/23/1982 1300 N
Total 3

Figure 11-5. *Master-detail interactive grids*

Editing Interactive Grids

In addition to behaving like a report, an interactive grid can also behave like a form. You enable editing in an interactive grid the same as you do in a form. In particular, go to the rendering tree for the interactive grid region, click its `Attributes` node, and look at the `Enabled` property in the `Edit` section. By default, this property is turned off. When you turn it on, additional properties will be displayed, as was shown in Figure 10-10. The checkboxes allow you to specify which editing operations the region should allow.

As with a form, you will not be able to edit an interactive grid until you specify its primary key column. In the `Sample Interactive Grids` page, you already specified the primary key column for the `Departments` grid (to support the master-detail linkage);

now you should specify that EMPNO is the primary key column for the Employees grid.
You should also turn off the Value Required property for these key columns; otherwise,
APEX will not be able to generate the key value for a newly inserted record.

Figure 11-6 shows the edit-enabled interactive grid for the Departments region. (I
hid the search menu and text box to save space.) When I enabled edit, APEX added two
new columns to the left of the grid: a checkbox column (named APEX$ROW_SELECTOR)
and a menu column (named APEX$ROW_ACTION). The toolbar also contains new buttons
labeled Edit, Save, and Add Row.

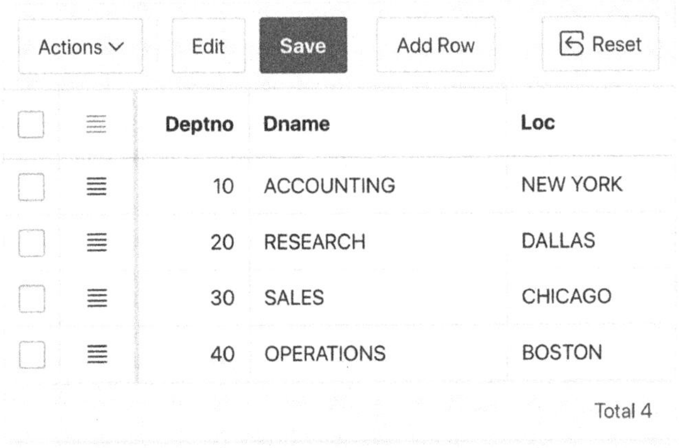

Figure 11-6. *An edit-enabled interactive grid*

You edit an interactive grid as follows: the Edit button toggles between view mode
and edit mode. Initially the button is white, as shown in Figure 11-6, denoting view
mode. Clicking it turns the button gray, which denotes edit mode. When in edit mode,
you can modify the value of cells. APEX denotes a modified cell by placing a small blue
triangle in its top right corner.

Clicking the Add Row button adds a new row to the grid. The initial value of its
primary key is a placeholder. You can either replace it with a desired value, or leave it as
is. If you leave it, then APEX will overwrite it with a generated value.

Clicking a row's APEX$ROW_ACTION icon brings up a menu of possible operations on that
row. For example, Figure 11-7 shows the row-action menu for the accounting department
row. In particular, selecting the Delete Row entry from this menu will delete its row.

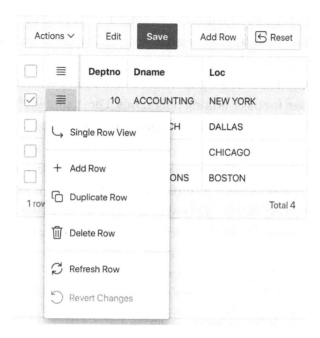

Figure 11-7. *The APEX row-action menu*

Figure 11-8 shows the interactive grid after performing three operations: I changed the name of department 20 from RESEARCH to OUTREACH, I deleted the SALES department, and I inserted a new record for the FINANCE department. APEX uses color-coding to indicate these changes—edited rows are blue, deletions are gray, and new rows are green.

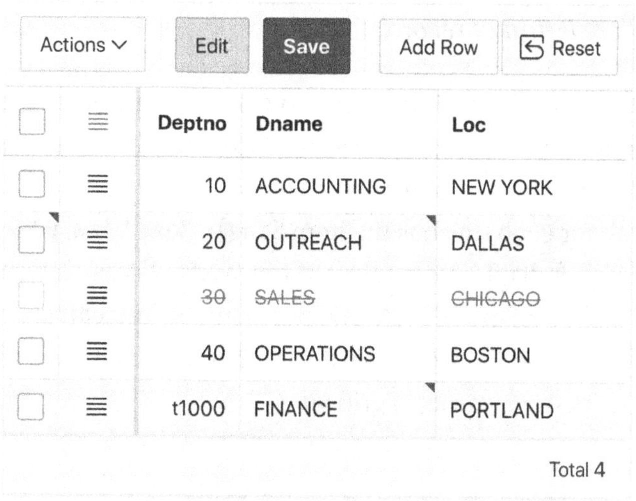

Figure 11-8. *Changes to the interactive grid*

None of these actions are permanent until you click the Save button. Until then, you can undo the change to a row by selecting the Revert Changes item from its row-action menu (as shown in Figure 11-7).

The row-selection column of the grid is the leftmost column, containing checkboxes. This column is not used for basic editing operations. For example, clicking the Save button in Figure 11-8 will save the three changed rows even though their row-selection boxes were not checked.

The purpose of the row-selection column is to support bulk operations, such as deletion. To use it, first select several records. Then, go to the row-action menu in the grid header, as shown in Figure 11-9. Choosing the Delete Rows menu item will flag the selected records for deletion. To finalize the deletion, you must then click the Save button.

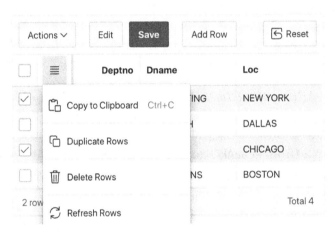

Figure 11-9. *Bulk deletion of records*

An alternative way to perform bulk operations is to use the Actions button in the toolbar above the grid. It has a submenu named Selection, whose menu items are identical to the header's row-action menu.

The action menu for each row has the item Single Row View, which you can see in Figure 11-7. Clicking it displays the selected row as if it were in a form. Figure 11-10 shows the single row view of the ACCOUNTING department. You can see the buttons to navigate to the next and previous row, as well as a button to return to the report. The other buttons work the same as in grid view.

Actions
Edit
Save
Add Row
Reset
Report View
Row 1 of 4
Deptno 10
Dname ACCOUNTING
Loc NEW YORK

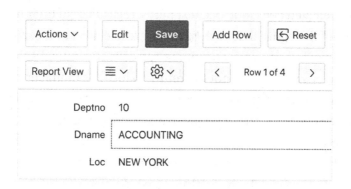

Figure 11-10. *Single row view*

A cell in a grid lives a dual existence. Normally, it displays its value as text, just like in a report. But when the cell has been selected in edit mode, it turns into an item. The type of the item is determined by the `Type` property of the cell's column. For example in the `Employees` grid, set the type of `Job` and `Mgr` to be `Select List`, the type of `Hiredate` to be `Date Picker`, and `Offsite` to be `Radio Group`. Figure 11-11 shows the list that pops up after clicking the `Job` cell for employee `MILLER`.

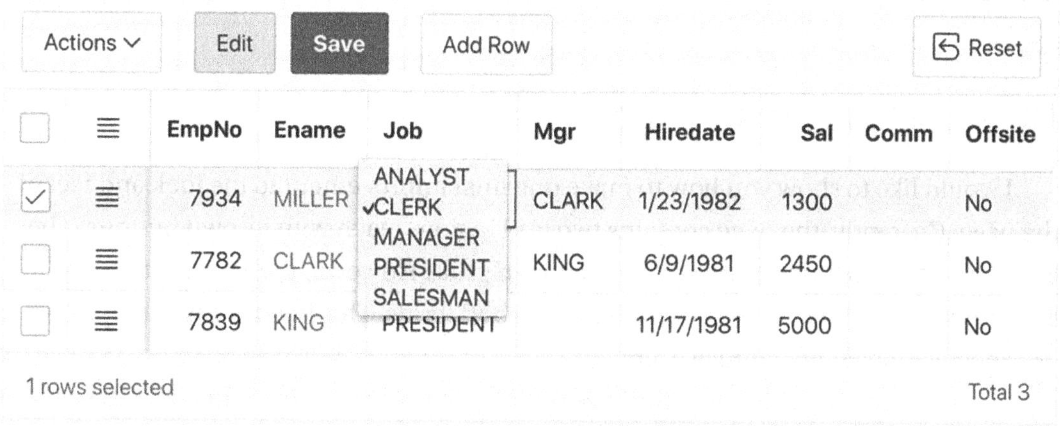

Actions
Edit
Save
Add Row
Reset
EmpNo Ename Job Mgr Hiredate Sal Comm Offsite
7934 MILLER CLARK 1/23/1982 1300 No
ANALYST
✓CLERK
MANAGER
PRESIDENT
SALESMAN
7782 CLARK KING 6/9/1981 2450 No
7839 KING PRESIDENT 11/17/1981 5000 No
1 rows selected
Total 3

Figure 11-11. *JOB formatted as a select list*

Note that nonselected cells look like text fields, regardless of their type. For example, you cannot tell from the figure that each Mgr cell is a select list and each Offsite cell is a radio group. However, you can see that the Mgr cells show the display value of the column (the manager's name) and not the return value (the manager's employee number). Similarly, the Offsite cells show the display values of the column ('No') and not the return value ('N'). The best way to learn about the different cell types is to experiment with them.

Each column has a property section named Default, which is where you can specify default values for a new record. In the Employees region, you should specify default values for the columns HIREDATE, COMM, and OFFSITE. Figure 11-12 shows the specification for HIREDATE, which is simply a call to the SQL function current_date. These default values will appear in the insert row, and the user can modify them before clicking the Save button.

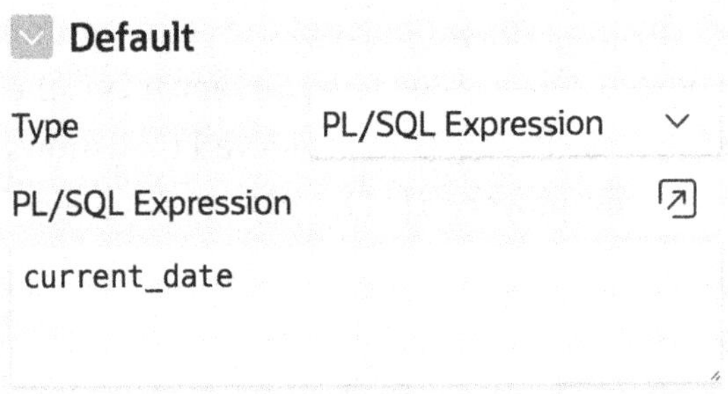

Figure 11-12. *Specifying the default value of a column*

I would like to show you how to make one final improvement to the look and feel of the page. Currently, the page contains two grid regions, each with its own buttons. The Edit and Add Row buttons affect only their own grids. However, the Save buttons are redundant—each one saves the changes from both grids. This behavior is somewhat unexpected and could confuse users.

The solution is to realize that the Save buttons do not have special functionality—their action is equivalent to a page-wide Submit operation. Therefore, it is possible to create your own Save button and display it anywhere you want on the page. My choice was to create a new static content region, titled Employees by Department, to be the parent of the two interactive grid regions. I then created a button in the new region labeled Save, set its position to Edit, turned on its Hot property (so that it is displayed in blue), and gave it the action Submit Page. You should do the same.

After you verify that the button works, you can hide the Save buttons on the region toolbars. Go to the rendering subtree for the Departments region, click the Attributes node, and find the Toolbar section in the properties editor (as was shown in Figure 11-3). Uncheck the Save Button entry. Then repeat the process for the Employees region. Figure 11-13 shows the resulting page.

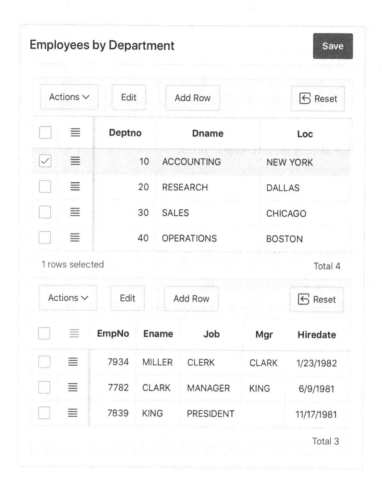

Figure 11-13. *The completed Interactive Grids page*

Ensuring Consistency

Chapter 8 discussed ways that a page can preserve data consistency. One way was to use validations to check for inappropriate item values; another was to restrict the values that can get entered. The following subsections show how these solutions can be applied to interactive grids.

Grid Validations

A validation in an interactive grid is an assertion that must be true for each row of the grid. You define an interactive grid validation the same as an item-based validation; the only difference is that it will apply to every row in the grid instead of just one.

   As an example, consider how to create a validation to ensure that the manager of an employee is either the president or an employee in the same department. To create this validation, go to the Processing tab of the page editor, right-click the Validating node, and select Create Validation. Figure 11-14 shows the relevant property values you should specify:

- Set the name of the validation to Mgr in Same Dept.

- Set the editable region to Employees.

- Set the validation type to Rows returned, having the query

  ```
  select * from EMP
  where EmpNo = :MGR
  and (DeptNo = :DEPTNO or Job = 'PRESIDENT')
  ```

- Give an appropriate error message.

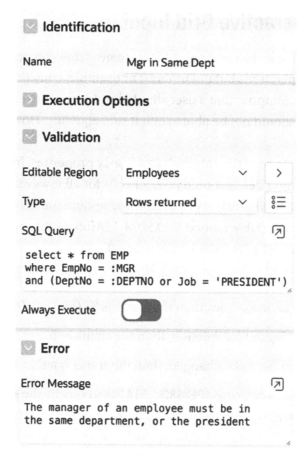

Figure 11-14. *Properties of a grid validation*

The critical property here is Editable Region. By providing a value for this property, you are specifying that this is an interactive grid validation and not an item-based validation. So when a submit action occurs (such as by clicking the Save button), APEX will apply the validation to each changed row of the grid.

Given an employee row, the validation query returns the employee's manager, provided that the manager is either the president or in the same department as the employee. In other words, if an output record exists, then the row has a proper manager and thus satisfies the Rows returned validation type. Note that the query references the values of the modified row using bound variable syntax; that is, it treats the cells of the modified row as if they were items.

Restricting Interactive Grid Input

One problem with using an interactive grid for update is that you might want a cell to be updatable for some operations but not others. For example, consider the EName column in the Employees grid. Suppose that a user should be able to enter an employee name during insertion, but should not be able to edit it subsequently. How to enforce this restriction?

The idea is to make use of the column's Read Only properties. In particular, you want to specify that the column's cells should be read-only for all rows except update rows. To express this specification, you will need to know the update status of each row.

APEX has a built-in variable named APEX$ROW_STATUS for this purpose. It has a value for each row of the grid, which can be one of four values:

- If the row has been edited, then the status is 'U'.

- If the row is an insert row, then the status is 'C' (for "created").

- If the row is flagged for deletion, then the status is 'D'.

- If the row has not been changed, then the status is null.

Figure 11-15 shows how to use APEX$ROW_STATUS to specify the Read Only SQL expression for the EName column. Note also that the value of the Execute property is For Each Row, which tells APEX to apply this expression to each row in the grid.

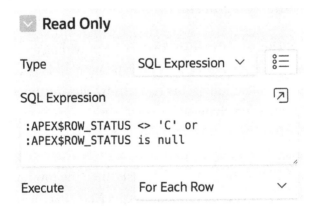

Figure 11-15. *Specifying when EName values can be entered*

The preceding example shows how to protect column values. The next example shows how to protect row values. Suppose that you want users of this page to not be able to delete managers and to not be able to edit or delete the president. The idea here is to make use of a grid's `Allowed Row Operations Column` property. This property appears in the `Edit` section of the grid region and is shown in Figure 11-16.

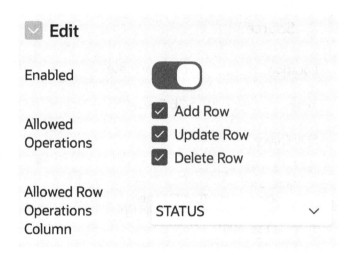

Figure 11-16. *Enabling row-specific updates and deletes*

This property also exists for forms (see, e.g., Figure 10-2), but until now none of the pages you created needed it. Its purpose is to indicate the column of the source query whose values denote allowable row operations, if one exists. In such a column, the value 'U' denotes that the row is update-only, 'D' denotes delete-only, and 'UD' denotes that both update and delete are allowed. Any other value denotes that no operations are allowed on the row. For example, here is my revised source query for the Employees region:

```
select EMP.*,
    case Job
        when 'PRESIDENT' then ''
        when 'MANAGER' then 'U'
        else 'UD'
    end as Status
from EMP
```

The Status column values are determined by the employee's job. The value for the president will be the empty string, denoting that it cannot be changed; the value for a manager will be 'U', denoting that managers can be updated only; and the value for all other employees will be 'UD', denoting that updates and deletes are allowed. Figure 11-17 shows the revised Source section for the region.

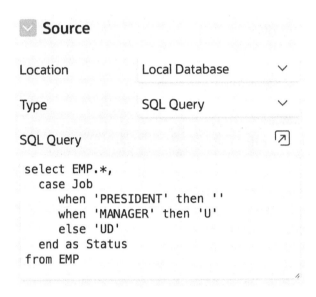

Figure 11-17. *Adding a row operations column to the grid's source*

By default, this new source column will be displayed in the grid as a text field. This column can be a useful debugging aid. But eventually, you will want to set its type to Hidden.

Figure 11-18 shows the result of running the page. You can see the row for the president is grayed out, indicating that those cells are not editable. (The cells in the Ename column are gray because of the read-only specification shown in Figure 11-15.) Not shown are the row-action menus for CLARK and KING, in which the Delete Row menu item is grayed out.

		EmpNo	Job	Ename	Mgr	Hiredate	Sal	Comm	Offsite
☐	≡	7934	CLERK	MILLER	CLARK	1/23/1982	1300		No
☐	≡	7782	MANAGER	CLARK	KING	6/9/1981	2450		No
☐	≡	7839	PRESIDENT	KING		11/17/1981	5000		No

Actions ∨   Edit   Add Row   ↺ Reset

Total 3

Figure 11-18. *Row protection in action*

Grid Processes

Each grid region comes with its own ARP process, which implements the database modification operations for that region. If you want your grid to have additional functionality, then you need to create additional processes for it.

The processes discussed in Chapters 7 and 10 execute once per submit request. Processes for an interactive grid, however, need to execute once per modified row of the grid. For an example, consider the LogChanges process from Listing 7-13. That process was used in the Revised Employee Data Entry page—whenever a user clicked the Delete, Insert, or Update button, the process inserted into the EMPLOG table a record denoting the request, the user, and the date.

You can easily re-create this process for the Interactive Grids page. Figure 11-19 shows the relevant process properties. These property values are exactly the same as for the Chapter 7 process, except for one—the Editable Region property now has the value Employees. This value tells APEX that when the process executes, its code should be applied to each changed row in the Employees grid.

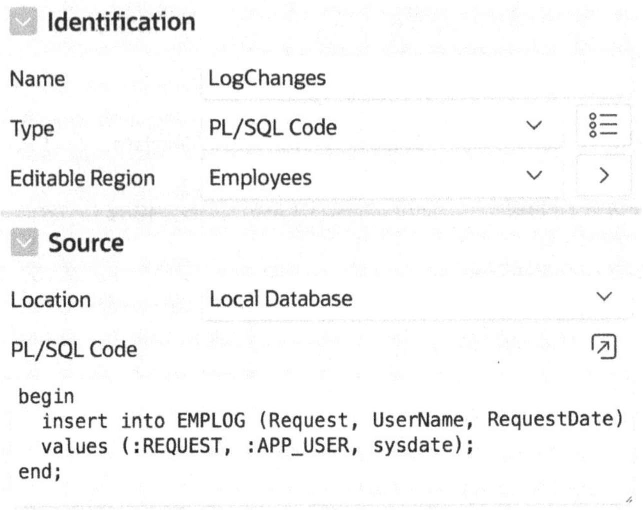

Identification

Name	LogChanges
Type	PL/SQL Code
Editable Region	Employees

Source

Location	Local Database
PL/SQL Code	

```
begin
  insert into EMPLOG (Request, UserName, RequestDate)
  values (:REQUEST, :APP_USER, sysdate);
end;
```

Figure 11-19. *The LogChanges process*

Test your process by making some changes to the Employees grid and then looking at the EMPLOG table from the SQL Workshop. The table should have a record for each modification you made. Unfortunately, all the records look the same—the Request values are either APEX_AJAX_DISPATCH (if you used the built-in SAVE button on the toolbar) or SAVE (if you used the SAVE button that you wrote for Figure 11-13). That is not good enough; the value of the Request field ought to be more informative.

Consequently, let's revise the process code so that the value of the Request field contains the row status and EmpNo value of the modified row, as in "update of 8830" or "insertion of 8200." Listing 11-1 contains the revised code. Note that it uses APEX$ROW_STATUS to determine which operation occurred.

Listing 11-1. PL/SQL Code for the Revised LogChange Process

```
declare
v_request varchar(20);
begin
  case :APEX$ROW_STATUS
    when 'U' then v_request := 'Update ';
    when 'C' then v_request := 'Insert ';
    when 'D' then v_request := 'Delete ';
  end case;
  v_request := v_request || :EMPNO;
```

```
  insert into EMPLOG (Request, UserName, RequestDate)
  values (v_request, :APP_USER, sysdate);
end;
```

Another situation you may encounter is that the grid's built-in database modification code does not do what you want. In this case, APEX lets you write your own PL/SQL code to replace it.

For a simple example, consider the problem of inserting a new row into a grid that does not contain all the fields of the table. The built-in insertion process will assign null values to the missing fields. But what if this isn't good enough? What if the new record needs non-null default values?

To explore this issue, create a new region in the Interactive Grids page. Name it CustomEmps, give it the type Interactive Grid, and set its template to Standard (so that it matches the Employees by Department region above it). Its source should be

```
select EmpNo, EName, Job, Sal, DeptNo
from EMP
```

Don't forget to turn on the Primary Key property of the EMPNO column and turn off its Validation Required property. Then go to the Attribute node's Edit section and enable editing. Figure 11-20 shows the top of the resulting region.

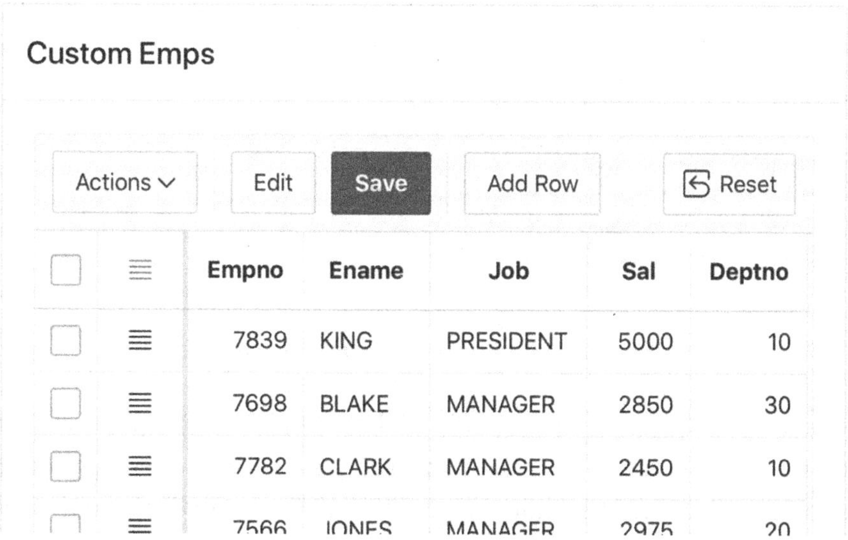

Figure 11-20. *The Custom Emps grid region*

The task at hand is to change the region's insertion code so that it places default values into the missing fields. Here is how to do it.

Go to the Processing tab of the page editor and select the process node named Custom Emps-Save Interactive Grid Data. This is the built-in ARP process for the Custom Emps grid region. Figure 11-21 shows its Identification and Settings properties. The critical property here is Target Type in the Settings section. The default value, Region Source, tells APEX to use the built-in modification process. To replace it with your code, change the property value to PL/SQL Code. The property editor will display a text box where you can enter the code.

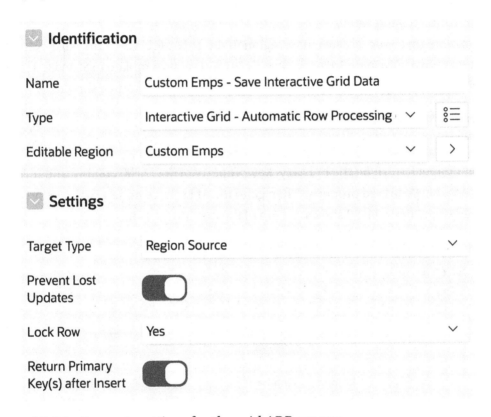

Figure 11-21. Property settings for the grid ARP process

Your custom PL/SQL code must handle all three modification operations, even though you are only changing insertion. Listing 11-2 shows my code. It uses a case statement to determine the operation that needs to be performed. The code for deletion and update are straightforward SQL commands, no different than what the ARP process would do. The code for insertion determines the default values for the four missing columns: the manager of a new employee is the president, the hire date is today, initial commission is 0, and the employee does not work offsite. The `returning` clause at the end of the `insert` statement causes the newly generated employee number to be saved in the grid's session state.

Note that your process only needs to handle a single row. APEX will loop over the grid, calling your code for each changed row and handling lost update detection.

Listing 11-2. Custom Interactive Grid Modification Code

```
begin
    case :APEX$ROW_STATUS
    when 'C' then
        insert into EMP(EName, Job, Sal, DeptNo,
                        Mgr, HireDate, Comm, Offsite)
        values (:ENAME, :JOB, :SAL, :DEPTNO,
                7839, sysdate, 0, 'N')
        returning EmpNo into :EMPNO;
    when 'U' then
        update emp
        set EName  = :ENAME,
            Job    = :JOB,
            Sal    = :SAL,
            DeptNo = :DEPTNO
        where EmpNo  = :EMPNO;
    when 'D' then
        delete emp
        where EmpNo = :EMPNO;
    end case;
end;
```

Summary

This chapter focused on interactive grids—what they are, what they can do, and how to build them. It began by examining their report-like characteristics. In this aspect, they look and behave a lot like interactive reports. Interactive grids also have some additional features, most importantly the ability to link two grid regions in a master-detail relationship.

The chapter then considered the issue of how to use an interactive grid to update the database. Interactive grids have a sophisticated, easy-to-use interface, in which you can tentatively edit values in place, add rows and initialize their values, and delete existing rows, and then undo or save these changes when desired.

Ineractive grids have validations to ensure appropriate user input. You specify these validations the same as in Chapter 8. The difference is that APEX applies the validation code to each modified row of the grid. You can also use the Read Only properties of a grid to restrict users from changing the value of specified rows or columns.

Each interactive grid has a built-in process that handles the database insert, delete, and update operations. If you need additional functionality, you can write your own processes. As with validations, the code of the process refers to just one row of the grid; APEX applies the process to each modified row of the grid. In fact, you can even swap out the default database processing code and replace it with your own.

Dynamic SQL

In this book, you have seen many ways to use session state values to customize a page. For example, the SQL source query of a report is a good candidate for customization, as is an SQL statement in a process that accesses the database. Much of this customization involves bound variable references in SQL statements.

However, there are limits to what can be customized. A reference to a session state variable can replace a constant in the SQL query, but it is not allowed to replace a table name or a column name. This chapter examines a technique called *dynamic SQL*, which overcomes this limitation by using PL/SQL code to construct and execute an SQL statement at runtime. You will see how to use dynamic SQL as the source of a report or the contents of a process and look at three examples that require dynamic SQL.

Dynamic Reports

Consider the Report Builder page shown in Figure 12-1, which is page 43 of the Employee Demo application. The items in the top region enable a user to specify a report. A user chooses the desired table, selects the columns to display, and then enters the text of the filtering condition. Clicking the submit button displays the report in the bottom region.

© Edward Sciore 2020
E. Sciore, *Understanding Oracle APEX 20 Application Development,*
https://doi.org/10.1007/978-1-4842-6165-1_12

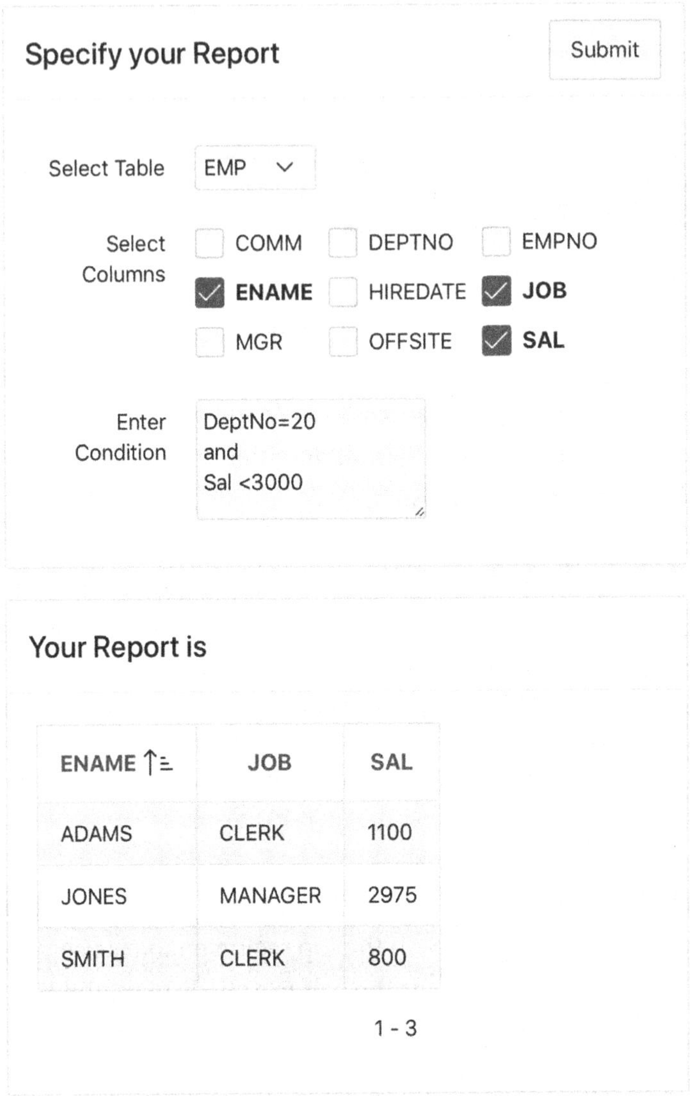

Figure 12-1. *Report Builder page*

What does it take to implement these two regions? The Specify Your Report region is relatively straightforward. The region has three items and a button. The Select Table item is named P43_TABLE. It is a select list that displays the names of relevant tables and has no action when selected. When I built the page, I specified the list of table names as the static values [EMP, DEPT]. Another possibility is to specify the list via the following query, which makes use of Oracle's User_Tables table:

```
select Table_Name as DisplayVal, Table_Name as ResultVal
from User_Tables
order by DisplayVal
```

The Select Columns item is named P43_COLS. It is a checkbox group that displays a checkbox for each column of the selected table. Its values are defined by the following query, which makes use of Oracle's User_Tab_Cols table:

```
select Column_Name as DisplayVal, Column_Name as ResultVal
from User_Tab_Cols
where Table_Name = :P43_TABLE
order by DisplayVal
```

This query references P43_TABLE, which means that its list of displayed columns will vary according to what table is selected. To get this list to update when P43_TABLE changes, use the cascading lists technique of Chapter 6. That is, go to the Cascading List of Values section for P43_COLS and set its Parent Item(s) property to P43_TABLE.

The item P43_WHERE is a text area in which the user enters the filtering condition. This condition will be used as the where clause of the report's source query.

Finally, the button in the Specify your Report region executes a submit action when pressed. This action causes the values of the three items to be saved in the session state.

The Your Report Is region displays a report customized by the values of these items. This region is not so straightforward to implement. Suppose that you tried to create the region as a classic report; its source query would look something like this:

```
select :P43_COLS
from   :P43_TABLE
where  :P43_WHERE
```

The problem is that such a query is not syntactically legal. The rule is that a bind variable can be used only to reference a constant, and this query is trying to reference columns, tables, and SQL code. To solve this problem, set the source type of the report to be PL/SQL Function Body returning SQL Query. The source of such a report is a PL/SQL function that computes the desired SQL query and returns it as a string. Listing 12-1 shows the code for the Your Report is report.

Listing 12-1. PL/SQL Code to Generate an SQL Query

```
declare
  v_table varchar2(20)  := :P43_TABLE;
  v_cols  varchar2(100) := replace(:P43_COLS, ':', ',');
  v_where varchar2(100) := '';
begin
  if :P43_WHERE is not null then
    v_where := ' where ' || :P43_WHERE;
  end if;
  return 'select ' || v_cols || ' from ' || v_table || v_where;
end;
```

This code constructs the desired SQL query string piece by piece. The construction of the column list is perhaps the only nonobvious part. Recall that P43_COLS is a multi-value list item, which means that its value will be a string containing the selected column names separated by colons. In the query, however, the column names need to be separated by commas. So all you need to do is use the replace function to replace each colon by a comma and then assign that string to the variable v_cols.

The technique of using code to construct the source query is called *dynamic SQL* because the query is computed dynamically at runtime. Dynamic SQL is appropriate whenever the source query can vary in ways that go beyond simple customization by constants. Figure 12-2 depicts the Identification and Source properties for the Your Report Is region.

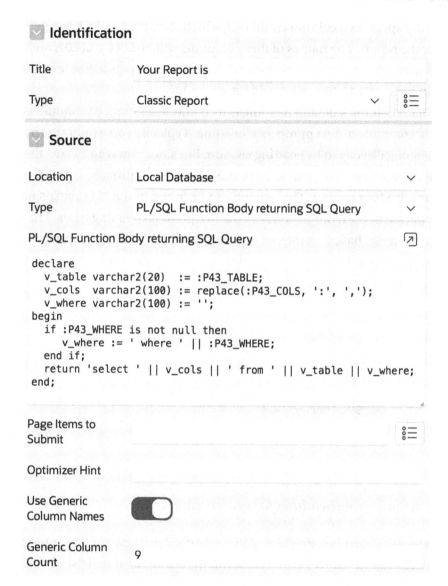

Identification

Title	Your Report is
Type	Classic Report

Source

Location	Local Database
Type	PL/SQL Function Body returning SQL Query

PL/SQL Function Body returning SQL Query

```
declare
  v_table varchar2(20)  := :P43_TABLE;
  v_cols  varchar2(100) := replace(:P43_COLS, ':', ',');
  v_where varchar2(100) := '';
begin
  if :P43_WHERE is not null then
     v_where := ' where ' || :P43_WHERE;
  end if;
  return 'select ' || v_cols || ' from ' || v_table || v_where;
end;
```

Page Items to
Submit

Optimizer Hint

Use Generic
Column Names

Generic Column
Count   9

Figure 12-2. *Implementing the Report Builder report region*

One of the consequences of using dynamic SQL is that the columns of the report may not be known until runtime. In this case, you must tell APEX to define *generic* column names for the report. You do so via the property Use Generic Column Names, which can be seen at the bottom of Figure 12-2. When that property is turned on, the property Generic Column Count appears for you to specify how many generic columns to create.

Figure 12-2 specifies a column count of 9, which means that APEX will generate 9 columns for the report. The names of these columns will be COL01, COL02, and up to COL09. This specified count is a maximum; if the report happens to use fewer columns (as shown in Figure 12-1), the others will be ignored.

Recall that a column's default heading is its name. Therefore, you should give each generic column a more appropriate heading. Typically you would specify a column's heading directly in its Heading section. But since you won't know the meaning of each column until runtime, you need to use a different approach. This is the purpose of the report's Heading section. This section can be found in the Attributes node of the report's rendering tree. Figure 12-3 shows the five possible heading types. The first three types create headings based on the column names, which is not appropriate here, and the last type specifies no headings. Thus, the best choice for handling generic columns is to use the heading type PL/SQL Function Body.

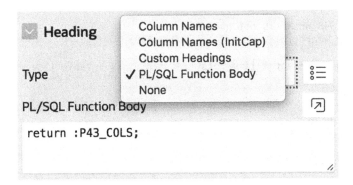

Figure 12-3. *Specifying headings for generic columns*

When you select that heading type, APEX will display a text area for entering PL/SQL code; that code should return a string containing a colon-separated list of the column headings. In this example, the checkbox group P43_COLS contains exactly what you need, so your code can simply return its value, as shown at the bottom of Figure 12-3. In more complex situations, you can write a PL/SQL block to compute the desired string.

When you run your page, the report will display the following error message until you choose at least one column:

```
failed to parse SQL query: ORA-00936: missing expression
```

The reason is that when P43_COLS is empty, the SQL string generated in Figure 12-2 begins "select from ...", which is not legal SQL. A good way to avoid this unpleasantness is to render the report region conditionally. In particular, set its Condition Type property to

P43_COLS is not null

Dynamic Processes

Chapter 7 demonstrated how easy it is to execute an SQL statement from a PL/SQL block: you simply place the statement directly within the block and parameterize it using bind variables. However, that syntax is not sufficient for dynamic SQL. This section explores the issues and their solution.

For an example, consider the Count and Delete page shown in Figure 12-4, which is page 44 of the Employee Demo application. This page contains two regions that have essentially the same functionality. In each case, a user chooses a table and specifies a filtering condition on it. Each region has the same two buttons: the Count button displays a message giving the number of records satisfying the condition, and the Delete button deletes those records from the table. Figure 12-4 shows the result of clicking the Count button in both regions.

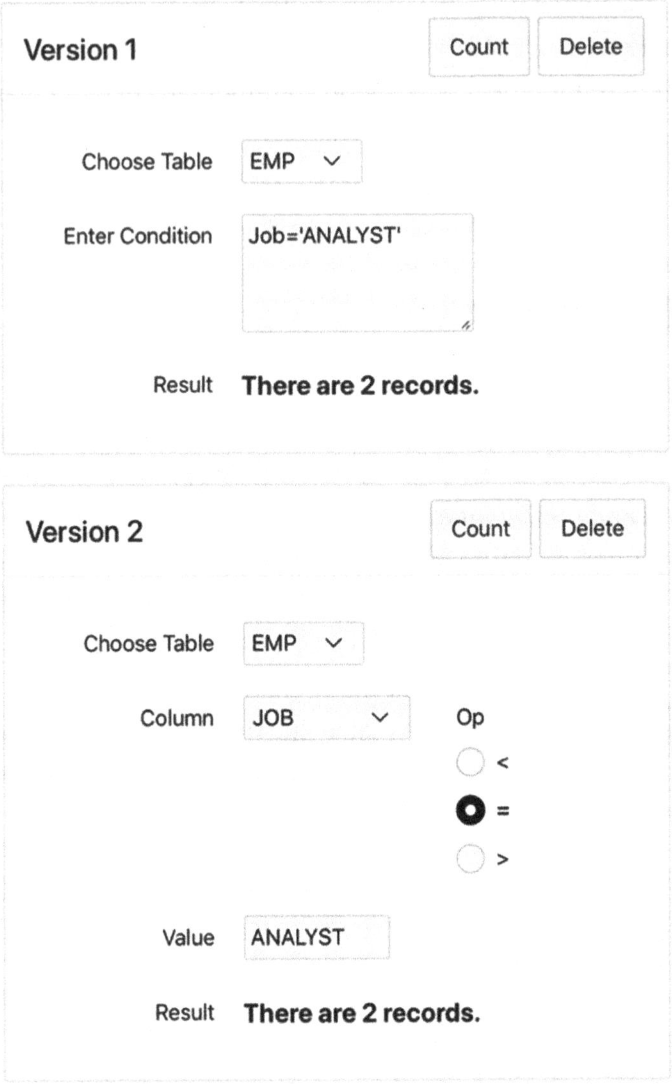

Figure 12-4. *Count and Delete page*

Both regions in Figure 12-4 display the same filtering condition: employees who are analysts. These two regions differ only in how the user specifies the condition. In the Version 1 region, the user can enter an arbitrary condition, similar to the Report Builder page. In the Version 2 region, the user composes the condition by choosing a specific column, operator, and value. This second way of specifying the condition doesn't require knowledge of SQL syntax and is perhaps more user-friendly, but it limits the kinds of conditions that can be expressed.

The creation of the items and buttons on this page is straightforward. The Version 1 region has three items: item P44_TABLE1 is a select list having the static values [DEPT, EMP], item P44_WHERE1 is a text area, and P44_RESULT1 is display-only. Its buttons are named Count1 and Delete1, and their actions are Submit Page.

The Version 2 region has five items. The item P44_TABLE2 has the same definition as P44_TABLE1. The item P44_COLUMN2 is a select list having P44_TABLE2 as its cascading parent; its values are defined by this SQL query:

```
select Column_Name as DisplayVal, Column_Name as ResultVal
from User_Tab_Cols
where Table_Name = :P44_TABLE2
order by DisplayVal
```

The item P44_VALUE2 is a text field, and P44_RESULT2 is a display-only item. Item P44_OP2 is a radio group with the three static values [<,=,>]. Its Template property is Optional-Above, so that the label can appear above the radio group. The region's buttons are named Count2 and Delete2, and their actions are Submit Page.

The most interesting aspect of the page is how to write the processes for the four buttons. Each process performs the same three tasks:

- It constructs a string containing the appropriate SQL command.

- It executes that string.

- It uses the result of the execution to formulate the output message.

The source code for a dynamic report needs to perform only the first task because APEX executes the query string when it renders the report. A process, on the other hand, does not have this luxury and it has to explicitly execute the SQL string.

The PL/SQL command to execute an SQL string is called *execute immediate*. This command is somewhat intricate to use—in fact, each of the four button processes uses it slightly differently. Let's examine each process in turn.

First, consider the button Delete1. Its process, also named Delete1, needs to execute an SQL deletion command. Most of the time, you can write the command directly as a PL/SQL statement; but in this case you won't know the table and its where clause until runtime. Thus, you need to use the execute immediate command, as shown in Listing 12-2.

Listing 12-2. Code for the Delete1 Process

```
declare
  v_cmd varchar2(100);
begin
  v_cmd := 'delete from ' || :P44_TABLE1 || ' where ' || :P44_WHERE1;

  execute immediate v_cmd;

  :P44_RESULT1 := SQL%rowcount || ' records were deleted.';
end;
```

The first statement constructs the SQL deletion command as a string using the chosen table and specified condition. The second statement uses the execute immediate command in its most basic form: you simply pass the SQL string to it. The third statement assigns a value to the result item by using the SQL%rowcount function (which was introduced in Listing 7-11).

Now consider the button Count1. Its process, named Count1, needs to execute a query to calculate the record count and save the retrieved value in a variable. Listing 7-4 showed how to use the into clause of an SQL query for that purpose. For example, if you did not have to use dynamic SQL, you could write the query corresponding to Figure 12-4 like this:

```
select count(*) into v_count
from EMP
where Job = 'ANALYST'
```

In dynamic SQL, however, the into clause is associated with the execute immediate command instead of with the SQL query. Listing 12-3 shows the proper code.

Listing 12-3. Code for the Count1 Process

```
declare
  v_query varchar2(100);
  v_count integer;
begin
  v_query := 'select count(*) from ' || :P44_TABLE1 ||
             ' where ' || :P44_WHERE1;
```

```
  execute immediate v_query
  into v_count;

 :P44_RESULT1 := 'There are ' || v_count || ' records.';
end;
```

Now consider the process for the button Delete2, which is also named Delete2. The main issue with writing this process is how to handle string constants. Note that the value ANALYST in Figure 12-4 is not in quotes. Thus, the straightforward approach, shown in Listing 12-4, will not work.

Listing 12-4. Incorrect Code for the Delete2 Process

```
declare
  v_cmd varchar2(100);
begin
  v_cmd := 'delete from ' || :P44_TABLE2 ||
           ' where ' || :P44_COLUMN2 || :P44_OP2 || :P44_VALUE2;
  execute immediate v_cmd;
end;
```

The issue is how to get a query to place quotes around the value if it is a string, but not if it is a number. The solution, as you saw in Chapter 3, is to use a bind variable reference. For example, the query you would like to generate for the Delete2 process should look like this:

```
select count(*) from EMP into v_count
where Job = :P44_VALUE
```

However, the execute immediate command is fussy about bind variables. In particular, the command does not allow bind variables in the generated query; instead, it has a using clause especially for this purpose. Listing 12-5 gives the correct code for the Delete2 process.

Listing 12-5. Correct Code for the Delete2 Process

```
declare
  v_cmd varchar2(100);
begin
  v_cmd := 'delete from ' || :P44_TABLE2 ||
           ' where ' || :P44_COLUMN2 || :P44_OP2 || ' :1';
```

```
execute immediate v_cmd
using :P44_VALUE2;

:P44_RESULT2 := SQL%rowcount || ' records were deleted.';
end;
```

Note that the generated query has the expression ":1" where the bind variable belongs. This expression is a placeholder. When the execute immediate command runs, it will replace the placeholder with the value in its using clause. If the query requires more than one bind variable, then it uses multiple placeholders and the bind variables in the using clause are separated by commas.

In Listing 12-5, there is only one placeholder, namely, :1. A placeholder has the same function as the formal parameter of a procedure. In effect, the execute immediate statement "calls" the SQL statement, passing it the value of each bind variable reference. The names of the placeholders are irrelevant. APEX will assign the values from the using clause to the placeholders in the order in which the placeholders appear in the SQL statement.

Finally, the process for the button Count2, also named Count2, appears in Listing 12-6. Note that the constructed string is a query and uses a bind variable; thus, the execute immediate command will use both the into and using clauses.

Listing 12-6. Code for the Count2 Process

```
declare
  v_query varchar2(100);
  v_count int;
begin
  v_query := 'select count(*) from ' || :P44_TABLE2 ||
             ' where ' || :P44_COLUMN2 || :P44_OP2 || ' :1';

  execute immediate v_query
  into v_count
  using :P44_VALUE2;

  :P44_RESULT2 := 'There are ' || v_count || ' records.';
end;
```

Combining Dynamic Reports and Processes

For a final example, I want to reconsider the Single Row View page from Figure 7-17, which is page 20 of the Employee Demo application. Recall that this page displays a report of all employees, sorted by EName. When a user selects an employee, the page turns into single row mode, displaying the data of the selected row and providing buttons to navigate to the previous and next row in sorted order.

The task is to modify the page so that a user can dynamically change the sort order of the rows. Figure 12-5 illustrates the new page, called Sortable Single Row View, which is page 45 of the demo application. The page is identical to the Single Row View page except that it also has a select list for specifying the desired sort field. Selecting a sort field will cause the report to be redisplayed in that sort order; in addition, clicking the Previous or Next button will use that sort order to determine the new current row.

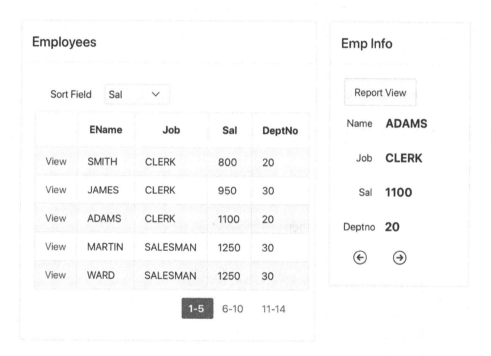

Figure 12-5. *Sortable Single Row View page*

As with Figure 7-17, Figure 12-5 shows both the Employees and Emp Info regions, even though only one of them is displayed at a time.

The easiest way to create this page is to copy page 20. This operation was discussed in Chapter 7 (see Figure 7-8). To review, go to the page designer for any page, click the + icon near the top, and select Page as Copy to initiate the Page Copy wizard. If you have trouble following the wizard, refer back to Chapter 7.

When copying a page, you must ensure that its various item references are updated. It turns out that item references within the PL/SQL code get updated, but references produced by the link builder do not. Thus, the target of the link for the EMPNO column incorrectly redirects to page 20 and sets the value of P20_EMPNO. In general, you should correct these values, but in this case there is no need because you are about to replace these columns with new ones.

After you have successfully copied the page, you can modify it. The first modification is to add a select list to the Employees region so users can choose the sort field. This select list is named P45_SORTFIELD and has the static values [EName, Job, Sal, DeptNo]. Its action should be Redirect and Set Value.

The presence of a changeable sort field affects two parts of the page: the source query for the report and the process that computes the next/previous records in single-record mode. You need to use dynamic SQL in both cases. The report's source query is generated by the PL/SQL code of Listing 12-7.

Listing 12-7. PL/SQL Source Code for the Employees Report

```
declare
  v_sort varchar2(20);
begin
  if :P45_SORTFIELD is null then
    v_sort := 'EName';
  else
    v_sort := :P45_SORTFIELD;
  end if;
  return 'select EmpNo, EName, Job, Sal, DeptNo from EMP ' ||
         'order by ' || v_sort;
end;
```

This query uses dynamic SQL to construct the appropriate query, based on the selected sort field. If no sort field has been selected, EName is the default. Because you are using dynamic SQL, you should enable the Use Generic Column Names property and specify a Generic Column Count of 5. APEX will create five columns, named COL01 through COL05. Because the column headings in this report will be the same regardless of the sort field, you can hardcode them into the report's Heading section. In particular, the value of the PL/SQL Function Body property will be

```
return ':EName:Job:Sal:DeptNo';
```

This string begins with a colon because the heading of the first column is empty.

You also need to specify the link for the first column. Recall that its name is COL01 even though it contains EmpNo values. So select COL01 from the rendering tree and set its type to Link. Click its Link Target property and configure the Link Builder wizard as shown in Figure 12-6. Then set the column's Link Text property to **View**.

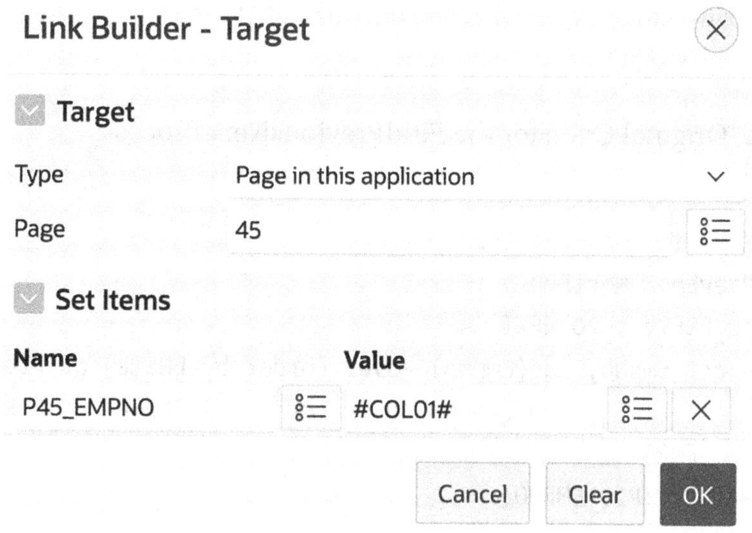

Figure 12-6. *Specifying the behavior of the column link*

You also need to configure the sortability of the report's columns. Recall from Chapter 3 that each column in a classic report has a property named Sortable—turning on its value enables users to sort on that column by clicking its header, and turning it off disables sorting on that column. The issue is how APEX should handle sortability when the source query also has an order by clause. APEX resolves this issue differently, depending on whether columns are generic or not. If columns are not generic, then the order by clause takes precedence—the Sortable property of each column will be turned off and cannot be turned on. On the other hand, if the columns are generic, then their `Sortable` properties take precedence—they are turned on by default, and the `order` by clause of the source query is ignored. APEX will only recognize the `order` by clause when the `Sortable` property of each column has been turned off.

In other words, if you want your report to be sorted according to the value of P45_ SORTFIELD, then you must turn off the `Sortable` property for each of the five generic columns in the `Employees` report.

You should now have a working sortable report. Test it out. Selecting a sort field should cause the report to re-render with the new sort order, and clicking the link for a row should display the `Emp Info` region for the selected row.

The remaining issue is that the `Previous` and `Next` buttons still use `EName` as the sort field. You need to modify the process that underlies those buttons so that it refers to P45_SORTFIELD instead of `EName`. This process was called `FindPreviousNext` in Chapter 7, and its code appeared in Listing 7-18. For reference, Listing 12-8 reprints that code.

Listing 12-8. Original Code for the FindPreviousNext Process

```
begin
  if :P20_EMPNO is not null then
    select PrevEmp, NextEmp
    into :P20_PREV, :P20_NEXT
    from (select EmpNo, lag(EmpNo)  over (order by EName) as PrevEmp,
                       lead(EmpNo) over (order by EName) as NextEmp
          from EMP)
    where EmpNo = :P20_EMPNO;
  end if;
end;
```

The revised code appears in Listing 12-9. Although this code seems complex, it is essentially the original code broken into pieces and translated into dynamic SQL. The initial if-statement handles the case in which no sort field has been chosen.

Listing 12-9. Revised Code for the FindPreviousNext Process

```
declare
  v_subquery varchar2(200);
  v_query    varchar2(250);
  v_sort     varchar2(20);
```

```
begin
  if :P45_EMPNO is not null then
    if :P45_SORTFIELD is null then
      v_sort := 'EName';
    else
      v_sort := :P45_SORTFIELD;
    end if;

    v_subquery :=
      'select EmpNo, ' ||
            'lag(EmpNo)  over (order by ' || v_sort || ') as PrevEmp, ' ||
            'lead(EmpNo) over (order by ' || v_sort || ') as NextEmp ' ||
      'from EMP';

    v_query := 'select PrevEmp, NextEmp ' ||
              'from (' || v_subquery || ') ' ||
              'where EmpNo = :1';

    execute immediate v_query
    into :P45_PREV, :P45_NEXT
    using :P45_EMPNO;
  end if;
end;
```

Summary

This chapter examined some situations in which it was necessary to customize the table names and column names in an SQL query. You saw how to handle such situations by using dynamic SQL to construct and execute an SQL query string at runtime. In the case of customizing a report, you learned how to use a PL/SQL function to generate the source of the report. In the case of customizing a PL/SQL process, you learned how to use its execute immediate command.

Dynamic SQL forces APEX to validate and process the query string at runtime; this additional overhead increases the time it takes to process the page. Moreover, in the next chapter, you shall see that the use of dynamic SQL can open a window for potential security breaches. Consequently, dynamic SQL should be used only of necessity. Such situations occur rarely, but it is good to know how to handle them when they do occur.

Security

When you created your `Employee Demo` application, you chose to restrict access to those who have an account on your workspace. This restriction is one of several APEX facilities for limiting access. These facilities can be divided into *authentication*, which identifies the legal users, and *authorization*, which specifies what information each legal user is allowed to see. This chapter will examine these facilities, as well as the related issue of how to protect the data from malicious users.

Authentication

Authentication is the ability to identify the current user of an application. APEX users identify themselves by providing a username and password. APEX supports several possible *authentication schemes*, which maintain the user/password list in different ways and at different organizational levels.

Here are four common authentication schemes, in order from the most general to least general:

- *LDAP Directory scheme*: The user/password list is maintained within an organization's LDAP directory. This scheme allows an organization to assign a single account to each person to be used for all systems that it maintains. The resulting ease of administration often makes LDAP the authentication scheme of choice for many organizations.

- *Database Accounts scheme*: The user/password list is maintained within the Oracle database system. This scheme allows a user to have a single account for multiple Oracle-based systems (including APEX applications). The downside of this scheme is that users will also have direct access to the Oracle database, which might not be desirable.

© Edward Sciore 2020
E. Sciore, *Understanding Oracle APEX 20 Application Development*,
https://doi.org/10.1007/978-1-4842-6165-1_13

- *Application Express Accounts scheme*: This is the current authorization scheme for the Employee Demo application. The user/password list is maintained within the application's workspace. The APEX administrator for a workspace manages the list for that workspace. If a person needs to access applications from different workspaces, the person needs an account for each workspace.

- *Custom scheme*: The owner of the application maintains the user/password list. A person will need a separate account for each such application. Custom schemes are often used by applications that allow people to create and manage their own accounts.

In addition, there is the scheme in which the application does not perform any authentication. APEX considers this to be a *No Authentication* authentication scheme.

Managing Authentication Schemes

An APEX application can contain multiple authentication schemes, but only one scheme can be current at a time. To create a scheme, go to the home page for the application, click the Shared Components button, look for the Security section, and select Authentication Schemes.

You are taken to a screen that lists the authentication schemes that have been created for your application. You should have one scheme listed, which is the scheme that you selected when you created the application; see Figure 13-1.

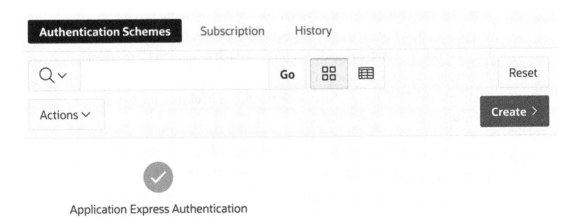

Figure 13-1. *Authentication Schemes screen*

To create other schemes, click the `Create` button. The first screen of the creation wizard is shown in Figure 13-2.

Create Authentication Scheme

Method

When you create a new authentication scheme, you have several options. Most let you reuse implementations that already exist in your application or in other applications within your workspace. There are even some pretested schemes you can copy to get you up and running immediately.

Create Scheme: ● **Based on a pre-configured scheme from the gallery** ⓘ
  ○ As a copy of an existing authentication scheme

〉 **Information**

Cancel   Next 〉

Figure 13-2. *The first Create Authentication wizard screen*

Select the option `Based on a pre-configured scheme from the gallery` and click `Next` to get to the second wizard screen, shown in Figure 13-3. The screen asks you to give your new scheme a name and choose a scheme type. Depending on the type, you may have to fill in additional information. Then click the `Create Authentication Scheme` button to create the scheme.

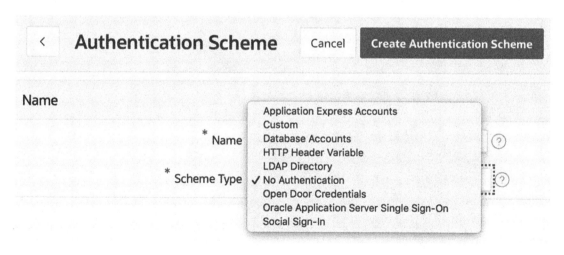

〈   ## Authentication Scheme   Cancel   **Create Authentication Scheme**

Name

    * Name   Application Express Accounts
                    Custom
                    Database Accounts
                    HTTP Header Variable
                    LDAP Directory
    * Scheme Type   ✓ No Authentication
                    Open Door Credentials
                    Oracle Application Server Single Sign-On
                    Social Sign-In

Figure 13-3. *The second Create Authentication wizard screen*

Each time you create a new authentication scheme, APEX makes it the current scheme. If you want to switch to a different scheme, go back to the list of schemes, click the icon corresponding to the scheme, and then click the Make Current Scheme button. If you want to delete a scheme, make sure that it is not current, click its icon, and then click the Delete button.

For fun, create a No Authentication scheme and make it current. When you run your application, you will be taken to the first page immediately, without having to go through a Login page.

If you have an Oracle database account, create a Database Accounts scheme, make it current, and log in that way.

If you have access to an LDAP server, you can try creating an LDAP Directory scheme. You will need to enter the necessary configuration information into the creation screen, such as the hostname of the LDAP server and the distinguished name string. Note, however, that LDAP servers are often inside firewalls. If the APEX server runs in a different domain from the LDAP server, you might encounter firewall issues that make this scheme unworkable.

Finally, create a Custom authentication scheme. When you select the scheme type Custom in Figure 13-3, the wizard will display additional sections named Settings and Source. Figure 13-4 shows these sections with the critical properties filled in.

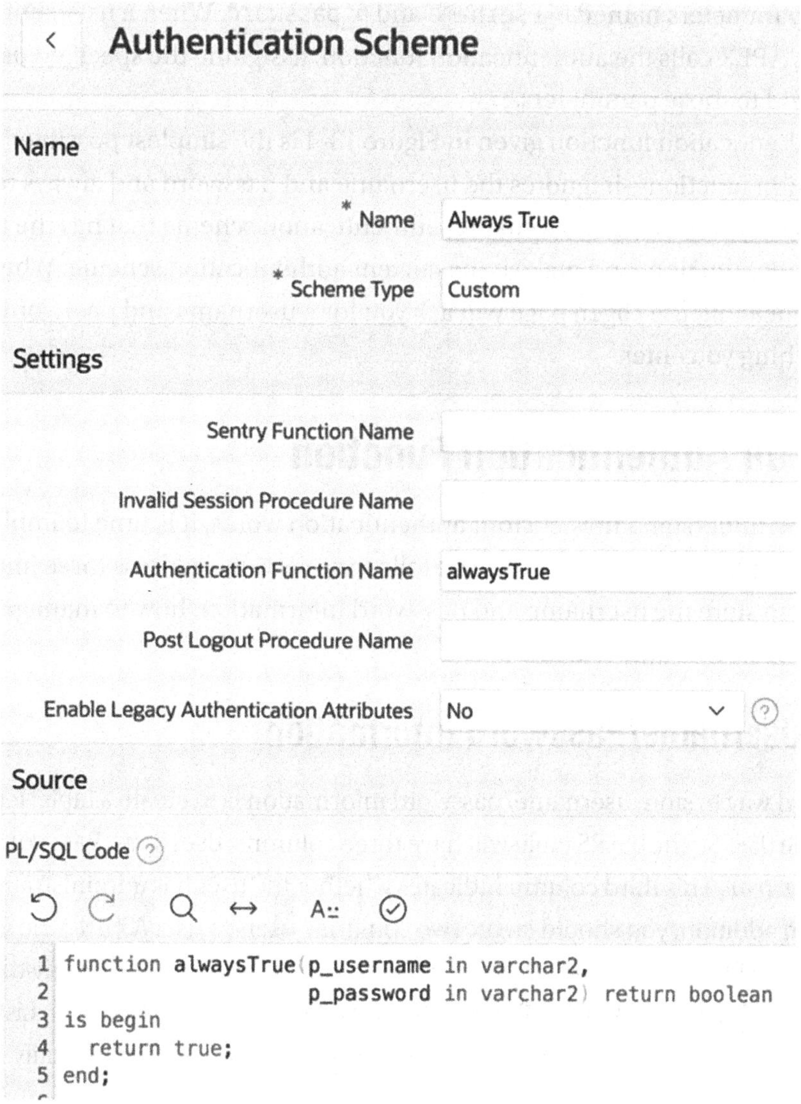

Authentication Scheme

Name

* Name	Always True
* Scheme Type	Custom

Settings

Sentry Function Name	
Invalid Session Procedure Name	
Authentication Function Name	alwaysTrue
Post Logout Procedure Name	
Enable Legacy Authentication Attributes	No

Source

PL/SQL Code ⑦

```
1  function alwaysTrue(p_username in varchar2,
2                      p_password in varchar2) return boolean
3  is begin
4    return true;
5  end;
```

Figure 13-4. *Properties for a Custom authentication scheme*

The Settings section allows you to specify four functions, but only the Authentication Function Name property is typically used. The authentication function is called each time a login is attempted. Its return value will be true or false, indicating whether the login should succeed or not. The Settings section asks only for the name of the function; APEX expects that the function will be defined elsewhere. Typically, the function will be defined as a stored procedure in the database, but if not, the Source section provides a place for you to enter the desired code. The authentication function must have parameters named p_username and p_password. When a user submits the Login page, APEX calls the authentication function, assigning the specified username and password to those parameters.

The authentication function given in Figure 13-4 is the simplest possible authentication function—it ignores the username and password and always returns true.

Try this for yourself. Create a custom authentication scheme that has the alwaysTrue authentication function, and make it the current authentication scheme. When you run the application, the Login page will ask you for a username and password, but will accept anything you enter.

Writing an Authentication Function

Now that you understand how custom authentication works, it is time to implement a more useful authentication function. The following sections address three important issues: how to store the username and password information, how to manage user accounts, and how to authenticate a user.

Storing Username/Password Information

The standard way to store username/password information is to create a table; let's call this table USERS. The USERS table will have three columns: UserName, Password, and IsAdministrator. This third column indicates whether the user has administrative privileges. In addition, you should create two "built-in" users: a user ADMIN, who is an administrator with the password 1234, and a user GUEST, who is not an administrator and has a null password. These tasks can all be performed in the SQL command tool. Listing 13-1 gives the corresponding SQL statements, which should be executed individually.

Listing 13-1. SQL Statements for the USERS Table

```
create table USERS (UserName varchar2(12), Password varchar2(1000),
                    IsAdministrator char(1));

insert into USERS (UserName, Password, IsAdministrator)
values ('ADMIN',
        apex_util.get_hash(apex_t_varchar2('ADMIN','1234'), null),
        'Y');
```

```
insert into USERS (UserName, Password, IsAdministrator)
values ('GUEST',
        apex_util.get_hash(apex_t_varchar2('GUEST',null), null),
        'N');
```

The treatment of passwords requires some explanation. For security, passwords should always be stored in an encoded form, not in plaintext. Listing 13-1 uses the function apex_util.get_hash to perform the encoding. This function was introduced in Chapter 7 and used for lost update detection. Recall that the function takes a collection of values as input and produces a string as output. The constructor function apex_t_varchar2 creates the collection of values from its arguments. For example, the encoded password for ADMIN is the output of calling the hash function with the collection ['ADMIN','1234'] as input.

The reason to use a hash function for password encoding is that it obfuscates its input value—given the output of the function, there is no practical way for someone to determine its input. So you can feel safe knowing that even if the database system were compromised (e.g., if the hard drive were stolen), the intruder could not easily make use of the encoded password information.

The hashed passwords in Listing 13-1 include the username as part of the hash value. This technique increases safety somewhat by thwarting the following attack: An intruder creates an account and then creates a sequence of passwords for it, noting the hash value of each one. The intruder can then compare these hashed passwords with the passwords stolen from the USERS table. Suppose that a match is detected. If the username is not part of the hash value, the intruder has most likely discovered a user's password. However, if the username is part of the hash value, detecting a match tells the intruder nothing.

The apex_util.get_hash function has two arguments: the first is the collection of values to be hashed, and the second argument is a Boolean value. The second argument in Listing 13-1 is null, which is treated as false. In Chapter 7, the function was called with only one argument, which implied a second argument value of true.

The second argument indicates whether the function should add the session ID to the input values. The hash value will be more secure if it includes the session ID, but it then will be of use only within the scope of that session. Because lost update detection occurs within a single session, it was reasonable to use a second argument of true, which is what occurred in Chapter 7. However, password encoding spans sessions, and so a second argument of false (or null) is mandatory.

Adding User Accounts

Your Employee Demo application needs a way to add other rows to the USERS table. Figure 13-5 shows a page called Manage Users that serves this purpose; it will be page 46 of the application. The page has two regions: the All Users region lists the records from USERS, and the Create User region lets you add a user to that table. (Note that the screenshot cuts off the password values in the All Users region to save space.)

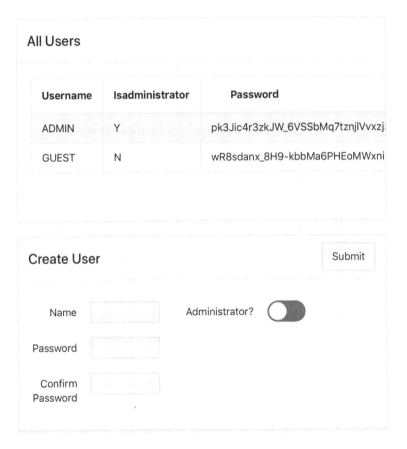

Figure 13-5. *Manage Users page of the demo application*

The `All Users` region is a classic report whose source is the SQL query:

```
select UserName, IsAdministrator, Password
from USERS
```

I put the encoded passwords in the report for demonstration purposes only. In a real application, encoded passwords should not be displayed—the values serve no useful administrative purpose, and displaying them increases the probability of their being cracked.

The `Create User` region contains four items and a submit button. The items are defined as follows:

- `P46_NAME` has the type `Plain Text`.

- `P46_ADMIN` has the type `Switch`.

- `P46_PASSWORD` and `P46_CONFIRM` have the type `Password`.

Figure 13-5 shows the contents of this page just prior to adding a non-administrator user named `JOE` having the password "`joe`". Although this username was entered in lowercase, it will get saved in the table in uppercase to ensure that usernames are case insensitive. And, of course, the password will be saved as an encoded string using the hash function.

When you click the submit button to create the new user account, two validations and a process get executed. One validation ensures that the chosen username does not already appear in the USERS table. This validation has the type `No Rows returned` and is defined by the following query:

```
select * from USERS
where UserName = upper(:P46_NAME)
```

The other validation ensures that the two passwords are identical. This validation has the type `SQL Expression` and is defined by the following code:

```
(:P46_PASSWORD = :P46_CONFIRM) or
(:P46_PASSWORD is null and :P46_CONFIRM is null)
```

The second line of the validation accounts for the possibility that the password can be `null`.

The process converts the username to uppercase, hashes the password, and inserts a record into the USERS table. Its code appears in Listing 13-2.

Listing 13-2. Code to Create a New User

```
declare
   v_username      varchar2(20) := upper(:P46_NAME);
   v_valuesToHash apex_t_varchar2 :=
                          apex_t_varchar2(v_username, :P46_PASSWORD);
begin
   insert into USERS (UserName, Password, IsAdministrator)
   values (v_username,
           apex_util.get_hash(v_valuesToHash, null),
           :P46_ADMIN);
end;
```

Authenticating Users

Now that you have a way to create users, you need to create a scheme to authenticate them. Return to your application's Authentication Schemes screen and create a new Custom scheme having the authentication function shown in Listing 13-3.

Listing 13-3. Custom Authentication Function

```
function custom_authentication (p_username in varchar2,
                                p_password in varchar2) return boolean
is
   v_userName      varchar2(20) := upper(p_username);
   v_valuesToHash apex_t_varchar2 :=
                          apex_t_varchar2(v_username, p_password);
   v_userCount     int;
begin
   select count(*) into v_userCount
   from USERS
   where UserName = v_userName
   and   Password = apex_util.get_hash(v_valuesToHash, null);

   return v_userCount = 1;
end;
```

This authentication function converts the provided username to uppercase to ensure that usernames are case insensitive. It then executes a query that sees whether there is a record in the USERS table having that username and encoded password. If so, it returns true.

After you have created this authentication scheme, make it current. Then run your application. Practice logging in as ADMIN, GUEST, and JOE. Go to the Manage Users page and create another user, and then log out and log back in as that user.

Public Pages

Consider an application whose authentication scheme is something other than No Authentication. When an unauthenticated user attempts to access any page of the application, that user will be directed to the Login page and will not be allowed to proceed until authenticated.

However, web applications often contain public pages that require no authentication, as well as the private pages that do. The APEX property Authentication lets you specify the pages that should be public.

For example, suppose that you want the home page of the Employee Demo application to be public. Go to the property editor for the page and scroll down until you find the Security section. Its Authentication property has two values: Page Requires Authentication (the default) and Page is Public. See Figure 13-6.

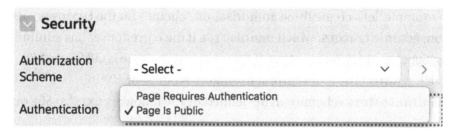

Figure 13-6. *Specifying a public page*

Change the value to Page is Public and save the page. To test the change, log out of the application. You will find that APEX enables you to visit the application's home page, but if you try to access any other page, you will be requested to log in.

Authorization

An authentication scheme specifies which users are allowed to access the non-public pages of an application. It is a good start, but often is not sufficient. A web application can have several types of users, with certain pages (or parts of pages) appropriate only for certain types. So you need a way to specify which users can access what information. This aspect of security is called *authorization*.

APEX implements authorization by allowing each page or page component to have an associated *authorization scheme*, which specifies a set of allowed users. If a page (or component) has an authorization scheme, it will be visible only to the users specified by that scheme.

Creating an Authorization Scheme

Recall that the built-in variable APP_USER holds the username of the current user. An APEX authorization scheme is defined by a Boolean expression, typically involving the value of APP_USER; a user is authorized when the expression returns true.

Authorization expressions are similar to validation expressions, and their types are similar. For example, the Exists SQL Query type returns true if the query output contains at least one record. The type PL/SQL function returning Boolean is PL/SQL code that explicitly returns true or false.

As an example, let's create three authorization schemes for the Employee Demo application: Administrators, which returns true if the current user has administrative privileges; Guests, which returns true if the current username is GUEST; and Built-in Users, which returns true if the current username is GUEST or ADMIN.

The Administrators scheme can be defined by the following Exists SQL query:

```
select *
from USERS
where UserName = :APP_USER and IsAdministrator = 'Y'
```

The Guests scheme can be defined by the following PL/SQL function:

```
return :APP_USER = 'GUEST';
```

The Built-in Users scheme can be defined by the following PL/SQL function:

```
return :APP_USER = 'GUEST' or :APP_USER = 'ADMIN';
```

To create an authorization scheme, go to the home page for the application, click the Shared Components button, and then select Authorization Schemes from the Security section. You are taken to a screen that lists the authorization schemes that have been created for your application; my initial screen is shown in Figure 13-7. My APEX server automatically creates the Administration Rights scheme for each application I create. My Employee Demo application doesn't need it, so I chose to delete it. Feel free to delete yours if your application also has one.

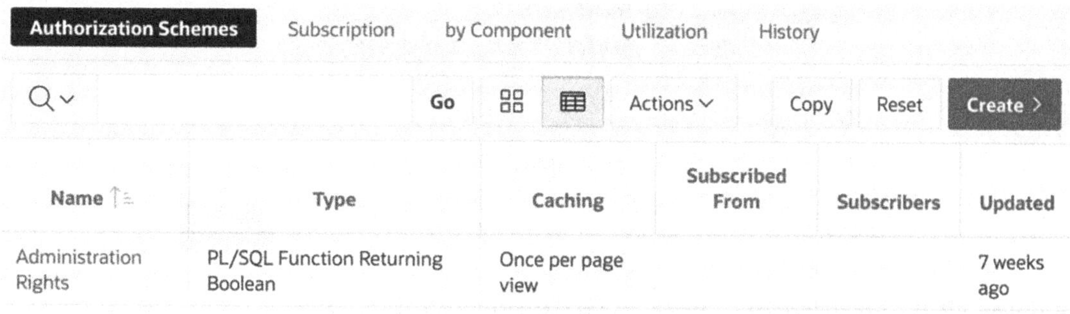

Authorization Schemes	Subscription	by Component	Utilization	History

Q ∨		Go	🔲	⊞	Actions ∨	Copy	Reset	Create >

Name ↑≜	Type	Caching	Subscribed From	Subscribers	Updated
Administration Rights	PL/SQL Function Returning Boolean	Once per page view			7 weeks ago

Figure 13-7. *The initial Authorization Schemes screen*

Clicking the Create button brings up the first screen of the authorization scheme wizard, which is shown in Figure 13-8. Specify that you want to create the scheme "from scratch." Clicking the Next button will bring up the second page of the wizard. On this screen, give the scheme a name, select its type, and enter the specification in the appropriate box; Figure 13-9 shows these specifications for the Administrators scheme.

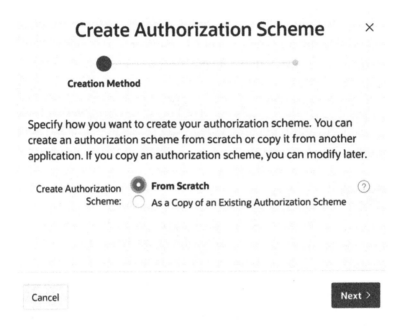

Figure 13-8. First screen of the Create Authorization wizard

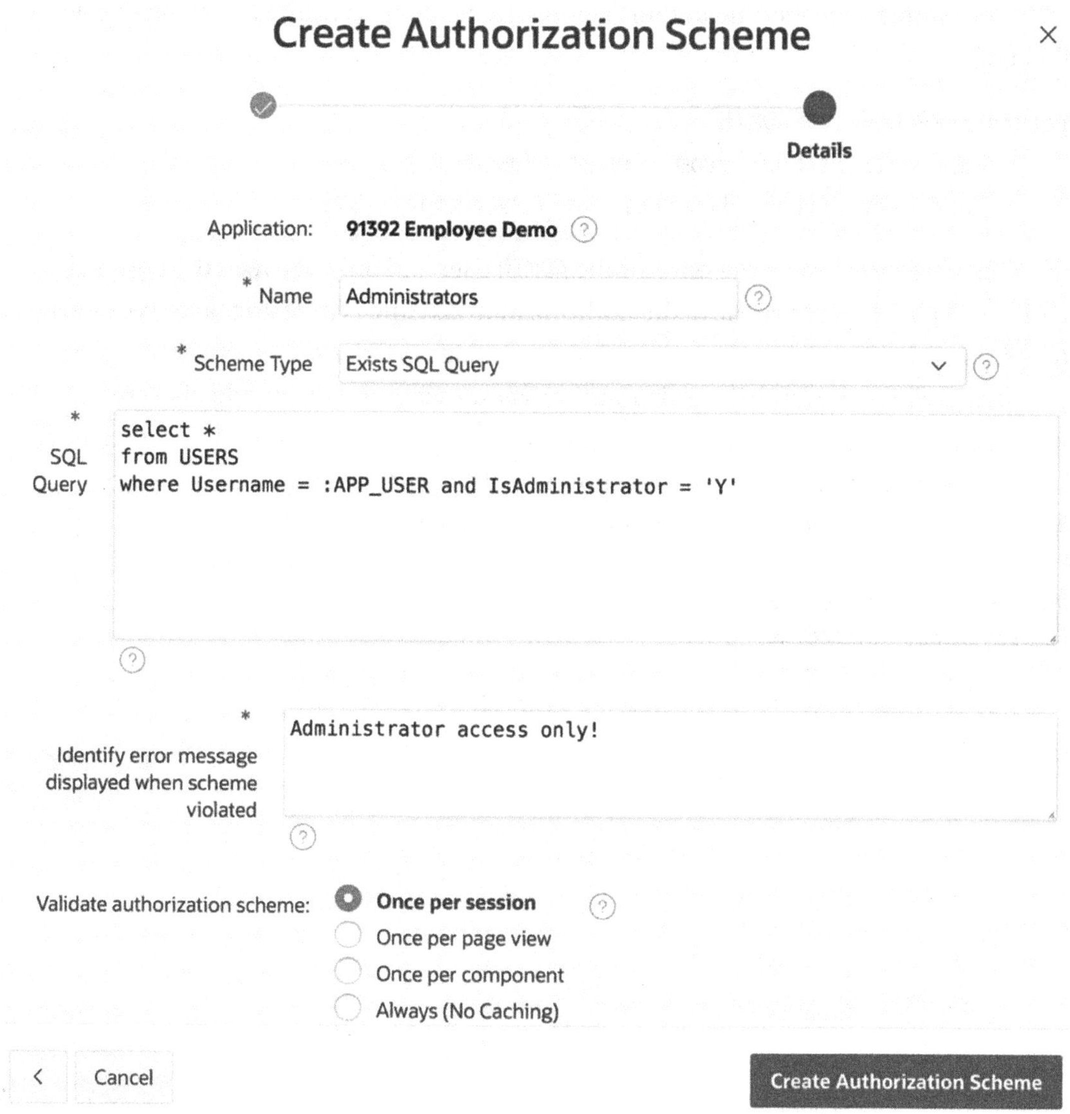

Create Authorization Scheme   ✕

Details

Application: **91392 Employee Demo** ⑦

* Name   Administrators   ⑦

* Scheme Type   Exists SQL Query   ⌄ ⑦

*
SQL
Query

```
select *
from USERS
where Username = :APP_USER and IsAdministrator = 'Y'
```

⑦

*
Identify error message
displayed when scheme
violated

```
Administrator access only!
```

⑦

Validate authorization scheme: ⬤ **Once per session**   ⑦
                                 ○ Once per page view
                                 ○ Once per component
                                 ○ Always (No Caching)

‹   Cancel   **Create Authorization Scheme**

Figure 13-9. *Second screen of the Create Authorization wizard*

The second wizard screen also asks you to provide an error message (such as **Administrator access only**) and to specify how often the authorization scheme should be validated. Two common choices are Once per session and Once per page view. Evaluating the scheme once per session is far more efficient and is the default. You would choose to evaluate once per page view only if the authorization condition is likely to change within the session.

For example, consider the authorization scheme defined by the following PL/SQL function:

```
return :APP_USER = 'ADMIN'
      and extract(hour from current_timestamp) >= 9
      and extract(hour from current_timestamp) < 17;
```

This scheme returns true only for the ADMIN user and only between the hours of 9 a.m. and 5 p.m. If the purpose of the authorization scheme is to restrict access to those times, its evaluation point needs to be Once per page view.

After creating the Administrator authorization scheme, you should also create authorization schemes for Guest and Built-In Users using the conditions described earlier. Assuming that you deleted the pre-built Administrator Rights scheme, your Authorization Schemes screen should now look like Figure 13-10.

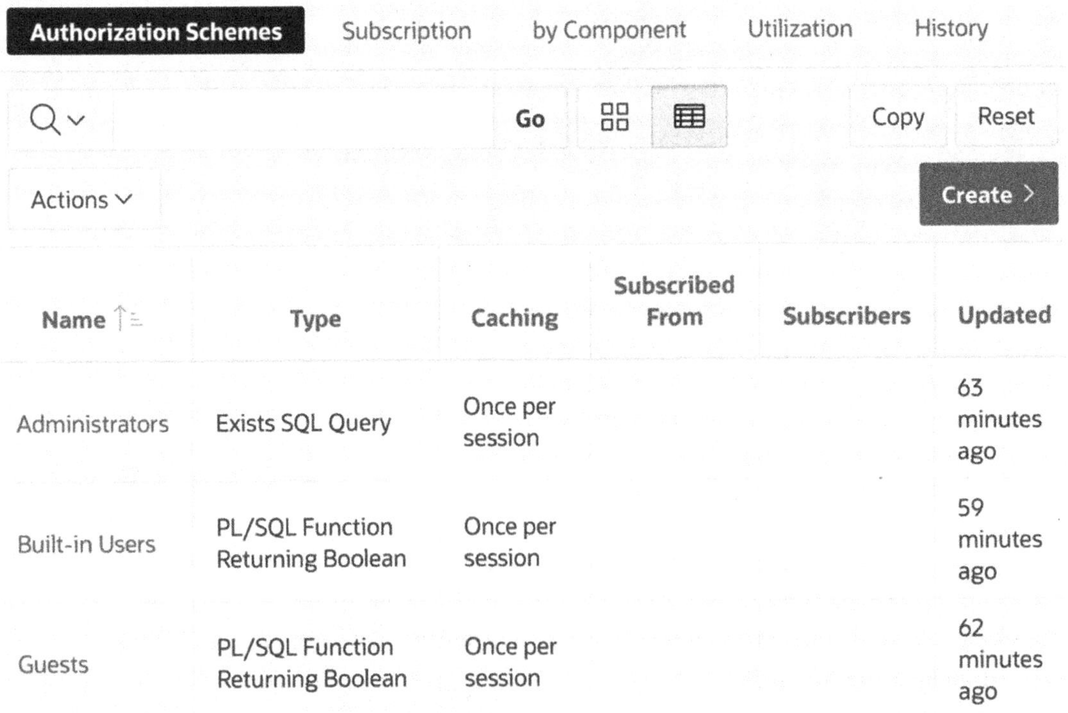

| Authorization Schemes | Subscription | by Component | Utilization | History |

| | | Go | | | Copy | Reset |

| Actions ∨ | | | | Create > |

Name ↑⹀	Type	Caching	Subscribed From	Subscribers	Updated
Administrators	Exists SQL Query	Once per session			63 minutes ago
Built-in Users	PL/SQL Function Returning Boolean	Once per session			59 minutes ago
Guests	PL/SQL Function Returning Boolean	Once per session			62 minutes ago

Figure 13-10. *The current Authorization Schemes screen*

Component Authorization

Every page component has a property `Authorization Scheme`, which appears in its `Security` section. You assign an authorization scheme to the component by choosing from a select list. Figure 13-11 depicts this select list for my `Employee Demo` application.

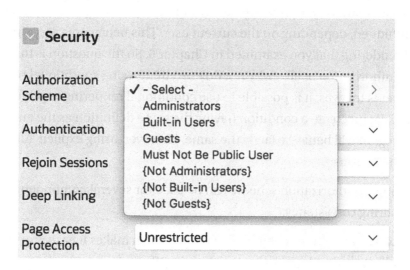

Figure 13-11. *Assigning an authorization scheme to a component*

The first option is `-Select-`, which denotes that no authorization is required. The next three options are the three authorization schemes I created. The last three options are the negations of these, which are automatically generated by APEX. The `Must Not Be Public User` scheme is built in to APEX and will be discussed later.

For an example, consider the `Employee Data Entry` page from Figure 7-5. Recall that this page has four regions: a region to display a report of the EMP table, plus regions to delete, insert, and update table rows. Assume that anyone can view the employee report, but guests are not allowed to modify it. In this case, you would assign the authorization scheme `Not Guests` to the delete, insert, and update regions and assign `-Select-` to the report region. The result is that users authenticated as GUEST will see only the report region; the other three regions will be hidden from them.

For a second example, consider again the `Manage Users` page of Figure 13-5. If you want the two regions on the page to be accessible only to administrators, assign the authorization scheme `Administrators` to each of them. As a result, administrators will see the page as shown in the figure; non-administrators will see a page having a navigation bar and menu, but no content.

Because displaying an essentially blank page to a user is awkward, the page ought to display something to the non-administrators. One solution is to create a region that displays the message **This page is for administrators only** and assign the authorization scheme Not Administrators to it. Another solution is to assign an authorization scheme to the entire page, as discussed later.

Assigning an authorization scheme to a component causes that component to be displayed or hidden, depending on the current user. This behavior is very similar to the conditional rendering that you examined in Chapter 6. So the question is this: why use component authorization at all—why not do everything using conditional rendering?

The answer is that yes, it is possible to use conditional rendering to perform authorization. If you create a condition having the same definition as the authorization scheme, the region will behave exactly the same. However, using explicit authorization is better for three reasons:

- A single authorization scheme can be used for several components, ensuring consistency.

- Each authorization scheme has a name, which makes it easier for the application developer to understand the effect of the authorization condition.

- Authorization and conditional rendering have entirely different purposes in an application, and it is clearer if they are kept separate.

Page Authorization

Instead of assigning an authorization scheme to the components of a page, you can assign it to the page itself. Each page has the property Authorization Scheme in its Security section, with the same options as in Figure 13-11.

For an example, let's build a page named Change Password, which will allow users to change their own password. This page is shown in Figure 13-12 and will be page 47 of Employee Demo.

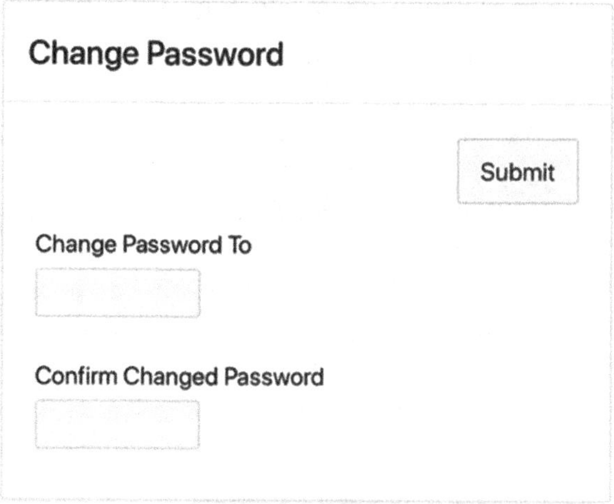

Change Password

Submit

Change Password To

Confirm Changed Password

Figure 13-12. Change Password page

This page consists of a static content region having two items of type Password:
P47_PASSWORD and P47_CONFIRM. Clicking the submit button invokes a validation and a
process. The validation uses the following SQL expression to ensure that the two entered
passwords are identical:

```
:P47_PASSWORD = :P47_CONFIRM
```

The process updates the USERS table via the following PL/SQL code:

```
declare
  v_valuesToHash apex_t_varchar2 :=
                        apex_t_varchar2(:APP_USER, :P47_PASSWORD);
begin
  update USERS
  set Password = apex_util.get_hash(v_valuesToHash, null)
  where UserName = :APP_USER;
end;
```

How should this page be authorized? Assume that everyone should be allowed to
change their own password except for the built-in users GUEST and ADMIN. Thus, the
authorization scheme for the page should be Not Built-In Users.

Assigning an authorization scheme to a page makes it inaccessible to unauthorized
users. In particular, if an unauthorized user attempts to render the page, APEX instead
displays an error message. Figure 13-13 shows the error message that results when a

built-in user tries to access the `Change Password` page. Clicking the OK button on the message returns the user to the previous page.

Built-in users only

Access denied by Page security check

Figure 13-13. *Result of unauthorized page access*

This error message does the job, but not very well. The error message is somewhat harsh. (In fact, the message is backward—APEX uses the error message defined for the `Built-in Users` scheme because the negated scheme, being automatically generated, has no error message.) A much more user-friendly approach is to simply hide the page from an unauthorized user. In the case of the `Change Password` page, this amounts to not displaying its navigation menu entry to an unauthorized user. This is easily done by changing the `Authorization Scheme` property of the list entry.

To find the property, start at the application's `Shared Components` screen and navigate to the `Desktop Navigation Menu` list, as shown in Figure 4-2. Scroll down to its `Change Password` entry; clicking that entry will bring up its `List Entry` screen as shown in Figure 4-3. The property you want is in the `Authorization` section; choose the `Not Built-in Users` authorization scheme and click the `Apply Changes` button. Then run your application. Note that if you are logged in as `ADMIN` or `GUEST`, the entry for the `Change Password` page will be missing from the navigation menu.

A good rule of thumb is this: if a page has an authorization scheme, its associated navigation menu entry should have the same authorization scheme.

Not Public User Scheme

The authorization scheme `Not Public User` is built into APEX. It returns `true` for any logged in user and `false` if the user has not logged in. Its primary use is to selectively hide components on public pages.

For example, suppose that your application's home page is a public page. However, suppose that not all of the page should be public; in particular, the Quick Link region should be visible only to logged in users. This situation can be handled by setting the authorization for that region to Not Public User.

Avoiding Malicious Use

A web application's authentication and authorization schemes form a detailed specification of who is allowed to access what components of which pages. Each authenticated user has a well-defined, limited interface to the data—provided, of course, that the user accesses the pages in the intended manner.

The problem is that there are various ways for users to subvert the intended functionality of a web application. This section focuses on three such techniques: SQL injection, cross-site scripting, and URL modification. With *SQL injection*, a user submits an SQL code fragment that masquerades as input data and alters the query that is processing this pretend "data." With *cross-site scripting*, a user saves a malicious JavaScript code fragment as part of a table's data value; when another user subsequently displays that value, the JavaScript code also executes. With *URL modification*, a user sends a URL to the server in a form that the server expects; however, the action requested by that URL is something that the user is not supposed to do.

APEX has several properties to help you guard against malicious use. In fact, it is relatively straightforward to use these properties to build a tamper-proof application. To take advantage of them, however, you need to understand what the threats are and how APEX can guard against them.

SQL Injection

Recall the Report Builder demo page from Figure 12-1. The intent of this page is to display a subset of either the EMP or DEPT table based on a condition entered into the Enter Condition text area. However, it is possible for a malicious user to enter a condition that causes the page to display data from other tables in quite unintended ways. For example, Figure 13-14 shows a condition that displays the contents of the USERS table.

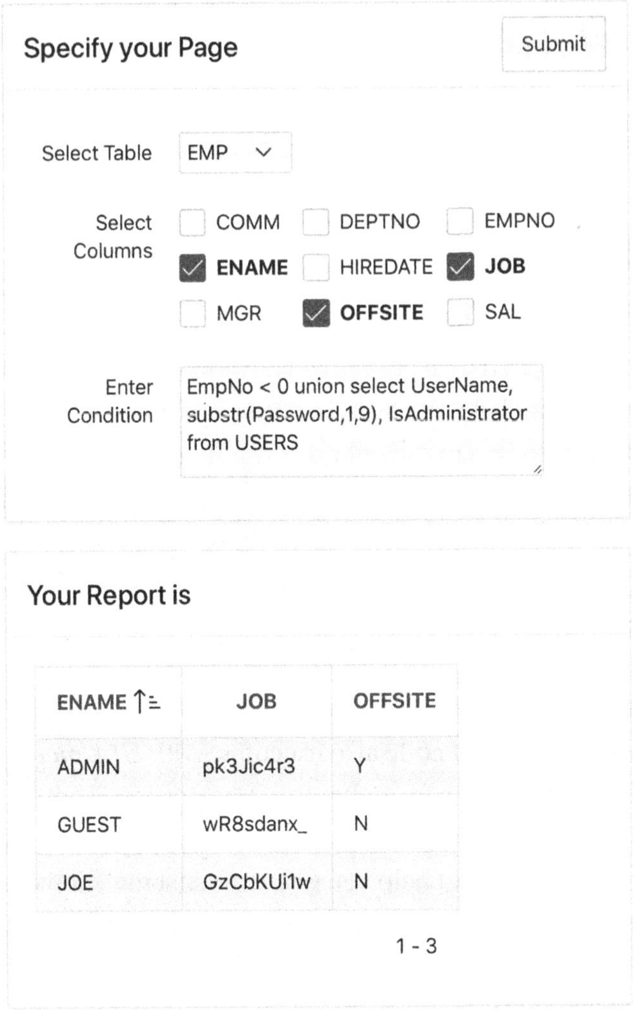

Figure 13-14. *Unintended use of the Report Builder page*

Note that the string typed into the Enter Condition item is not a legal SQL condition. Instead, it consists of a legal condition, EmpNo<0, plus some additional SQL code. To understand the purpose of the input, you have to know how the PL/SQL function of

Listing 12-1 constructs the report's source query. Recall that the code generates the beginning of a query for EMP and then appends the specified condition to the end of it. So the source query generated for Figure 13-14 becomes the following:

```
select EName, Job, Offsite
from EMP where EmpNo < 0
union
select UserName, substr(Password,1,9), IsAdministrator
from USERS
```

Note that the user has taken advantage of the union keyword to broaden the scope of the query. The intended query on the EMP table is now just a subquery of the overall query. Moreover, the condition EmpNo<0 causes that subquery to return no output records, which means that the output of the overall query comes entirely from the second subquery.

This second subquery can be arbitrary, subject only to the restriction that it must have the same number of columns as the first subquery, and each output value must match the type of the corresponding column of the first subquery. This restriction explains why the second subquery extracts only the first nine characters of the password—the Job column is defined as varchar2(9), so attempting to select additional characters would generate an SQL error.

A malicious user might use this exploit to obtain the encoded passwords of users, in order to subsequently crack them and gain unauthorized access to the application. Of course, having only the first nine characters of the encoded passwords is not sufficient. The malicious user could, however, discover the remaining characters by running the exploit several more times, each time grabbing the next nine characters of the password.

This technique is called *SQL injection*. SQL injection occurs when a malicious user enters SQL into a text-based item to change a query from its intended purpose. The preceding example shows that SQL injection can have serious consequences. Thus, application developers must be aware of the possibility of SQL injection and avoid it at all costs.

In a sense, the Report Builder page was asking for trouble because the Enter Condition item expected SQL code. The real perniciousness of SQL injection is that it can succeed even when an item expects a value. For example, let's build a page titled SQL Injection, which will be page 48 of Employee Demo. Figure 13-15 shows an intended use of this page.

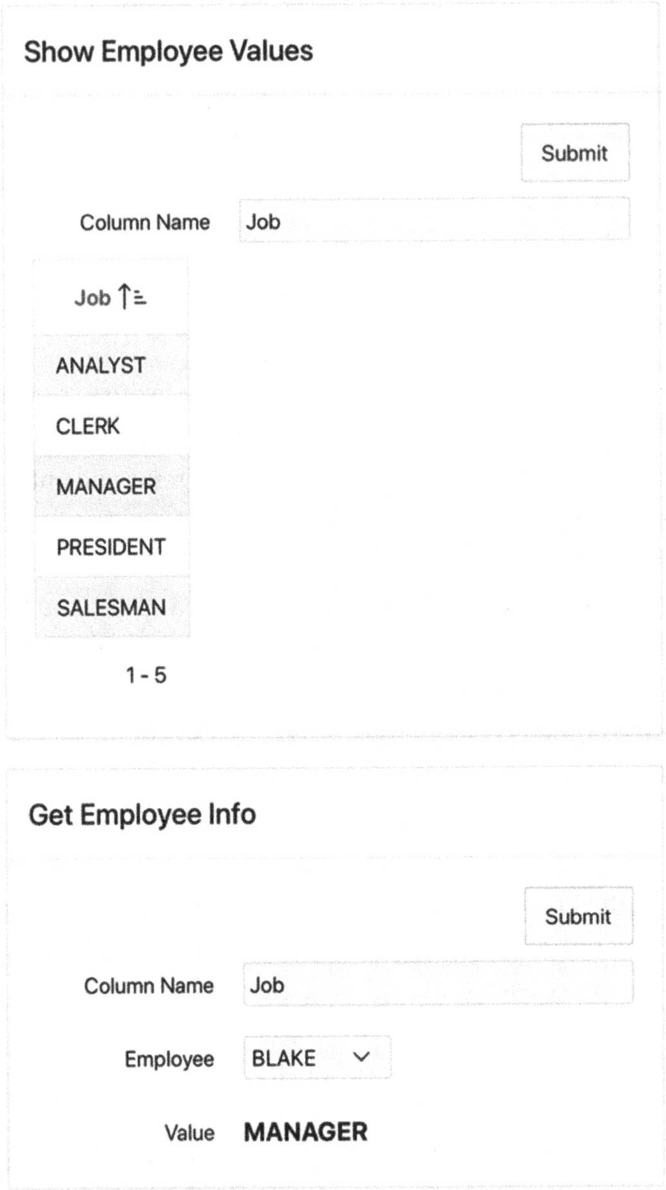

Show Employee Values

Submit

Column Name   Job

Job ↑≞

ANALYST

CLERK

MANAGER

PRESIDENT

SALESMAN

1 - 5

Get Employee Info

Submit

Column Name   Job

Employee   BLAKE   ∨

Value   **MANAGER**

Figure 13-15. *Intended use of the SQL Injection page*

The page contains two regions. The input to the Show Employee Values region is a column name from the EMP table; clicking the Submit button then displays a report of the distinct values for that column. In Figure 13-15, the report displays the five jobs appearing in the EMP table.

The Get Employee Info region is similar. Its input is a column name and employee number; clicking the submit button displays the value of that column for the selected employee. In Figure 13-15, the region tells you that Blake is a manager.

Let's first consider how to implement the Show Employee Values region. It will have a single item: a text field named P48_COLUMN1. The region will have the type Classic Report and will use dynamic SQL as described in Chapter 12. That is, its source will have the type PL/SQL Function Body returning SQL Query and have the code shown in Listing 13-4.

Listing 13-4. PL/SQL Code for the Show Employee Values Report

```
return 'select distinct ' || :P48_COLUMN1 || ' from EMP';
```

Because the report uses dynamic SQL, you will also need to configure some of the report properties, as follows:

- Enable generic column names.

- Specify a column count of 1.

- Set the column heading type to PL/SQL Function Body, having the expression return :P48_COLUMN1;.

Now let's consider how to implement the Get Employee Info region. It is a static content region having three items: P48_COLUMN2 is a text field, P48_EMPNO2 is a select list that displays employee names and returns employee numbers, and P48_VALUE2 is a display-only item.

The region has a process associated with the submit button; the code for this process appears in Listing 13-5. The code first constructs a query string to retrieve the value of the specified employee. It then uses execute immediate to retrieve the specified value for the employee P48_EMPNO2 and place it in the display-only item P48_VALUE2.

Listing 13-5. Process Code for the Get Employee Info Region

```
declare
  v_query varchar2(100);
begin
  v_query := 'select ' || :P48_COLUMN2 || ' from EMP where EmpNo = :1';
```

```
execute immediate v_query
into  :P48_VALUE2
using :P48_EMPNO2;
end;
```

Although the regions on this page seem innocuous enough, they are vulnerable to SQL injection. Figure 13-16 shows how either region of the page can be used to display the entire encoded password of the ADMIN user. (The screenshot cuts off the encoded passwords to save space.)

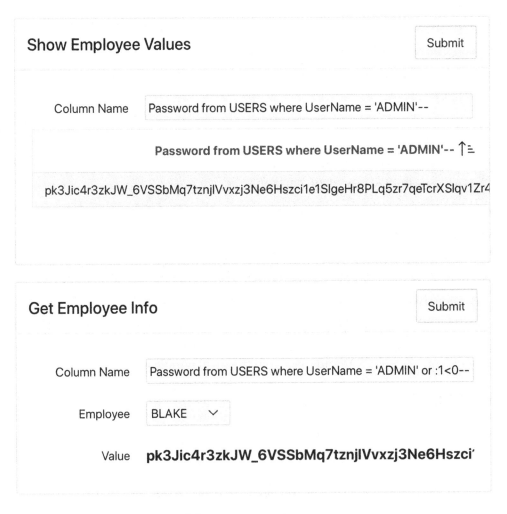

Figure 13-16. *Malicious use of the SQL Injection page*

The value for `P48_COLUMN1` in Figure 13-16 is this:

```
Password from USERS where UserName = 'ADMIN' --
```

When APEX uses this string to construct the source of the report, it gets the following SQL query:

```
select distinct Password from USERS where UserName = 'ADMIN' -- from EMP
```

Recall that the character "`--`" denotes a comment in PL/SQL. Thus, the `from EMP` part of the SQL code is totally ignored. In other words, the SQL injection transformed a query on the EMP table into a query on the USERS table.

The `Get Employee Info` region uses essentially the same injection trick. The value for `P48_COLUMN2` in Figure 13-16 is the following:

```
Password from USERS where UserName = 'ADMIN' or :1 < 0 --
```

When APEX uses this string to construct the source of the report, it gets the following SQL query:

```
select Password from USERS
where UserName = 'ADMIN' or :1 < 0 --from EMP where EmpNo = :1
```

Again, everything after the comment characters is ignored, so the injection winds up creating a query on the USERS table instead of the EMP table.

Note that the malicious user must carefully craft the injected code so that the resulting SQL string is legal. Consider the `Get Employee Info` example. The `execute immediate` statement passes an employee number to the SQL query; although the malicious query will not use this value, it still needs to have a formal parameter to receive it. The expression `:1<0` achieves this goal. The specified employee number is assigned to the parameter `:1`. Because employee numbers are always positive, this expression always evaluates to `false`, so it does not affect the output of the query.

In general, SQL injection is possible whenever a query string is constructed from raw, unchecked user input. In such cases, a malicious user might be able to enter a code fragment as input that changes the purpose of the constructed query. Therefore,

an application developer should always check user input to ensure that it is in the
intended format. Here are three strategies:

- *Avoid text-based input.* Note that the SQL injection technique of
  Figure 13-16 would not work if the user were forced to choose a
  column from a list (although the URL modification technique could
  circumvent this strategy, as you will see later).

- *Write an APEX validation for the input that detects possible code
  fragments.* For example, in Figure 13-16, you might refuse to accept
  column names that contain spaces or comment characters.

- *Translate the input into a "cleansed" form.* That is, write a function to
  transform a user value into an acceptable one. In Figure 13-16, the
  function might remove all spaces from the input or it might convert
  each space into the escaped HTML character .

Let's see how these strategies can be used to improve the Report Builder page
shown in Figure 13-14. The issue, of course, is that the text-based item Enter Condition
requires the user to enter SQL code. The first strategy suggests that you try a non-text-
based way to specify the condition. The Version 2 region of the Count and Delete
demo page (shown in Figure 12-4) showed how this could be done, at least for simple
conditions. The APEX *query builder* provides a more complex solution.

Note   If you have never used the query builder, you should try it. Starting from the
APEX SQL Workshop, click Utilities and then Query Builder. Click a table
name to include it in the query, and explore.

The second strategy suggests you write a validation that rejects condition strings that
contain suspicious keywords such as union or select. This strategy seems reasonable
here.

The third strategy won't work well for an item that expects SQL code as input, as in
Figure 13-14. However, it is useful for items that expect values, as in the SQL Injection
page of Figure 13-15. In particular, a good strategy for the Show Employee Values
region is to remove all spaces from P48_COLUMN1 in the source of the report, as shown
in Listing 13-6.

Listing 13-6. Revising Listing 13-4 to Avoid SQL Injection

```
return 'select distinct ' || replace(:P48_COLUMN1, ' ', '') || ' from EMP';
```

Similarly, you can improve the Get Employee Info region by removing all spaces from P48_COLUMN2 in the code for the submit process.

Cross-Site Scripting

In the *cross-site scripting* technique, a malicious user saves JavaScript code as part of a database value. The code acts like a booby trap: when another user displays a page containing that value, the user's browser executes the JavaScript code without the user's knowledge. The JavaScript code might do things like emailing the user's session information to the attacker (thereby letting the attacker pretend to be the user) or having the APEX server execute a specified function.

What makes cross-site scripting so evil is that the JavaScript code gets executed *with the victim's level of authorization*. So if an administrator falls prey to a cross-site scripting attack, the attacker would obtain administrator-level access to the database.

A successful cross-site scripting attack has three requirements: first, some table must have a column of type varchar2(N), where N is large enough to hold the JavaScript code; second, some page of the application must have a text-based item used for data entry into this field; and third, some page of the application must be configured to display the tainted value in "raw" unescaped form.

As it stands, the Employee Demo application is not susceptible to cross-site scripting because neither EMP nor DEPT has a sufficiently large column. So for the purpose of this example, you should alter the DEPT table by expanding the column Loc to varchar2(80). The required SQL is this:

```
alter table DEPT
modify Loc varchar2(80)
```

Now you can build a page to demonstrate cross-site scripting attacks. The Cross-Site Scripting page is page 49 of Employee Demo and is shown in Figure 13-17.

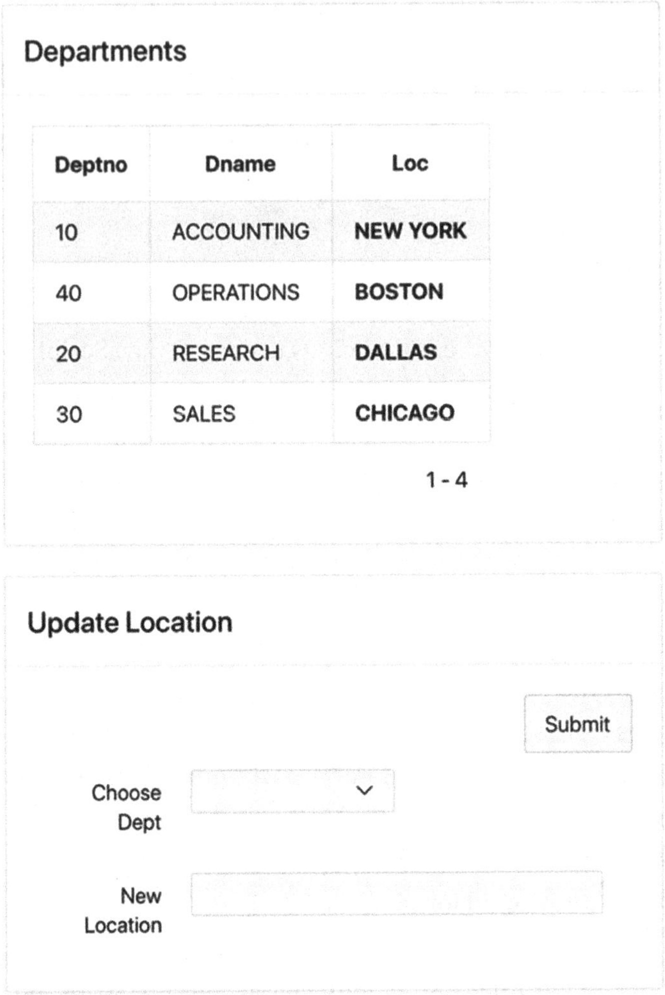

Figure 13-17. *Cross-Site Scripting page*

This page has two regions. The Departments region is a classic report having the source query

```
select * from DEPT
order by DName
```

The Update Location region is a form having the source

```
select DeptNo, Loc
from DEPT
```

You should customize the form region using the techniques of Chapter 10. In particular:

- Turn on the form's `Edit Enabled` property, and select `Update Row` as the only allowed operation.

- Create a button whose action is `Submit` and whose database action is `SQL UPDATE action`.

- Specify that the item `P49_DEPTNO` is the primary key. Also, change its type to be `Select List`, having the list-of-values query.

  ```
  select DName, DeptNo
  from DEPT
  ```

The page needs one further configuration to match Figure 13-17, namely that the values in the Loc column should be formatted in bold. Chapter 3 showed how to use the column's `HTML Expression` property to wrap a column value inside HTML tags. For example, you could use the HTML expression for the LOC column to be this:

```
<b>#LOC#</b>
```

For the purposes of this example I want to use a different technique, which is to use the report's source query to format the column. In particular, change the source of the report to this:

```
select DeptNo, DName, '<b>' || Loc || '</b>' as Loc
from DEPT
order by DName
```

Note that the query wraps HTML tags around the department name, meaning that the value of LOC is the HTML expression. The idea is that when I display the report, the LOC values should be formatted in bold. However, it doesn't quite work. If you run the page, the HTML tags appear as part of the value, as shown in Figure 13-12.

Departments

Deptno	Dname	Loc
10	ACCOUNTING	<b>NEW YORK</b>
40	OPERATIONS	<b>BOSTON</b>
20	RESEARCH	<b>DALLAS</b>
30	SALES	<b>CHICAGO</b>

1 - 4

Figure 13-18. *Report displays the HTML tags*

If you think about it, this result makes some sense—after all, the report is just displaying the output of the query. However, the situation is actually more complex than that. Consider how APEX renders a report: it generates an HTML table and places the output values within it. So, for example, the HTML code to display the first row of the report would look like this:

```
<tr><td>10</td>
    <td>ACCOUNTING</td>
    <td><b>NEW YORK</b></td></tr>
```

Although the <b> and </b> tags were entered into the table as data, the browser will wind up treating them as HTML. In order for APEX to display the tags in the report, it must do extra work. In particular, it transforms the < and > characters into different characters that happen to display the same. This transformation is called *escaping the special characters*. In particular, the character < is replaced by < and the character > is replaced by >.

Each report column has the property Escape special characters in its Security section. By default it is turned on, which causes APEX to escape the special characters and display the HTML tags as in Figure 13-18. Now go to the Loc column and turn off the property. The tags in the Loc values will not be escaped, and will thus be treated as HTML. The report will now look like Figure 13-17.

This ability to format data within the SQL source query is quite powerful and lets you do things that are not possible via the HTML Expression property. For example, you can choose to format certain values in a column as text, and other values as a link or an image. This power, however, comes with a price. As soon as you turn off a column's Escape special characters property, you open yourself up to a cross-site scripting attack. The help screen for this property is particularly vehement on this point; see Figure 13-19.

Escape special characters

To prevent Cross-Site Scripting (XSS) attacks, always set this attribute to **On**. If you need to render HTML tags stored in the page item or in the entries of a list of values, you can set this flag to **Off**. In such cases, you should take additional precautions to ensure any user input to such fields are properly escaped when entered and before saving.

Figure 13-19. *Help text for the Escape Special Characters property*

To demonstrate, let's see how easy it is to use this page to compromise the application. From the Update Location region, choose any department, such as OPERATIONS. The Location field should show the current value, which is BOSTON. Change that value to this:

```
BOSTON<script>alert('Your application has been compromised')</script>
```

This new value is a string consisting of the location, followed by a script that calls the JavaScript function alert. When a browser renders this string, it will display "BOSTON" and then call the script. In other words, the update will have no visible effect on the report. However, the script will run each time someone renders the page.

Click the Submit Changes button. Before the page reloads, your browser will display an alert similar to Figure 13-20. Now navigate to a different page and come back to this one—the alert will again be displayed. It is a bit chilling to realize that without this alert, you would have had no idea that your application was already seriously compromised.

Figure 13-20. *Cross-site scripting attack succeeded*

The preceding JavaScript code is not malicious. The `alert` function just displays an alert window in the user's browser. A malicious JavaScript string will almost certainly not throw an alert and will do something far more sophisticated and nasty. In all likelihood, you will not discover the problem until it is too late. It is therefore up to you to ensure that this cannot happen.

The only way for an application to eliminate cross-site scripting is to ensure that a page does not display unescaped data. Three approaches are possible, which will be considered in turn:

- Reject inappropriate data

- Escape the data before saving it in the database

- Escape the data before it is displayed

Reject Inappropriate Data

In any data entry page, it is good practice to keep inappropriate data from being entered into the database. This is what database constraints and APEX validations are all about. The act of checking input data for unexpected HTML follows the same principle. There are two approaches you can take.

The first approach is to use the property `Restricted Characters`, found in an item's `Security` section. This property lets you specify which characters are allowed in the input. Figure 13-21 shows the possible choices. You can require that the input be only alphanumeric, or you can restrict the use of certain special characters.

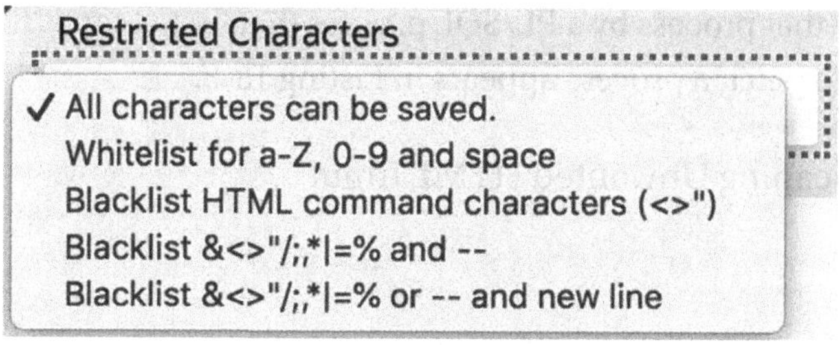

Figure 13-21. *Choices for the Restricted Characters property*

In the current example, suppose that department locations are alphanumeric; in that case, it would make sense to set the Restricted Characters property for P49_LOC to be Whitelist for a-Z, 0-9, and space. If not, then you should at least set it to Blacklist HTML command characters.

The second approach is to write an APEX validation to perform the restriction. APEX provides a function called apex_escape.html, which takes any input string and turns it into a visibly identical string that contains no HTML characters. For example, Listing 13-7 shows the PL/SQL code for a validation that returns false if the input to P49_LOC contains HTML characters.

Listing 13-7. Validation to Guard Against Unwanted HTML Input

```
declare
  v_LocEscaped varchar2(100);
begin
  v_LocEscaped := apex_escape.html(:P49_LOC);
  if :P49_LOC = v_LocEscaped then
    return true;
  else
    return false;
  end if;
end;
```

Escape Data Before Saving It

Instead of rejecting HTML-based input, you can instead transform it to a version without HTML characters. The apex_escape.html function is useful here as well. For example, in the Cross-Site Scripting page, the form generated the process to update the database.

You could replace that process by a PL/SQL process that first escapes the values before saving. The code for such a process appears in Listing 13-8.

Listing 13-8. Escaping Unwanted HTML Input

```
begin
  update DEPT
  set Loc = apex_escape.html(:P44_LOC)
  where DeptNo = :P44_DEPTNO;
end;
```

Escape Data Before Displaying It

An application might not be able to guarantee that the database does not contain any HTML code, because users might have other ways to enter data. So to ensure against cross-site scripting, it is a good idea to always escape data before displaying it on a page. That is what the Escape Special Characters property is all about (refer back to Figure 13-19). If every column in your report has this property turned on, your report is immune to cross-site scripting attacks.

However, if a column of your report needs to turn this property off, you must escape the necessary characters. Again, the apex_escape.html function is very useful. For example, Listing 13-9 gives the original source for the example report, and Listing 13-10 shows a revised version in which the data has been escaped.

Listing 13-9. Original Source Query

```
select DeptNo, DName, '<b>' || Loc || '</b>' as Loc
from DEPT
order by Dname
```

Listing 13-10. Revised Source Query

```
select DeptNo, DName, '<b>' || apex_escape.html(Loc) || '</b>' as Loc
from DEPT
order by DName
```

URL Modification

The third type of malicious attack takes advantage of the way that web pages are accessed. In a typical, non-malicious scenario, a user types the URL for an application's home page into a browser. From there, URLs are largely irrelevant; the user clicks tabs, links, and buttons to navigate to the other pages.

This scenario corresponds to the intended use of the application. The navigational links on a page are designed to help the user decide what pages to examine next. In fact, one criterion for measuring the quality of an application is the extent to which navigational aids contribute to a coherent user experience.

Of course, a user need not follow this scenario. A user who knows the URL structure of an application can access an arbitrary page by simply constructing a valid URL to it. This possibility presents several difficulties for APEX developers. The following subsections examine these difficulties and their solutions.

APEX URL Structure

APEX applications support two different URL formats: a legacy syntax and a newer "friendly" syntax. The syntax used in this book has been the legacy syntax, in which applications and pages are specified by their number. For example, the number of my `Employee Demo` application is 91392 and the number of the home page is 1. Thus, the legacy URL of my home page is

```
apex.oracle.com/pls/apex/f?p=91392:1
```

Instead of numbers, the friendly URL syntax specifies the workspace, application, and page by their names. For example, the friendly URL of my home page is

```
apex.oracle.com/pls/apex/understanding_apex/r/employee-demo/home
```

Although I will continue to use legacy URLs in this chapter, most of these concepts also apply to friendly URLs. (And even if you prefer friendly URLs, you still need to be aware of how a malicious user can abuse legacy URLs.)

A legacy URL supports nine colon-separated arguments; if the value of an argument is missing, a default value is used. You already know the first three arguments: the application id, the page id, and the session id. The other two relevant arguments are the seventh and eighth, which are used for setting the session state.

For an example of these arguments, consider the Employees by Department page of Chapter 6, which appears again in Figure 13-22.

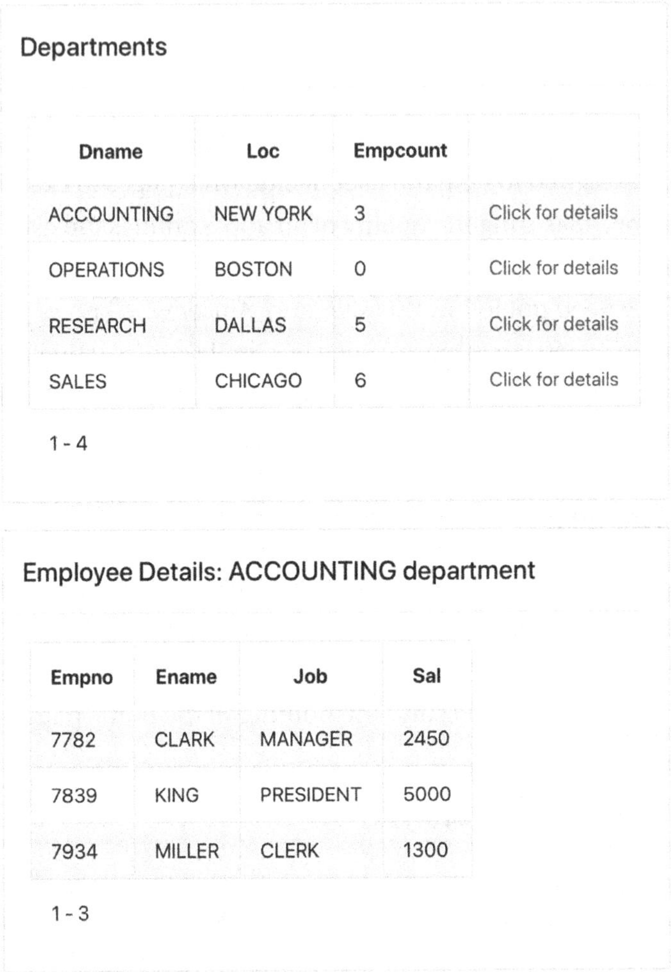

Departments

Dname	Loc	Empcount	
ACCOUNTING	NEW YORK	3	Click for details
OPERATIONS	BOSTON	0	Click for details
RESEARCH	DALLAS	5	Click for details
SALES	CHICAGO	6	Click for details

1 - 4

Employee Details: ACCOUNTING department

Empno	Ename	Job	Sal
7782	CLARK	MANAGER	2450
7839	KING	PRESIDENT	5000
7934	MILLER	CLERK	1300

1 - 3

Figure 13-22. *Employees by Department page*

Recall that when you click a Click for Details link, a redirect occurs, the session state values of P12_DEPTNO and P12_DNAME are set, and the page is re-rendered. Listing 13-11 shows the legacy URL that arises from clicking the link for ACCOUNTING, assuming that the session id is 98765. (I omitted the URL's common prefix to save space.)

Listing 13-11. URL for Employees by Department Page

```
f?p=91392:12:98765:::::P12_DEPTNO,P12_DNAME:10,ACCOUNTING
```

This listing illustrates the purpose of the seventh and eighth arguments of a URL. The seventh argument is a comma-separated list of the items whose values are to be set (P12_DEPTNO and P12_DNAME), and the eighth is a list of the values they will be set to (10 and ACCOUNTING).

GET vs. POST

Requests that a browser makes to a web server can be of different types. The two most common types are GET and POST, which differ in how they pass information to the server. A POST request places the information in a specific area within the request packet. A GET request, on the other hand, passes information to the server via its URL.

In APEX, POST requests are made by submit operations. To process a submit, the browser extracts the values of the page items, packages them into the POST request, and sends it to the server. The server then uses these values to change the session state. If you want to verify this, go to any page with a submit button (such as Filter by Job and Department). Click the submit button and observe that the URL does not change. This demonstrates that the input to the computation is not part of the submitted URL, which is also the reason why you cannot bookmark the result of a submit operation.

On the other hand, redirect operations in APEX make GET requests. Redirections are performed by several kinds of APEX components, such as buttons, list-based items, column links, and branches. As part of the redirection, APEX lets you assign values to specified items in the session state. For example, in the Employees by Department page of Figure 13-22, the Click for Details column link sets P12_DEPTNO and P12_DNAME to the department number and name of the current record, respectively. The browser sends this information to the server by encoding it within the URL, as was shown in Listing 13-11.

Because the structure of an APEX URL is well-known, it is possible for an authenticated user to construct a URL that accesses the application in a way the application developer did not intend. The following sections consider two techniques.

Page Scanning

The first technique is called *page scanning*. A user constructs a sequence of URLs to access every possible page, just to see what page (if any) shows up. The possibility of page scanning means that you cannot make a page inaccessible just by hiding it. For example, consider the Change Password page from Figure 13-12, which is page 47 of Employee Demo. In that section, you saw how to hide the page by assigning an authorization scheme to its navigation menu entry. Although it is a good design strategy, it doesn't make the page inaccessible because any user could access the page via the URL

```
apex.oracle.com/pls/apex/f?p=91392:47.
```

Because there is no good way to eliminate page scanning, a developer's only recourse is to use authorization to limit accessibility. In other words, the fact that page scanning is possible means that it is absolutely essential to define an authorization scheme for each page, regardless of its visibility from the navigation menu.

Item Modification

The second technique, *item modification*, can be used to attack pages that set item values via a URL. A user takes an existing legitimate URL for that page, modifies the assigned values, and submits the modified URL.

For example, suppose that the company has a fifth department, whose department number is 50 and name is SECRET. Suppose that you don't want the membership of this department to become public, so you set the source of the Departments report in Figure 13-22 so that it excludes that department. Unfortunately, it is easy to use URL modification to obtain this hidden information. A user only needs to modify the URL of Listing 13-11 so that it requests the contents of department 50, as follows:

```
f?p=91392:12:98765::::P12_DEPTNO,P12_DNAME:50,SECRET
```

For another example, consider the Form Update page of Figure 10-9. Figure 13-23 displays its Update Employees region after I selected BLAKE from the Choose Employee item. This item, named P30_EMPNO, performed a Redirect and Set Value action. The URL generated by the redirect action is

```
f?p=91392:30:98765:::::P30_EMPNO:7698
```

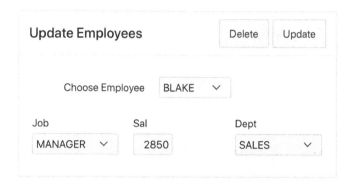

Figure 13-23. *The Update Employees region*

This URL redirects to page 30, setting the session state value for the select list to 7698, the employee number for BLAKE. Once I understand this, I can modify this URL to retrieve the information for any employee. For example, if I enter the same URL into my browser, changing the last four characters to 7782, I will see the information for employee CLARK.

At first glance, this modification seems like no big deal. After all, why should I go out of my way to type a value into the URL when I can use the select list to do it for me instead? The real point of this technique is that it works regardless of how the item is implemented on the page.

In Figure 13-23, P30_EMPNO is a select list that displays all employees. But suppose instead that it displays only the employees in the sales department, because the application developer wants users to be able to modify the records of only those employees. It doesn't matter, because I can bypass the select list by entering any employee number directly into the URL. It makes absolutely no difference what the type of P30_EMPNO is or even if it is visible.

Item modification can also be applied to pages that use submit instead of redirect. That is, you can use item modification to change the value of items that are passed via POST and don't even appear in the URL. Consider again the Filter by Job and Department page of Figure 6-5, which appears in Figure 13-24. Suppose that you choose Job and Dept values (say, CLERK and RESEARCH) from the select lists and then submit. The URL will be

```
f?p=91392:9:98765:::::
```

That is, the values for items P9_JOB and P9_DEPTNO do not appear in the URL because the input is being sent via a POST request.

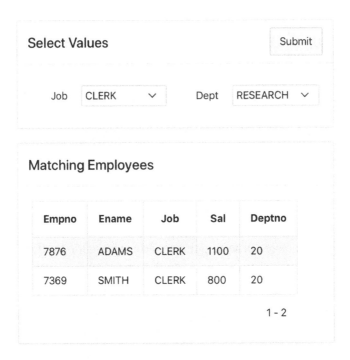

Figure 13-24. *Filter by Job and Department page*

Suppose now that I modify the URL by adding item names and values to the last two arguments, as follows:

```
f?p=91392:9:98765:::::P9_JOB,P9_DEPTNO:MANAGER,10.
```

APEX executes the request as follows. It first performs the submit by copying the item values from the browser to the session state; it then copies the specified values from the URL to the two specified items and renders the page. Thus, the values of P9_JOB and P9_DEPTNO that were chosen on the page will be overwritten by the values from the URL. That is, the resulting report will list the manager of the accounting department, regardless of the values displayed in the select lists!

The possibility of item modification means that you cannot depend on list-based items to enforce any kind of restriction on input data. This has ramifications for SQL injection and cross-site scripting. Recall that the discussion of those techniques noted that an attacker needs a sufficiently long text-based item for data entry, so the use of list-based items was preferred. However, an attacker can use item modification to enter the attack code directly into the URL. Thus, the use of list-based items cannot provide security (and, in fact, gives a false sense of security) unless there is a way to prohibit item modification.

Guarding Against Item Modification

APEX has functionality called *page access protection*, whose sole purpose is to prevent item modification attacks. There are several levels of protection. This section will discuss only the most general-purpose one: Arguments Must Have Checksum. It works as follows.

Suppose that a page is protected at this level. If a URL for that page assigns item values, that URL must also contain a checksum for those values. When the APEX server receives a request, it extracts the argument values, computes their checksum, and compares it with the checksum within the URL; the request is rejected if they differ.

The idea is that the checksum function is known only to APEX. When APEX generates the URL for a redirect operation, it calculates the checksum and adds it to the URL. If the user modifies the item values in any way, the existing checksum will no longer be correct; moreover, the user will have no way of knowing how to compute the correct value. Similarly, a user cannot create an item-saving URL from scratch because there is no way to determine its checksum. Thus, item modification is impossible.

There are two steps to enabling page access protection for a page. The first step is to enable the application's Session State Protection property. Starting from the application's home screen, click the Edit Application Properties button and then click the Security tab. The property is in the Session State Protection section. Most likely, the property is already enabled; if not, select Enabled. The second step is to go to the page properties for the page. The Page Access Protection property is in the Security section; select the option Arguments Must Have Checksum.

As a test, set up page access protection for the Employees by Department page. Then go to the page and click the link for the accounting department. You should see a URL similar to this:

```
f?p=91392:12:98765::::P12_DEPTNO,P12_DNAME:10,ACCOUNTING&cs=1OFzVgvoxRFQBVR
nEe9Ww2QSzoVM
```

Note that this URL is the same as in Listing 13-11, except for the checksum information at the end. Now try to perform item modification on this URL (with or without changing the checksum value). APEX detects the modification, returning the error message shown in Figure 13-25.

Session state protection violation: This may be caused
by manual alteration of a URL containing a checksum or
by using a link with an incorrect or missing checksum. If
you are unsure what caused this error, please contact
the application administrator for assistance.

Contact your application administrator.

Figure 13-25. *Detecting an attempted item modification*

There is one additional complication: if you want page access protection, you will
need to enable it for every page of your application because a URL for one page can set
the items for another. For example, suppose that the Employees by Department page
(page 12 of the demo, Figure 13-22) has been protected. Now consider the home page of
the application, which is page 1. Because it does not have any items, you might assume
that there is no need to require a checksum. But a clever user could issue this URL
request:

```
f?p=91392:1:98765:::::P12_DEPTNO,P12_DNAME:10,ACCOUNTING
```

This request sets the session state value for P12_DEPTNO and P12_DNAME before
loading the home page. The user can then navigate normally from the home page to the
Employees by Department page. If those items get their source from the current session
state value (as is typical), the page will be rendered with the user-specified values. In
other words, the user will have successfully performed item modification despite your
good intentions.

Summary

This chapter focused on the question of how to ensure the security of an application. It discussed how to configure the application so that each user can do only what that user should be able to do—no more and no less. There are three aspects to the security issue: authentication, authorization, and establishing safeguards.

Authentication ensures that an application knows the identity of its users. Users identify themselves by supplying a username and password; the application's authentication scheme is responsible for matching the username/password against a master list. APEX supports several authentication schemes, which differ according to the part of the organization that manages the user/password list. You saw how to build a custom authentication scheme in which the application itself is responsible for the list.

Authorization specifies what each authenticated user can do. The fundamental authorization mechanism is the authorization scheme. Each authorization scheme specifies a set of users. By associating an authorization scheme with a page (or page component), you restrict access to that page (or component) to the users specified by its authorization scheme.

Safeguards are necessary to keep users from doing things they are not authorized to do. This chapter covered three well-known techniques: SQL injection, cross-site scripting, and URL modification. In SQL injection, a user submits an SQL code fragment as "data" in a way that causes the underlying process to execute the wrong query. In cross-site scripting, a user saves a malicious JavaScript code fragment as "data"; the malicious code then executes when another user attempts to display that data. With URL modification, a user sends a URL to the APEX server in a form that the server expects; however, the action requested by that URL is something that the user is not authorized to ask for. You examined ways to guard against each of these techniques. The bottom line is that if you are aware of the risks, it is relatively straightforward to ensure the complete security of your application.

Index

A

alert function, 400

apex_escape.html
  function, 401, 402

Appearance property, 14

Applications and Pages
  accessing built-in help, 32
  APEX page designer, 25, 26, 28
  APEX, running page outside, 22
  APEX, running page within, 19–21
  application creation, 13–16
  Create Page wizard, 22, 24, 25
  Delete This Application, 19
  editing application properties, 17–19
  property editor, 28–31

Authentication
  definition, 367
  managing schemes, 368, 369, 371, 372
  public page, 377
  schemes, 367, 368
  writing function
    authenticating users, 376
    store username/password
      information, 372, 373
    user accounts, adding, 374, 375

Authorization
  APEX authorization
    scheme, 378, 380–382
  component, 383, 384
  definition, 378

Not Public User scheme, 386

page, 384–386

B

Behavior properties, 292

Branches
  filtered employees region, 264–266
  process creation, 266
  separate pages, input and output, 263
  session state, 280
  Submit button, 265
  target, 267
  wizard-like interfaces (*see* Wizard-like
    interfaces)

C

Cascading list
  Classic Report, 188
  Employee Demo application, 187
  property, 190
  query, 189

Chart drill-down, 182–184

Chart regions
  chart series, configuring, 75, 77
  configuring, 75
  definition, 71
  employee counts, 72
  multiple series, 78, 79, 81–83
  rendering tree, 74

E. Sciore, *Understanding Oracle APEX 20 Application Development*,
https://doi.org/10.1007/978-1-4842-6165-1

Printed in the United States
By Bookmasters